Foundations of
Home Economics
Research
A Human Ecology Approach

Foundations of Home Economics Research

A Human Ecology Approach

by

NORMA H. COMPTON
Dean, School of Home Economics
Auburn University
Auburn, Alabama

and

OLIVE A. HALL
Counselor, El Camino College
Torrance, California

BURGESS PUBLISHING COMPANY   •   MINNEAPOLIS, MINN. 55415

Preface

This book focuses on theories and methods of research appropriate for the study of man in interaction with his near environment. "Human ecology" has been used by several disciplines and interdisciplinary groups since its introduction by Park and Burgess in 1921. Out of their theoretical scheme of applying plant and animal ecology to the study of human communities, the classical position has developed which views competition as the basic process of human relationships, largely involving a struggle for space. Human ecology emerged in studies of the spatial distribution of interrelated social variables. Geography was one of the sources from which it developed. However, the social and geographical parts developed in relative isolation from each other. (Theodorson, 1961)

By 1950 the classical position had been subjected to sharp criticism for more than a decade. It is virtually without proponents today in its original form. Today human ecology has a broad, interdisciplinary meaning:

> The term human ecology presents difficulties of concept and definition. It sometimes appears to be a subdivision of sociology, it has been closely related to biomedical and health sciences, and it has been treated as a field of interdisciplinary study. Organized in different ways in different colleges and universities, human ecology does not appear to be conceived as a distinctive, integrated discipline.... Human ecology requires some form of extradepartmental or interdisciplinary structuring. Since there has not appeared to be an obviously "right" way to organize the study of human ecology, arrangements vary from university to university. (Caldwell, 1968)

Pioneers in home economics once considered the name human ecology for their field but abandoned it. Early in its history home economics was defined as "the study of the laws, conditions, principles, and ideals which are concerned on the one hand with man's immediate physical environment and on the other hand with his nature as a social being, and a study specially of the relation between these two factors." Some schools of home economics are focusing on this man-environment relationship and are changing their names to human ecology, human development, human resources, or other titles denoting similar interests. But whatever the name under which these schools operate, the man-environment relationship approach is important to their survival in a rapidly changing world. In this context, it may be thought of as a creative approach to a better life.

The 1971 *Annual Guides to Graduate Study* has added a section of "institutions offering graduate work in human development and home economics, including child development, clothing and textiles, and household economics and management." That publication states: "These sciences have in part grown out of or replaced some formerly isolated academic areas and now constitute a single study of human ecology and are therefore presented here as a new discipline for the first time."

The Association of Administrators of Home Economics has examined the current status of research and projected directions for future emphases, specifically by establishing five long-range research goals with relevant research problem areas. Researchers and administrators concluded that lack of trained personnel is their greatest deterrent to research productivity, followed by lack of sufficient research funding. They emphasized that a new and higher priority must be assigned to research. This must begin with identifying and motivating potential researchers in the *undergraduate years*, possibly through a research methodology course for upper level students. Thesis-based graduate degree programs with supporting courses such as research methods, statistics, and computer applications in research were favored.

The authors hope that this book will help to implement these ambitious research projections. It is designed not only for the graduate student but for the potential graduate student as well — for juniors and seniors in various disciplines related to human ecology. These students can contribute much to new knowledge by participating in research projects. The book is directed also to the consumer of research who needs to understand, interpret, evaluate, and apply the research conducted in his field.

At no time in history have so many demands been made on fields of knowledge encompassed by human ecology. Families, communities, and nations are faced with problems of change and adjustment requiring decision-making skills. Solutions can be sought to these pressing problems through research and service.

The primary focus of the book is on theories and methods of research appropriate for the study of man in interaction with his *near environment* — housing, home furnishings, household equipment, clothing and textiles, food, and family. Man is viewed as an organism who responds to varied stimuli in this environment. The stimuli emanating from this environment include colors, textures, shapes, tastes, noises, temperatures, and pressures. Man responds to these stimuli by certain physiological responses and by psychological and social behaviors which may take the form of self-concepts, relationships with other humans, etc. These stimuli also influence his decision-making processes as a consumer as well as his learning processes. In turn, those psychological and social behaviors influence his reactions to physical environmental stimuli.

The book is based upon several premises: (1) Scientific research is but a structured and controlled form of the investigations conducted in solving problems and making decisions in daily life, whether it is choosing a specific piece of household equipment, selecting a marriage partner, or choosing a college field of study or life career; (2) A researcher need not be overwhelmed by what Lurie (1958) terms "statistical embellishments." A few statistical tools will be presented in terms of scientific reasoning and the rationale for their use; and (3) Research can be creative, serving as a means of self-expression for the individual. Through the pursuance of well-planned research, the individual student can experience the *excitement of discovery*.

The authors are deeply grateful to their colleagues, former professors, and students who have challenged their thinking and offered frank criticisms of the manuscript. The book evolved from the authors' experiences in teaching research methods courses in several universities and research and statistical methods courses taken in the fields of business, physiology, psychology, education, and home economics. The methods should be applicable to research related to these and other disciplines.

The book is organized in five parts:

Part I. *Research Planning* focuses on human ecology as a problem-solving discipline and sets forth selected research goals and problem areas. It provides conceptual and theoretical frameworks as bases for research in several aspects of man's near environment. Guidance is offered on selecting and formulating a problem as well as on reviewing related literature.

Part II. *Research Types or Settings* describes documentary, experimental, survey, and field study research methods. Examples of research studies from various human ecology areas are included.

Part III. *Sampling and Measurement* discusses principles of sampling and determination of the reliability and validity of measuring instruments.

Part IV. *Methods of Data Collection* includes the use of observations, questionnaires and interviews, objective tests and scales, and projective methods.

Parts V and VI. *Analysis and Interpretation of Results* and *Research Communication* cover the statistical significance of data, writing research proposals, and communicating the results of research.

This book is unique in its theoretical framework, interrelating various areas of human ecology, and in its use of actual research studies as illustrations of research methodology. Nevertheless, a book of this type has obvious limitations. Research skills must be developed through experience. Therefore, a book can only serve as a guide by informing the researcher of available tools and general rules to be applied in using them. Each research project should be unique if it is to contribute new knowledge to the field. Just as the artist uses his basic materials to create a painting or a sculpture, the researcher uses his basic research tools to explore possible solutions to unsolved problems. May each of you find the challenge and self-fulfillment that can come through conducting creative research in an area in which you are vitally interested.

May, 1972   Norma H. Compton
                                                                                            Olive A. Hall

Contents

LIST OF FIGURES

LIST OF TABLES

Research Planning

Discovery through research is an adventure akin to that of exploring an isolated, mountainous island. There will be interesting, pleasant, and easy areas to travel but there may also be many hours of loneliness and despair as the researcher struggles to find his way through canyons and over mountain peaks. In his humorous map, Harbury encourages researchers to face the realities as well as to recognize the potential pleasures of discovery on "The Island of Research."

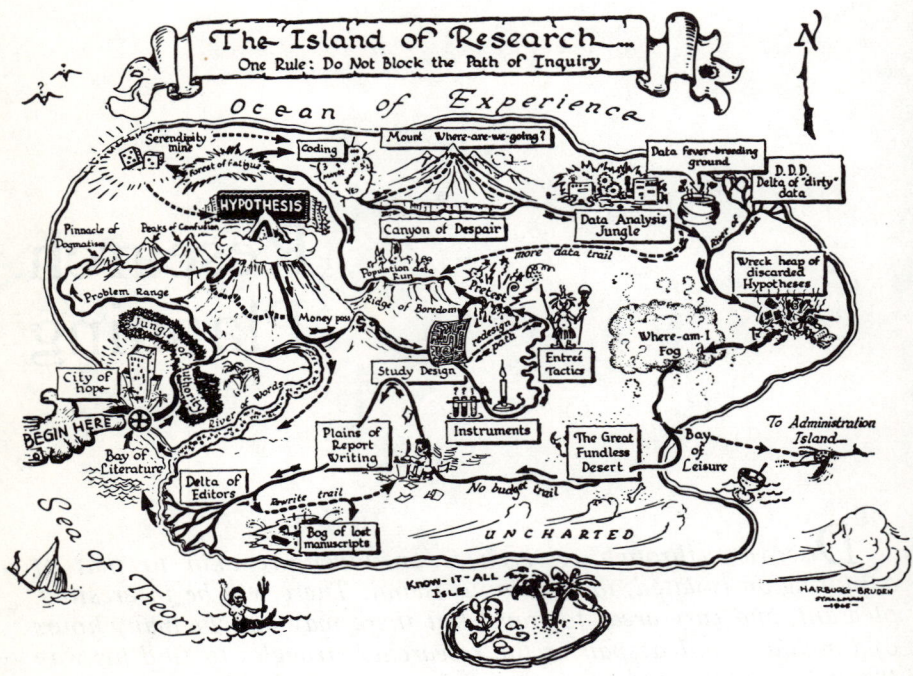

Figure 1. The Island of Research (From American Scientist, 54, 4, 1966). Reprinted with permission of Ernest Harburg, University of Mich., Ann Arbor.

CHAPTER 1

Invitation to Research

Creative thought is of great significance in today's society. Many advances that are accepted as commonplace, with no thought of their origin, arose from the ability of an individual to perceive a problem and think of an original solution. Homes and families today enjoy many physical conveniences and health safeguards that are practical applications of someone's search for a better way of living.

Although individuals and groups have access to a great body of scientific facts on which to base their decisions, man can no longer make decisions solely on the basis of what seems best for himself and his family. The complicated relationships between man and his environment must be studied if individuals are to adapt to environmental change, retain their humanness, and fulfill their responsibilities toward preserving natural resources for future generations.

Research can cast light on the technological, economic, psychological, socio-logical, political, and ethical issues involved in the study of man in his environ-ment. Its aim is the discovery of new facts and their correct interpretation. To fulfill this purpose, an investigation must be purposeful, systematic, adapted to scientific ways of problem solving, and carried out with a genuine desire to know the truth rather than to prove a point.

RESEARCH AS DISCOVERY

At this time in our society young people are challenging the entire educa-tional enterprise in terms of its resistance to change and lack of relevance to the problems of the individual, the community, and the nation. More than ever before, students are searching for expression of their individuality, for a commit-ment, and for a voice in the solving of social problems. At the same time, they are calling for faculty to leave the research laboratory and return to the classroom. The real question is not whether the faculty member should leave the laboratory and return to the classroom, but whether his research and his teaching should be better coordinated, with students included as participants in both enterprises.

Conant (1951) has stated that in the scientific world there are two broad views of science — the static and the dynamic. These views can be applied to both teaching and research. The static view seems to influence most laymen and students, hampering their understanding of the thinking and activities of the scientist and scientific research in general. According to this view, the scientist explains the present set of laws, theories, and principles and adds new facts to this already existing body of information.

The dynamic view, on the other hand, regards scientific teaching and research as an activity of the scientist. This view has been termed *heuristic*, meaning *to discover*. A heuristic method of teaching emphasizes students discovering things for themselves. Such a method is to be favored in contrast to the fact-oriented lecture approach. Unquestionably, a similar approach to research would recruit many of today's students. As McLuhan says: "We are entering the new age of education that is programmed for discovery rather than instruction." (McLuhan, 1964, p. x). Heuristic methods involve problem solving with an emphasis on imaginative, not routine, problem solving. Established facts are important to the heuristic researcher only as they help lead to new theories and discoveries.

HUMAN ECOLOGY AS A PROBLEM-SOLVING DISCIPLINE

Human ecology, as presented in this book, is the study of man in interaction with his near environment. His near environment includes his housing, home furnishings, household equipment, clothing and textiles, food, and family.

> Human ecology focuses on the individual and his reciprocal relationships with other men and technology in the settings most critical for human development: the family, home, and community. Its basic mission is to improve the quality of human life. The subject matter . . . is both commonplace and of great social concern, for the ways in which men live, eat, spend their money, and raise their children determine not only individual and family well-being, but the welfare and stability of society as well. (Knapp, 1970, p. 3)

To carry its objective of improving the well-being of families through education, research, and community service, human ecology applies and synthesizes theories from the physical and behavioral sciences, humanities, and arts. Its researchers must work as part of a team with members of other disciplines on complex social problems requiring multidisciplinary approaches toward improving the quality of living in an increasingly polluted environment. "It requires the analysis of actual human situations and the use of experimental models reproducing some selected aspects of these situations." (Dubos, 1968, p. 19)

Figure 2 provides a model for a man-environment approach to research in

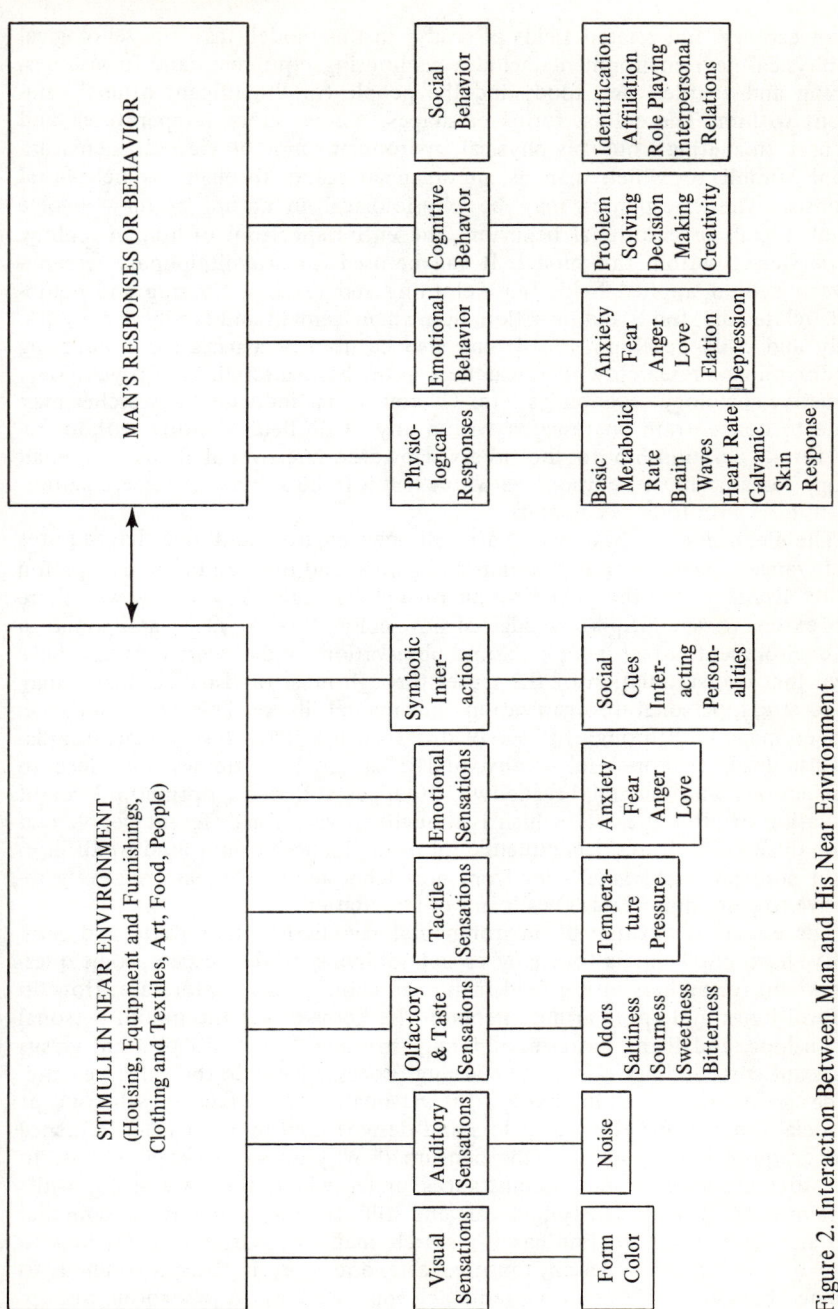

Figure 2. Interaction Between Man and His Near Environment (An Integrative Conceptual Framework for Human Ecology)

human ecology and related fields of study. In this model, man's psychological and physical near environment includes his housing, equipment and furnishings, clothing and textiles, art, food, and the people (or "significant others") important to him. The colors, forms or shapes, noises, odors, temperatures, and pressures emanating from this physical environment may be viewed as environmental stimuli to which man as an organism reacts through his behavioral responses. These responses may be physiological in nature or may involve mental, social, or emotional behavior. The entire spectrum of human ecology can be viewed within this model. It can be used for interdisciplinary research between several applied fields (e.g., clothing and textiles, housing and equipment, related art, foods and nutrition, home management and family economics, family and child development). It can also be used as a basis for conducting interdisciplinary research with researchers in the basic disciplines of psychology, chemistry, sociology, economics, etc. Of course, an individual researcher may decide to concentrate on research within any single field of study without regard for its relationship to the others. However, the overall focus in human ecology research must be upon the whole if it is to be a dynamic research enterprise in tune with today's demands.

The electronic age has created a totally new environment, one that requires a wide range of awareness of materials and colors, and that requires participation and involvement with things and people on a global scale. As yet, however, there is no extensive scientific knowledge of how color, texture, taste, and sound in this environment affect people. Some observations and research studies have shown that overstimulation of the senses through noise or visual confusion may lead to stress, personal disorganization, and mental illness. This overstimulation has been magnified through the use of drugs, such as LSD. Insufficient stimulation also leads to boredom, apathy, and if carried to extremes, may lead to hallucinations and mental breakdown. It appears that an optimum level of stimulation or arousal exists, which is thought to vary for different people and among different cultures. Delinquents, for example, have been found to differ in certain perceptual characteristics from non-delinquents. They are relatively insensitive to pain, noise, and other forms of stimulation.

The effects on people of environmental stimulation, its novelty and complexity, have implications for many aspects of living. In this respect, some questions which researchers in the field of human ecology can explore are: How do the furnishings and space arrangements in the home affect the mood, personal relationships, and living patterns of family members? How do pleasant versus unpleasant surroundings affect the learning process? How do the color, texture, and design of one's clothing express his personality and affect his self-concept and social interaction? How do colors and designs used in advertising influence the decision-making process of the consumer? Why do some people choose to adapt to surroundings and circumstances under which they are living while others move to a more satisfying locale and still others are committed to mental hospitals? Based upon the findings of research, man may learn ultimately how to utilize or control color, design, texture, taste, and noise in the environment to influence human reactions in a predictable manner toward promoting the optimum development and adjustment of each individual and family.

RESEARCH GOALS AND PROBLEM AREAS

In 1970 the Association of Administrators of Home Economics sponsored a major nationwide endeavor to examine the current status of research in its fields and to project directions for future research emphases. Using an ecological model as a base, three task forces worked on broad scope objectives within different areas of emphasis as follows:

Task Force I: Physical/biological aspects of man and his environment
Task Force II: Sociopsychological needs and development of human beings
Task Force III: Relation between man and the technological setting in which he develops and lives

Five major research goals were presented to a group of active researchers and administrators as the framework for a research workshop in March 1970. Broad research problem areas and specific research questions were also developed for each goal. This document is available in published form. (Schlater, 1970) The five goals and suggested broad research problem areas are presented here as a guide for the researcher. It is suggested that the reader refer to the original publication for additional detail. The authors hope that the researcher will find these goals and problem areas helpful, but not restrictive, to his innovations and creativity. These areas are considered important by current researchers and administrators *now*.

GOAL I.   *Improve the conditions contributing to man's psychological and social development*
Research Problem Areas
    1.   Social-emotional development
    2.   Cognitive development
    3.   Family structure and function
    4.   Roles and role behavior
    5.   Husband-wife relationships
    6.   Parent-child relationships
    7.   Family planning
    8.   Social and technological change

GOAL II. *Improve the conditions contributing to man's physiological health and development*
Research Problem Areas
    1.   Nutrient requirements and metabolism
    2.   Nutritional status
    3.   Food quality, composition, and safety
    4.   Food patterns
    5.   Health-related variables
    6.   Food service systems

GOAL III. *Improve the physical components of man's near environment*
Research Problem Areas
    1.   Housing and environs: human needs
    2.   Housing and environs: psycho-socio-cultural aspects
    3.   Housing and environs: aesthetic aspects

4. Housing and environs: economic aspects
5. Textiles and textile products: properties and performance
6. Clothing: human needs
7. Clothing: psycho-socio-cultural aspects
8. Clothing: economic aspects
9. Clothing: creation and design

GOAL IV. *Improve consumer competence and family resource use*
Research Problem Areas
1. Consumer service needs
2. Consumer choice making and behavior
3. Consumer and the marketing system
4. Values and behavior
5. Management, decision-making processes, and situations
6. Resource development, allocation, and use
7. Levels of living

GOAL V. *Improve the quality and availability of community services which enrich family life*
Research Problem Areas
1. Community program needs
2. Health, safety, and recreation programs
3. Continuing education programs
4. Housing programs
5. Day care programs for preschool children
6. Family influence on and response to public programs

SUMMARY: LOOKING TO THE FUTURE

The "Invitation to Research" is an invitation to discovery — discovery of solutions to many of the problems facing individuals, families, communities, and nations. Innovative or creative research can also lead to self-discovery and fulfillment, as it provides an individual with a medium for expressing himself.

Looking at human ecology as a problem-solving discipline in terms of man and his environment and at the research goals and problem areas suggested by the leaders in the field raises a question to challenge the thinking of administrators and researchers: How can these systematically-determined research goals facilitate rather than limit and confine the production of researchers in basic, applied, and action research?

The paths are open to many types of research and many methods of data collection. By starting with a carefully selected and specific research problem that has not been solved previously, basing it upon a sound theoretical framework with a well-structured research design, and planning early the method of analyzing the data, a research study should make a valuable contribution.

CHAPTER 2

Conceptual and Theoretical Frameworks as Bases for Human Ecology Research

The first step toward mastery of any scientific discipline is the mastery of its basic concepts. Concepts are working tools, embodying the important ideas of a field of study. They are mental images of what is known, thought, and felt about an idea. Conant defined science as "an interconnected series of concepts and conceptual schemes." (Conant, 1951, p. 25) It is from such a body of relationships among variables that theories are built. Kerlinger defined theory as "a set of interrelated constructs (concepts), definitions, and propositions that presents a systematic view of phenomena by specifying relations among variables, with the purpose of explaining and predicting the phenomena." (Kerlinger, 1964, p. 11)

The following is an illustration of how words and sentences in ordinary speech may be likened to concepts and theories in science: (Brodbeck, in Gage, 1963, pp. 44-45)

Ordinary Speech	Science
Words	Concepts (name characteristics and relations; descriptive terms)
Sentences	Definitions, statements of facts, laws, generalizations (relationships between concepts)
Certain sets of sentences	Theories

As indicated, theories consist of defined and interrelated concepts and explain phenomena. Concepts and theories are important research tools, helping to determine gaps in knowledge and to think through and organize ideas. They provide a basis for rigorous testing and help to fit pieces of knowledge together.

A variety of conceptual frameworks and theories exists for every discipline. A multitude of meanings may exist for a given concept and the theories may appear contradictory. However, if these concepts are accompanied by clearly stated definitions and deductively formulated theories, the problem need not be great. The value of research should be based upon its contribution to theory or its relationship to other research.

The following examples of conceptual or theoretical frameworks are not intended to be all-inclusive but may serve as an indication of some of the recent thinking in human ecology fields and to illustrate the forms which such frameworks can take. It is hoped that the student will develop his own framework after a thorough study of the concepts basic to his major field of interest and that he will then contribute to further development of his theories through research.

THE FAMILY AS AN ECOSYSTEM

The family is an example of an ecosystem — a group of organisms interacting with each other and their environment. Families, like organisms, do not exist in isolation; they occupy an environmental niche or microenvironment. Just as an ecosystem tends toward self-regulation, a family can learn to maintain itself somewhat like a balanced aquarium. Basic resources provide energy input which can be absorbed, stored, gradually consumed, and dissipated as heat. Associated with the flow of energy is a cycling of nutrients enabling the ecosystem to be balanced and self-contained. As a life support system, the family receives physical sustenance from the natural environment and is dependent upon the social environment for its affectional and socialization needs.

An ecosystem is affected by an environmental catastrophe as well as by the invasion of a new species. The birth of each child, the addition of an in-law or stepparent, the hospitalization or death of an individual family member affect some of the members more than others. Some individuals respond to opportunities afforded them and others suffer restraints to their further development. The better-adapted species tend to survive and increase while the less well adapted ones are unable to survive the competition for space, nutrients, or other needs. The stability of an ecosystem, or its ability to adapt to invasion or catastrophe without a period of instability or major change, is related to its diversity. In the same manner, a family with little diversity among its members and its investment of resources is vulnerable to changing social and economic conditions.

Nature obtains stability by allowing energy to flow smoothly through the ecosystem, by retaining and recycling nutrients, and by encouraging diversity of species. Both the species and the environment have remarkable ability to change. Since the family is not a closed system, it must be resilient and adaptable to change, while maintaining its family organization as an ecosystem. The continued well-being of an ecosystem depends upon keeping the natural recycling mechanisms intact. The family needs to recognize that its resources are finite and must be conserved. The maintenance of environmental quality and the development of attitudes and values necessary to solve problems within the microenvironment can be a trust for one's children.

MAN'S INTERNAL ENVIRONMENT

The power of population is infinitely greater than the power in the earth to produce subsistence for man. (Malthus, 1766-1834)

The well-being of an individual is affected by both his external and internal environment. Today's researchers are concerned with the interrelationships among the biophysical, psychosocial, and economic aspects of nutrition and food.

Physiological and Metabolic Processes

The understanding of man's behavior rests upon some knowledge of man's physical structure and how it functions physiologically. Food nourishes his body, enabling man to survive and adapt to his environment.

Energy. Energy may be regarded as a broad, unifying concept in studying man's relationship to his environment. Every event that takes place in the universe, whether physical, biological, or cultural, is an expression of energy.

According to the Second Law of Thermodynamics, *entropy* (an inactive or static condition in which energy may become useless) tends to increase as the universe becomes older. As it increases, the universe and all closed systems tend naturally to deteriorate — to move from a state of organization and differentiation to a state of chaos and sameness. But human beings are not isolated, closed systems. They take in food, which generates energy from outside themselves, and are, as a result, parts of that larger world that contains the sources of vitality or energy. They also take in information through their sense organs and act on the information received. (Wiener, 1954) This is in accord with the Second Law which holds that living organisms can oppose the drift and move in a direction opposite to that specified for the cosmos as a whole, developing more complex structures and greater concentrations of energy.

Homeostasis. The human organism combats entropy or resists the general stream of decay through the process of *homeostasis.* "It is the pattern maintained by this homeostasis which is the touchstone of our personal identity." (Wiener, 1954, p. 96) Originally this concept was applied by Bernard to strictly physiological processes. It has since been applied to psychological and social areas. In the physiological sense, homeostasis consists of dynamic automatic forces operating within the organism to maintain a fairly rigid constancy or stability within its internal environment. These forces are under the control of the autonomic nervous system and therefore operate quite automatically. However, man can consciously assist the natural forces in some cases by altering his external or internal environment (i.e., through surgery, clothing and shelter provisions, etc.).

The nature of these "forces" that keep homeostasis operating can best be explained by the biochemist. The key word is probably *enzyme.* A prominent chemist once defined life as "a system of cooperating enzyme reactions." As Cannon indicated in his classic book, *The Wisdom of the Body:*

The blood proteins (on which the very existence of the normal blood volume depends), the blood calcium (of primary importance for the proper functioning of the neuromuscular system), and the red corpuscles of the blood (essential for the oxygen supply to the tissues) are examples of factors in the fluid matrix, all of which exhibit homeostasis to a surprising degree. Marked change in their concentration brings about alarming disturbance in the organism. (Cannon, 1932, p. 289)

Man needs to learn more about the relations of his body to the total environment. The human being is an open energy system. There is no separating him from his environment. "Living is capturing, controlling, and using energy. Each human is designed to capture and transform the energy stored in foods into the complex processes of living, growing and behaving." (Dildine, 1950, p. 252) The only form in which energy can be taken from the environment in significant amounts by higher animals is the chemical energy of food. This chemical energy is converted into other forms of energy (mechanical, electrical, heat) by biological transducers. Every organ in the body plays a part in energy flow within the body. The end result of these processes is body activity.

Body's Utilization of Energy. The body utilizes four kinds of energy: (1) mechanical — expressed through muscular contractions; (2) electrical — expressed through nervous impulses; (3) chemical — digestion of food; and (4) heat — by-product of chemical reactions. One-half of man's energy pool is used for maintenance of body organs and functions. Assessment of the utilization of energy for body maintenance is made through measurement of the BMR (*basic metabolic rate*). The other half of an individual's energy pool is available for growth and for activity or behavior.

Factors affecting an individual's amount of energy and its use are:

1. *Endocrine efficiency.* Thyroid controls the rate of burning of body fuels.

2. Place in *growth cycle.* Among growing children a great deal of energy is needed for this function.

3. The individual's *reality.* There is a relationship between the utilization of energy for handling one's emotions and conflicts and the amount of energy available for activity and learning.

4. *Carbohydrate* from foods.

$$\text{Glucose} + \text{Enzymes} + O_2 \rightarrow CO_2 + H_2O + \text{ATP}$$

ATP is a high energy phosphate compound that makes energy available to cells.

Nutrition and Foods

The effects of hunger and malnutrition are far reaching, causing problems in health, mental development, learning, motivation, employment, and human relations. These problems affect not only the individual's mental health but his adjustment to society. Therefore, food and nutrition play a significant role in the health of families and nations around the world.

Adaptation Through Nutrition. "Adaptation is the most important dynamic concept in human ecology." (Klausner, 1971, p. 27) Through adaptation, an organism gains control over its environment and may change its own character in the process. (Hamley, 1950) Hamley defined culture as the prevailing techniques of adjustment by which a population maintains itself in its habitat.

The *principle of population* is a principle of survival resting on the relation of numbers of people to food. Population, unless checked, increases in a geometrical ratio while the food supply increases in an arithmetical ratio. Few resources are tied as directly to survival as is food. (Klausner, 1971) "The most pressing factor now limiting the capacity of the earth to support Homo sapiens is the supply of food." (Ehrlich and Ehrlich, 1970, p. 65)

To understand fully the nutritional problems of the millions of hungry people throughout the world one must be familiar with problems of agricultural development and production, agricultural economics, food distribution patterns and food preferences of different cultural groups. "But above all, the nutritional needs that are common to all people, regardless of what they recognize as 'food,' must be understood." (Ehrlich and Ehrlich, 1970, p. 66)

Figure 3. Nutritional Deficiency Disease
Used with permission from the Wellcome Museum of Medical Science, London.

To this end, concepts developed by a subcommittee of the Interagency Committee on Nutrition Education should be apropos. Recognizing that the development of nutrition constitutes one of the greatest advances toward controlling man's environment in relation to health, this subcommittee was appointed to develop some broad research-based statements considered to be needed by everyone in making decisions about food to promote a desirable level of health and growth. The statements are expressed in lay language to ensure clarity of meaning for the public. They summarize all the nutrition knowledge that is applicable to food-for-people-for-health and reflect the research findings that constitute the newer knowledge of nutrition. (Leverton in USDA, 1968)

These nutrition concepts are presented here as they were reviewed from the standpoint of content and intent by Leverton:

1.   "Nutrition is the food you eat and how the body uses it."

This generalizes the knowledge of the relation of food to health, including the processes of digestion, absorption, and metabolism, and the interaction with enzymes, hormones, and other components of the internal environment. This is a short version of the definition formulated by Lusk in 1917 and still accurate today: "Nutrition may be defined as the sum of the processes concerned with growth, maintenance and repair of the living body as a whole or of its constituent parts." (Lusk, 1917, p. 69)

Most important now is that this concept gives a dynamic definition of nutrition, indicating that it is more than just food — it is the food eaten and how the body uses it. It also gives the scope of nutrition and it does so in terms of the food a person eats. It is positive; it is forward looking; and it involves individual action to a large extent under individual control — eating. There is nothing here to imply that nutrition is eating "what you don't like because it is good for you." Here nutrition is put into the context of a means or a process to a desirable goal — to live, to grow, to keep healthy, and to have energy. Many of the barriers faced today in nutrition education exist because this concept is missing in the minds and experiences of the clientele.

2.   "Food is made up of different nutrients needed for growth and health."

This concept generalizes on the composition of food, its nutritive value, its need by the body, and the flexibility in choice to achieve an adequate diet. Each of the five subconcepts contributes to the idea of the need for a variety of foods and the interdependence among foods, and among the nutrients furnished by them. Most important is that food is the best source of nutrients and, therefore, individuals can and should get their nutrients from food.

Food analysis is a key science on which man is becoming increasingly dependent as he learns about newly identified nutrients and the body's need for them. Without the expertise and dedication of scientists in this often unrecognized field of service, man would not be able to translate nutritional needs into foods he eats.

The essential tool for developing and applying this concept is a daily food guide. Such guides represent the consensus among a group of experts as to the best translation of nutrient needs into reasonably flexible patterns of food selection. Probably the most widely used one today is the United States Department of Agriculture's "Food for Fitness, A Daily Food Guide," successor to the "Basic Seven." Because this concept emphasizes food as an adequate source of nutrients, comprehension and application of this concept constitute one of the strongest defenses that individuals can have against food faddism.

3. "All persons, throughout life, have need for the same nutrients, but in varying amounts."

This concept generalizes on the Recommended Dietary Allowances of the Food and Nutrition Board. The allowances are themselves a research-based quantitative concept of nutrient needs of healthy people of different age, sex, size, and activity. Like most present-day concepts, they were developed by a group of experts representing the best and broadest knowledge of the times. Of course, the Recommended Dietary Allowances include a measure of compromise but they are a consensus of fact and judgment, intended as a guideline, and are of great usefulness to all who have need of quantitative values.

Nutrition clientele will seldom have occasion to need to know these quantitative values except those for energy where the balance between requirement and use is both crucial and manageable. The translation of the nutrient allowances into food guides has provided an indispensable tool — one that permits the maximum freedom in choosing what a person will eat that is consistent with safeguarding his nutrient intake.

This concept, like the one before it, aims to protect clientele from charlatans or self-proclaimed specialists by stating that nutrition scientists are the ones to make the suggestions about the kinds and amounts of food needed.

4. "The way food is handled influences the amount of nutrients in food, its safety, appearance, and taste."

This, the last of the concepts, generalizes on the preservation of nutritive value and eating quality at every stage in the field-to-table food chain. Nutrient content, appearance, and taste are not to be viewed as constant, rigid attributes unaffected by technological assault and immune to destruction or damage. These attributes are vital, responsive components of food and must receive proper care if their values are to be preserved for man's benefit and enjoyment. Research-based directions for the selection, care, and preparation of food combine procedures that ensure safety, maximize eating quality, and minimize damage to nutritive value. Nutritive value sometimes has to be sacrificed in the interest of safety. There can be no compromise here. Compromises are possible and frequently desirable, however, between maximum nutritive value and eating quality in the interest of acceptability.

A consensus among any group of experts, such as the Interagency Committee on Nutrition Education and its counterparts, is both a milestone of accomplishment and a springboard for future efforts. A bright future is predicted for those who use these nutrition concepts and those who acquire these concepts to guide their food selection. The concepts can be the content or subject matter of what is communicated. The next step is to gain skill in how to communicate — how to create a climate for learning that will promote behavioral changes in eating habits, and how to use the appropriate techniques for reaching people of different ages, cultures, and economic levels.

Concepts are as dynamic as the research findings on which they are based. Like the dietary allowances and the food guide, they will need to be reviewed from time to time. As research establishes more facts, the concepts may require some expansion, or revision of wording, or change in emphasis to keep the interpretation of research sound. But, like the definition of nutrition given by Lusk 50 years ago, these basic concepts of nutrition for nutrition education can remain useful and dynamic during the decades ahead.

Nutrition and Communication. As indicated previously, human beings may combat entropy in that they are open rather than closed systems, taking in food to generate energy from outside themselves. The importance of food and nutrition to such environmental adaptation has been summarized. As also indicated, human beings can combat entropy through communicating with their environment, taking in information through their sense organs and acting on the information received. Such communication and action is controlled by the *nervous system.*

The primary function of the nervous system is to adjust the organism to its environment. Such adjustment is achieved through: (1) the coordination of sustaining systems; (2) learning or habit formation; (3) reflective thought and planned adaptation. As already emphasized, the autonomic nervous system functions to regulate visceral activities (hunger, sex, elimination) and maintain their balanced coordination and stability (homeostasis). Emotions are also expressed through the autonomic nervous system. The central nervous system, comprised of the brain and spinal cord, functions to maintain the adjustment and coordination of afferent and efferent nerve impulses. Afferent nerve fibers receive *stimuli* from the environment, in the form of visual, auditory, affectory, gustatory, and tactile sensations, and carry these sensory impulses to the central nervous system. Efferent nerve fibers convey outgoing or motor impulses from the central nervous system to organs of *response* such as the muscles of limbs, speech organs, etc.

The importance of nutrition to the operation of homeostasis within the body as controlled by the autonomic nervous system has already been discussed. Nutrition is also of primary importance to central nervous system functioning. Learning may be a matter of protein synthesis within the neurons and in relation to other neurons. The protein-producing system is poorly developed in mentally disordered persons. Mental disturbances invariably accompany the physical symptoms of pellagra (absence of nicotinic acid in the diet). Similar disturbances may occur in beriberi, caused by lack of Vitamin B_1. There is a correlation between these vitamins and the functioning of the brain. The source of energy for the brain is the metabolism of sugar. These vitamins are coenzymes in the various steps of that metabolism. Whether the stresses on a brain are emotional or chemical (resulting from absence of dietary essentials), the consequential symptoms are apparently very similar.

Normally, the process of communication with one's environment proceeds as follows:

Nerve cells have long thin threads leading from the spinal cord to the various muscles in the body. Messages (from *sensory stimuli*) are sent along this net-

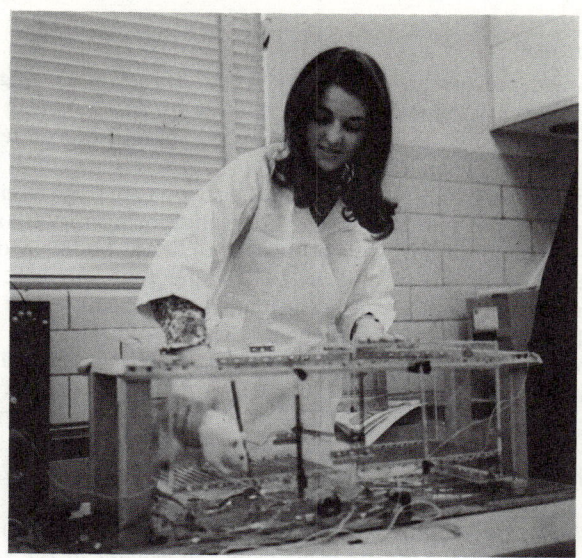

Figure 4. Measurement of Learning Performance Study on "Brain Enzyme Activities, Nucleic Acid Concentrations, and Learning Abilities of Rats Fed Varying Levels of Pyridoxine."

work, ordering muscles to perform their function (response). There is a gap between the end of the nerve fiber and the muscle. A chemical acetylcholine is released to send messages across this gap (or synapse). Once the message is delivered to the muscle cells, an enzyme in the blood rips apart acetylcholine into fragments and the stage is set for new communication.

Summary

"Living organisms are open systems communicating and in circular process with their environments." (Grinker, 1956, p. 4) They take in energy from food in their environment and in turn utilize that energy to interact with that environment, responding through their nervous systems to stimuli such as colors, smells, tastes, sounds, and temperatures. "We can conclude that the organism not only selects the energy (stimulation) it accepts from the environment, but it also maintains its own rate of responsiveness." (Grinker, 1956, p. 6)

PSYCHOLOGICAL AND SOCIAL DEVELOPMENT

The individual's psychological and social development — the formation of his "tentative self" — is the summary of the interaction of his organic heritage, his cultural heritage, the social groups of which he has been a part, and his personal experiences.

Organic Heritage

As mentioned previously, man's nervous system is an amazing circuit that coordinates his various sense organs and enables him to function as a whole. Information is constantly being received by the brain, interpreted, analyzed, stored, and acted upon when appropriate.

Nervous System. At the outset of life, behavior is biological and a number of well-defined response patterns are set up in the organism. Very important to the operation and equilibrium (homeostasis)* of these bodily processes is the autonomic nervous system, fully developed at the time of birth. The central nervous system is immature at birth and represents a blank tablet upon which environmental factors make impressions as experienced. However, the impressions made are in turn dependent upon further and continuous maturing of the nervous system. Thus, the nervous system serves as the integrating point of the organism and sets the limits or capacities of the individual for learning. Physical maturity and the amount of prior learning set the rate. The section on Man's Internal Environment discussed the relation of food and nutrition to the functioning of the nervous system.

Differentiation-Integration. It is a general concept of human growth and development that *development proceeds from the general to the specific*, from the diffuse to the well-ordered. At first, there is for the infant no body as a whole but rather an "undifferentiated blur ... probably simply moving spots, unstructured sounds, pains, warms and colds, muscular strains and relaxations, all ill defined, fleeting and confused." (Murphy, 1947, p. 184) He is self-centered in the sense that he does not know where he ends and the world begins. The visual mechanisms are poorly developed in the first weeks while the sense of touch operates almost from birth. Therefore, visceral and kinesthetic preoccupations and concern with the body predominate in this early period of development. However, for many months it is not recognized as self. In this respect, disagreement exists regarding the age at which a conscious body-self occurs. Through the differentiation-integration process, the organism organizes the world into definable objects and people, and then further into more refined categories.

Research on infancy has developed rapidly during the past decade. Questions regarding the early months of a child's life have been raised with reference to whether there are innate means by which the child perceives the world and organizes his experiences; whether his behavior develops through relating stimulus and response or whether he actively directs his approaches to the world; whether the amounts and types of his experience set boundaries for his later intellectual development, whether there are critical periods in infancy during which a child must have certain types of experiences without which he cannot develop appropriately, etc. Some of these questions can be partially answered. Others are still merely guesses. (CRM Books, 1971)

---

*See the previous section for a discussion of homeostasis.

Cultural Heritage

The child is born into a society with well-established material and non-material components, through which the "progress" or complexity of the society may be determined. The material components of culture consist of housing, clothing, food, tools, and concrete presentation of ideas such as books and paintings. Nonmaterial components include the ideas and techniques behind these objects as well as ways of thinking and behaving, values, language, science, law, and religion.

Socialization Process. The relationship between material technology and the self will be discussed in the section on Physical Components of Man's Near Environment. With respect to the nonmaterial cultural heritage, the child is conditioned, through the socialization process, to conform to society's well-established patterns of thinking and behaving. Whether he accepts these patterns with ease or whether they must be forced upon him depends upon other factors (organic heritage, social groups, and his personal experiences). His reaction to these cultural environmental pressures plays an important part in his future psychological adjustment.

Environmental Stimulation. Probably the greatest significance of the cultural heritage to the development and adjustment of the self in its environment lies in its provision of supplies or resources for reaching potentialities. Early environmental stimulation in the form of visual and tactile stimuli, communication with other humans, etc., are considered essential to cognitive and emotional development. Opportunities lost during the early years may never be regained fully.

Social Groups

Studying the nature of social influences on the development of personality gives insight into the effects of growing up in different social contexts. Another important area for study is how social factors are transmitted, both through formal education and informal means such as parent-child relations, adult models, and peer groups.

Organization and Adaptation. The social groups in a society are organized and held together by a common cultural heritage. For human ecologists the concept of *organization* is central. The modes of organization among people affect their impacts on their environment. The overarching process is *adaptation.* These two central ecological concepts are linked. Along with population size and the amount of subsistence resources available, the way populations are organized influences the level of living attained by them. At the extreme, such organization may affect their very survival — that is, their adaptation. (Klausner, 1971)

The Family. The family is an important social group and the most important molder of personality. Family members exert a primary influence on the individual's concept of himself and of the environment and on his development and adjustment to the environment.

Love relationships among family members are the most important and

Figure 5. A Study of Parent-Child Emotional Environment

effective means toward socialization and future personality development of the child, for these relationships help to orient the self to mankind, to the universe, and to God. The privation of love in childhood may result in harmful physical as well as psychological effects. An individual cannot live without interpersonal relations, as many case studies have shown.

Gradual independence from the family becomes important as the individual performs the various developmental tasks toward adulthood. This is a natural adaptation based upon a secure feeling about the self in relation to other people. Too great a dependence upon parents will result in retardation of development.

The Peer Group. A step toward independence begins with peer group interaction. The peer group provides the beginning for genuine relations with others in the broader environment outside the child's family. He is required to play rather specific roles in the peer group. He measures himself as others react to him in terms of the number of roles he has won and his skill in playing these roles.

Personal Experiences

Organic heritage, cultural heritage, and social groups have important meanings for the individual. These meanings are derived from the individual's interpretations of his unique experiences, based upon what these experiences imply for need-satisfaction.

Ecologists may sometimes reduce culture to patterns of instinctual or conditioned responses to environmental conditions. Such a reduction ignores the interpretative or subjective aspects of meaning. The fact that societal as well as individual responses to the similar environments vary indicates that these environments alone do not determine responses. The older evolutionary framework is therefore modified. (Klausner, 1971)

Giving meaning to the environment implies having emotions and making evaluations about it. Thus, the environment may be interpreted as being comfortable or uncomfortable, friendly or hostile, beautiful or ugly, etc. Individuals tend to interpret the environment in terms of its relevance to the self — in terms of the extent to which it satisfies their needs and aspirations.

The Tentative Self

The tentative self is the end product of the interaction of a person's organic and cultural heritages, his social groups, and his personal experiences. It takes such forms as attitudes, values, goals, drives, levels of aspiration, self-concepts, and codes of conduct, which are fairly consistent with one another.

Self-Control. The word "tentative" indicates that no life pattern is static. The self, once organized, exerts itself in self-control. Although a human being is never completely free of the influence of social and physical factors, he is not a passive component in an adaptive system. He does not simply *react* to his environment. He *responds* to it. Moreover, his responses are not always aimed at blindly adapting to the environment. They often reflect rather a need for exploration, activity, and manipulation. These three drives have much in common and have therefore been classified under the single concept of *competence.* This opened the way for considering those aspects of behavior in which stimulation and contact with the environment seem to be sought, in which raised tension, mild excitement, novelty, and variety are enjoyed for their own sake.

Perception. Through the process of perception the individual tends to protect his already achieved self-organization. Through selective perception he selects stimuli supportive of his present self-development.

The individual must master or "come to terms with his environment" because it affords the means by which self-actualization can be achieved but it also contains obstructions in the form of threats and pressures which hinder self-actualization. Dealing with the environment is the most fundamental element of motivation. (Woodworth, 1958)

Summary

The individual is a product of his environment (his organic heritage, his cultural heritage, the social groups in his life) with respect to his psychological and social development. If he is to realize or actualize his full potential as an individual, he must come to terms with his environment. He must master it because, if the discrepancy between his goals and the realities of his environment is too high, he either must give up some of his aims or break down.

An individual masters his environment largely through the processes of differentiating-integrating, valuing-evaluating, and perceiving. Through the differentiation-integration process, the human being organizes the world into definable objects and people; then he refines the categories further. Valuing-evaluating includes the feeling tones accompanying experiencing. The individual sees himself as an entity and assigns values to himself, probably in relation to how he feels other people evaluate him on the basis of their actions toward him. Perceiving operates to aid in protecting the already achieved self-organization. Perceiving processes select what stimuli will be acted upon by the individual and screen out those that are out of tune with the present rhythm of the individual's self-development.

PHYSICAL COMPONENTS OF MAN'S NEAR ENVIRONMENT

Of all living things, man alone is capable of creatively cooperating with the natural processes to insure his continued survival and progress. Yet, he has used the earth's resources as though he could heedlessly exploit, contaminate and alter the world about him without endangering the stability and harmony of the system of which he is a part. (U.S. Department HEW, 1970, p. 1)

Technology and Man

The world is saturated with the idea that technological progress is for the benefit of man and his environment. Man has operated with a conviction that he can accomplish anything by suitable manipulation of the environment. Now he must learn to use technology in understanding his world better and in finding ways of maintaining the biological and mental health required to live in a technological society.

Technology and Adaptation. Man need not accept his natural environment as a fixed and final aspect of his existence. Through his technology he can alter and transform this environment to meet his needs. Societies differ widely in the efficiency and complexity of their technologies and hence in the degree to which they may fully exploit (or overexploit) their environmental resources. As Frank said:

The outstanding characteristic of our time is the headlong rush of technology and science. Scientists and engineers are prying new secrets out of nature and remaking our lives at a breathtaking and ever accelerating rate. The adverse effects on society of their efforts could be referred to as social diseases, although we have preferred the term social issues. (Frank, 1966, p. 1)

Energy and Technology. The concept of energy has already been referred to as a unifying concept in studying man's relationship with his environment. (See the section on Man's Internal Environment, p. 11.) Energy is also an important concept with which to describe the functioning of technology in relation to cultural development. Since cultural systems are dynamic, not static, energy as well as matter is involved. The primary function of culture is to harness and control energy so that it may be put to work to serve man's needs. This function is accomplished by means of technological instruments. According to this theory, the degree of cultural development is largely a measure of the amount of energy harnessed per capita per year and the quality and efficiency of tools employed in the expenditure of that energy. Culture advances as the proportion of nonhuman to human energy increases or as the amount of human need-serving goods and services produced per unit of human labor increases. (White, 1949)

Using clothing and textiles as a technological medium for studying cultural development under this theoretical framework, one could assume that societies whose textile and apparel items are produced by the human organism alone have not reached a very high degree of cultural development.

Technological, Sociological, and Ideological Systems. White (1949) defined a *technological system* as the material, mechanical, physical, and chemical instruments, together with the techniques of their use, by means of which man, as an animal species, is articulated with his natural habitat (tools of production, means of subsistence, materials of shelter, instruments of offense and defense). According to White, a primary role is played by the technological system in relation to the other two subsystems of culture (sociological and ideological systems). Man, and consequently culture as a whole, is dependent upon the material, mechanical means of adjustment to the natural environment. A *social system* is the organized effort of human beings in the use of the instruments of subsistence, offense and defense, and protection. *Ideological or philosophical systems* are organizations of beliefs in which human experience finds its interpretation. But experience and interpretations are conditioned by technologies. Philosophies express technological forces and reflect social systems. For example, ideals of beauty in women may be correlated closely with mode of subsistence as technologically determined. In cultures where technological control over food supply is slight and food is scarce, a fat woman is often regarded as beautiful. Where food is abundant and women work little, obesity is likely to be regarded as unsightly.

Mechanical Technology and Human Relations. Some observers come close to seeing technology as the master of human relations. Changes in technology often bring with them changes in human relationships. For example, handicraft manufacturing consists of producing through the use of human power alone or with hand-and-foot operated machines. It tends to be family-anchored. However, under commercial manufacturing conditions, relations with non-kin build up around the fabrication of goods and the work may shift from the home to a factory. Emphasis is put on finding the right man for the job, the most efficient method of production, and the most economical number of workers. Traditional allegiance to kin, tribe, or caste has little priority when efficiency is the goal. (Honigmann, 1959)

The ideal person is the one who can get along with a variety of strangers and who does not upset the applecart by becoming temperamental, adopting radical ideas, or fighting for causes. The style of life common in America in the mechanistic age is not easy to acquire in a community just beginning to industrialize. People find it difficult to work methodically, by the clock, and conscientiously under impersonal conditions.

Electronic Technology. Automation brought about by electronic technology, with instant communication and retrieval of information, is replacing the preceding mechanical technology. This instant communication requires a total environmental field approach, with the simultaneous use of all of man's senses. Such a technology appears to have resulted in a rejection of standardized goods, scenery, and education in America. Moreover, according to McLuhan, fashion may be "an attempt to adjust the sensory life to a changing technological environment." (McLuhan and Fiore, 1968, p. 163)

Environment-Behavior Relations

Environmental or ecological units should be defined and measured in terms of both their physical and psychological or behavioral components. These two components should be described and measured independently in order to study environment-behavior relations. The ecological environment has an objective reality, with physical and temporal attributes apart from the behavior with which it may be linked. On the other hand, the study of the linkage between the two necessitates an interchange across a common boundary. Physical and chemical attributes of objects may, through interpretation by people, share a boundary with social and psychological facts. (Klausner, 1971) For example, clothing is an extension of the skin and as such can be seen both as a heat-control mechanism and as a means for defining the self socially. Housing extends the inner heat-control mechanisms of the organism (McLuhan, 1964) and also defines the family socially, especially in terms of community status and roles to be played both within the family and the larger society.

Housing-furnishings and textiles-clothing will serve as specific examples of the physical environment for further elaboration of the conceptual framework.

Housing and Furnishings.

We shape our buildings, and afterwards our buildings shape us.
(Winston Churchill)

Housing and its furnishings may be viewed as a combination of many factors. A few of them are given here as examples:

1. Organization of space and furnishings for privacy and for social interaction
2. Functionality in meeting physical needs
   Noise (or noise insulation)
   Lighting and ventilation
3. Design elements (form, color, texture): aesthetics
4. Human energy conservation in maintenance of home

Although not all of these factors will be discussed here, they form a physical home environment to which people respond.

Organization of space and furnishings. For thousands of years man had the open spaces of his natural environment for individual privacy and solitude. Today, his home is the last refuge he has from the hazards of street traffic and from the noise, stress, and dust of the outside world.

Research to provide understanding of how people use and respond to space is essential to designing and arranging physical home environments that promote the healthy psychological and social development and adjustment of people.

Territoriality. Although studies on the relation between man and physical space have been conducted in many fields of social science, more is understood about animal spatial behavior. One of the most important concepts emerging about animal studies is that of territoriality. The concept is also applicable to human societies. Territoriality is a basic characteristic of living organisms. Territory is the space or area to which an animal (or man) lays claim and which he defends against others of his own species. (Plihal and Brown, 1969) An individual's or family's territory (usually consisting of his home and its grounds) may be protected by laws preventing its search or seizure, by the installation of fences or planting of hedges, constructing walls, etc. The psychologist Jung believes that territory for man is an expression of his basic need for roots:

> The need for roots is the need for a sense of safety, identity, and belonging, a feeling of wanted security and steadiness. If a person has a physical area or territory which is his own, the familiarity of it, the feeling of being "at home" or belonging there meets the need for roots. People may satisfy the need in other ways but territory is one way. (Jung, 1965, p. 2)

Crowding. The degree of crowding in the rooms of a home is regarded as an important index of housing conditions. "Crowding and congestion is pollution of living space and we must look at human beings as potential environmental insults." (Linton, 1968, p. 92) The same space may feel more or less crowded depending upon number of persons per room, how furniture and equipment are arranged in it, how the occupants of the space organize themselves, and the types of activities or social interaction taking place within the space. The concept of crowding may also be as much an attitude on the part of people as it is physical in nature. Some recent studies suggest that individuals who commit violent crimes may have a low tolerance for crowding. Rates for violent crimes have been positively correlated with actual population densities in American cities. (Ehrlich and Ehrlich, 1970)

Social interaction. In addition to the importance of providing space for privacy, the organization of space is important to social interaction:

> The dwelling unit is the locus of the initial socialization of the child; it is there that his character-structure is largely shaped. Not only are patterns of socialization typically enacted *within* the home; they appear in part to be oriented *toward* the house and its contents. (Merton, 1951, p. 181)

Physical distance carries social interactional meaning with people tending to arrange themselves at distances from one another on the basis of the social action in which they are engaged. (Klausner, 1971) Space and furniture arrangements in a room may be classified as *sociofugal* (discouraging interaction among people) or *sociopetal* (encouraging interaction). (Plihal and Brown, 1969)

Functionality in meeting physical needs. According to Etter (1971), "A dissonant world has a way of producing dissident people. Noise is the ultimate insult. It belittles us. . . . It kills what is left of many things we have loved — music, beauty, friendship, hope, and excitement — and the reassurance of nature."

In this discussion, functionality will be approached from the standpoint of noise, lighting, and ventilation:

1. Noise. A professor of environmental medicine has stated that "Sonic booms, jackhammers and garbage trucks may needle your nerves like a hypodermic but it is the dishwasher, vacuum cleaner and hi-fi that endanger disposition." (Cromie, 1967, p. A13) Noisy appliances and electronic status symbols

Figure 6. Measurement of Sound

raise the sound level in some homes to the point where it threatens health and well-being and can aggravate ulcers, allergies, and emotional problems. Exposure to the noise also leads frequently to fatigue and to disharmony among family members.

Few interior designers give sufficient thought to the problem of noise. Yet, research studies show that sound can be minimized by textile fabrics and manner of hanging draperies in relation to the amount of wall surface covered.

Noise is usually measured in decibels. Silence is represented by zero decibels and the threshold of hearing at one decibel. A food blender measures 80 decibels. Recently there has been growing evidence that irreversible changes in the autonomic nervous system may result from noise in the 90-decibel range. (Ehrlich and Ehrlich, 1970)

2. Lighting and ventilation. Lighting and ventilation are other physical components of the environment affecting health and functioning. For example, one's sense of spaciousness tends to increase with lowered temperatures. Crowding tends to be more noticeable under conditions of high temperature and humidity. These environmental conditions also relate to work production and accident rates. Work performance has been found to be highest and accident rate lowest in a temperature from 67° to 81° F., 50% humidity.

Quality of lighting encompasses chiefly the distribution of brightness within the visual field. The important contribution of lighting to the environment is the provision of conditions that will provide maximal visual and mental relaxation and proper conditions for seeing where human safety is involved. Level of illumination influences visual acuity, frequency of blinking of the eye, nervous muscular tension while reading, heart-rate, and fatigue of the ocular muscles. (Luckiesh and Moss, 1937) "Life may be said to begin with light and to be sustained by light. As man-made environments increase in size and extent, man-made light sources acquire great importance and demand new understanding and development." (Birren, 1969, p. 9)

To McLuhan, housing is an extension of man's bodily heat control mechanism and techniques of lighting and heating give new flexibility and scope to this mechanism, enabling him to attain some degree of equilibrium in a changing environment. (McLuhan, 1964)

Design elements: aesthetics. Aesthetics has been described as "a field of inquiry in search of a method." (Pratt, 1961, p. 87) It exists as an interaction between material reality and human observers. Aesthetic experience is grounded in perception and is psychologically quite complicated. Aesthetics has been defined as the perception of an object just for the sake of perceiving it. It applies not to one sensation alone but to many (e.g., visual, tactile, kinesthetic). It is experienced not only at the sensual level, however, but is a harmonious blend of feelings and emotions, judgment and reasoning, motivation and personality. Through aesthetic communication (with form, color, texture), the impersonal aspects of one's technological and scientific environment may be altered by reviving the concept of individual existence and expression. Art has been considered the primary means of adjusting to the environment. An individual selects what he will perceive and creates his own world. A base of knowledge and understanding is needed of specifically how people perceive and react to their aesthetic surroundings.

Textiles and Clothing.

Clothing as an extension of the human skin is as much a technology as the wheel or the compass. (McLuhan and Fiore, 1968)

The human body and its extension through textiles and clothing have been referred to as the subject and object of perception (as both a stimulus and a response). As such, it is part of man's near environment.

A textile or clothing item is a product, which Newman defined as: "a symbol by virtue of its form, size, color, and functions. Its significance as a symbol varies according to how much it is associated with individual needs and social interaction. A product, then, is the sum of the meanings it communicates, often unconsciously, to others when they look at it or use it." (Newman, 1957, p. 100)

As products, textile and clothing items have physical realities in terms of form, color, texture, weight, etc., even though these components may be perceived and interpreted differently by individual observers. Textiles are usually composed of fibers, yarns, and finishes to provide different effects in the end-product. They may be constructed into many shapes in garment form. An understanding of the physical characteristics of textiles is important in fabricating, choosing, and consuming products to meet the individual's needs. Mathematical, chemical, physical, and biological concepts must be applied to effect such understanding. Textile chemists or laboratory technologists are generally concerned only with the physical aspects of products under varying conditions. The associated problems of defining human responses to these physical stimuli challenge only those who have worked with an interdisciplinary team on a broad conceptual design. Participation and contribution in these evolving areas of research and application should be encouraged. "People should become involved with the discipline of psychophysics, and to be enthused about the future prospects of design by discovering its reality through their conscious experience of the environment." (Halldane, 1970, pp. 8-13)

Textiles. Brand arbitrarily divided fabric character into four categories: aesthetics, comfort, convertibility (tailorability), and performance (functionality). In Figure 7 these categories are shown in overlapping circles to show their interdependence. (Brand, 1964, p. 794)

1.   Aesthetics. Fabric aesthetics is a complex response made by people, not machines. The only alternative is its measurement by people. The concept of aesthetics must be related to at least one of three main physiological sensations (visual, tactile, or kinesthetic). They can be evaluated subjectively and some of them, in addition, may be quantified by physical measurements. Figure 8 illustrates criteria for defining aesthetic concepts.

Examples of aesthetic concepts, their relationships, and subconcepts are shown in Figure 9.

McLuhan sees fashion as an attempt to adjust the sensory life to a changing

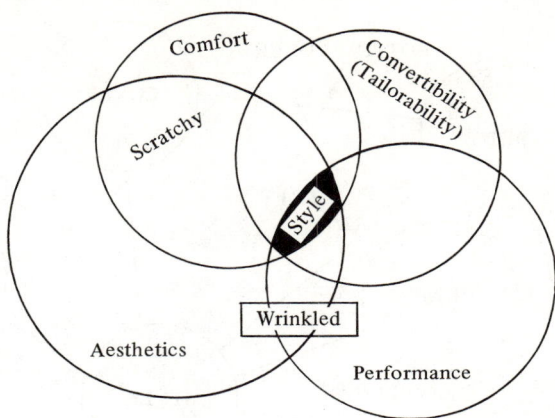

Figure 7. Fabric characteristics are interrelated, as suggested in the above diagram, and they are meaningful only with respect to specific fabric styles. The same common quality words (wrinkled, scratchy) can be used in reference to several characteristics. Fig. 3, p. 794, from "Measurement of Fabric Aesthetics," by R.H. Brand, reprinted with permission from *Textile Research Journal,* September, 1964, pp. 791-804.

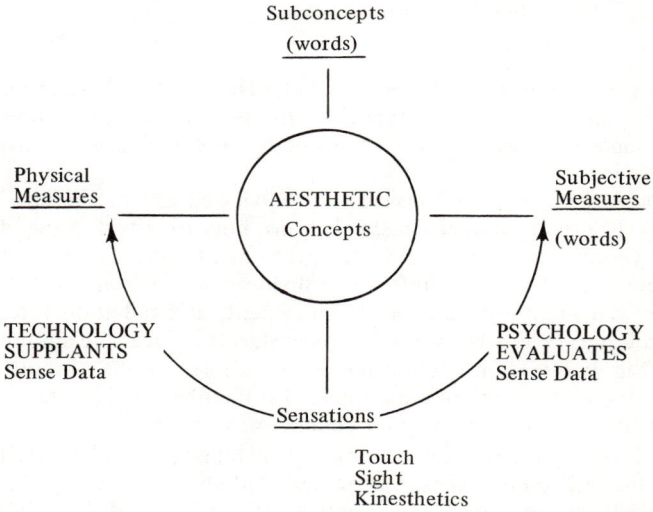

Figure 8. Criteria for Defining Aesthetic Concepts
Fig. 4, p. 795, from "Measurement of Fabric Aesthetics," by R.H. Brand, reprinted with permission from Textile Research Journal, September, 1964, pp. 791-804.

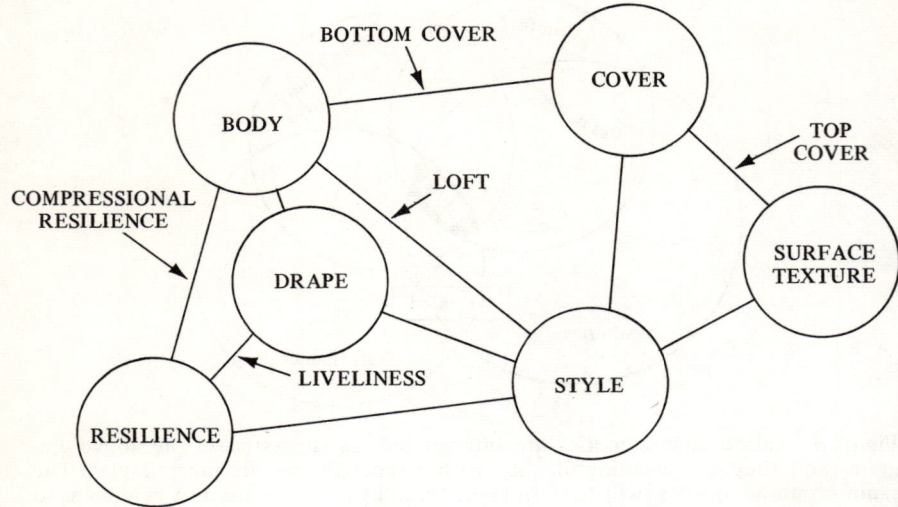

Figure 9. Concept Structure of Aesthetics. The minimum number of aesthetic concepts (in circles), their relationships and subconcepts identified by associated words, i.e. loft, liveliness, top cover, etc. Fig. 5, p. 795, from "Measurement of Fabric Aesthetics," by R.H. Brand, reprinted with permission from *Textile Research Journal*, September 1964, pp. 791-804.

technological environment. (McLuhan, 1968) Hence, the experiencing of not only a wide range of colors in fabrics today but also of many textures and sculptural shapes in dress relates to man's desire to experience the environment in its entirety with all his senses.

2. Comfort.* An apparel textile may be viewed as an extension of a person's bodily heat-control mechanism, helping him to attain some degree of equilibrium (homeostasis) in a changing environment. Such thermal equilibrium relates to comfort. Thermal comfort is influenced by environmental factors of temperature and humidity, rate of air movement, and radiation intensity. An apparel textile serves as a barrier to heat transfer. It reduces the amount of heat lost from the body to the atmosphere and decreases the amount of heat absorbed by the body from the atmosphere. Textile fibers and air trapped within them are excellent insulators and poor conductors of heat.

Thermal comfort characteristics of textile fabrics must be determined in relation to the environmental factors enumerated above as well as the porosity of the fabric itself and the distance between the fabric and the skin (e.g., the geometry of the fabric and the manner in which it is worn on the body). Other

---

*Although Brand included comfort and performance among his four fabric categories, he did not elaborate on them in this article. Therefore, the ideas presented on comfort and performance in this book may not represent his thinking.

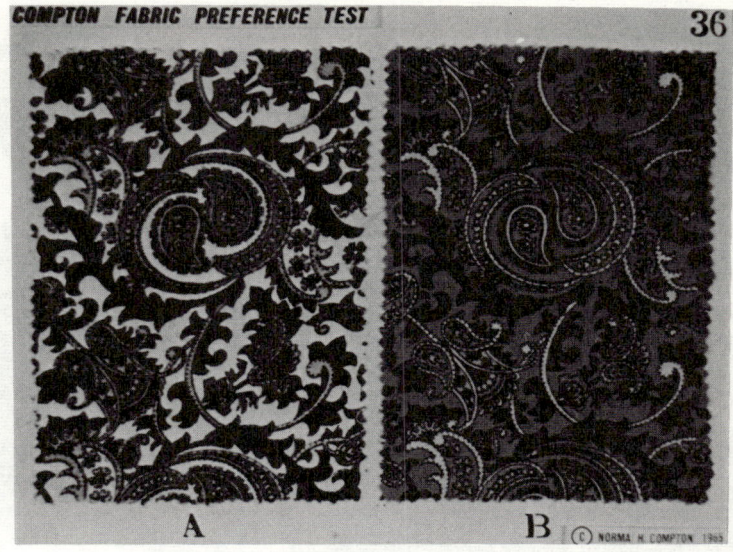

Figure 10. Measurement of Color Preferences
(From Compton Fabric Preference Test, © 1965)

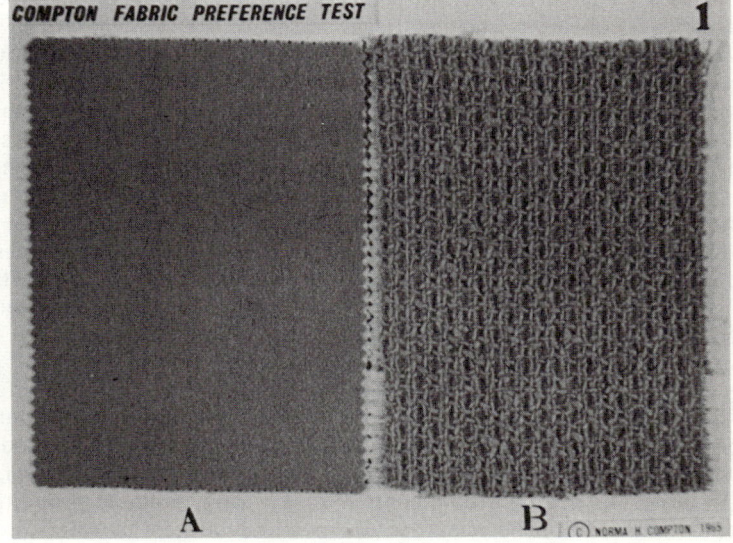

Figure 11. Measurement of Texture Preferences
(From Compton Fabric Preference Test, ©1965)

Figure 12. Psychophysical Responses to Texture

factors to be considered for thermal comfort are fabric weight, finish and color, number of layers of fabric, and the design and fit of the garment. All of these factors combined play a part in determining the insulating value of clothing, expressed by the unit of measurement called the *clo*.

In addition to thermal comfort, textile fabrics can provide a comfortable (or uncomfortable) tactile sensation through their surface textures. Factors contributing the most to people's subjective evaluations of the feel or the "hand" of fabrics are stiffness-limpness, roughness-smoothness, and thickness-thinness. Responses to such factors may relate both to physical and psychological comfort. For example, skin irritations may result from stiff, rough fabrics but psychological needs for contact, affection, and dependency may also be satisfied through fabric texture. (Klopfer et al, 1954; Harlow, 1958) Concealed needs for affection and dependency have been suggested to increase the degree of sensitivity with respect to texture. (Ainsworth and Kuethe, 1961)

3. Performance. In order to fulfill their purposes satisfactorily, fabrics must be planned for specific end-uses. More laboratory test methods must be developed which will adequately predict end-use performance and producers should carefully weigh and balance the various properties of textile fibers and fabrics in order to obtain a combination of as many desirable properties as possible. Communication between consumers and producers in order to determine consumer needs and preferences is also needed if maximum performance and acceptability are to be attained.

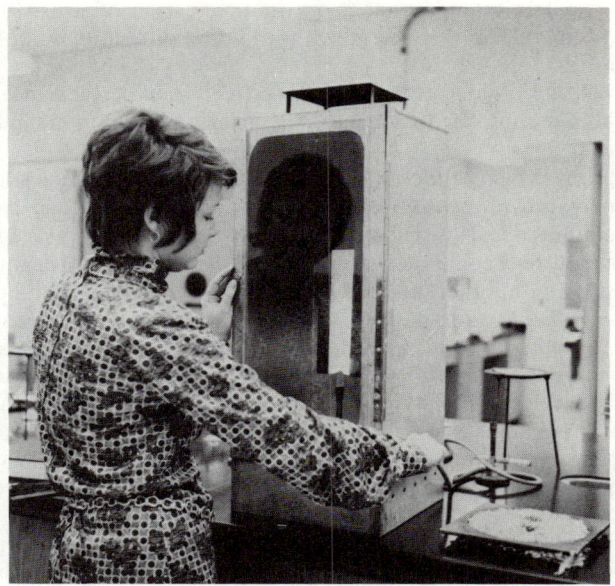

Figure 13. Measurement of Fabric Flammability

4. Environmental safety. Safety in textiles and clothing products is sufficiently important to warrant treating it as a separate category. Probably no textile apparel item is as essential to survival as the aluminized pressure space suits worn by the astronauts. These aluminized suits function to maintain air pressure surrounding the body and can withstand temperatures up to 800°F. and reflect back most of the sun's radiation. It is likely that many of the innovations developing from space travel research will eventually be adapted to civilian use. (Horn, 1968)

Fabric flammability is an area related to fabric safety, which is already of primary consumer concern. However, at the present time, there is no single textile fiber inherently resistant to flame that is acceptable to the consumer for apparel use.

Clothing. Unlike other animals, man supplements the body covering provided by nature with clothing — a second skin. Clothing thereby becomes a very personal aspect of one's environment, linking him to the larger physical and social environment in which he lives.

The properties of seamed fabrics are a function of properties inherent in the fiber, the structure of the yarn and fabric, and the modification of these factors by the construction of the seams. Geometric relations among fibers and yarns in the fabric are changed by cutting, puncturing, bending, and compressing them during the seam construction process. (Lindberg, 1961, pp. 664-669)

To provide serviceability of a garment, a seam should absorb the energy imparted to the fabrics and garment by the application of stress (under conditions of wear) and release this energy without fabric or seam failure. (Hamburger et al., 1952)

Seam construction factors purported to affect seam performance are type of thread, needle size, number of stitches per inch, seam direction, and amount of ease in the seam.

Clothing serves many functions for the individual. Through aesthetic characteristics, it may provide *sensory satisfaction*. Its other social and psychological functions are numerous. It is one aspect of culture and can serve as a medium for the study of culture. People need to establish *identification* with the values and patterns of living within their society and clothing helps them in the process.

A person develops as an individual by identifying with other people through *role playing*, usually accomplished through the use of costume. The self tends to take on characteristics prescribed or approved by social groups but an individual also needs to develop a life style of his own that incorporates social characteristics but which is unique.

Clothing becomes important in establishing *self-awareness* very early in life. Such awareness is at first related to kinesthetic sensations and awareness of the physical body. Clothes become closely identified with the body and affect body sensations. Through the *differentiation process* people learn to separate their bodies from their environment and the clearness of this demarkation may have important behavioral implications throughout their lives. Clothing plays an important part in this demarkation. Clothing that extends the physical dimensions of one's body tends to be felt as part of the body. The stiffness, thickness, and strength of clothing fabrics are also imparted through body sensations.

One's *personal identity* tends to become more firmly established as other people evaluate him. In discussing the psychological functions of clothing, Flugel wrote that "the essential purpose of decoration is to beautify the bodily appearance so as to attract the admiring glances of others and fortify one's self-esteem." (Flugel, 1950, p. 20)

The place of *self-fulfillment* or *self-actualization* in the development of the individual may be considered in terms of Maslow's theory of personality and motivation. This theory has important implications for viewing clothing in relation to human development. Briefly, the substance of the theory is that man has basic needs which can be organized into a hierarchy of relative potency. It is paramount that the lower level needs be reasonably satisfied before the individual is likely to pursue the fulfillment of the next need in the hierarchy. At the base of the hierarchy are needs based on physiological drives of hunger, thirst, etc. Next to these needs in relative strength is the need for safety, followed by belongingness and love, the need for self-esteem, and finally, self-actualization, cognitive, and aesthetic needs.

In terms of clothing, once the individual has adequate clothing for physical health and safety he can be concerned with clothing for more culturally refined purposes, such as belonging and self-esteem. These are the levels at which most individuals in American society seem to be operating. Clothing is selected largely to win belonging in groups and to achieve self-esteem, usually through conformity to the dictates of fashion. Mass production technology and advertising media tend to reinforce this orientation.

A few individuals are at the stage of striving in terms of the highest needs — self-actualization, cognitive (curiosity), and aesthetic needs. It is at these levels that creativity finds expression. This expression is often revealed through clothing. Having their needs for belongingness and self-esteem reasonably satisfied, individuals become less preoccupied with conformity and impressing other people and become more independent, expressing their individuality and creativity. Clothing thereby is interrelated with other forms of creative expression and can serve as a medium for artistic perception and expression for the individual.

Summary

Through technology, man can alter his environment to meet his needs. Present electronic technology, with its instant communication and retrieval of information, requires the simultaneous use of all man's senses to experience the total environmental field. Through his housing, furnishings, and clothing, man may attempt to adjust his sensory life to a changing technological society. Today, one's home and personal space, including his clothing, may be his last refuge from the noise, stress, and chaos of the outside world. Through study of these variables, man may ultimately learn how to utilize or control color, design, texture, taste, noise, and pollutants in his environment toward promoting the optimum development and adjustment of each individual.

MANAGEMENT OF ENVIRONMENTAL RESOURCES

We are facing what some writers are calling an "eco-catastrophe" brought on by man's violating the unity or interrelationships of the systems. The only hope of avoiding the catastrophe is for man to reorder his value systems and restrain his life style of living. (Harris, in Scoby, 1971, p. 169)

Management Defined

"Management is management wherever it occurs whether applied to the home, to the firm, or to government; whether applied to individuals or to groups; or whether applied to our culture or other cultures." Schlater defined management as "a dynamic, ongoing process which encompasses those human actions directed toward the realization of values and goals . . . ." (Schlater, 1967, pp. 93-98). That values function as the most basic underlying force in directing managerial activity is an accepted proposition in management.

Trilling identified the crisis of the present age as a crisis of values, with the comment that no cliché has been so damaging to modern life and times as the notion that science has nothing to do with values, for if consideration of values is to be the exclusive concern of religion and the humanities, a scientific understanding of human behavior is impossible. (Trilling, 1955)

Management operates in all aspects of the home and family environment. Although it was formerly considered to be task-centered and confined to the work of the household, it is now viewed in a human behavioral context in relation to all aspects of the home and the wider community of which it is a part.

While home management used to concern itself with the management of physical energy expended in household tasks to control fatigue, a deeper understanding and control of fatigue has now largely supplanted this concern. Fatigue resulting from the expenditure of physical energy is less important to many homemakers today than fatigue caused by psychological problems such as boredom and frustration. (Gross, 1966, pp. 448-452)

All management problems involve the use of some kinds of resources as inputs to produce some kinds of outputs. These resources usually have alternative uses and a cost is sustained in using the resource. The output, or benefit, from using the resource also has value. Therefore, management seeks to minimize the costs and maximize the benefits associated with a given use of resources. (Miller and Starr, 1967)

Economic Framework

Using an economic theoretical framework for study of the family, the output (or benefit) may be viewed in terms of the consumption of goods and services that leads to family welfare, as shown below: (Rice, 1966, pp. 254-257)

Use of Family
RESOURCES
is determined by

WANTS, NEEDS, ATTITUDES, CUSTOMS, HABITS

leads to

CONSUMPTION
of
GOODS and SERVICES

which determines or is determined by

STANDARDS	STATUS	BEHAVIOR
Values Income	Occupation Education Income	Utility Value

producing

STANDARD OF LIVING	SOCIOECONOMIC STATUS	LEVEL OF LIVING AND CONSUMER BEHAVIOR

considered in relation to

ECONOMIC CONDITIONS OF THE SOCIETY

leads to

FAMILY WELFARE

Figure 14 shows in perspective the economic subsystems of the family in relation to the social-psychological-physiological subsystems of the family, to the outside environment, and to the socioeconomic institutions of the community, state, and nation. (Burk, 1970, p. 325)

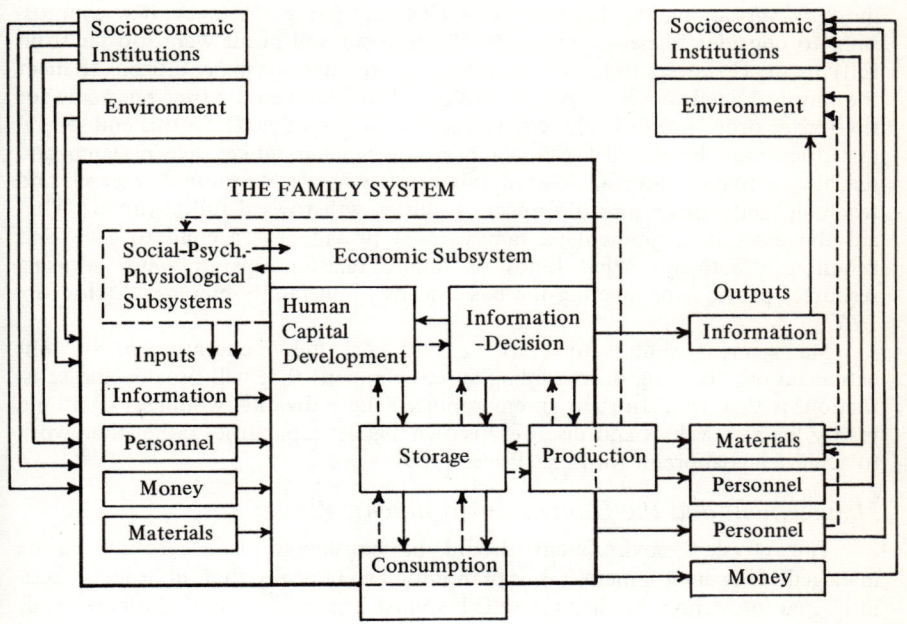

Figure 14. Flows and System Components of the Family Economy in Perspective. Fig. 3, p. 325, from "Food Economic Behavior in System Terms," by Marguerite Burk, from *Journal of Home Economics,* May, 1970, Vol. 62, copyright by the American Home Economics Association, Washington, D.C.

Consumption is a key concept in the economic framework, linking four areas of concentration (Rice, 1966, pp. 254-257:)

1. standards of living (sum total of things families consider essential as revealed through their consumption or aspirations
2. socioeconomic status
3. consumer behavior and the motivating forces behind consumption
4. economic conditions of society and the circumstances it imposes on the family.

The economic view of the family uses the household or consumer unit as a unit of reference in economic surveys. Such surveys or consumption patterns over long periods of time are important in analyzing fully the family cycle. Economic concepts such as those involving control of expenditures and division of labor within the household affect power structure and roles within the family.

Management for Self-Actualization

In the preceding presentation of the economic framework, emphasis was placed upon management of resources to produce a high standard of living, primarily through consumption. At a time when men and women were required to toil unceasingly to meet their families' barest survival needs and when mothers were dying in childbirth and babies were dying in infancy, it was impossible to consider higher-order needs. Physical survival needs were too far from fulfillment. However, today means are being provided for many citizens to meet the physical needs of food, shelter, clothing, and health so the time has come for the higher order need of self-actualization to be considered. To this end several questions may be posed for researchers and teachers alike: Are research and teaching activities directed toward this primary goal? Do present research and teaching really make any difference in the growth toward full selfhood? What are the essential ingredients a family must provide for a child to grow and function effectively? What kinds of family relationships or ways of using resources provide for meeting the basic needs of all family members? (Hodson, 1967)

Management should have as its end goal the encouragement of self-actualization, focusing on providing an environment that will provide the satisfaction of this need. In such an environment the individual would seek out and justify his own values and discover his own highest capabilities rather than work to achieve a goal preset for him. (Price, 1969)

Management and the Human Environment

The physical environment should be considered as a resource to be managed. This environment has been modified so radically that, in order to exist in it, man must now modify himself. He must become aware of the new needs the environment has imposed upon him as well as the new means at his disposal for meeting these needs. (Wiener, 1954) It may be necessary to develop a new "environmental ethic," with the establishment of new values, to guide in making the difficult choices that must be made. (McClintock, 1971; Scoby, 1971) Such an environmental ethic would apply to all facets of society producing and consuming goods.

Such an ethic could provide a voluntaristic theory for negotiations between man and his environment, based on rational decision making. Examples of topics and questions on which decisions must be reached for future survival are: (McClintock, 1971)

1.   Limitations on human population, how they could be applied, and attitudes toward such limitations. "Family planning is not designed to destroy families. On the contrary it is designed to save them." (Robert McNamara)

2.   Profit motive in business.

3.   Living with nature and conserving natural resources.

Since demands for the affluent life have created a breakdown in natural balances, consumption levels must be restrained. The environment is being transformed rapidly into forms of matter that cannot be consumed, used, or reactivated, with no concern for the waste and pollution created.

Management has tended to stress the raising of the level or quality of living of families. While it should remain concerned with the values and goals of individuals and families, it also can play an important role in a broader context by considering the effects on the environment of high levels of product consumption, thus helping to solve environmental problems in society. Man's very survival may depend upon his decisions in this regard.

Management as Decision Making*

"Operations research and the decision-theory framework are part of a current worldwide *management science movement*." (Miller and Starr, 1967, p. 10) Such research is problem-oriented and is used to produce rational decisions and logical plans of action. Although management science usually employs quantitative methods, if problems cannot be quantified they may be handled qualitatively.

The organization to be studied, whether it be a business firm, a school, or a home should be viewed as a communication network — a collection of points between which information is transmitted. The information coming into the organization from the outside world is *input*. The responses of the organization (i.e., buying of products, etc.) are *outputs*. An input-output model for management within the family is presented in Figure 15.

A specific decision by a manager depends upon his analysis, interpretation, and evaluation of information available to him. Proper categorization of data is important in this process. The decision process is a complex one. The quantitative analysis of a decision problem necessitates measurement in the form of a numerical description of each alternative strategy.

The economic concept of utility has been adopted by decision theorists. Utility is thereby used as a measurement of the degree to which satisfaction (or attainment of objectives or goals) is obtained. Alternative choices or modes of action are compared to determine which choice yields the greatest amount of utility. Some decision problems are more easily quantified than others. For example, if an objective can be expressed in dollars such as gross profit received, degree of satisfaction of the objective is easily measured. If it can be predicted

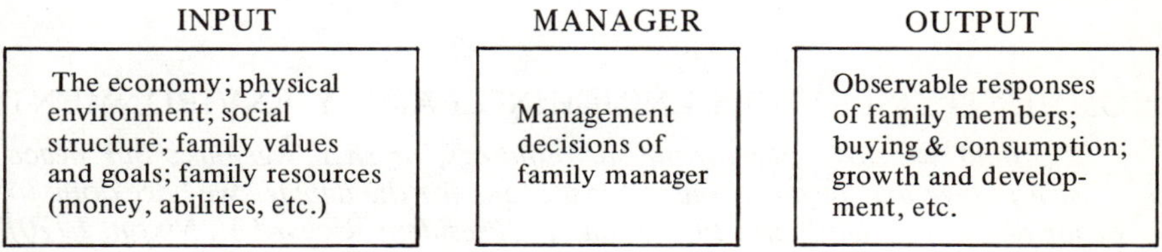

INPUT	MANAGER	OUTPUT
The economy; physical environment; social structure; family values and goals; family resources (money, abilities, etc.)	Management decisions of family manager	Observable responses of family members; buying & consumption; growth and development, etc.

Figure 15. Input-Output Model for Management Within the Family

---

*Ideas are based upon the theory presented by Miller and Starr, 1967.

that profit increases as items sold increase, an attempt can be made to control number of items sold to maximize profits. Variables not so easily controlled may be studied in terms of frequency distributions. Some of the problems involved in the "decision procedures of individuals involved in the business of living" have been summarized by Miller and Starr as follows:

1.   Being unable to satisfactorily describe goals in terms of one objective, people customarily maintain various objectives. Each is relevant to some phase of their life activities.

2.   Multiple objectives are frequently in conflict with each other, and when they are, a suboptimization problem exists.

3.   A particularly important aspect of the suboptimization problem is temporal. This means that (at best) we can only optimize as of that time when the decision is made. This will frequently produce a suboptimization when viewed in subsequent times.

4.   Typically, decision problems are so complex that any attempt to discover the set of optimal actions is useless. Instead, people set their goals in terms of outcomes that are good enough. (Simon's principle of bounded rationality.)

5.   Granted all the difficulties, human beings make every effort to be rational in resolving their decision problems. To help, they have a great store of past human experiences codified for them in the form of ethical principles. These principles, maxims, and heuristics are such that adhering to them is no guarantee of success — but they do afford guidance.

Summary

The family is an example of an ecosystem. Ecology is concerned with mutual relations among organisms and between them and their environment. When the family can maintain itself somewhat like a balanced aquarium, it is quite self-sufficient. This requires the family organization to remain intact. Man must recognize the inseparable relationship of all living things. To diminish the whole, whether it be the family or larger society, could destroy the part, the individual. Although the family is not a closed system, the family must recognize that its resources are finite and must be conserved. Solving environmental problems is a matter of attitudes and values, not technology alone.

COMMUNITY SERVICES ENRICHING FAMILY ENVIRONMENT

Shall we surrender to our surroundings, or shall we make our peace with nature and begin to make reparations for the damage we have done to our air, to our land, and to our water? (President Richard M. Nixon, 1970)

Urbanization: The Living Community

Large urban complexes sprawled across the nation constitute the environment in which more than 80 per cent of Americans live. It has been suggested that the place to begin solving America's problems is in the communities and, of course, communities are composed of families. Some kind of balance is always developed between the contributions made by the family to the larger community and the community services received by the family. Today interaction between family and society appears to be on the rise. Decreasingly is the family a unit that can sustain itself physically and intellectually. Decreasingly is it able to determine the destinies of its individual members. As the total social structure becomes more industrialized and urbanized, with massing together of people, opportunities for contacts with many people outside the family structure vastly increase.

Roles of Family Members

Probably changes in the American family constitute part of a differentiation process as society moves into more specialized subsystems. The loss of many traditional family functions becomes inevitable in many so-called "advanced societies." The family remains the basic reproductive and economic unit but many of its social functions are being partially relinquished — its educational function to the schools, its care of the physically dependent to hospitals and nursing homes, its social security function to the government.

Not only do the functions of the family change with social change, but the roles of family members also change. In earlier years the woman was director of home production, which was important in an agricultural economy. Today she has emerged as a colleague of her husband in the home and she has assumed the additional role of participant in community affairs and in the world of work in institutions outside the home.

Such role changes increase the need for and possibilities for provision of more services to the family in order to ease the burden of the woman who works outside the home. The report of the 1963 President's Commission on the Status of Women stated:

> If the family is to continue to be the core institution of society, as it has been for many centuries, new and expanded community services are necessary. Women can do a far more effective job as mothers and homemakers when communities provide appropriate resources and when they know how to use such resources for health, education, safety, recreation, child care, and counseling. (*American Women,* 1963, p. 18)

The Commission also emphasized that child care facilities are a primary need. Family counseling, homemaker services, and education in homemaking skills for inexperienced housewives are other aids that the community can provide.

Research in this area should include "defining and accomplishing community goals and programs which contribute to the well-being of families and to larger societal goals." (Schlater, 1970, p. 50)

The Quality of Human Life

A healthy individual will postpone an immediate pleasure or tolerate pain in order to obtain a greater pleasure in the future. Community services need to be directed toward goal-setting, creativity, and reality principles. Effective ways of promoting individual action and cooperative efforts for community betterment need to be determined in areas that could have potentially disastrous effects on the quality of life. Among the concerns requiring concerted effort are population growth, racism and problems of minorities, materialistic goals that measure success in terms of ever-increasing consumption, pollution and the reckless destruction of the environment, unemployment, growing size of impersonal institutions, and decreased opportunities for creative and effective individual action.

OPENNESS TO ENVIRONMENTAL EXPERIENCES

> *The real revolution will be a revolution of attitudes. It must concern itself with the meaning of "progress," and, if it is successful, cause man to see himself as interdependent with, and not plundering master of, his environment. (Luther Gerlach, 1970)*

Since an individual's openness to environmental experiences is related to his psychological and social development, this section could have been combined with the conceptual framework for that area. However, it is being considered separately for emphasis and to illustrate possible linkages between man and his environment through a common boundary. (See section on Environment-Behavior Relations, p. 24.)

The human personality with its needs and values determines one's perception of the physical and social environment. Ultimately, this perceptual frame of reference governs one's adaptive behavior to his environment. The conceptual framework presented here shows man's processing of the sensory environment through reduction or augmentation and the relationship between perceptions, feelings, and thoughts. Also, the importance of body percept is shown in relation to field dependence and body-image boundary.

Processing the Sensory Environment

Lowen pointed out a basic concept of bioenergetic theory:

> ... what a person really feels is his body. He cannot feel the environment except through its action upon his body. He feels how his body reacts to stimuli proceeding from the environment, and then he projects this feeling on the stimuli. Thus, when I sense that your hand is warm as it rests upon my arm, what I feel is the warmth in my arm that is produced by your hand. All feelings are body perceptions. If a person's body does not respond to the environment, he feels nothing. (Lowen, 1970, p. 55)

Reduction-Augmentation. People tend to differ in the manner in which they process their sensory environment. Petrie (1967) identified three kinds of persons who differ in this respect: (1) the *reducer*, who tends subjectively to decrease what is perceived; (2) the *augmenter*, who increases what is perceived; and (3) the *moderate*, who neither reduces nor augments but tends to leave unchanged that which is perceived. The reducer tends to strongly desire physical activity, movement, speed, bright colors, and company. He is relatively tolerant of pain. He has a need for change. The augmenter, who increases the intensity of stimulation, is relatively intolerant of pain, and tends to be quiet, inactive, avoiding activities, etc. In contrast to the reducer, the augmenter appears to have intense consciousness of himself and others, which may relate to his rich inner life coming into him from the environment. Free from sensory needs, he may be freer to cultivate his own mind. (Petrie, 1967)

Perception Consciousness. Lowen said that thinking and feeling are different aspects of the function of perception:

> A feeling is a sensory perception of a bodily process and carries an energetic charge or affect. ... A thought, on the other hand, is a psychic perception of a bodily process in the form of an image. The image itself carries no charge and has no quantitative aspect. ... The motive power or charge behind a thought is due to the feeling that accompanies it. (Lowen, 1970, p. 132)

The relationship between sensory perception and consciousness was clarified further in this way:

> It is our bodies that appreciate the freshness of a stream, the sweet taste of pure water, the sight of blue sky, the song of a bird, the smell of a flower, and so on. If we are in touch with our bodies, we enjoy being part of nature and being able to share its splendors. If we are identified with our bodies, we have soul, for through our bodies we are identified with all creation. (Lowen, 1970, p. 121)

Openness to one's experiences involves both the conscious and unconscious, according to Lowen:

> Pleasure has a large unconscious component, which accounts for its spontaneous character. It is not subject to command. It may appear in the most unexpected places: a flower that grows by the wayside, a conversation with a stranger, or an unwelcome social evening that turns out to be a delightful soiree. ... Whereas the response of pain involves a heightening of self-consciousness, the response of pleasure entails and demands a decrease of self-consciousness. ... To have pleasure one has to "let go," that is, allow the body to respond freely. A person who is inhibited cannot easily experience pleasure because unconscious restraints restrict the flow of feeling in his body and block his natural bodily motility. (Lowen, 1970, p. 32)

The Body Percept

A central idea appearing in various forms in the literature is the recognition of the interdependence of the structure of the bodily self and the structure of one's environment or of the characteristics of the person as a bodily entity and the characteristics of the world around him. It is to be assumed that there can be no perception of objects "out there" without a bodily framework and conversely there can be no perception of the body-as-object without an environmental frame of reference. There is constant action going on between them. (Wapner and Werner, 1965)

Field Dependence. Application of Witkin's concept of the "body as perceived" classifies people into those experiencing high sensitivity to stimuli from their bodies irrespective of outside environmental stimuli (field independent) and those experiencing high sensitivity to outside environmental cues (field dependent). The field independent person tends to be highly differentiated from his environment, perceiving his body as separate from the world of objects and tending to remain independent of it. He tends to be relatively unaffected by authority and to be guided by his own values and needs. The field dependent individual, on the other hand, relies on others for direction and guidance. (Witkin, 1962)

Body Boundary. A steadily mounting number of references has appeared in the literature regarding the psychological body image boundary concept. The basic idea expressed is that the individual must learn to differentiate his body from his environment and that the clearness of this differentiation or demarkation may have significant behavioral implications. (Fisher and Cleveland in Wapner and Werner, 1965)

The individual's boundaries play an important role in maintaining homeostasis in the course of the individual's transactions with the world. Some individuals experience their boundaries as definite and firm; others experience them as indefinite and weak. Individuals also differ with respect to where they set their boundaries. The body wall may be the reference point for some; clothing and other aspects of the environment (e.g., the automobile) may be included within the body image boundary for others.

The existence and importance of the body boundary are difficult to grasp because normally people experience little concern about their boundaries, knowing quite certainly where they end and the outer world begins. However, in various pathological states the individual loses his body boundary and its value in relation to his adjustments to objects and people in his environment becomes apparent.

The selection and formulation of a research problem are never simple matters. However, especially in the "discovery" or heuristic approach to research, both imagination and common sense are needed to find a proper problem, and extreme care must be exercised in expressing it. At the same time, because we tend to see only what we are looking for, the formulation must be clear and unequivocal if it is not to have the effect of guiding the researcher's thoughts in a direction which will eventually restrict his results.

CHAPTER 3

Selection and Formulation of a Research Problem

SELECTION OF RESEARCH PROBLEM AREA

Values are involved in the selection of every research topic just as they are involved in the selection of one's major field of study in college. Having chosen a major field, either at the undergraduate or graduate level, it should not be difficult to select a broad research goal such as those enumerated in Chapter 1. For example, a major in Family and Child Development may wish to select Goal I (Improve the conditions contributing to man's psychological and social development). The selection of a more specific research problem area within this broad goal may be a more difficult decision. This decision is based on the student's interest in the topic, the need for a solution to a problem in that area, and the student's knowledge of the subject matter, concepts, and theories from the basic disciplines underlying it. If the student does not currently possess such knowledge, he should seek it through additional course work or self-directed study. A major in Family and Child Development, for example, may be interested in Research Problem Area 8 (Social and technological change) but he may have had no background dealing with the problems of social change.

When selecting a problem area and clarifying a problem within that area, three basic questions should be considered:

1. Is the problem important?
Will the selected problem advance the knowledge of human ecology? Is it a new topic, or does it represent an original, timely approach in an area that has been studied previously? Is the field sufficiently limited to permit thorough treatment of the problem?

2. Is the investigator qualified?
Is the investigator sincerely interested in the general field and in the specific problem? Does he have adequate background in the field he has chosen, as well

as in related fields? Does he possess the necessary research skills to carry out the study, or can he equip himself with the skills which he lacks? Is he free from strong biases?

3.   Is the study feasible?

Are the time, energy, and money requirements compatible with the investigator's resources? Can the study be completed within a reasonable length of time and yet provide sufficient understanding of long range value? Can adequate and accurate data be obtained? Are the necessary library facilities and data-processing equipment available?

If the researcher looks upon his job as a creative, challenging experience, he will be conscious of many problems or obstacles which provide opportunity for research. If he learns to listen carefully and read critically, he will become aware of areas in which there are problems awaiting solution. If he enjoys trying different ways of doing a task, he will be opening the way for experimentation with, and evaluation of, various approaches.

Professional literature can help one select a problem and gain assurance that he has chosen a worthwhile area for study. Wide reading will enable him to keep up-to-date on completed research studies, the analysis of trends as viewed by experts in various fields, statements of needed research, and titles of research currently underway.

An important consideration regarding a research problem is that it must be transformed into a feasible research project that can be investigated by scientific procedures. Not every topic can be so investigated. For example, one student wished to conduct a project that reasoning determined could be investigated only by conducting a human post mortem. This was scientifically but not ethically feasible. Animals can sometimes be so sacrificed for the advancement of science but not humans. If the researcher is to show a true concern for human ecology research, he will be careful not to impoverish the environment which he is studying.

STATEMENT OF THE PROBLEM

Too often investigators jump from the selection of a topic to the collection of data. The first step in the formulation of research is to discover a problem in need of solution and then to make the problem concrete and explicit.

Stating a research problem may appear easier than it is in practice. In some respects, this is the most difficult and probably the most important part of the whole research process. The researcher may first have only a vague and confused idea of the specific problem he wishes to investigate. Nonetheless, he must bring his ideas out in the open and express them in some limited form.

The research problem must be of manageable size. Usually not all aspects of a problem can be studied simultaneously. The task must be reduced to one that can be handled in a single study, or it may be divided into sub-questions for separate studies by one or perhaps several researchers.

To assist in formulating his problem, the researcher studies the literature in his field and related fields and reviews his own experience and the experiences of others. (See Chapter 4.)

An analysis of the characteristics of several research problem statements may be helpful:

1. Is personality related to the consumer-decision process?
2. What are the effects of soil release finishes on the removal of soil from different fabrics?
3. "What is the relationship between a person's feelings about himself and his feelings about other people?" (Rosenberg, 1965, p. 168)

These problem statements meet three criteria (Kerlinger, 1964):

1. They express a relation between two or more variables.
2. They state problems clearly and unambiguously in question form. Questions are preferred because they tend to pose the problem directly.
3. They *imply* the possibility of empirical testing. This means that the variable can be measured in some manner. As indicated previously, questions that are not amenable to testing are not scientific.

"A *problem*, then, is an interrogative sentence or statement that asks: What relation exists between two or more variables? The answer to this question is what is being sought in the research." (Kerlinger, 1964, p. 19)

HYPOTHESES

Hypotheses are the researcher's guesses as to the probable outcomes of his study. They may rest on hunches, be based on findings of other studies, or stem from a body of theory leading to the prediction that if certain conditions are present, certain results will follow. Hypotheses serve as guides to the kinds of data to be collected and the method by which they should be analyzed. Statements of hypotheses should contain two or more variables that are measurable and should specify how the variables are related. The object of research is to test hypotheses and show them to be probably true or probably false.

Hypotheses may be stated in three primary forms:

1. *Declarative form.* This form usually states a relationship between the variables that the experimenter expects will emerge. Example: There will be a significant difference between scores on a measure of inferiority feelings of low I.Q. students compared to high I.Q. students.
2. *Null form.* This form states that no relationship exists between the variables concerned. The null form is best fitted to statistical techniques. Example: There will be no significant difference between scores on a measure of inferiority feelings of low I.Q. students compared with high I.Q. students.
3. *Question form.* This is often easiest for the inexperienced research worker to use because it states specifically the question the research will attempt to answer. Example: Is there a significant difference between the scores on a measure of inferiority feelings of low I.Q. students compared with high I.Q. students?

According to Barnes (1956, p. 6), a good hypothesis must:

"1. be clear and unequivocal. It must be worded in operational terms; *what* action, *who* is involved, what is the *prediction*, in what quantity or to what degree?

"2. be specific. Is it testable? Are the predictions and operations of the test spelled out? If sub-hypotheses are needed to detail the test, are they provided?

"3. be directly related to empirical phenomena. Are the words 'ought,' 'should,' 'bad,' and other normative or moral judgments avoided? These concepts can't be tested.

"4. be related to available techniques. If the hypothesis satisfies all other tests, it is still worthless if procedures for testing it are not known.

"5. be related to knowledge or theoretical constructs concerning the original problem area. Professional knowledge or acquaintance with other relevant research studies can help sharpen a hypothesis."

Moral, ethical, or value judgments have no place in the statement of a problem or hypothesis. The following statement contains such value judgments and therefore is not scientific: "The lecture method of teaching leads to *poor* learning." "Decreased problem-solving behavior" or some other expression implying measurement possibilities should be substituted for the word "poor."

Vague generalizations and definitions should also be avoided, e.g., "Team teaching is an enriching experience"; "Creativity is a function of the self-actualization of the individual." While the latter may be an interesting problem, it should be more specifically defined.

Whenever possible, it is desirable to formulate hypotheses before commencing a study, but the timing may vary with the nature of the problem and the extent of prior knowledge about it. In some fields of study, particularly in those dealing with social relations, much exploratory research is needed before hypotheses can be formulated. In these instances, objectives may be listed at the beginning of the study and hypotheses formulated at the conclusion of the project.

DEFINING CONCEPTS

In order to organize his data to perceive relationships among them, a researcher must make use of concepts. As indicated in Chapter 2, concepts embody the important ideas of a field of study. Some concepts are quite close to the objects or facts they represent and need little definition. For example, one's mental image of food may be easily illustrated by pointing to specific foods. Other concepts cannot be so easily related to the phenomena they represent. Such concepts as intelligence, creativity, management, and attitude fall into this category. These higher level abstractions are sometimes referred to as constructs, which are constructed from concepts at a lower level of abstraction. When there is a wide distance between one's concepts or constructs and the empirical fact to which they refer, care must be given to defining them, both in terms of the general meaning they are intended to convey and the operations by which they will be represented in the particular study. The latter type definition is referred to as an *operational* or *working definition*. Such a definition specifies the meaning of the concept by denoting the measuring operations used to identify it. Such definitions therefore reflect measurements. Operational definitions facilitate communication among scientists.

Thus, in a study dealing with mood, the literary definition of mood may be stated as follows: Mood is "a long-lasting affective state, usually mild in intensity." (Harriman, 1965, p. 110) In a specific research study, however, the operational definition could be that mood is a rating by the individual of how well he is feeling at the present time on a ten point scale ranging from "feel as bad as possible" to "feel as good as possible." The latter kind of operational definition could also be called a behavioral or observational definition. It defines or gives meaning to a variable by spelling out what the investigator must do to measure the variable. In making operational definitions the researcher must answer the question, "What will I accept as an indicator of my concept?" Underwood described the important role of operational definitions: "I would say that operational thinking makes better scientists. The operationist is forced to remove the fuzz from his empirical concepts. . . . Operationism facilitates communication among scientists because the meaning of concepts so defined is not easily subject to misinterpretation." (Underwood, 1957, p. 53)

Writing his own definitions may enable the researcher to convey the meaning he wishes to express for the specific situation in which his problem is to be studied. Definitions should be in harmony with other related concepts and should be stated in such a way as to give the reader a concise and complete understanding of the concepts. Definitions serve two purposes: to explain the meaning of a concept that might not be clearly understood otherwise and to restrict a concept that has more than one meaning.

A good definition fulfills the following criteria:

1. It gives the essence of that which is being defined.

2. It refers to the attributes possessed by, rather than those lacking in, the object being defined.

3. It contains the elements that are essential characteristics of what is being defined, but eliminates superfluous factors.

4. It is expressed in clear and direct language rather than in obscure or figurative terms.

5. The subject of the definition and the defining clause are reversible.

6. The defining clause contains words whose meaning is clearer than the word that is being defined, and it does not, directly or indirectly, contain the word that is being defined.

CHAPTER 4

Review of Literature

H ow much material should I read on my topic?" is a question confronting the researcher in planning a research study. Research experts do not agree. Some believe that a study should be planned rather completely before extensive reading, in order to promote original thinking on the problem. Others feel that wide reading is needed in order to evaluate the significance of a problem and to be sure that the problem has not already been solved satisfactorily.

In planning research, a survey of related literature is valuable for at least three reasons:

1. It reveals the importance of the problem. Only by making an intensive survey can one determine whether or not a problem has been solved satisfactorily in previous studies. The fact that a problem has been studied does not preclude another investigation. Valuable studies may result from deliberate repetition of a study. The conditions may be kept identical in order to verify the results, or they may be changed to provide for a comparison of two or more procedures. Repetition at regular time intervals enables the researcher to observe trends and developments.

2. It guides in the formulation of the problem. Knowing what others have tried and how successful their efforts have been can stimulate ideas and enrich a study. Methods, techniques, or instruments may be found that can be utilized. A combination of creative and informed thinking can lead to new approaches in problem solving without unnecessary waste of time or duplication of effort.

3. It aids in the interpretation of results. If the researcher's findings are in agreement with the results of other research studies, he may have greater confidence in his conclusions. When his results differ from the comparative data, he will be stimulated to find out in what respects they differ and to explain possible reasons for these differences.

THE SEARCH FOR RELATED STUDIES

Reference guides to periodicals, books, or bulletins can help in locating suitable materials on a specific topic. One source is the *library card catalog* which lists each book by author, title, and subject. Browsing among the books in a classification related to a problem may help one to find books that might be overlooked otherwise.

Encyclopedias

An encyclopedia may help to sharpen a problem and to locate significant research reports. Among those applicable to human ecology research are these:

The Encyclopedia of Biochemistry. Edited by Roger J. Williams and Edwin M. Lansford. New York: Reinhold, 1967. 876 pp.

The Encyclopedia of the Biological Sciences. 2nd ed. Edited by Peter Gray. New York: Van Nostrand, 1970. 1027 pp.

The Encyclopedia of Educational Research. 4th ed. Edited by Robert L. Ebel, Victor H. Noll, and Roger M. Bauer. A project of the American Educational Research Association. New York: Macmillan, 1969. 1522 pp.

The Encyclopedia of Human Behavior. Edited by Robert M. Goldenson. Garden City, New York: Doubleday, 1970. 1472 pp.

Yearbook of Science and Technology. New York: McGraw-Hill Book Co., 1971.

International Encyclopedia of the Social Sciences. Edited by David L. Sills. New York: Macmillan, 1968. 17 volumes.

Encyclopedia of World Art. New York: McGraw-Hill Book Co., 1967.

Indexes

Several indexes related to human ecology areas are available. These include:

Applied Science and Technology Index, dealing with periodicals on engineering, trade, business, and related subjects. Among its subject headings are acoustic impedance, air pollution, architecture, fibers, food additives, human relations, lasers, pesticides, and public health.

Art Index is a guide to art periodicals and museum bulletins. Its subject areas include archaeology, architecture, art history, arts and crafts, city planning, fine arts, graphic arts, industrial design, interior design, landscape design, photography and films.

Biological and Agricultural Index covers agriculture, biological sciences, ecology, food technology, and nutrition.

Business Periodicals Index refers to articles in business and economics, dealing with such topics as advertising, air pollution, attitude, clothing industry, computer-based services, consumer protection, decision making, detergent pollution of water, environmental policy, food industry, housing, management, and technological change.

Education Index covers periodicals, bulletins, monographs, yearbooks, and government publications on such topics as behavior modification, birth control, counseling, preschool education, culturally deprived, learning, nutrition education, sensitivity training, tests and scales.

Index of Economic Articles in Journals and Collective Volumes, under the auspices of the American Economic Association, deals with such subjects as motivation; value, price, and allocation theory; government and the economy; money, credits and banking; economic fluctuations; natural resources, population; labor economics; regional planning and development.

Index to Periodical Articles By and About Negroes is a guide to reference and research in Negro literature and history. Some of its topics are adoption, black power, civil rights, clothing and dress, designers, intermarriage of races, and women.

Public Affairs Information Service Bulletin deals with economics and public affairs on such topics as family allowances, communication, dissenters, family life, home ownership, and insurance.

Reader's Guide covers periodicals of general interest, published in the United States.

Social Sciences and Humanities Index lists scholarly American and foreign journals dealing with social and cultural activities of man. Its subject headings include adolescence, conflict of generations, clothing and dress, diet, family, interior decoration, and investments.

Abstracts and Annual Reviews

Abstract journals and annual reviews give the reader more information about the content of articles, but the additional time necessary to render this service often means that the references are not as current as those found in an index. Of particular value in human ecology research are the following:

Abstracts in Anthropology is divided into four sections: ethnology, linguistics, archaeology, and physical anthropology. Its topics include such areas as acculturation, adaptation, authority and power, cultural change and stability, culture of poverty, ecology, ritual and ceremony.

Abstracts for Social Workers, prepared by the National Association of Social Workers, can help in locating references on such topics as alcoholism and drug addiction, civil rights and civil liberties, economic security, health and medical care, group work, and mental health.

Annual Review of Psychology is broadly representative of the whole field of psychology. It includes such topics as developmental psychology; perception; the chemical senses; color vision; personality; attitudes and opinions; human abilities.

Biological Abstracts is valuable for specialized studies related to diet, nutrition, vitamins, food technology, genetics, gerontology, infancy and childhood.

Chemical Abstracts includes such topics as dyes and textile chemistry; foods; glass, clay products, enameled metals; building materials; fuels; waxes and detergents.

Child Development Abstracts and Bibliography has areas on biology; clinical medicine and public health; developmental and comparative psychology; experimental psychology, including learning; personality; sociology and social psychology; education and counseling; psychiatry and clinical psychology.

Environmental Abstracts (SERI) is a collection of annotated abstracts of literature dealing with the environment and human behavior. (Publication of the Architectural Research Laboratory, College of Architecture and Design, University of Michigan, 1965.)

Historical Abstracts has sections on methodology and research methods, philosophy and interpretation of history, social and cultural history, economic history, sciences and technology, and areas or countries.

Nutrition Abstracts and Reviews includes chemical composition of foodstuffs, vitamins, physiology of nutrition, human diet in relation to health and disease, and other topics related to nutrition.

Psychological Abstracts covers the major fields of psychology and related disciplines: experimental; physiological; animal; developmental; social; personality; clinical; educational; personnel and industrial. Specific topics include culture and social processes, drug usage and abuse, nutrition and digestive processes, family relations, environment and stress, sensory physiology, etc.

Review of Educational Research is a comprehensive summary and critical analysis of articles and trends covering all phases of education.

Sociological Abstracts, sponsored by the American Sociological Association, covers areas such as methodology, social psychology, group interactions, culture and social structure, complex organizations, social change and economic development, mass phenomena; political interactions, social differentiation, and rural sociology and agricultural economics.

World Textile Abstracts covers areas such as fibers; yarns; fabrics; chemical and finishing processes; clothing and made-up goods; mill engineering; management; analysis, testing, quality control; and polymer science.

In addition to these general sources, government agencies and other organizations publish summaries of research in their special fields of interest. For example, the Children's Bureau of the United States Department of Health, Education and Welfare publishes a bulletin of research relating to children.

Computer Storage and Retrieval of Data

ERIC (Educational Resources Information Center) is a national system for disseminating educational research results. ERIC acquires, abstracts, indexes, stores, retrieves, and disseminates significant information on research and leadership development. Several universities participate in this project in cooperation with the United States Office of Education. Each clearinghouse, or university center, handles information on a specific area. For example, the Ohio State University is responsible for vocational and technical education.

CRIS (Current Research Information System) is a service of the United States Department of Agriculture, providing communication of research and management information.

MEDLARS (Medical Literature Analysis and Retrieval System) is a similar type of service in connection with *Index Medicus*.

Science Citation Index is prepared by a computer and cites source authors as entries. Selected journals covering all the major disciplines and subdisciplines of mathematics, the life, physical, and chemical sciences, and engineering are included as basic inputs. The *Index* brings together all articles by a certain author that were cited in leading journals during a certain year.

Unpublished Dissertations and Theses

The American Home Economics Association* publishes useful research abstracts in such areas as: family economics-home management; institution administration; textiles and clothing; art, housing, furnishing, and equipment; home economics education; family relations-child development; and food and nutrition.

Dissertation Abstracts International is a compilation of doctoral studies from more than 270 cooperating institutions. These dissertations are available on microfilm or as Xerographic reproductions. The service provides separate volumes for: (1) the humanities and social sciences and (2) the sciences and engineering.

Masters Abstracts is a newer but similar type of service which accepts only those masters theses recommended by the graduate school of the cooperating institutions.

PREPARATION OF A REVIEW OF THE LITERATURE

Since human ecology is a relatively new field of research, little or no material may be found under this heading. However, specific topics related to human ecology can be located. Many of these topics are suggested in Chapter 2. Before reading extensively, the researcher should outline the types of literature which are related to his study.

An abstract is a good form in which to take notes of research reports. The essential parts of an abstract are: (1) purpose of the study; (2) method of procedure; (3) findings; and (4) conclusions. A desirable fifth step is an evaluation of the study, including brief comments on its quality or significance, pertinence to one's problem, and adequacy. File cards or a loose leaf notebook provide flexibility for adding or reorganizing materials and assembling a bibliography. Complete bibliographical information for each reference should be included. A subject heading at the top of each abstract aids in organizing materials.

If the studies located are in disagreement, a special effort must be made to present an unbiased review of the literature. Many persons find it easier to locate and present materials that support their own views.

An entire chapter may be devoted to a review of literature, or such a review may be combined with other material in an introductory chapter. A review

---

*American Home Economics Association, 2010 Massachusetts Avenue N.W., Washington, D.C. 20036.

probably will not contain all of the sources available on a topic. A comprehensive but selective summary should be presented.

REFERENCES AND FOOTNOTES

References should be given to support any facts or opinions that are borrowed, whether or not they are quoted directly. Several different styles of footnotes and bibliography are in use. The student should adopt one that is recommended by his graduate school or by the publication for which he is writing and follow it consistently and accurately.*

Quotations

A direct quotation may be used for several reasons. The most obvious use is when no change is possible for the sake of accuracy, as in a statistical formula, law, or official ruling. When a statement is unusually clear or beautiful, its exact wording may be the most effective way to present a significant thought. A direct quotation from a recognized authority may be a means of adding strength to one's paper.

Whenever a direct quotation is used, it must be reproduced exactly from the original publication. Even though changes in spelling or punctuation might make a quotation more in keeping with modern usage, no corrections should be made. If part of the original quotation is omitted, the break is indicated by the ellipsis (. . .). If the omission is at the end of a sentence, a fourth dot is added to represent the normal punctuation at the break. If anything is added to a direct quotation, the addition should be placed in brackets [ ] .

Footnotes

Footnotes serve two purposes: (1) providing additional information and (2) indicating the source of an idea. When the reader might need specific information which would disrupt the continuity of the regular text, details can be presented in a footnote. Footnotes should be as helpful as possible to persons who wish to refer to the sources of facts or opinions presented. Complete and accurate information is essential.

At least two styles are acceptable for indicating references in footnotes. The more traditional form is to number footnotes consecutively throughout a chapter. When a second reference to the same work is made on the same page or the following page, *ibid.* (meaning "in the same place") is used. When other references have intervened, *op. cit.* (meaning "in the work cited") may be used following the author's name.

A newer, but more simple technique, is the parenthetical style in which each item refers by the author's name to the appropriate reference in the bibliog-

---

*Among the widely used reference books are these:

William G. Campbell, *Form and Style in Thesis Writing*. 3rd ed. Boston: Houghton Mifflin Company, 1969.

A Manual of Style. 12th ed. Chicago: The University of Chicago Press, 1969.

raphy. This style eliminates duplicate listing of a reference in a footnote and in the bibliography.

Bibliography

A bibliography contains each reference that was cited in the research report and additional selected references that might be helpful to workers in that problem area. The bibliography is a complete, though not exhaustive, list.

Research Types or Settings

No research results are any better than the methods by which they are obtained. The maturity of a discipline can be gauged by the spread of sophisticated methodology among its members. In Part II, four major research types or settings are described in terms of characteristics and methods employed. Each research type is illustrated with examples from recent dissertations or published research articles representing the major fields of study in human ecology. Specific methods of data collection, with examples of research studies using these methods, are discussed in Part IV. Some projects combine several research designs and methods of data collection.

CHAPTER 5

Documentary Research: Historical

Documentary or historical research involves the discovery and analysis of records of previous events, interpretation of trends in the attitudes or events of the past, and generalization from these past events to help guide present or future behavior. From documentary research we may gain respect for early leaders, understanding of the relationship between various parts of our environment, insight into past mistakes that might be avoided in the future, understanding of contemporary problems, and awareness of possible new approaches that might be used in solving current problems.

DOCUMENTARY RESEARCH DEFINED

Documentary research consists of locating, integrating, and evaluating evidence from physical relics, written records, or documents in order to establish facts or generalizations regarding past or present events, human characteristics, etc.

This method of data collection and analysis may be considered the oldest form of true research, having been developed by the ancient Greek historians and philosophers. In modern times, the method has been greatly refined and made more exact.

The documentary method is often called the historical method because historians use it so frequently. However, it is also used in literature, art, philosophy, and other fields of study.

Sometimes documentary research is selected by students as an "easy way out." It may be regarded by some as an escape from experimental studies which some students resist. Such students do not realize that good documentary research demands objective methods and the setting up of specific testable hypotheses. These demands may be much more difficult to meet with documentary than with scientific methods because of the nature of the data. Of course, not all documentary historical studies meet these criteria. Critical analyses of a large sample of historical studies revealed that fewer than one-half met the requirements of true historical research. Too often the historian recites facts but does not synthesize or integrate them into meaningful generalizations. The mere recitation of established facts is not historical research.

Historical sources are classified in terms of physical objects (or relics) and of written or printed documents. The researcher's task usually is to formulate hypotheses and examine his data, in the form of documents or relics. Such data are his evidence to support his hypotheses and conclusions and this evidence must be based upon reliable observation. However, the historian does not usually make his own observations and those upon whose observations he depends are likely to be untrained observers. Therefore, one of his major tasks is to determine the accuracy of the reports made by others. In this critical evaluation of his documentary evidence, the researcher leans heavily upon scientific methods.

SOURCES OF DATA

Source materials that are used in documentary research are of two types: (1) primary — the original document or relic; and (2) secondary — an account or record that is one or more steps removed from the original source or document, prepared by someone who was not actually present to observe what he is describing. One of the basic rules of documentary research is: Always use primary sources. A scholar should never use a copy of a document if he has access to the original. Transcription and publication can result in many possible errors. A picture is not the same as the object itself, however carefully it is reproduced. The newspaper account may be a primary source if the reporter himself witnessed the event he describes. Material quoting an author from the writings of another author can never be considered a primary source. The researcher should search the original published or unpublished form of the quoted material before using the data. Like rumors, data that pass through several hands before they reach the investigator may bear little resemblance to the original versions.

Such materials as the following are likely to be useful in human ecology research:

Expressive documents. Angell and Freedman (1963, p. 302) divide expressive documents into three types: (1) personal letters, (2) life histories (i.e., diaries or autobiographies), and (3) accounts of small-group process. These documents are not always "spontaneous," for their production may sometimes be stimulated by the scientific investigator.

Personal letters are the most available type of expressive document. Information contained in personal letters is likely to be more intimate than that in public records. Thomas and Znaniecki (1927) used letters more than any other source in their comprehensive work, *The Polish Peasant in Europe and America.* Series of letters were collected by Thomas in the United States and by Znaniecki in Poland. A total of 764 letters are reproduced in the book. These letters are used mainly to throw light on the changes in Polish peasant primary groups brought about by industrialization of the peasants and immigration of family members. In no other study has this type of data been used so extensively. The value of letters in documentary research varies with the culture of the writers. Personal correspondence was likely to be more indicative of life situations in early America than it is today since, at that time, other means of communication that are available today were lacking.

Life histories in the form of diaries are a second type of expressive document which have been used extensively by historians and recommended by some psychologists. Cultural anthropologists have used spoken autobiographies more than any other group. Angell and Freedman (1963) indicate the remote possibility that, in the future, autobiographies can be obtained from enough people to control variables and test hypotheses. Nevertheless, they can be authoritative sources for verifying facts established through original sources.

Accounts by a participant of a small group process or behavioral interaction are rarely written spontaneously, so they have not been used as the basis of any large investigation. Occasionally such documents have been stimulated by the researcher. For example, Angell obtained from university students fifty documents on family life before and after the impact of the depression. The writers, who were paid a small fee, wrote from a broad outline which suggested aspects of family life to be emphasized. They were asked, for example, to "discuss the external conditions of your family's existence prior to the decrease in income; touch on the type of neighborhood, the house and yard, the family's material possessions, etc." Several hypotheses about family organization under stress were tested. (Angell and Freedman, 1963)

Expressive documents are most often used in exploratory research rather than in the final stages of the research process principally because such documents are rarely sufficiently controlled by the investigator to give a crucial test of specific hypotheses. The special value of such documents is that life is discussed in them in terms meaningful to those involved. To the degree that we need to understand the "definition of a situation" as seen by participants, such documents constitute an important source of scientific information.

To rely solely upon expressive documents would yield inadequate data because they may not furnish a sufficient number of cases. It is difficult to get a representative sample of people with expressive documents because some people are much more interested and willing to express themselves than others. Interviews, observation, or questionnaires can provide a better coverage of situations because they can be set up to obtain the information that is relevant to the hypotheses for many cases. Documentary evidence can constitute an excellent check on data obtained by these other methods.

Official records may include legal records (e.g., transcriptions of courtroom proceedings), laws and other legislative acts, legal instruments such as contracts and wills, court decisions, commission reports and proceedings, and committee reports showing the work of clubs and organizations. They provide excellent sources because of the care official bodies exert to make certain that such records are accurate, complete, and carefully preserved.

Newspaper and magazine accounts are very interpretive and often inaccurate but provide a more or less permanent record of day-to-day happenings in the world. They are used chiefly when official records do not exist. Be sure to consider whether the report was based on first-hand observation by the journalist or on information obtained through another person.

Eye-witness accounts of events. Such testimony may be given orally or in written form. Since human memory is uncertain, an eye witness account written down at the time of the event usually proves more reliable than efforts to recall incidents a long time after they have occurred.

Archaeological and geological remains, such as gravestones and cornerstone plaques, are not documents in the same sense as written records but they serve the same purpose.

Creative productions such as works of art, literature, and music may be important in some research. Researchers in human ecology might study such creations as pottery, utensils, houses, furniture, photographs, equipment, costumes, textiles, and other museum pieces.

Registration and census data. Numerous statistical data about human population have been collected by government, business, and private organizations. However, individual researchers often ignore the availability of such data when they plan their own research. The following list illustrates important activities which may be covered by registration data (Angell and Freedman, 1963, p. 310):

1. Vital events: Births, deaths, marriages, divorces, morbidity
2. Education: School attendance, grades, performance on psychological tests
3. Crime: Crimes known to police, arrests, court actions, prison records, parole records
4. Voting: Registration, voting
5. Social Security payments and benefits
6. Automobile registrations
7. Draft and Army service
8. Illness: Hospital and insurance data
9. Business activity: Payrolls, production records, absentee records
10. Formal organizations: Membership, office-holding committee participation

A census is a collection of data gathered periodically about a population, usually by a house-to-house canvass. Census data are often used in constructing area samples. They may also be used to select areas of communities as units for research study. Census data can sometimes be combined with other data:

> The Bureau of Census will compile statistics from scientific census schedules of lists of consumers, furnished by business concerns. A given firm may provide certain information about its clients which is transcribed and placed on punch cards along with information taken from the census schedules of the same persons. Cross tabulations are then prepared to show relationships between the characteristics known to the census and those

known to the enterprise. No data are given out in terms of individuals but only in frequencies or summary form. (Parten, 1950, pp. 14-15)

Caution should be taken in using registration data for research. These data are not generally collected for the specific purpose of such research. The definitions and tabulations used in calculating and processing the data may be different from those which the researcher would use if he were collecting his own data. The investigator cannot impose his own standards of validity and reliability on the data. In evaluating the validity of such data, the researcher must consider whether the person responding is able to give the information required and whether the recorder is likely to have secured the information accurately. In some cases, reports of death causes were apparently made by unqualified lay persons. The informant may have the necessary information, but the recorder of this information is not always properly motivated or instructed to get the correct information.

Published indexes. Many published indexes are available which are based on the combination of registration and/or census data. Illustrations are the Cost of Living Index, county level-of-living indexes, juvenile delinquency rates, F.B.I. crime rate index, vital statistics (birth and death rates). An individual investigator may construct indexes for a specific purpose by combining or manipulating series of such published data. Although such indexes often do not meet rigid scaling standards, they may be useful as rough measures of a variable.

APPRAISAL OF DOCUMENTS

The person who writes historical research has seldom witnessed the original events about which he is writing, and these events cannot be reproduced. Therefore, he must strive to determine the reliability of the evidence he obtains. The evidence may be incomplete, deliberately biased, or otherwise defective. Since an individual tends to record only what he considers to be of interest or value, or what he chooses to make known to others, great expenditures of time and money are often required to locate complete and accurate information.

Whether primary or secondary sources are used, the documents should be examined for their genuineness or authenticity (known as *external* criticism) and their meaning or credibility (known as *internal* criticism). The processes of external and internal criticism may overlap and be carried on simultaneously.

External appraisal or criticism is concerned with the validity or genuineness of the data. Documents are to the scholar as courtroom witnesses are to the lawyer. Just as the attorney must lay a foundation for the admissibility of a document in evidence in court, the researcher must determine the identity of the author and his connection with the document. Some of the questions to be raised in this connection are: Why, where, when, and by whom was the document written? Is the subject one in which the author should be competent? Is it reasonable to expect that he could have been in the place indicated at the time indicated? Did he originate the information in the document or copy it from someone else? Is this document consistent in style with the writer's previous works establishing him as the author? Did he write about events or places which would be familiar to a person living in that period?

Since forgeries are common, and there is always the chance of honest errors being made, the form and appearance of documents must be studied. In handwritten documents, authenticated examples of the supposed author's handwriting can serve as a check. Physical and chemical analyses of paper can be made inasmuch as papermaking has changed gradually over time. Ultraviolet rays and fluorescent photography are also used for examining documents, especially to detect alterations and erasures.

Just as hoaxes occur in documents, there are fakes that must be detected among remains such as antiques. Claims of antiquity can be questioned by careful study of such characteristics as odor, smudgy colors, circular saw markings, perfectly round pegs, and perfectly smooth glass doors.

Internal appraisal or criticism is concerned with what the document *says* whereas external criticism evaluates whether it really *is* what it purports to be. Once the document is determined to be valid or genuine, we must ask what it may contribute as a source of information or solution to a problem. What is the content, meaning, and accuracy of the document? Internal criticism seeks to answer such questions as: What was the writer's intent (his real meaning, not the literal meaning)? How should the obsolete terms and symbolic expressions be interpreted? Was the author capable of reporting accurately? Are there evidences that the writer was biased or illogical in his thinking? Were reliable sources used as the basis for his writing? Inaccurate reporting might stem from such factors as emotional stress, poor health, lack of intelligence, writing about an event after a lapse of time, political or other types of personal bias.

In working with documents of the distant past, the question of meaning or interpretation is likely to arise first. Such interpretation in some cases may require a thorough knowledge of history, economics, psychology, sociology, linguistics, political science, or other disciplines.

USE OF HYPOTHESES

When working on historical or documentary research, the researcher in either the natural or social sciences does not begin by testing hypotheses deduced from a general theory. Rather, he starts with a problem of interpretation of empirical material. Confronted with such a problem, he sets forth tentative hypotheses based upon his knowledge of theories related to the problem and then proceeds to test the hypotheses against his observations. (Social Science Research Council, 1954) He searches for documentary evidence that suggests answers to the questions raised. Contrary to this procedure, some students start their dissertations not with a problem and hypotheses but with a body of documents from which they intend simply to find out what is in them.

Historians often conduct descriptive studies in which they identify events which took place in a sequence. By the critical use of documents, credible evidence may be established regarding the *facts*. However, if the researcher does not go beyond this description to analyze *how* and *why* the events occurred, he is not performing a truly scientific function. "The analysis of interrelations goes on in all social science, but the attempt to make a general synthesis of all major factors at work in a given conjecture of events is peculiar to historical studies." (Social Science Research Council, 1954, p. 87) The significance of an event is related to a past and to a future. The fundamental problem of historical study is therefore the analysis of change over time. The process involves essentially determining accurately the events that have occurred in sequence, analyzing the interrelationships among these events, and finally, determining how and why they occurred in the specific sequence. The process is truly a study of the phenomenon of change.

To analyze the history of the American family, its internal structure should be studied (the interrelated roles of father, son, daughter, mother, uncle, and other kin), and its relationship to the society and culture to which it belongs (the effects of the emancipation of women, industrialization, urban living, and similar elements). Likewise, biography or autobiography may be considered historical research when the individual's life is placed in historical perspective with the society and events of his time. What were the social habits, emotional responses, and leading ideas around him?

An important deterrent to historical analysis of the family is that there are many "American families" at any given period:

> But the scholar striving to check theories and hypotheses regarding the family against historical data (and no one not so motivated should assay the task) will doubtless find many clues that have been concealed from the eyes of the conventional historian. Perhaps some day it will be possible to guess wisely at the degree to which group aggressions, political radicalism, or instability in mass reactions were due to the stresses and strains of a family conditioning that became unsuited in varying degrees to the changes in surrounding society. (Social Science Research Council, 1954, pp. 165-166)

Having a strong background in related disciplines can help the researcher interpret historical evidence. Studies may be made of the ways in which great personalities have influenced historical developments. The influences of scientific and technological knowledge on the existing economic and life activities may be examined. Ways in which economic institutions and processes affected social institutions and culture may be explored, as well as the causes and results of group life. The ultimate objective is to prepare a critical, truthful, and meaningful synthesis of available materials.

EXAMPLES AND ANALYSES
OF DOCUMENTARY RESEARCH

THE METHOD OF RECORD LINKAGE APPLIED
TO FAMILY DATA

HAROLD T. CHRISTENSEN

This report is to deal with a relatively new approach in research, accompanied by illustrations of its application to a few specific problems in the area of family phenomena. The method, which we have come to refer to as "record linkage," has been under development by the writer over a period of approximately two decades and some of the substantive findings have appeared in print previously.[1] However, none of these earlier publications discussed the method itself (except in a somewhat brief and descriptive manner) whereas *method is the focus* of the present paper.

Development of the Method

Briefly stated, record linkage consists of using documentary sources — in contrast to data obtained by questionnaires, interviews, or direct observation — and of cross-checking and matching these records against each other. Thus, as was the case in our own studies, marriage records may be linked with birth records and again with divorce records, to give a continuing family picture over time. Though limited to data found on the records, this method nevertheless provides a rather simple way to longitudinal analysis.

The writer conducted his first study in 1937, in Utah County, Utah; then repeated it, with alterations, about one decade later in Tippecanoe County, Indiana. In both of these studies, the central beginning interest was the phenomenon of child spacing, and most particularly the spacing of the first birth from marriage. This was pursued by comparing official marriage and birth

---

Reprinted with permission from *Journal of Marriage and Family Living*, Vol. 20, No. 1, February, 1958, pp. 38-42.

[1] See "The Time Interval Between Marriage of Parents and Birth of Their First Child in Utah County, Utah," *American Journal of Sociology*, 44 (January, 1939), pp. 518-25; "Rural-Urban Differences in the Time-Interval Between the Marriage of Parents and the Birth of Their First Child, Utah County, Utah," *Rural Sociology*, 3 (June, 1938), pp. 172-76; "Studies in Child Spacing: I — Premarital Pregnancy as Measured by the Spacing of the First Birth From Marriage," *American Sociological Review*, 18 (February, 1953), pp. 53-59; with Olive P. Bowden, "Studies in Child Spacing: II — The Time Interval Between Marriage of Parents and Birth of Their First Child, Tippecanoe County, Indiana," *Social Forces*, 31 (May, 1953), pp. 346-51; with Hanna H. Meissner, "Studies in Child Spacing: III — Premarital Pregnancy as a Factor in Divorce," *American Sociological Review*, 18 (December, 1953), pp. 641-44; "Rural-Urban Differences in the Spacing of the First Birth from Marriage: A Repeat Study," *Rural Sociology*, 18 (March, 1953), p. 60; with Robert Andrews and Sophie Freiser, "Falsification of Age at Marriage," *Marriage and Family Living*, 15 (November, 1953), pp. 301-4; with Hanna H. Meissner, "An Analysis of Divorce in Tippecanoe County, Indiana," *Sociology and Social Research*, 40 (March-April, 1956), pp. 248-252.

records so as to follow individual couples through from marriage to the birth of a first child. Before long, numerous other ramifications and possibilities for the method — not present in the original child spacing concept — developed. It became apparent, for example, that a linking of marriage records with divorce records (as well as with birth records) would provide additional data of interest to the family sociologist. Considering divorce as one index of marriage failure, it was now possible to determine how numerous factors, including various aspects of child spacing and premarital pregnancy, are related to the marital outcome.

Recent analyses have been upon the Tippecanoe County data derived from this triple linking of marriage, birth, and divorce records. Marriages occurring during the years 1919-21, 1929-31, and 1939-41 were studied, then matched with birth records searched for five years following the date of each marriage, and finally matched with divorce records searched for all years from the beginning of 1919 through the end of 1952 — all for this one county. Published findings include the following: on the average, first births occurred approximately one and one-half years after the wedding; the trend was toward an increase in length of this time-interval; disproportionately short intervals were found for those who married young, had a non-religious ceremony, and followed a laboring occupation; as might be expected, premarital pregnancy was disproportionately high for these same groups; approximately one-fifth of all births within marriage were conceived before marriage; the peak of marital conceptions was found to be about one month after the wedding, and of premarital conception, about two months before the wedding; premarital pregnancy cases were found to have disproportionately high divorce rates; early conceivers within marriage showed higher divorce rates than late conceivers; about one out of every twenty or twenty-five persons in the sample falsified their ages upward in order to get married.

Two Additional Illustrations

In addition to these previously published findings, there are several analyses using the method of record linkage which are still in process. Following are two examples:

Residence After Marriage. This first example has to do with matrilocal and patrilocal tendencies. By comparing marriage and birth records as to place of residence it is possible to study the moving habits of couples following the wedding. In our sample, 55 per cent of the cases showed residential homogeneity at the time of marriage; that is, husband and wife from the same locality. In 45 per cent of the cases, they were from different localities. But whether from the same or different localities at the start, they tended to remain in or return to the home town of either spouse for the starting of their families. This was true of 78 per cent of the couples. Of those who were heterogeneous in residence at the start, 19 per cent returned to the home town of the husband as compared with 14 per cent to the home town of the wife, showing a moderate patrilocal tendency.

Age seems to be a significant factor in this analysis; it was the younger couples who were most likely to be from the same locality at the time of marriage and to remain there for the starting of a family. Also, of those who were heterogeneous in residence prior to marriage, it was the younger ones who were most matrilocal, with the patrilocal pattern becoming more common in the higher age groups.

This is enough to show what can be done. A more complete analysis would need to take other factors into account, such as rural-urban residence and emigration from the county.

Infant Sex Ratio by Age of Mother. The second illustration pertains to a refinement we have been able to make in testing for a relationship between infant sex ratio and the age of mother. Most reported research on this problem indicates a tendency for the live birth sex ratio to decrease as the age of the mother increases (although not consistently).[2] Our data revealed this same irregular relationship. It is not difficult to understand why the infant sex ratio is lower with older mothers, since prenatal mortality, which is known to affect male more than female fetuses, is higher when older women are involved.

But why should this relationship, found so consistently in the various researches, be so consistently irregular? We decided to explore the problem by the use of time-interval data already made available through our method of record linkage. We reasoned that this relationship in sex ratio might be affected by the extremes in time-interval to first birth, since: (1) the very short intervals represent premarital pregnancy cases where abortion may have been attempted, and (2) the very long intervals may over-represent cases where the mother has had difficulty carrying her pregnancies through to completion because of a tendency toward spontaneous abortion. Since, as we have said, abortion is more frequent with the male than the female fetus, surviving fetuses would more likely be female than in cases where abortion (either induced or spontaneous) is not as apt to intrude. We hypothesized, therefore, that live birth sex ratios would be disproportionately low in cases having either extremely short or extremely long intervals to first birth.

Statistical tests found this supposition to be correct and we consequently eliminated the extreme interval cases from our analysis. Using the remaining, more normal, cases we again found a negative relationship between infant sex ratio and age of mother and this time the picture was quite clear, with the sex ratio decreasing consistently from 1.30 for mothers ages seventeen and under to .95 for mothers aged thirty and over. Our refinement had sharpened the analysis and made the results more conclusive. It would seem evident that future studies of sex ratio by age of mother will need to take into account this factor of time-interval to first child.

Advantages in Record Linkage

Experience with this tool has brought us to the conclusion that it has certain real advantages in family research.

---

[2] Cf. C.A. McMahan, "An Empirical Test of Three Hypotheses Concerning the Human Sex Ratio at Birth in the United States, 1915-1948," *Milbank Memorial Fund Quarterly,* 29 (July, 1951), No. 3, pp. 273-93.

1. Availability of Data. It utilizes data that have already been gathered, that are *relatively* uniform from locality to locality, and that are *generally* available for research purposes. This means that record linkage research may be less expensive than that involving primary field work. Even more important, perhaps, it means that approximately identical studies may be conducted with ease almost anywhere, thus facilitating the formulation and testing of broad theories — through replication on diverse populations.

2. Internal Checks on Reliability. Reliability of data is one of the first requisites of sound research. Though public records of events like birth, marriage, and divorce are officially gathered in compliance with the law, they are not free from omissions and errors. By linking comparable data from two or more sets of records, it is possible to estimate the numbers and kinds of errors involved and to make corrections in the analyses. Furthermore, with a knowledge of the specific type of errors contained in the records, it becomes more possible to protect the consumers of statistics against unwarranted assumptions or inferences and to assist planners in eliminating, or at least reducing, the sources of error for future data gathering.

Through record linkage, we have been able to identify and measure various discrepancies among different sets of records.[3] A brief mentioning of two kinds of "conscious errors" (involving wilful misinformation) will serve our present purposes. The first has to do with underaged boys and girls falsifying their ages in order to get married. By comparing calculated ages of brides and grooms on the marriage records with stated ages of parents on the birth records, and allowing for the time lapse, we were able to determine discrepancies and analyze the factors involved. Since most of these discrepancies were in the direction of upgraded ages at marriage, and since most of the upgrading put the bride or groom just over the legal minimum, the real nature of the phenomenon became obvious. Some 4 or 5 per cent of our sample misstated their ages in this manner. The second "conscious error" has to do with physicians sometimes falsifying birth records in order to cover up the fact of premarital pregnancy. We coped with this by taking births resulting from the 1939-41 marriages and classifying them into "term" or "premature" according to the physician's notation on the record. Only 3.8 per cent fell into the premature category. Yet, when we made this same classification for a premarital pregnancy subgroup (those with intervals of less than 196 days between marriage and first birth), it was found that 13.2 per cent fell into the premature category. This strongly suggests that some physicians are "cooperating" with the premaritally pregnant couples to make it appear that the child came early because of prematurity.

It should be noted, also, that record linkage has been in recent use by the United States Bureau of the Census. In 1950, several months after the field work for the regular census had been completed, specially trained interviewers went

---

[3] Some of these have been previously reported in the published articles. Under the writer's direction, Robert O. Andrews (now deceased) gathered extensive data from Defiance County, Ohio, for purposes of getting at errors in official records. Additional insights are forthcoming, once these data have been analyzed.

into approximately 3,500 small sample areas and carefully rechecked for omissions and errors. This was known as the Post-Enumeration Survey. Survey schedules were matched with the corresponding original census schedules and the discrepancies observed. Another project, known as the Infant Enumeration Survey, required census enumerators to fill out a special infant card for each child born during the first three months of 1950. These cards were then checked against birth records covering this same period, and matched where possible. Questionnaires were mailed to parents of infants for whom no census record could at first be found. This resulted in additional matchings and yielded information on the reasons some infants were missed in the original census. Still another project, referred to as "record check studies," has matched a sample from the Post-Enumeration Survey with several other record sources (the 1920 census files, birth registration files, Social Security Administration files, and Veterans Administration files) for the purpose of studying discrepancies in recorded ages of identical persons. These recent activities at the national level are illustrations of the usefulness of record linkage for studying and eventually improving our data gathering processes.

　　　3. *Studying Intimate Behavior.* There are certain phenomena revealed through record linkage which are either inaccessible or less precisely measurable by other approaches. This method has an advantage over both the questionnaire and the interview in that here official documents are used and people are not given a chance to either refuse an answer or prevaricate the information supplied. This is especially important when one is studying such a "sensitive area" as premarital pregnancy, for there is reason to believe that other methods of data collection run into the natural human tendency to cover up that which is socially disapproved, and so result in distortions of the truth.

　　　Record linkage permits the researcher to make deductions concerning certain previous behavior (for example, premarital conception) where an event (for example, birth) is related to a time-constant (for example, length of gestation). There is nothing on either the marriage or birth record, taken alone, that could reveal such a thing as the timing of conception in relation to marriage. But, considered together, these two records yield information on interval between marriage and first birth, which then makes possible the calculation of pregnancy timing and hence the determination of which couples were pregnant before marriage. Thus, record linkage lends itself to studying this kind of intimate information without asking anybody any questions — which means that it should be most reliable.

　　　There is good reason for believing that Kinsey underestimated the extent of premarital pregnancy in his sample. Apparently, he did not ask his parent respondents whether or not their first child was conceived out of wedlock; but for the single females who had had premarital intercourse, nearly 18 per cent had become pregnant.[4] Though he did not report premarital pregnancy figures for his total sample, he spoke of unwanted pregnancies before marriage as being

---

[4] Alfred C. Kinsey, *et al, Sexual Behavior in the Human Female*, Philadelphia: W.B. Saunders Company, 1953, p. 327.

only "occasional."[5] Our own reported research estimates premarital pregnancy to constitute around 20 per cent of all first birth cases.

4. *Conducting Longitudinal Analyses.* The need for observing a given sample over time, where the same persons are followed through from one stage to the next, has long been recognized by students of human development. This, in contrast to a cross-sectional approach, is the best way for getting at the processes of personality growth and social change. Longitudinal study avoids such problems as "rationalization" and faulty memory, which are present in retrospective data obtained by requiring the subjects to remember back into their pasts. It is for this reason that longitudinal analysis is better able to get at and to clarify the cause-effect relationships that may be involved.

But longitudinal design requiring long-time observation and/or interviewing is generally complicated and expensive, with the result that many investigators and supporting agencies have hesitated to go into it. One difficulty has been the problem of maintaining continuity among personnel, which is important from the standpoints of cooperation from the subjects and consistency in the investigation. It is also difficult to maintain continuity with respect to the subjects, because of migration and dropouts over the period of the study, and with respect to the research concepts and methods employed, since these change with developments over time and there is always the question of whether to adopt the newer developments or to stay with the older concepts and methods for the sake of comparability. Still another problem is the possibility that repeated observation or interviewing will tend to "contaminate" the subjects, affecting their motivations and orientations in ways that will alter the outcome of the research.

Record linkage permits longitudinal research without most of the above named difficulties. Though the analysis cuts across time, there is no necessity for waiting for time to pass or for the subjects to act. They have already acted and their acts have been recorded on official records, which are studied — ex post facto. Furthermore, there is no researcher-respondent relationship to be concerned about. One simply locates his subjects at different points in time on the time-separated records that are available, and then studies the changes and relationships that are revealed. In our own research, for example, each married couple has been labeled and then traced through from the wedding to the starting of the family and finally divorce — providing these latter two were a part of the experience. We have been able to see what our couples do over time, to get at developmental sequences, to study the dynamics of spacing and duration.

Limitations and Next Steps

There are also certain disadvantages in our method of record linkage and we suggest only that it supplement, not supplant, other approaches.

One limitation is that this type of research is restricted by the nature, completeness, and accuracy of the data supplied on existing and available records. Hence, not every problem can be studied by this method; and of the problems studied, not every one can be carried through to its ultimate solution.

---

[5] *Ibid.,* p. 320.

Certain problems must either be let alone, explored superficially, or turned over to other methods of attack — simply because available record data may be quite insufficient for the insights needed.

Another limitation has to do with possible biases through cases lost in the searching process. In our own research, for example, we somewhat arbitrarily have had to limit our search to records of the one county and to births occurring within five years of the date of marriage. This means that certain cases (those who moved out of the county sometime during the periods studied and those who waited longer than five years to have their first child) have been missed. We have explored and reported ways for estimating these losses, but have had no means for accurately measuring them or for determining precisely the amount of bias introduced.

Record linkage could be further developed and perfected as a research tool by simply expanding the scope of its application. In the first place, additional data from the marriage, birth, and divorce records could be utilized, such as studying the spacing of second and subsequent births, and relating decisions on child custody to the phenomena of family size and child spacing. Secondly, additional sources, such as employment records, public welfare records, and death records, could be utilized for various other linkages and analyses. Thirdly, with adequate financing, both the time and space limits could be greatly expanded, which would improve the reliability of results. For example, if a study of this kind could include several counties and/or states, there would then be a better basis for estimating, and correcting, migration losses in future studies.

Our final suggestion is that record linkage be teamed with other research tools in ways that will produce results more definitive than would be possible by any one approach alone. In a preliminary attempt, we already have combined record linkage with field interviews on the problem of premarital pregnancy. And this effort, though exploratory, was productive of new insights into the personal and situational factors responsible for adjustment or maladjustment of couples when faced with the problem of pregnancy before marriage.[6]

Of methodological interest is the possibility of using records and record linkage for studying the data-gathering efficiency of the questionnaire and the interview. Individuals who had been studied by record linkage could also be interviewed or given a questionnaire, and any discrepancies in information could then be analyzed; this would lead to a better understanding of biases introduced into samples by either lack of response to soliciting questions or by falsification in the information supplied. To illustrate, with a preknowledge of premarital pregnancy *via* record linkage, the researcher could approach these same persons to see if the same information would be readily, correctly, and completely supplied *via* the questionnaire and/or interview.

---

[6] See Harold T. Christensen and Bette B. Rubinstein, "Premarital Pregnancy and Divorce: A Follow-up Study by the Interview Method," *Marriage and Family Living*, 18 (May, 1956), pp. 114-123.

ANALYSIS OF DOCUMENTARY RESEARCH EXAMPLE

The Method of Record Linkage Applied to Family Data

Christensen states in his article that "record linkage consists of using documentary sources — in contrast to data obtained by questionnaires, interviews, or direct observation — and of cross-checking and matching these records against each other."

Source of Data. Christensen cites several studies in which he has used the documentary method. In each instance data were collected from official public records of events (e.g., marriage, birth, and divorce records).

Appraisal of Documents. Accuracy of the data obtained from the public records was determined by linking comparable data from two or more sets of records. For example, by comparing calculated ages of brides and grooms on marriage records with stated ages of parents on the birth records and allowing for the time lapse, discrepancies have been determined.

Use of Hypotheses. The following null hypotheses are examples of those which may be deduced from Christensen's discussion of studies conducted by him using the documentary method:

1. There are no significant relationships between premarital pregnancy and marriage outcome.

2. There are no significant relationships between child spacing and marital outcome.

3. There are no significant differences between matrilocal and patrilocal residence patterns at time of starting of a family.

4. There is no significant relationship between infant sex ratio and age of mother.

PRE-INDUSTRIAL PATTERNS IN THE COLONIAL FAMILY IN AMERICA: A CONTENT ANALYSIS OF COLONIAL MAGAZINES*

HERMAN R. LANTZ, MARGARET BRITTON, RAYMOND SCHMITT, AND ELOISE C. SNYDER

It has been a widely accepted opinion that modern courtship and mate selection are products of urbanization and industrialization. Freedom in mate choice and romantic love as bases for marriage are thought to have been made possible because family control and rules of endogamy had less impact in an individualistic milieu.

This essentially passive view of the family as a reacting agent has been

Reprinted with permission from the *American Sociological Review*, Vol. 33, 1968, pp. 413-426.

*The authors are indebted to the staff of the Morris Library, Southern Illinois University, for assistance in obtaining the source materials necessary for this project.

criticized by Greenfield (1967:312-322) and Goode (1963:ch. 1) who question the assumed relationship between family change and industrialization, and suggest that in reality some of the characteristics of the modern family may have been present prior to industrialization.

Furstenberg (1966:326-327) has been perhaps the most recent writer to cast doubt on the origin of modern courtship and mating practices (also Udry, 1966:19-22; Wilkinson, 1962:678-682; Mott, 1965:294-295). He points out that several of the characteristics of the modern family, such as freedom of choice, romantic love, and permissiveness in parent-child relations, were observed by European travelers in the United States during the first half of the nineteenth century.

Investigations of the emergence of particular family practices are helpful in coming to terms with history, but from a more strict sociological point of view, it is imperative that we understand what given developments in the social structure, such as industrialization, are related to what consequences in the institutional configuration.

The effort to explain contemporary social behavior presupposes a linkage between given forms of social behavior and different kinds of social structures. However, if given forms of social behavior or characterological types have always been in existence through varying social structures, the fact would raise questions about the usefulness of contemporary sociological explanations concerning many types of social behavior, and it would set a somewhat different course for the pursuit of sociological inquiry. Many issues regarding the evolution social change would be reopened, and a reexamination of the relationships between social structure, social behavior, and social change would be necessitated.

The Problem

Any sociological reinvestigation of history presents formidable problems with respect to available source materials and method. Travel accounts and diaries, though interesting and worthwhile, are still merely suggestive. There are difficulties in evaluating the bias of the reporter and the extent to which the contents are representative. Another troublesome but potentially significant *source of available data* is the newspaper and the magazine. In the present study, the investigation of family patterns in the pre-industrial period involved a systematic examination of colonial magazines, with a view to determining whether or not particular characteristics of the modern family existed during this earlier era. Specifically, we examined the following features of the American colonial family structure: power patterns present in the man-woman relationship, types of attitudes and actions toward premarital and extramarital sexual involvement, and motivations for entering into the marital relationship. The research did not attempt to cover other important phases of the family and *is limited to these aspects*. These particular variables were selected because the traditional view of the relationship between industrialization and the family structure posits that each of them was influenced considerably by the advent of industrialization. Hence, we gathered evidence concerning these variables during the 1741-1794 period.

Source, Method, and Procedure

Our investigation of the American colonial period centered about a content analysis of fifteen magazines which were published during the years 1741-1794.[1] These time limits were based upon Mott's work (1930), *A History of American Magazines*. Mott, a leading authority on the history of journalism, divided his history into five periods: 1741-1794, 1794-1825, 1825-1850, 1850-1865, 1865-1885, and 1885-1905. Before 1741, Americans read British magazines rather than publishing their own. In fact, even during the period from 1741-1794, the British influence upon American magazines was great, with much material being reprinted directly from the British magazines. This period ended in 1794 with the Postal Act, which allowed magazines to be sent through the mails and thus increased circulation and influence. Mott's initial period included the Late Colonial Period, The Period of the Revolution, and The Early Years of the New Nation; the period in which America was developing its own customs and traditions.

Mott's work also guided our decision to study the American colonial family structure on the basis of a content analysis of fifteen magazines. He indicated that the 1741-1795 period was characterized by a circulation of thirteen *important magazines*.[2] A magazine was defined by Mott (1930) as a bound pamphlet issued more or less regularly; it contained a variety of reading matter and possessed a connotation of entertainment. Magazines were judged important or unimportant by Mott (1930) on the basis of their literary worth, circulation, and influence upon the reading public. Six of these magazines were of particular interest to women, while the remaining seven were oriented toward the general public. Mott also listed two additional magazines which were of particular concern to women. Although he does not label them important, we have also

---

[1] The standard source with respect to this method is still Berelson (1952). For a more recent discussion of this method see De Sola Pool (1959).

We also divided this time period into two subperiods in order to examine any changes that might have occurred in the family structure during this critical period of history. The year 1776 was used as a breaking point due to its historical importance.

[2] These thirteen magazines were: *The American Magazine*. December, 1787-November, 1788. *The American Magazine and Historical Chronicle*. September, 1743-December, 1746. *The American Magazine and Monthly Chronicle for the British Colonies*. October, 1757-October, 1758. *The American Magazine, or A Monthly View of the Political State of The British Colonies*. January, 1741-March, 1741. *The American Museum, Or Repository of Ancient and Modern Fugitive Pieces, etc., Prose and Poetical (The American Museum, or Universal Magazine*, 1790-1792). January, 1787-December, 1792. *The Christian's, Scholar's and Farmer's Magazine*. April-May, 1789-February-March, 1791. *The Columbian Magazine, or Monthly Miscellany (The Universal Asylum and Columbia Magazine*, 1790-1792). September, 1786-December, 1792. *The General Magazine, and Historical Chronicle, For All the British Plantations in America*. January, 1741-June, 1741. *The Massachusetts Magazine or Monthly Museum of Knowledge and Rational Entertainment*. January, 1789-December, 1796. *The New York Magazine or Literary Repository*. January, 1790-December, 1797. *The Pennsylvania Magazine or American Monthly Museum*. January, 1775, July 1776. *The Royal American Magazine, or Universal Repository of Instruction and Amusement*. January, 1774-March, 1775. *The Worcester Magazine Containing Politicks, Miscellanies, Poetry and News*. First week of April, 1786-Last week of March, 1787.

included them in our study, since they were designed especially for women and contained references to the existing family structure of the period.[3]

Two characteristics of these fifteen magazines should be noted. (1) The magazines were primarily written for the middle and the upper classes. The data indicate that the typical subscriber to these magazines had servants, participated in leisurely recreation, entertained often, and was well-educated. Since the writers most likely wrote with these people in mind, the articles probably reflect the upper and middle class subcultures of the period more than the lower class subculture. (2) The magazines were all published in New England and were circulated primarily in the Northern section of America. Problems in distribution prevented extensive circulation in distant areas. Hence, conclusions of this study can *most legitimately be applied to New England's middle and upper classes during the period 1741-1794.*[4]

The universe comprised all issues of the fifteen magazines that were published during the years 1741-1794.[5] A total of 98 issues were published during the years 1741-1776, while 448 issues were published during the years 1776-1794. The entire 546 issues constituted our sample.[6]

Since it would have been extremely time consuming to read the 546 issues in their entirety, article titles were used as indicators of the relevance of the article. As the variables being coded were rarely explicitly mentioned in the titles, we considered an article to be relevant if the title indicated that it pertained to women.[7] Each of these articles was read for its general content and then reread in detail if it seemed pertinent.

The unit of analysis in content analysis may be words, themes, characters, items, etc. (Berelson, 1952:135-146), but the only unit of analysis used in this study was the *explicit discussion* of one of the variables being coded. Reliability was approached in a manner similar to that used by Sebald (1962:318-322) in his study of national character. Sebald suggests that reliability of content analysis may be approached by a consistent application of criteria for classification. This involves both specific statements and overall explicit meaning. He believes that a sufficient degree of objectivity and reproducibility may thus be achieved.[8]

---

[3] These two magazines were entitled *Boston Magazine*, and *Lady's Magazine and Repository of Entertaining Knowledge.*

[4] However, this is a conservative position. The conclusions *may* also extend to the lower class of New England and/or to other regions of the United States.

[5] Six of the magazines were published in the 1741-1776 period and nine in the 1777-1794 period.

[6] We felt that this procedure would eliminate any sampling error with respect to the selection of issues.

[7] This criterion was selected for two reasons: (1) The variable being coded, power patterns present in the man-woman relationship, the presence of the romantic love complex in the man-woman relationship, types of attitudes and actions toward premarital and extramarital sexual involvement, and motivations for entering into the marital relationship, all involved women. (2) If authors were ignoring women during any part of this period of history, this criterion should offset this bias somewhat. Mott (1930:64-67) discusses this point.

[8] However, a *blind reliability check* was undertaken on a random sample of the magazines previously examined with respect to *one* of the variables considered in the *initial*

A schedule was employed to examine each issue in the sample. This schedule was used to record the presence of a discussion, bibliographical data concerning each magazine, and known biases of the publishers or editors. In addition, distinctions were made between fiction and non-fiction and between an advocated pattern and existent pattern.

Once the data were tabulated, tests of significance were applied at various points in the analysis.[9] The formula for testing the difference between two proportions for uncorrelated data was used when comparisons *between* time periods were of interest.[10] The total number of issues in each of the two time periods were expressed as N_1 and N_2 in this formula.[11] The chi-square goodness-of-fit test with a correction for continuity was used for comparisons *within* time periods.[12] The assumption here, of course, was that if there is no difference between the number of discussions in the categories, the expected frequencies should equal the total number of discussions divided by the number of categories. In some instances, the latter test could not be applied because the total number of discussions was too small.

The Results

Power in the Man-Woman Relationship. Since the female has been traditionally viewed as occupying a subservient position relative to the male in the U.S. prior to industrialization, various aspects of the power relationships between male and female during the 1741-1794 period were investigated.

For our purposes, power was defined as the ability of one individual to dominate another or others, to coerce and control them, obtain obedience, interfere with their freedom, and compel their action in particular ways. The various categories of power were dictated by the magazine content. They

---

analysis, i.e., the romantic love complex. This check *suggested* that the initial results may have been *slightly* conservative. (A correlation coefficient was not calculated since we felt it might tend to *overemphasize* the *exactness* of the check.) *If* this conservatism did tend generally to characterize our initial results, it would in fact strengthen our conclusions *in most instances*. The reader should, of course, evaluate each *specific* conclusion in light of this footnote.

[9] As we had included the whole universe of issues in our sample, our data did not actually represent a random sample. Nevertheless, we felt it was legitimate to use tests of significance since this universe could realistically be viewed as a random sample from some *hypothetical* universe, i.e., the universe of all important published material during this period. Hagood (1941: ch. 17) discusses this. Two-tailed tests were used at all times.

[10] Since many of our proportions were extreme, i.e., less than .10, we based the standard error of the difference on the proportion in the two groups combined. Downie and Heath (1965:148-151) discuss this.

[11] Although this formula standardizes for the difference in the number of issues between the two periods, the possibility exists that the lengths of the issues may have varied.

[12] Although at times several discussions occurred in a single article, the discussions generally represented independent events, i.e., the classification of the $N + 1$ discussions were not *systematically* dependent upon the classification of the initial discussions. However, independence of units has been a problem in content analysis studies (for example Osgood, 1959:65) and some readers may wish to view the statistical results only as benchmarks.

included general discussions of power, i.e., explicit discussions of power that did not pertain to a particular form of behavior, power over morality, i.e., power over sexual, gambling, or drinking behaviors, power in the handling of finances, power in the courtship situation, and power in certain other situations, i.e., child rearing, minor decision making, etc.

As we were interested in male-female comparisons with respect to each of the power categories, the source of power was considered in all instances. Power was coded as being exerted overtly by the male, overtly by the female, subtly by the female, or by both cooperatively.[13] Subtle female power refers to situations where the female is in control but where the male may not be fully aware that he is being manipulated. These data are presented in Table 1.

Attention was first given to a comparison of those discussions wherein power was *exerted overtly* by the male and by the female. There were *136 such discussions* in the male category for the total period and *42 discussions* in the female category for the same period. The resultant p of the chi-square test was less than .001. When the male-female totals are examined in the ten *exists* columns of Table 1, it can be seen that there were significantly more discussions involving the male as the source of power in the general power category (p < .001) and in the morality category (p < .001) during the later time period. However, the differences between males and females in the finance, courtship, and other categories, during the later period were not significant at the .05 level. The difference between males and females in the general power category during the earlier period also was not significant at the .05 level. The remaining four totals could not be meaningfully tested.

The number of discussions *advocating* that overt power should be held by the male or the female were practically nil except for the general power category. For both time periods, there were more discussions involving the male. The difference for the latter period, which could be tested statistically, was significant below the .01 level.

This analysis lends considerable support to the traditional view of the male-female power relationship before industrialization. In four instances, the male was involved in significantly more discussions than the female,[14] and in no instance was the female involved in significantly more discussions than the male. Nevertheless, it should be noted that in some power categories there was no evidence that the male possessed more overt power than the female.[15] It should also be emphasized that there were 42 discussions over the total period that either indicated that the female possessed overt power or advocated that she should possess it.

Attention was next given to those discussions that reflected subtle power on the part of the female. As we were essentially interested in the overall power position of the woman relative to the power position of the male, the discussions

---

[13] Instances of subtle male power were almost never discussed.
[14] This includes the comparison that was made between male and female overt power for the entire period. It is also noteworthy that 63 per cent of the discussions involving overt male power occurred in non-fiction.
[15] The reader is cautioned to keep in mind the possibility of a Type II error.

TABLE 1. VARIOUS DIMENSIONS OF POWER IN THE MAN-WOMAN RELATIONSHIP AND SOURCE OF POWER BY CHARACTER OR DISCUSSION (FICTION OR NON-FICTION), STATE OF POWER (ADVOCATED OR EXISTENT) AND TIME PERIOD.(IN FREQUENCY OF DISCUSSIONS)

Source of Power	Power in General 1741-1776 Advocated F^a N^b T^c		Exists F N T		1777-1794 Advocated F N T		Exists F N T		Power over Morality 1741-1776 Advocated F N T		Exists F N T		1777-1794 Advocated F N T		Exists F N T	
Overtly by Male	3 4 7		4 4 8		4 12 16		18 38 56		0 0 0		0 1 1		0 0 0		19 8 27	
Overtly by Female	0 0 0		1 3 4		2 0 2		2 6 8		0 0 0		0 0 0		0 0 0		0 2 2	
Subtly by Female	1 1 2		0 4 4		2 3 5		4 17 21		0 6 6		0 1 1		5 10 15		5 19 24	
Mutual Cooperation	0 3 3		0 0 0		2 10 12		1 3 4		0 0 0		0 0 0		0 0 0		0 0 0	

Source of Power	Power in Courtship 1741-1776 Advocated F^a N^b T^c		Exists F N T		1777-1794 Advocated F N T		Exists F N T		Power over Finances 1741-1776 Advocated F N T		Exists F N T		1777-1794 Advocated F N T		Exists F N T	
Overtly by Male	0 0 0		0 1 1		0 0 0		1 5 6		0 0 0		0 0 0		0 0 0		1 5 6	
Overtly by Female	0 0 0		1 0 1		0 0 0		0 5 5		0 2 2		0 1 1		0 0 0		6 5 11	
Subtly by Female	0 2 2		1 2 3		0 2 2		2 12 14		0 0 0		0 0 0		0 1 1		0 0 0	
Mutual Cooperation	0 0 0		0 0 0		0 2 2		0 0 0		0 0 0		0 0 0		0 1 1		1 0 1	

Source of Power	Power in Other Areas 1741-1776 Advocated F^a N^b T^c		Exists F N T		1777-1794 Advocated F N T		Exists F N T		Row Sum
Overtly by Male	0 0 0		0 0 0		0 0 0		0 8 8		136
Overtly by Female	0 1 1		0 0 0		0 0 0		1 4 5		42
Subtly by Female	0 0 0		0 0 0		0 1 1		1 3 4		105
Mutual Cooperation	0 2 2		0 0 0		0 8 8		2 3 5		38

[a] F is fiction.　　[b] N is non-fiction.　　[c] T is total.

that indicated either *overt or subtle* female power were compared with those discussions that indicated overt male power.[16]

There were *136 discussions of male overt power* during the entire period and *147 discussions of female power* (overt and subtle) for the same period. The resultant p of the chi-square test was not significant at the .05 level. When the male-female totals are examined in the ten *exists* columns of Table 1, it is found that there were significantly more discussions involving the male *only* in the general power category during the later period (p < .01), and there were significantly more female discussions in the courtship category during the later period (p < .02). Also, there were no significant differences at the .05 level between males and females in the morality, finance, and other categories during the later period. Nor was there any difference at this level of significance in the general power category during the earlier period. The remaining four totals could not be meaningfully tested.[17]

With respect to the courtship category during the later period, the data suggest that the male had the power of choosing whom to court (or who was to court his daughter), but the female may have had control of the relationship through the threatened, or actual withholding of affection and through "playing the coquette." The data also suggest that the female controlled the courtship process, similar to Willard Waller's principle of least interest, by which the one with the least interest in the continuance of a relationship controls it.

The implications of our data are that authority was normatively vested in the male (the initial analysis of male and female overt power implies this), but that this authority was not *de facto* always exercised by the male. More often by the use of subtle power rather than by overt power, the female apparently was able to exercise influence in various areas (Becker and Hill, 1955:135). The data indicate that she exerted significantly greater influence than the male in the area of courtship during the later period, and that she may have had an equal influence in the finance, morality, and other categories during the later period. There were also significantly more discussions advocating that the female should have power rather than the male in the area of morality during the later period.[18]

---

[16] These combined totals are not presented in Table 1. However, the reader can easily obtain these totals from the given data if he so desires. For example, there were 42 discussions over the total period that reflected overt female power, and there were 105 discussions for the same period that indicated subtle female power. Hence, there were 147 discussions of overt or subtle female power for the entire period.

[17] Comparisons were also made between the male overt power totals and the combined female subtle and overt power totals in the ten *advocates* power columns in Table 1. Only two of these totals were large enough to test statistically. In these instances, it was found that (1) there were significantly more discussions advocating that the female have power rather than the male in the morality category during the later period (p < .001), and (2) while there were more male discussions in the general power category during the later period, the difference was not significant at the .05 level.

[18] The necessity of power in the hands of the widow hints at Lantz's (1958:ch. 5) hypothesis that "a mother-centered, or mother-dominated home, is believed to have developed out of situations in which the continuation of the father's role was in danger."

The existence of subtle female power does not necessarily indicate that the family in this period was not male dominated. The pattern of subtle female power may be viewed as a reaction to or a way of dealing with male authority. Our findings do suggest areas of delineation in regard to how power may have been distributed and expressed by husband and wife. The data also raise relevant questions about the role of subtle female power. If power represents the ability to move others, then obviously the female possessed power. The basic questions raised by our findings are as follows: How much subtle female power can be said to be present before power shifts from the man to the woman? Did subtle female power ever reach a point where the woman was, in fact, in control? Does the marked evidence for subtle female power suggest that the colonial family was in a period of dynamic change prior to industrialization?

Certainly it is true that the impact of industrialization was to enable subtle power to be supplanted by more open patterns of assertion and persuasion. Was this necessarily a change in actual power, or a change in the form in which power was expressed, or both? These are questions to be raised; our study provides no answer for them, however.

The Romantic Love Complex. It is commonly believed that the romantic love complex which presently forms the basis for marriage in our society was essentially a consequence of industrialization (Goodsell, 1938:215-216; Furstenberg, 1936:326-327). We have already noted that Goode (1936) has raised doubts in this regard. Furstenberg (1966:330) notes in his study of European travelers to the United States during 1800-1850 that "most of the observers praised the American marriage system because it permitted young people to select mates whom they loved and with whom they could enjoy a happy marriage." Stewart (1954:182) has similarly stated, regarding the court-ship process during the latter part of the colonial period, that ". . . in general, the attitude toward marriage might be termed 'moderately romantic.'" Our universe of magazines was examined for evidence concerning the romantic love complex. Romantic love has been defined in terms of five dimensions.

(1) *Idealization of the Loved One* (Bell, 1963:107).
(2) *The One and Only.*
(3) *Love at First Sight.*
(4) *Love Wins Out Over All.*
(5) *Glorification of Personal Emotions.*

Examples of discussions depicting romantic love from the data are:

When I am not with her in the day, her enchanting image pursues me; and when I retire to sleep, she fills my every idea; I slumber . . . I wake, and starting up in agony, wander round my chamber maniac-like. . . .[19]
Here uncontroul'd foll'wing nature's voice,
The happy lovers make the unchanging choice,
While mutual passions in their bosoms glow,

[19] The Drone, XXI, *The New York Magazine*, April, 1794, p. 198.

> While soft confessions in their kisses flow,
> While their free hands in plighted faith are given,
> Their vows accordant reach approving Heaven.[20]

The frequency of discussions occurring in each of these categories is presented in Table 2. The character of the discussion (poetry, other fiction, and non-fiction) and the time period in which the indicator occurred are also shown in Table 2.

The most significant aspect of Table 2 is the unexpected number of discussions which portrayed the romantic love complex. There were *337 discussions* for the entire period.[21] Each of these discussions (poetry, other fiction, and non-fiction) described the romantic love complex as being in existence. There were only nine *other* discussions (not included in Table 2) wherein the authors indicated that romantic love did not exist. Eight *other* discussions advocated that the romantic love complex be made the basis for the man-woman relationship, while nine *other* discussions opposed romantic love as the basis for marriage. The majority of the 337 discussions occurred during the later period ($p < .001$). A significant number of these discussions occurred in fiction (poetry and other fiction) rather than in non-fiction ($p < .001$). The discussions during both periods were fairly evenly spread across the five categories in Table 2. However, the idealization category and the love-wins-out-over-all category con-

TABLE 2. INDICATORS OF THE ROMANTIC LOVE COMPLEX AND
CHARACTER OF DISCUSSION (POETRY, OTHER FICTION,
AND NON-FICTION) BY TIME PERIOD (IN NUMBER OF DISCUSSIONS)

The Indicator	1741-1776				1777-1794				
	Poetry	Other Fiction	Non-Fiction	Total	Poetry	Other Fiction	Non-Fiction	Total	Row Sum
Idealization of the Loved One	2	1	6	9	24	52	17	93	102
The One and Only	0	1	2	3	12	42	5	59	62
Love at First Sight	0	1	2	3	2	21	3	26	29
Love Wins Out Over All	2	1	7	10	12	46	17	75	85
Glorification of Personal Emotions	0	0	1	1	23	29	6	58	59
Total	4	4	18	26	73	190	48	311	337

---

[20] "A Poem on the Happiness of America," *Boston Magazine*, August, 1786, p. 351.

[21] It should also be noted that there were 57 discussions of individualism in marriage choice, i.e., the selection of the marriage partner by ego rather than by someone else, during the entire period. Although individualism is not a *sufficient* condition with respect to the existence of the romantic love complex, it is a *necessary* condition with respect to its existence. For this reason, we did not consider it to be an unquestionable indicator of the romantic love complex. However, the existence of the 57 discussions on individualism indicates that the romantic love complex *could have been* in existence.

tained the highest frequencies during both periods. The love-at-first-sight category during the later period had the lowest frequency.[22]

The data certainly indicate that the romantic love complex was known in colonial American society and that, indeed, it may have been a common pattern among large sections of the upper status groups. Thus, with regard to the impact of industrialization, it may well be that industrialization *facilitated* the development of a romantic love complex already in *existence*. Finally, presence of the romantic love complex must be seen in the broader context of the emergence of individualism and the role of personal wishes as an important basis in mate choice.

Although the romantic love complex was often discussed, other motivations for marriage existed, and these were considered. It was found that only three motives of this type were discussed with any regularity in the magazines — *happiness*, *wealth*, and *status*. We noted whether these motives were held by the individuals entering into the marital relationship or by their parents. The motive of happiness was indicated when the person in courtship or the parents perceived enjoyment as a major reason for marrying a particular person. The motive of wealth was indicated if selection was based primarily on financial aspects. The motive of status was indicated if the end of marriage was primarily to acquire a mate from a family with an *equal* or *higher* social standing. Social status was indicated in the literature by such expressions as "from a good family," or "people of an equal rank and fortune," etc. The data are presented in Table 3.

Although the reader may wish to make a more detailed analysis of Table 3, the final row sums are of primary interest to us at this point. For the entire period, there were *ninety-seven discussions* that indicated that *happiness* was regarded as a motive for entering marriage; *fifty-two discussions* indicated that wealth was regarded as a motive for entering marriage, while only *fifteen discussions* gave any indication that social status was a motive for entering into the marital union. It should be observed that there were significantly more discussions of these three motives during the later period ($p < .001$), and a significantly greater number of these discussions occurred in fiction ($p < .001$).

The frequency with which personal happiness as motivation for marriage appears (a motivation compatible with the romantic love complex), adds weight to our previous conclusions with respect to the existence of the romantic love complex in America during the colonial period. Moreover, this result is in direct contrast to the traditional discussions of strong economic and utilitarian goals that were said to characterize the marital union in the pre-industrial period.

---

[22] Although it should be viewed only as a *post hoc* suggestion, the idea occurred to us that if one were to hypothesize concerning the *development* of the romantic love complex in a particular social system, it would be logical to suspect that various components of the *complex* might be likely to emerge before other components. Further, it might be argued that the emphasis on *love* and the emphasis on love *toward the loved one* would precede other indicators of love, such as love at first sight. In other words, one would not suspect the courtship system to be characterized by "love at first sight," *unless* love, and the loved one, were already emphasized as desirable in the culture. It so happens that our data fit this hypothesis.

TABLE 3. MARITAL MOTIVE AND HOLDER OF
MOTIVE BY CHARACTER OF DISCUSSION (FICTION AND NON-FICTION)
BY TIME PERIOD (IN NUMBER OF DISCUSSIONS)

1741-1776

| The Motive | Fiction | | | Non-Fiction | | | Total |
	Parent	Ego	Not Specified	Parent	Ego	Not Specified	
Happiness	0	0	1	0	6	3	10
Wealth	0	0	0	3	1	2	6
Status	0	0	0	0	0	0	0
Total	0	0	1	3	7	5	16

1777-1794

| The Motive | Fiction | | | Non-Fiction | | | Total | Row Sum |
	Parent	Ego	Not Specified	Parent	Ego	Not Specified		
Happiness	13	40	5	4	11	14	87	97
Wealth	22	12	3	5	2	2	46	52
Status	11	2	0	1	1	0	15	15
Total	46	54	8	10	14	16	148	164

Sexual Standards. The traditional view holds that industrialization tended to liberalize the sexual norms in the American social system. The belief is that the conservative sexual norms of the post-industrial period were modified by the industrial revolution *and* the corresponding movement towards urbanization. Reiss (1960:67), for example, in his consideration of premarital sexual standards in America, maintains this position:

> Another consequence of city life was the lessening of social controls and resultant increases in divergent viewpoints. In short, the city did not have the intimacy, the control by reputation and gossip which the farm or the small town had. People hardly knew their neighbors and were not as strongly concerned with their opinions. Then, too, in the small town, there was usually general agreement on what was proper; in the city, this agreement was often lacking, so that if one group of people criticized a person, it would not be difficult to find another group supporting him in his position. Thus, individualization of behavior was encouraged. *This situation, of course, helped destroy many of the older sexual standards and made possible the growth of newer, more liberal and equalitarian standards.*[23]

---

[23] Our italics.

Since there were few direct references to the actual sexual normative structure of the period, certain indirect indices of the prevailing sexual norms of the period had to be used. Consequently, we decided to analyze the content of the magazines in terms of the sanctions that were exhibited towards those individuals who deviated from the existing sexual mores of the period. Sanctions were selected as the indicator for two reasons: (1) They appeared to be a reasonable indicator of the existing sexual normative structure. (2) They were discussed in the magazine content.

There were three forms of sanctions that appeared with any regularity in the important magazine content of the period: (1) punishment, (2) ostracism, and (3) sympathy.[24] At times, these discussions indicated that the particular sanction *had been* implemented toward the person mentioned in the article, while in other instances, the writers indicated that the particular sanction *should* be implemented toward the person being discussed in the article. Hence, the three forms of sanctions were classified into one of two categories — *behavior* or *attitudes*. The data are presented in Tables 4 and 5.

These tables concern only the 1777-1794 period, since there were only three discussions of sanctions during the 1741-1776 period. Two of these indicated that the female had been ostracized for deviating from the sexual mores, and one advocated that the male should be ostracized for his deviation. Each of these discussions occurred in non-fiction.[25]

There were seventy-five discussions during the 1777-1794 period advocating that our three designated sanctions *ought to be implemented* towards the sexual deviator (see Table 4). Thirty-nine of these occurred in fiction, while thirty-six

TABLE 4. ATTITUDES THAT SANCTIONS SHOULD BE IMPLEMENTED
TOWARD INDIVIDUALS INVOLVED IN
PREMARITAL OR EXTRAMARITAL SEXUAL RELATIONS
DURING THE 1777-1794 PERIOD BY CHARACTER OF DISCUSSION
AND BY SEX (IN FREQUENCY OF DISCUSSIONS)

Sanction (Attitude)	Male			Female			Row Sum
	Fiction	Non-Fiction	Total	Fiction	Non-Fiction	Total	
Punishment	0	1	1	0	0	0	1
Ostracism	14	19	33	2	0	2	35
Sympathy	0	0	0	23	16	39	39
Total	14	20	34	25	16	41	75

[24] A discussion which indicated that a person should or did receive understanding when premarital or extramarital sexual relations occurred because he was a victim of circumstances beyond his control (force) or because he became involved as a result of sincerity and trust in others was included in one of the sympathy categories.

[25] This represents the same pattern that was observed during the later period (see below).

TABLE 5. SANCTIONS IMPLEMENTED TOWARD INDIVIDUALS
INVOLVED IN PREMARITAL OR EXTRAMARITAL
SEXUAL RELATIONS DURING THE 1777-1794 PERIOD
BY CHARACTER OF DISCUSSION AND
BY SEX (IN FREQUENCY OF DISCUSSIONS)

Sanction (Behavior)	Male			Female			Row Sum
	Fiction	Non-Fiction	Total	Fiction	Non Fiction	Total	
Punishment	1	0	1	4	5	9	10
Ostracism	0	0	0	26	18	44	44
Sympathy	1	2	3	3	1	4	7
Total	2	2	4	33	24	57	61

occurred in non-fiction. There was only one indication that physical punishment should be given to those involved in premarital or extramarital sexual affairs, and the indication was that the male should receive this punishment. There were, however, thirty-five instances in which it was proposed that the deviator should be ostracized. Interestingly, thirty-three of these discussions concerned the male, whereas only two concerned the female ($p < .001$). Fourteen of the discussions involving the male occurred in fiction, while nineteen appeared in non-fiction. On the other hand, there were no advocates of sympathy for the male offender, although sympathy was indicated for the female in thirty-nine instances ($p < .001$). Twenty-three of these discussions occurred in fiction and sixteen occurred in non-fiction. Thus, the data suggest that with respect to attitudes toward the sexual deviator, *the male was to be ostracized and the female was to receive sympathy.*

There were sixty-one discussions during the 1777-1794 period which indicated that our three designated sanctions had been *implemented* towards the sexual deviator (see Table 5). Thirty-five of these occurred in fiction, while twenty-six appeared in non-fiction. There was only one indication that physical punishment was inflicted upon the male, and this was a fictional episode that concerned self-inflicted punishment: suicide. There were nine instances, however, wherein physical punishment was inflicted upon the female ($p < .05$). Five of these negative sanctions were suicide and four were legal punishments, i.e., fines, jail sentences, or whippings. Similarly, there were forty-four discussions wherein the female was ostracized, but there was not a single discussion that indicated that the male was ostracized for his sexual deviation ($p < .001$). Seven discussions fell into the sympathy category, and these were divided approximately evenly between males and females. Thus, the data suggest that with respect to behavior toward the sexual deviator, *the female was physically punished or ostracized, while the male was not.*

Although one must exert caution in generalizing from the quantity and quality of these presentations to conclusions regarding the normative sexual structure of the period,[26] the evidence implies that the prevailing norm(s) of the period concerning premarital and extramarital sexual relationships were of the *ancient double standard type and/or of the formal standard of abstinence type* (Reiss, 1960:chs. 4 and 9). The following reasons are offered for this conclusion: (1) The only sanctions that were discussed with any regularity in the literature were negative ones. If a liberal or semiliberal normative structure had existed with regard to the behaviors under consideration, this *probably* would not have been the case. Physical punishment and ostracism were advocated for, and implemented against, the sexual deviator, and these sanctions are typically considered to be rather severe overt negative sanctions. Even sympathy cannot be viewed as a positive sanction since it was typically advocated or given only if the person had engaged in premarital or extramarital sexual relationships due to circumstances out of his control (force) or because he had become involved as a result of his sincerity and trust in others. This implies that such behavior was culturally prohibited. It should also be noted that many of the discussions involving sanctions occurred in non-fiction. (2) The sanctions were differentially applied toward the male and the female. Although punishment was advocated for the male and sympathy for the female, the literature also indicates that the female was physically punished or ostracized, while the male was not. The following quote is indicative of a discussion reflecting the double standard which seemed to be well entrenched.

> Nothing but an unjust custom has rendered vice in a man less odious than in a woman; and shall we smile upon, and approve of a custom that is so encouraging to them, and so destructive to us? Were those in particular, who glory in seducing, and betraying innocence, to meet with the contempt they deserve, and the neglect of every person of virtue, they would soon be ashamed of their practices, and reduced to the necessity of quitting their unlawful pursuits. But while they are caressed, and admitted into the best companies they find restraint unnecessary . . . women are said to be the weaker vessel; and but few men will allow them to be equal in strength of mind; yet is the uprightness and rectitude of angels expected from them: instead of imputing their errors to the defect of their judgment, and the inferiority of understanding they pretend to reduce them to, they view every failing in an aggravated light, and for one false step forever deprive them of all that renders life valuable, and, although (as is often the case) their mistake may be owing to ignorance, inexperience, or a credulity that results from an honest heart, their persons are despised, their company avoided and their characters sacrificed . . . while the base betrayer is suffered to triumph in the success of his unmanly arts, and to pass unpunished even by a frown . . . surely compassion is due to misfortune, even if it arises from misconduct.[27]

---

[26] A twofold caution should be exercised at this point. We not only have the problem of making inferences from the magazine content to the real world but we also have to make inferences from our working definitions (sanctions) to our concept (sexual norms).

[27] Letter to the Editor, *Boston Magazine*, August, 1784, p. 419-420.

(3) There was no substantial evidence in the literature that the female was expected to be, or allowed to be, permissive in her sexual behavior before or outside of marriage.[28] There were no recurrent discussions of positive sanctions for such behavior, nor were there any indications that the female should have such rights.[29] This is particularly noteworthy because of the traditional view that industrialization tended to liberalize the sexual norms of our society in that the female, more than the male, was accorded additional rights and privileges in the area of sex (Reiss, 1960:Chs. 2, 5, 6). (4) Certain other evidence not presented in Tables 4 and 5 also lends support to this conclusion. There were, for example, fourteen discussions of illegitimacy. These were generally very sentimental and moralizing with great emphasis placed on the *dire* consequences of sexual deviance. Ten other discourses emphasized the dire alternatives that were open to the female who had engaged in premarital intercourse.[30]

Summary and Implications

The primary goal of this research was to examine *selected* aspects of the colonial American family structure via the content analysis procedure in order to determine whether certain facets of current family structure which have been attributed largely to the effects of industrialization were in evidence earlier.

Some aspects of the American family structure usually attributed to the effects of industrialization were noted in the important magazine content of the pre-industrial period. This appears to be the case regarding the existence of the *romantic love complex*, and the influence which this may have had on personal freedom in mate selection. Although there was some evidence to support the traditional view that economic goals and parental control in mate selection were present in the colonial courtship process, there was a considerably greater number of discussions that involved a component of the *romantic love complex*. Similarly, the findings with respect to motive in mate choice indicate the importance placed on *personal happiness* in contrast to traditional economic concerns.

The results regarding power indicate a patriarchal pattern with considerable subtle female power. These findings raise interesting questions regarding the meaning and significance of subtle female power in the family. It seems important to understand more about the dimensions of power in the pre-industrial family: Was power a single or multi-faceted phenomenon? Under what conditions and in what manner was power, overt and subtle, *exercised and expressed.* Finally, was subtle female power ever developed to a point where control did, in fact, rest with the woman of the house?

Although the evidence dealing with romantic love raises important questions regarding some patterns of the pre-industrial family, the data on sex do not. The evidence here is consistent with the general view regarding the conservative

---

[28] Of course, the possibility of a Type II error exists.

[29] Certain of the discussions, however, expressed dissatisfaction with the "extreme" rights of the male in the sexual area.

[30] It should be noted that a majority of the discussions referred to under point four occurred in non-fiction.

nature of sexual norms, including some evidence for the existence of the double standard.[31]

To be sure, the results obtained in this report should be interpreted with caution for several reasons. In this regard, there is always the problem of the limitations. *Not all aspects of the colonial family were studied.* The peculiar strategical decisions of the study should be evaluated. The inherent restrictions of the content analysis procedure must be kept in mind. The use of literary documents presents limitations with regard to our ability to generalize about social behavior, but such a difficulty, more pronounced in research of this type, is a general problem we confront in social research. All we may add is that the prevalence of particular points of view in magazines concerned with sex, marriage, and family behavior suggest a *concern for*, and *preoccupation with* these areas among a section of the populace. While one might expect occasional articles to appear on any subject, the *frequency of discussions*, as indicated in this paper, clearly suggests that some patterns consistent with the modern industrial family were present in the colonial period, although we recognize that frequency of themes may not always be a reliable indicator.[32]

In addition, while the class bias of the magazines must be recognized, it may be that the more privileged classes represented a model upon which other groups may have patterned their behavior. It may also be that the magazines studied that were published in England represented the views of a more highly industrialized society than was the case in the colonies at the time. Nevertheless, the problems presented by an empirical reexamination of the family in an earlier period are so formidable that the task is one of seeking out innovative ways of dealing with the data while making efforts to refine and improve such methods.

Why is history so relevant in this regard? As sociologists, we may be inclined to view the past, in this instance the colonial family social structure, as more homogeneous, integrated and consistent than it was in fact, forgetting, for example, even the significance of class differences. We are aided in this view by a rural myth of simplicity and homogeneity. Yet we also realize that *consensus*, *integration*, and *change* reveal themselves in varying ways, depending at what point in time the investigation is undertaken. The colonial family was undoubtedly a family in transition, perhaps in some areas a *more marked transition* than is commonly recognized.

Unless we can document the past with *base lines*, it becomes difficult to differentiate the dimensions and the extent of change. Such investigations might

---

[31] It should be observed that with respect to differences in the proportion of discussions of various aspects of the family structure between the two periods — 1741-1776 and 1777-1794 — it was typically observed that more discussions occurred during the later period. However, we cannot be sure *why* this happened. It may be a function of the American Revolution, or of an increased interest in the family structure, or of certain other factors. Perhaps future research will illuminate this point.

[32] Albrecht (1956:722-729), dealing with contemporary media, believes short stories in wide circulation reflect cultural norms and values (of family) but cautions against the frequency of themes as a reliable basis for such an assumption. Backman (1956:729-733) also discusses this.

be especially helpful in refining our understanding of the relationship between industrialization and the family.

REFERENCES

Albrecht, Milton C.
    1956 "Does literature reflect common values?" *American Sociological Review* 21:722-729.
Backman, Carl W.
    1956 "Sampling mass media content: the use of the cluster design." *American Sociological Review* 21:729-733.
Becker, Howard and Reuben Hill (eds.).
    1955 *Family, Marriage and Parenthood.* 2nd ed. Boston: D.C. Heath and Company.
Bell, Robert R.
    1963 *Marriage and Family Interaction.* Homewood, Illinois: The Dorsey Press, Inc.
Berelson, Bernard.
    1952 *Content Analysis in Communication Research.* New York: Free Press of Glencoe.
De Sola Pool, Ithiel (ed.).
    1959 *Trends in Content Analysis.* Urbana, Illinois: University of Illinois Press.
Downie, N.M. and R.W. Heath.
    1954 *Basic Statistical Methods.* 2nd ed. New York: Harper and Row.
Furstenberg, Frank F., Jr.
    1966 "Industrialization and the American family: a look backward." *American Sociological Review* 31 (June):326-337.
Goode, W.J.
    1963 *World Revolution and Family Patterns.* New York: Free Press of Glencoe, Ch. 1.
Goodsell, Willystine.
    1938 Pp. 215-216 in Bernhard J. Stern (ed.), *The Family in the Nineteenth Century.* New York: Appleton Century Crofts.
Greenfield, Sidney M.
    1967 "Industrialization and the family in sociological theory." *American Journal of Sociology* 67:312-322.
Hagood, Margaret Jarman.
    1941 *Statistics for Sociologists.* New York: Henry Holt and Company.
Lantz, Herman R.
    1958 *People of Coal Town.* New York: Columbia University Press.
Mott, Frank Luther.
    1930 *A History of American Magazines: 1741-1850.* Vol. 1. New York: D. Appleton and Company.
Mott, Paul E.
    1965 *The Organization of Society.* Englewood Cliffs, New Jersey: Prentice-Hall.
Osgood, Charles E.
    1959 "The representational model and relevant research methods." P. 65 in Ithiel De Sola Pool (ed.), *Trends in Content Analysis.* Urbana, Illinois: University of Illinois Press.

Reiss, Ira L.
1960 *Premarital Sexual Standards in America.* Glencoe, Illinois: The Free Press.
Sebald, Hans.
1962 "Studying national character through comparative analysis." *Social Forces* 40 (May): 318-322.
Stewart, George R.
1954 *American Ways of Life.* New York: Country Life Press.
Udry, J. Richard.
1966 *The Social Context of Marriage.* New York: J.B. Lippincott.
Wilkinson, Thomas O.
1962 "Family structure and industrialization in Japan." *American Sociological Review* 27:678-682.

ANALYSIS OF DOCUMENTARY RESEARCH EXAMPLE

Pre-Industrial Patterns in the Colonial Family in America: A Content Analysis of Colonial Magazines

Source of Data. This study of the American colonial family structure consisted of a content analysis of fifteen magazines which were published during the years 1741-1794. The complete list of these magazines is given in a footnote to the research article. Eight of the magazines were of particular interest to women and seven were oriented toward the general public. The magazines were primarily written for the middle and upper classes and were all published in New England and circulated primarily in the northern section of America.

The universe studied comprised all issues of the fifteen magazines published during 1741-1794. Six magazines were published in the period 1741-1776 and nine in the period 1777-1794. The entire 546 issues published during these periods constituted the sample. Article titles were used as indicators of relevance of the article. Articles were considered relevant and were read for content if they pertained to women.

Appraisal of Documents. The selection of the time period and thirteen of the magazines used in this study was based upon Mott's work. Mott was a leading authority on the history of journalism. He judged thirteen magazines of the period to be important on the basis of their literary worth, circulation, and influence upon the reading public. The two additional magazines included in this study, while not labeled as important by Mott, were designed especially for women and contained references to the existing family structure of the period.

The authors recognized that the newspaper and the magazine are "another troublesome but potentially significant *source of available data*." A schedule was used to examine each issue in the sample. Bibliographical data concerning each magazine and known biases of the publishers or editors were recorded. Distinctions were made between fiction and non-fiction and between advocated and existing patterns.

Content Analysis. The unit of analysis used in this study was the explicit discussion of one of the variables being coded. The following features of the American colonial family structure constituted the variables: patterns present in the man-woman relationship; types of attitudes and actions toward premarital and extramarital sexual involvement; motivations for entering into the marital relationship.

Use of Hypotheses. The following null hypotheses are examples of many which may be deduced from discussion of results:

1.   There are no significant differences between the number of discussions involving the male as the source of general power and the number of discussions involving the female as the source of general power.

2.   There are no significant differences between the number of discussions involving the male as the source of power over finances and those involving the female.

3.   There are no significant differences between fiction and non-fiction sources with respect to number of discussions portraying the romantic love complex.

4.   There are no significant differences between behavior (or sanctions) directed against the female sexual deviant and those directed against the male sexual deviant.

5.   There are no significant differences among the motives for entering marriage of happiness, wealth and social status.

Statistical tests of significance were applied at various points in the analyses (e.g., chi-square).

This study appears to be descriptive rather than analytical. The authors stated that the magazines were studied to examine the extent to which certain pre-industrial patterns of the family may have been present. However, they also indicated that "it is essential to establish base lines in history in order to make meaningful comparisons about the impact of given social phenomena, industrialization, or particular social institutions like the family." Their primary purpose in conducting this study was "to determine whether certain facets of current family structure which have been attributed largely to the effects of industrialization were in evidence earlier." Their results indicated that some facets did in fact occur at an earlier period. Thus, the study may have shed new light on previous assumptions regarding the effects of industrialization on the family and the colonial family as one in "more marked transition than is commonly recognized."

As indicated earlier in this chapter, the fundamental problem of historical study is the analysis of change over time. It is suggested that the study of pre-industrial patterns in the colonial family in America is a study involving such an analysis of change.

CHAPTER 6

Experimental Research: Laboratory and Field

The purpose of controlled experimental research is to test hypotheses about the effects of certain treatments on specific characteristics of individuals or objects. When an experiment is carefully controlled, it can be repeated by another investigator, or by the same investigator on another occasion, with nearly identical results.

LABORATORY EXPERIMENTS

In the ideal situation, the experimental method is the application of logic or reason to observations made in a completely controlled situation where one variable alone is permitted free play. Control can be achieved either by: (1) holding constant the variables that are extraneous to your hypothesis to prevent them from changing; or (2) deliberately causing a variable that is pertinent to your hypothesis to change in a prescribed manner.

Components of Laboratory Study

Most studies consist of three components for, in effect, we ask the question: "If something happens to something, what difference can we detect?" This final difference or observation is important but the factors which are involved in producing the final observation are also important. This is where the logic of science must be used. Schematically, the three components of a study are represented in Figure 16. (Shindell, 1964, p. 47)

Referring to Figure 16, *Component 1, Population to be studied:* the "population" or "universe" means all the members of any class of people, events, or objects. A population of consumers of hand lotion would be all people consuming this product. A population of electric refrigerators currently on the market would include all refrigerators in this category.

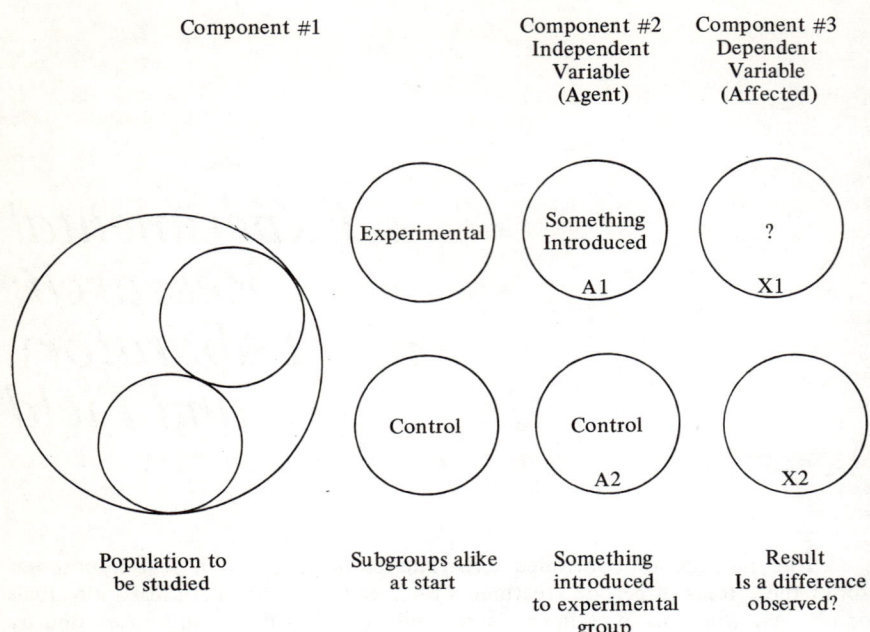

Figure 16. Schematic Representation of Components of Typical Comparative Study. Adapted from *Statistics, Science and Sense,* by Sidney Shindell, p. 47, by permission of the University of Pittsburgh Press. © 1964 by the University of Pittsburgh Press.

Another part of Component I is *"Subgroups alike at start."* These groups constitute the "sample." Obviously, it is not practical to study every member of a large population, i.e., *all* consumers of hand lotion or electric refrigerators. Therefore, a group of cases, or sample, is observed or studied. As Chapter 9 explains in greater detail, a sample of a population must be representative of that population in order to permit generalizations. Most of the world's knowledge is based upon samples, often inadequate and/or unrepresentative samples, from which opinions and attitudes are formed. For example, take the statement: "Adolescents are delinquent." Such a statement obviously is based upon an inadequate and/or unrepresentative sample.

Figure 16 shows the importance of subgroups being alike at the start. An experiment ordinarily has two groups, one called the experimental group and the other called the control group. A variable (i.e., a drug, a food product, a method of teaching, etc.) is introduced to the experimental group and the effects which the variable has on that experimental group are compared with the effects the absence of the variable has on the control group. For example, if we wish to study the effect of a drug on blood pressure, we would give the drug to the experimental group and not give it to the control group. If the experimental group had lower blood pressure readings at the start than the control group, and the results of the experiment showed that the experimental group (to whom the drug was given) had lower blood pressure than the control group, we could not conclude that the drug lowered the blood pressure, for the results could have been caused by the initial difference in the two groups. In some studies, instead of giving nothing to the control group, another drug could be given to compare its results with those of the first drug given to the experimental group.

Component 2 in Figure 16 involves primarily the *factor being introduced*, often called the *independent* or *experimental variable*. This is the variable that is introduced by the experimenter to the experimental group. The attempt to isolate this factor in order to study its influence alone is called "controlling other variables." One of the principal purposes of having a second group with which to compare (control group) is to enable the specific factors introduced to be isolated from all other similar influences. Therefore, the experimental and control groups must be treated alike except for the introduction of the experimental factor to the experimental group. Methods of control will be discussed later in this chapter.

The *third component* is the final observation itself or the *results of the experiment*. This component is often called the *dependent* (or *affected*) *variable*. An experiment raises this question: "Is a difference observed?" As indicated, an experimenter starts with two groups and introduces the variable into one of the two. If the final result is different and the groups were comparable at the beginning, the difference resulted presumably from the introduction of the variable. Experiments proceed from left to right in the diagram. In contrast, surveys usually start by observing a difference in two groups and seeking to know what happened at some previous point in time to account for this difference. In effect, surveys proceed from right to left in the diagram.

Much use will be made of the term "value," which is ordinarily used to refer to the numerically expressed result of a measurement, as "104°F. body temperature." It will be used here to refer also to the verbally expressed result of an observation, as "high fever."

An experiment to determine the effect, if any, of change in body temperature on heart rate may be used in identifying the essential features of an experiment. Such an experiment consists of making several measurements of heart rate at one body temperature, and several at some other, and comparing the two sets of measured values (assuming that they are comparable) to see if there is any significant difference.

There are two *variables* in the experiment — body temperature and heart rate. *Every experiment has two variables.* The first of the two is suspected of being causally related to the second, in the sense that a change in the value of the first, it is believed, may possibly cause a change in the value of the second. Every experiment tests for the existence of a causal relationship between two variables.

The first variable in such a pair is known as the "agent" (or independent) variable and is designated by the letter "A"; the second as the "affected" (or dependent) variable, and is designated by the letter "X." (See Figure 16.)

The structure of an experiment may now be redescribed: An experiment consists of giving the agent variable any chosen value (call it A_1) and making several or many measurements of the affected variable to yield a group of X_1 values; and in giving the agent variable some other chosen value (A_2) and making several or many measurements of the affected variable to yield a group of X_2 values. The X_1 and X_2 groups of values are then compared for any significant difference that may be found between them and a conclusion is sought as to the cause of the difference.

The following questions may serve as a guide in dealing with experimental studies (Shindell, 1964, p. 49):

> In terms of *Component 1*: From what population is the sample drawn? How are samples obtained? Are all possible sources of bias eliminated? Are the subgroups comparable?
>
> In terms of *Component 2*: Is there adequate control of the variables which may obscure the effect of the one being tested?
>
> In terms of *Component 3*: Is the observation being made relevant to the variable which is being investigated? Is there distortion in measurement or classification? Is there a difference not accountable on the basis of chance alone?

In answer to the last question, "Is there a difference not accountable on the basis of chance alone?," the probability that the results of an experiment were due to the experimental variable and not to chance may be determined by statistical tools. The time to be concerned with the use of statistics is before one begins a study, not after the collection of the data. The use of statistics in research will be discussed in Part V of this book.

The Six Unities in Research

The following discussion centers around one rule from the principles of experimental method: "Observe the six unities." This rule may be expanded to become: "See to it that there is unity of time, place, material, procedure, personnel, and mental attitude in the design of your experiment." This rule is directed toward reduction of errors in the design of an experiment. Since it is sometimes impossible or inconsistent ethically to observe all six unities, one or more may have to be violated in an experimental study. However, the logical penalty is the same, whether the violation is from carelessness or necessity. The six unities are necessary for correct experimental design. Without their observance, the conclusions from experiments are less secure. What might have been proved conclusively by an experiment may be weakened even down to a mere possibility.

Each of the six unities will be discussed in some detail. For unity of any one of the conditions of measurement, there must be identity, or near identity, between the average and range of the condition as it affects the X_1 group of values and the average and range of the condition as it affects the X_2 group.

1.   *Unity of Time.* In the case of *time*, if the collection of the X_1 group requires six months to complete, identity of *time range* demands that collection of the X_2 group of values also occupy not far from a six-month period. If identity of range were the only requirement, the two six-month periods might be in different years or decades; but identity, or near identity, between the *mean dates* of collection of the X_1 and X_2 groups is also required. This should be achieved to a sufficient degree by having the two time periods run *concurrently*.

There must be unity of time if any significant difference between the two groups of measured values is to be attributed with security to the difference in treatment employed (difference between A_1 and A_2). If the required unity is lacking, there is opportunity for some event or some trend, acting in the time interval, to affect the measurements and, thus, possibly to be the cause of any difference observed between X_1 and X_2 groups.

In comparing two sulfa drugs in a respiratory epidemic in camp, unity of time demands that both kinds of treatment be in progress concurrently. If sulfathiazole were used in the first six weeks, and sulfadiazine were then used on to the end of the epidemic, a trend in the virulence of the disease might alone account for any difference observed between the results of the two treatments.

If a new mode of therapy in congestive heart failure is to be tested for comparison with an older treatment, unity of time requires that both treatments be tested concurrently from the start. Tossing a coin for each successive patient will decide which treatment he is to receive. If the investigator should, instead, give the new therapy to all patients and compare the results with those of collected cases from his earlier practice or from the literature, when he came to draw his conclusions he would be plagued by the possibility that some trend or event, acting in the time period, was the cause of his results.

The "before and after" experiment, if the pairs of measurements are always made in a *fixed sequence* (as X_1 always first, and X_2 second), is affected by lack of unity of time. The mean dates of the two groups will differ by an interval equal to the average time interval separating the two measurements in a pair. If, however, the sequence can be reversed, becoming $X_2 X_1$ instead of $X_1 X_2$ in approximately every other pair, the "before and after" experiment can be saved from this error.

If an experiment unavoidably lacks unity of time, it may be possible to compensate for the error, provided that the two time ranges are not completely separated, but are concurrent over part of their course. The two groups of values (or other "results") should be examined for any trend in the values *along the time range* within either group. If the earlier versus later measured values within each group show no tendency either to rise or fall, but follow a horizontal time course, it may be believed that the difference observed between the results of the two modes of therapy has not arisen from the lack of unity of time.

2.   *Unity of Place.* Unity of place is achieved if the average of place distribution is the same for the X_1 group as for the X_2 group values. The range of place, like that of time, may be as extensive as the investigator cares to make it. He may roam the country in the course of his investigation and make measurements in every locality.

If his experiment is paired in respect to place, he will make both an X_1 and an X_2 measurement at every stop. If it is not a paired experiment, he can make the same stops, but will let the toss of a coin determine for each measurement whether it shall be for the X_1 or X_2 group. Note that random selection — "letting chance decide" — is preferable always to simple alternation.

If the experiment is confined to a single city, the X_1 subjects must not be drawn from the river section and the X_2 group from the hill section of town. A difference in locality can affect the outcome. If it is conducted in a hospital, the X_1 group of patients and the X_2 group must not come from different wards. If rats are the subjects of study instead of patients, there must be no consistent difference in the positions of the X_1 and X_2 cages in the animal room. A different location may bring with it a difference in illumination, or temperature, or disturbance from passing personnel, all conceivably capable of affecting the outcome of the experiment.

It will be seen that Doctor X cannot compare his results with those of Doctor Y in a different city without taking account of the lack of unity of place when he essays to draw conclusions from the comparison.

3.   Unity of Material. Unity of material is realized if the average and range of each of the characteristics of the material used in the X_1 group are duplicated, more or less closely, in the X_2 group.

Unity of material is achieved with the greatest economy of effort if paired design can be used. If a number of pairs of identical twins are available, one twin for the X_1 observation and the other for the X_2 observation, only a few pairs of measurements may be required to arrive at unity of material as between the two groups. More measurements must be made if the twins are not identical; still more are required if the two persons in each pair were merely of the same race, as in an experiment in which two Americans, two Chinese, two Eskimos, two Indians, etc., were used.

An important subvariety of the paired experiment is the "before and after" experiment, paired on the basis of unity of material by making both measurements in the pair on the same person or animal. An instance would be the test of a new drug for its possible effect to lower blood pressure. The A_1 dose (a placebo dose) is given, followed by the X_1 measurement of blood pressure; the A_2 dose of the drug (the actual dose) is then given to the same person, who is again measured to obtain the X_2 blood pressure reading and thus complete the pair of values. Comparison of the rate of gastric secretion before and after section of the vagus nerves in cases of hypersecretion associated with ulcer is another instance of a before and after experiment, as is comparison of the exercise tolerance before and after removal of the thyroid gland in patients with cardiac insufficiency.

In experiments with rats, unity of material is usually sought by using a number of pairs of rats, each pair from the same litter ("littermates") and making an X_1 observation on one rat, and an X_2 observation on the other in each pair.

Pairing is usually based on identity (or near identity) in some characteristic or group of characteristics of the *material*, but may be based on any of the conditions of measurement — time, place, material, procedure, personnel, and mental attitude.

The sulfathiazole versus sulfadiazine study in camp might, with some difficulty, be constructed of paired measurements. To begin, the doctor would have to find two patients alike in severity of illness, or in age, or race, or some other characteristic, or alike in a combination of any of these, to make a pair. Pairing would here be on the basis of material. The doctor would toss a coin to decide which treatment (A_1 or A_2) to give the first man in the pair, and would give the other treatment to the second. When he finally measured the affected variable, days of hospitalization, for each, he would have a pair of values, X_1 and X_2. He would then have to find other pairs of patients and construct his entire study out of such pairs, always giving one treatment to one man in each pair and the other treatment to the other. It is obvious that the paired construction is not too well suited to this experiment.

The statistically minded reader will recognize that if measurements are paired, the values in the X_1 group will be correlated with those in the X_2 group. If the condition of the measurement on which the pairing is based is highly relevant to the measurement, the correlation will be high (unless all other relevant conditions are also held constant). If the pairing should be based on an irrelevant condition of measurement (as on the basis of length of head hair in males, in an experiment in which the affected variable was blood pressure), no correlation would appear between the two groups of values. In such an experiment, which might be called an irrelevantly paired experiment, the investigator would have performed, unwittingly, an experiment constructed of independent (uncontrolled) measurements.

In many experiments the paired design is impracticable. Where this is the case and the two groups of values are independent (uncorrelated), all that is required to achieve unity of material is to make a sufficiently large number of measurements. The material is, of course, drawn from the same population and "coin tossing" is used in assigning treatment.

In a study to compare two modes of therapy for congestive heart failure, as additional patients are added by random selection to the two groups, the average and range of ages will approach the same value for the two groups, the proportion of males to females will undergo the same approach to identity, the average and range of severity of the disease will come to be the same in the two groups, or nearly the same, and identity or near identity will develop in the other details of the material. There is no need to restrict such an experiment to heart disease of a given severity or to patients of the same sex or of any narrow age limit. The investigator can take all patients who come.

The procedure followed here — collection of two randomly selected groups — leads to unity of time and place as well as unity of material. The three are related. If either unity of time or place is violated, as by collecting the X_1 measurements in one year and the X_2 measurements in a subsequent year, or in a different city, unity of material can never be assured. On the other hand, the physician could make one or more measurements in every locality in a trip around the world and still expect at the end to have two groups of the same or nearly the same average and range of racial stocks, severity of disease, education, politics, or whatnot. All that would be necessary would be that he select cases for the X_1 group and the X_2 group by random selection.

If the investigator has found himself unable to build into his experiment the requisite unity of material, and if there is a considerable range of material in each group, he may examine each group of measure values (X_1 and X_2) for any *trend* in the values that may extend along the range of the material. If, for example, there is lack of unity in the average age of the two groups of patients, each group contains quite a wide range of ages, he may examine each group of values of the affected variable (X_1 and X_2) to see if they have any tendency to rise or fall with age. If no trend is found it may be believed that, in spite of the lack of unity of material in respect to age, the error in design has not affected the outcome of the experiment.

4. Unity of Procedure. Unity of procedure requires that the average and range of procedures leading up to the measurements in the X_2 group shall be duplicated, or nearly so, in the procedures leading up to the measurements in the X_1 group. The difference in procedure that constitutes the essential difference in the two methods of therapy, A_1 and A_2, is, of course, excepted.

In many clinical studies, medical ethics make it impossible to achieve unity of procedure. On the other hand, some situations offer no difficulty. In a study to determine the effect, if any, of a new drug on blood pressure, unity of procedure demands that a placebo (A_1) be given prior to the X_1 measurement. Administration of the placebo (A_1) can easily be made to resemble in every respect the administration of the actual dose (A_2).

If the study is one to establish the comparative merits of a high choline intake (A_2) versus an ordinary choline intake (A_1) in cases of cirrhosis of the liver, there would be little difficulty in giving the same average and range of diet in the two groups, instituting the same hospitalization and nursing care and prescribing the same average and range of activity, with the addition of placebo capsules for the X_1 patients to match the choline capsules given the X_2 patients. Unity would be assured if the collection of cases in the two groups were continued long enough.

In general, no difficulty arises when comparison is made between the results of the best routine of therapeutic measures previously known, and the same routine plus some simple additional element that, it is believed, may improve the results.

In a study, however, such as that of the effect of thyroidectomy (A) on exercise tolerance (X) of patients with cardiac insufficiency, achievement of unity of procedure is out of the question. The study may establish that *something* in the complex of procedures involved in the thyroidectomy has improved the exercise tolerance of the patients, but to identify the stoppage of thyroid function as the single effective element in the complex, from the evidence furnished by the experiment alone and without use of collateral evidence, would require that a sham thyroidectomy be performed on approximately every other patient, for comparison with the removal of the gland.

The same difficulty would exist in a study to determine the effect of section of the vagus nerves on gastric hypersection in cases of ulcer. The fasting gastric secretion (X_2) after such an operation might be significantly less than that (X_1) before, but a sham vagotomy would have to be performed on approximately every other patient for comparison with the real vagotomy, to permit a firm conclusion, from the experimental evidence alone, as to just what element in the total complex of procedures was the cause of the result.

Ethical principles are often found in conflict with the principles of correct experimental design. When they do conflict, experimental design must yield.

The "before and after" experiment offers a peculiar difficulty in achieving unity of procedure. In an experiment to test the effect of a new drug upon blood pressure, the X_2 measurement is the end of a train of events that includes *making the X_1 measurement.* The X_1 measurement is not preceded by any such rehearsal. Such a difference in procedure — rehearsal for one measurement and not the other — is itself conceivably capable of bringing about a difference between the two measured values in a pair.

A comparable difficulty in regard to unity of *time* was solved by reversal of the sequence of the measurements in approximately every other pair. The same solution applies here. If the sequence of measurement, $X_1 X_2$, can be reversed to become $X_2 X_1$ in approximately half the pairs, unity of procedure in this respect is achieved.

Such reversal is possible in the test of the new drug on blood pressure, as there is no difficulty about first giving the actual dose of the drug (A_2) and making the X_2 measurement, and some time later following it with the placebo dose (A_1) and the X_1 measurement. The sequence is not reversible in any situation where application of the therapeutic agent makes a permanent change in the material.

As in the case of the other conditions of measurements so far discussed, procedures may vary over a wide range within a group. The only condition, aside from exercise of the researcher's best judgment in all cases, is that whatever diversity of procedure exists in one group shall also exist in the other.

If unity of procedure is unavoidably lacking in an experiment, little benefit is likely to be had from examining the measurements in each group for evidence of a trend along the range of procedures within a group. The difference existing between the two groups in respect to procedure is not likely to be bridged within either group by the procedure differences to be found there.

Where unity is lacking, each item of procedure affecting one group that is not matched in the procedures affecting the other group (each "associated agent") must be examined separately for its possible effect upon the result of the experiment. Assuming that a sham operation containing the item is ruled out by medical ethics or other considerations, the investigator may have recourse to animal experimentation to obtain collateral evidence that may aid him in coming to a conclusion. Or, he may draw upon his past experience for collateral evidence in regard to the effects of each of the associated agents upon other patients. Thus, in the vagus experiment, he may be able to summon experience with anesthesia and laparotomy in other cases of gastric hypersecretion, due to ulcer cases in which the vagi were not interfered with. Furthermore, positive collateral evidence favoring the agent under test may be strong enough to leave little doubt in the conclusions. In the vagus and ulcer experiment, such evidence is furnished by the known functions of the vagus nerves. It should be understood that reliance upon collateral evidence is seldom as satisfactory to the investigator and his audience as is possession of crucial evidence from a correctly designed experiment.

In the absence of specific experience or other collateral evidence in regard to any of the unmatched items of procedure (associated agents), the investigator may be able to invoke the "principle of inconceivability." In the vagus experiment, it may be deemed inconceivable that anesthesia for an hour could cause a reduction in the rate of gastric secretion, observable perhaps weeks after exposure to the anesthetic. Such associated agents as cannot be crossed off on such grounds (inconceivability of effect) must remain to weaken the investigator's conclusions.

5. *Unity of Personnel.* Unity of personnel is achieved if the average and range of personnel connected with the X_1 measurements are the same or nearly the same as the average and range of personnel for the X_2 group.

The simplest way to bring about this unity is to see that the same persons are engaged in all the activities connected with both groups of measurements. In a study of two sulfa compounds in a respiratory epidemic in camp, the patients under the two treatments must not be separated into two different wards with different nurses, doctors or attendants, or even cooks. Any one nurse must take care of approximately the same number of X_1 and X_2 patients; one chef must preside over the preparation of food for approximately the same number of each; each doctor must take care of approximately equal numbers of X_1 and X_2 patients, and the same even division of attention must extend to laboratory technicians, X-ray personnel, and others.

If it should be necessary in some experiment that only one patient be assigned to one doctor, with the result that the X_1 patients were handled by a group of X_1 doctors and the X_2 patients by a group of X_2 doctors, unity of personnel could still be achieved. All that would be required would be that random selection (coin tossing) be used in deciding which type of patient, X_1 or X_2, each doctor was to have, and that the numbers involved – patients and doctors – be sufficiently large to assure that the group of X_1 doctors and the group of X_2 doctors were identical, or nearly so, in average and range of skill, temperament, etc. In short, there would have to be "unity of material" as between the two groups of doctors.

Lack of unity of personnel is one of the least likely to arise in an experiment. The need for such unity should not be forgotten, however, when Doctor X essays to compare his results, using one treatment, with those of Doctor Y, who has used another. The difference in doctors, rather than a difference in treatments, may be the cause of any difference in results.

6. *Unity of Mental Attitude.* This final unity has to do with the mental attitude of all persons involved in the collection of the X_1 and X_2 groups of values. The mental attitude of patients and personnel must be the same in average and range for the two groups of measurements.

For unity of mental attitude in the patients, neither group should be aware that there is an older accepted treatment and a newer but as yet untried treatment that promises to be better. If knowledge of the existence of two treatments is unavoidably current in the two groups, no patient should have reason to doubt that he is getting the treatment best suited to his case.

It will be seen that unity of mental attitude in the patients cannot be achieved without unity in all personnel having contact with the patients. If Doctor X should have charge of one group and Doctor Y have charge of the other, a difference in the personality of the two men may conceivably affect the mental attitude of the two groups and through it affect the outcome of the study.

The doctor must also have unity of mental attitude. To achieve it, he should not know which treatment each patient is receiving until measurement of the affected variable (X) has been completed for that patient. It is seldom possible to meet this requirement.

The study of the two sulfa compounds in an epidemic in camp happens to be one in which this unity could be achieved. By the device of a code name for the treatments, the dispensing pharmacist could be the only person who knew the identity of drug "X" and drug "Y" until the study was over, and unity of mental attitude could thus be assured for all personnel — doctors, patients, and others — whose mental attitude was capable of affecting the outcome of the experiment.

With the cooperation of the manufacturer of the drug, the same device could be employed to achieve unity of mental attitude on the part of both doctor and patient in a test of the addition of testosterone administration to the best previous therapeutic management in cases of angina pectoris. The investigator could explain to each patient that during a portion of the time he would have to administer only the solvent, without the drug, in order to evaluate properly his results and possibly save needless continuation of an expensive treatment if it should prove to be of no avail. The identity of preparation "X" and preparation "Y," one of them being only a placebo, would remain known to the manufacturer alone until the end of the study.

In other studies it may be possible for the doctor to have a colleague evaluate the results of the treatment. If the results are observable by X-ray or by some laboratory measurement, the X-ray consultant or laboratory director may complete his evaluation of each patient before knowing what therapy each has received.

The best way to assure unity of mental attitude is to make sure that all persons whose mental attitude may be capable of affecting the X_1 and X_2 measurements are deliberately kept uninformed as to the difference in therapy until the measurements are completed. This is not always possible to do.

In summary, six conditions of measurements have been discussed for which identity or near identity is required as between the two groups of measurements or observations that go to make up an experimental study. If identity or near identity is impossible to achieve in one or more of the conditions of measurement, the investigator must attempt to evaluate the relevancy of the condition, either from internal evidence within the two groups of measured values or observations, or from collateral evidence from other experience with the condition of measurement in question, or from general experience — the conceivability or inconceivability of the condition's affecting the outcome of the experiment. If identity or near identity is lacking, and the condition is relevant to the outcome of the experiment, it may be impossible to arrive at a firm conclusion.

EXAMPLES AND ANALYSES
OF LABORATORY EXPERIMENTS

BEHAVIORAL ABNORMALITIES IN YOUNG ADULT PIGS CAUSED BY MALNUTRITION IN EARLY LIFE[1]

RICHARD H. BARNES, A. ULRIC MOORE AND WILSON C. POND

Previous publications from our laboratories have described behavioral abnormalities observed in rats and pigs several months after nutritional rehabilitation from malnutrition imposed during the immediate postnatal period (1-6). In both rats and pigs protein-calorie malnutrition during early life resulted in poorer learning performance in several types of test procedures. Moreover, it was also noted that these animals had elevated excitatory responses to stressful situations such as anticipated electric shock (2), sudden immersion in cold water (1), or the availability of food for a short period of time when the animal was extremely hungry (4). Furthermore, all of these behavioral differences were found in animals after long periods of complete nutritional rehabilitation. In order to understand and interpret the decreased learning performance of previously malnourished animals it will be necessary to evaluate behavioral characteristics such as motivation, drive, frustration, fright and other factors which will affect learning performance. Hopefully, this may lead to the ultimate assessment of the contribution, if any, of impaired capacity as a factor influencing the animal's poor learning performance.

Other features of the malnutrition-behavior interrelationship that can be evaluated in experimental animals are the influence of the age at which protein-calorie malnutrition is imposed and the relative effects of protein deficiency as compared with calorie deficiency. In the present communication these factors are examined utilizing the pig as the experimental animal.

Materials and Methods

Male Yorkshire piglets at 3 weeks of age (with the exception of one group which will be described later) were weaned from their dams and divided into five groups according to the schedule: four experimental groups of 4 pigs each and a control group of 6 pigs. Insofar as possible, littermates were distributed evenly within the groups. At an early age the experimental groups were subjected to protein or calorie deprivation. Protein deprivation (groups labeled low protein) was achieved by feeding a diet containing approximately 2.5% protein (3%

Reprinted with permission from *Journal of Nutrition*, Vol. 100, pp. 149-155, 1970.

[1] Supported in part by funds provided through the State University of New York and by Public Health Service Research Grant no. HD-02581 from the National Institute of Child Health and Human Development.

Note: This research was discussed by Dr. Barnes in relation to human beings in "Effects of Malnutrition on Mental Development," *Journal of Home Economics* 61:671-676; November 1969.

casein). Calorie deprivation (groups labeled restricted) was achieved by restricting the quantity of the control diet in such a manner that the body weight of the piglets remained at the level established at the time of initiating the restricted dietary intake. The one exception to weaning at 3 weeks of age mentioned above was in group 4 (see below). This group was made up of piglets taken from sows at 3 days of age. They were kept in wire screen-bottom chick brooder cages for 3 weeks and were fed 40 ml homogenized, vitamin D-fortified cow's milk four times daily. This amount of food was found to be sufficient to maintain body weight constant and not permit an appreciable gain. At 3 weeks of age these piglets were transferred to pens in the experimental barn and the purified control diet was fed in such an amount as to prevent an appreciable gain in weight over an additional 5 weeks. Dietary deprivations were for 8-week periods according to the schedule: group 1, restricted from 3 to 11 weeks of age;

TABLE 1. DIET COMPOSITION

	Control 18% casein diet	Low protein 3% casein diet
	g	g
Major components		
Casein[1]	18.0	3.0
Glucose monohydrate[2]	47.6	62.6
Dextrine[3]	25.0	25.0
Corn oil[4]	3.0	3.0
Mineral mixture	5.4	5.4
Vitamin mixture	1.0	1.0
Total	100.0	100.0

Minor components

Vitamin Mixture			Mineral Mixture	
Vitamin A	572	IU	$CAHPO_4 \cdot 2H_2O$	1.54 g
Vitamin D	66	IU	$CaCO_3$	1.23 g
Thiamin	4	mg	KH_2PO_4	1.72 g
Riboflavin	0.99	mg	NaCl	0.61 g
Niacin	6.6	mg	$CuSO_4 \cdot 5H_2O$	57 mg
Ca pantothenate	4.0	mg	$FeSO_4 \cdot 7H_2O$	66 mg
Choline dihydrogen citrate	396	mg	$MnSO_4 \cdot H_2O$	18.5 mg
Vitamin B_{12}	6.6	μg	$ZnCO_3$	66 mg
Vitamin E	10	IU	MgO	82 mg
Inositol	22	mg	KI	0.04 g
Folic acid	0.22	mg	$CoCl_2 \cdot 6H_2O$	1.1 mg
Menadione	0.44	mg	Na_2SeO_3	0.05 mg
Pyridoxine	0.33	mg		
Biotin	0.033	mg		
Glucose to make	1.0	g		

[1] Crude, 30-mesh, National Casein Company, Riverton, N.J.
[2] Cerelose, Corn Products Company, Argo, Ill.
[3] Nutritional Biochemicals Company, Cleveland, Ohio
[4] Mazola, Corn Products Company, Argo, Ill.

group 2, low protein from 3 to 11 weeks of age; group 3, low protein from 7 to 15 weeks of age; group 4, restricted from 3 days to 8 weeks of age; and group 5 was fed the control diet ad libitum from 3 to 11 weeks of age. The composition of the control and low protein diets is given in table 1. Following completion of the experimental periods all pigs were fed a practical pig ration ad libitum. This was a corn-soybean meal ration with minerals and vitamins added to meet NRC recommendations. Growth curves presented in figure 1 further illustrate the experimental design.

Results

During the depletion period the pigs which were either protein or calorie deprived developed a gaunt, unthrifty appearance. The protein-depleted animals consumed very little food while the calorie-depleted pigs retained their appetite. In fact, it became necessary to remove bedding from the concrete pen floors because the restricted animals ate the wood shavings and one animal in group 4 (restricted 0-8 weeks) died with a large intestinal impaction which was composed of shavings. Surprisingly, these "marasmic-like" pigs remained active throughout the 8 weeks of depletion and when let out of their pens each morning during a

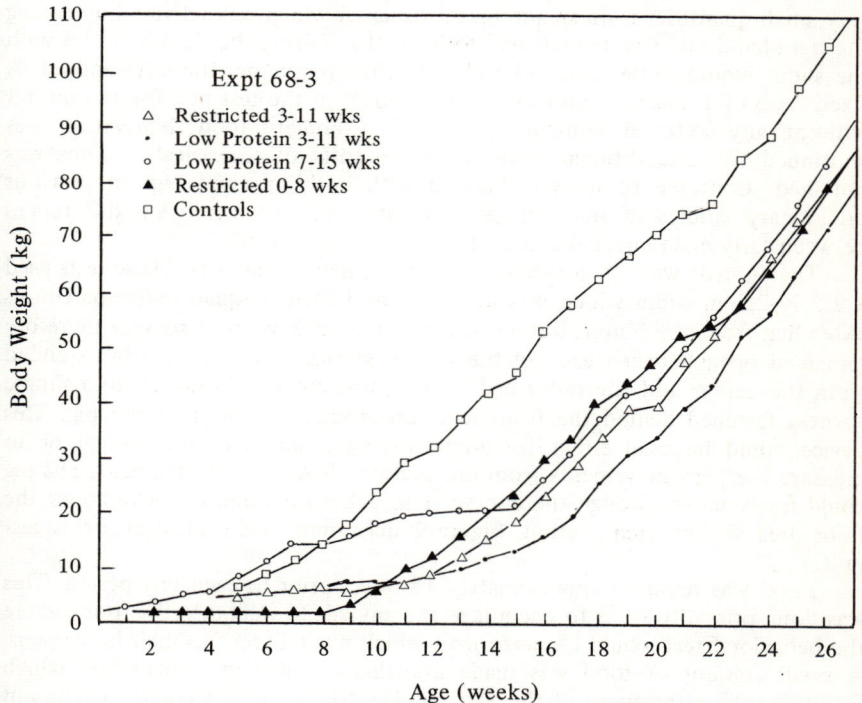

Fig. 1. Growth curves illustrating depletion and rehabilitation for the five dietary treatments.

clean-up period, they would run up and down the corridor between the pens. The pigs were kept in pairs in the pens since this has been found to be an important factor in maintaining the young animals during the period of their severe nutritional deprivation. When released in pairs while their pens were being cleaned, the malnourished pigs frolicked and explored the new surroundings during their brief freedom in much the same manner as the control animals. When the experimental animals were switched to the normal commercial swine ration, they were individually penned and remained one to a pen for the remainder of the study. The pens were approximately 180 by 120 cm with solid plywood partitions about 100 cm high.

When the animals were approximately 6 months of age and had been nutritionally rehabilitated for about 3 months, they were subjected to a battery of behavioral tests devised on the basis of several years of studies in our laboratories. The first procedure was an operant test involving a food reinforcement. The pigs were fasted for 24 hours and then placed in a specially designed cage with two devices at one end of the cage. These devices resembled the lids on feeder boxes. They were familiar to the animals since the pigs had been fed from dispensers with these lids during their entire rehabilitation. Under the lids were pans, but only the left pan provided food which was dropped into the pan in very small quantities from an automatic dispenser which was activated by raising the right-hand lid. The animals had to learn that raising the right-hand lid with the snout would cause food to be placed in the pan under the left-hand lid. A fixed ratio of 1 was used and each pig remained in the test pen for 14 minutes without any external stimulation or aid. Complete food deprivation was continued for 2 additional days so that a total of three test sessions was obtained. Contrary to results obtained with both rats and pigs in previous preliminary studies of the same general nature (7), no significant differences between early malnourished and control pigs were obtained.

The animals were then submitted to three behavioral tests. These tests used a 2.5 × 2.5 m room which was divided into 4 smaller squares with partitions extending from the center, but not reaching the outer walls. A passage therefore remained open between each of the smaller sections. A rotating arm extended from the center and the outer end of this arm could be attached to a simple harness fastened behind the front legs and around the chest of the pig. This device could be used either for administering a shock to the animal or to measure the pig's movements from one section of the room to the next. The pig could freely move through the doorways in either direction or move about the floor area within each section. Figure 2 diagrammatically illustrates this test unit.

Food was removed approximately 18 hours prior to each test period. This was done primarily so as to encourage the animals to walk into the room where the behavioral test would be performed which was adjacent to their home pens. A small amount of food was made available to them in a small stall which facilitated the attachment of the harness. The harnessed pigs could then be put into the testing room and the harness connected to the swivel arm.

The first test with this facility was to place the pigs in the room with wood

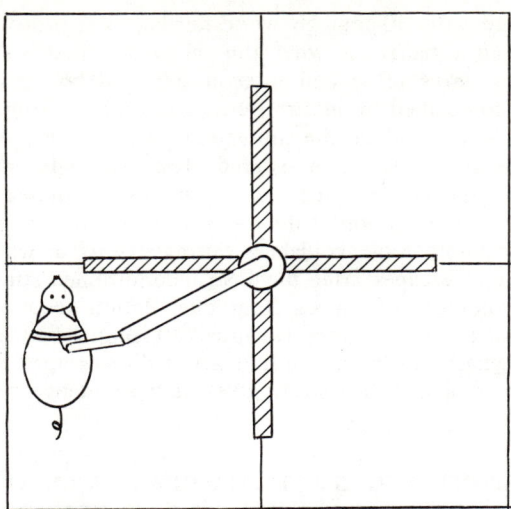

Fig. 2. Diagram of the behavioral testing unit. The doorways joining the four sections contained either minimal obstacles (7.5-cm-high wood braces) or 30-cm-high hurdles.

braces, each 7.5 cm high, placed on the floor in each doorway. This was the animal's first exposure to the harness and to the room. It was obviously a stressful and frightening experience. All pigs rapidly moved from section to section. They frequently vocalized and exhibited a general attitude of excitement. There were very noticeable differences between the control animals and most experimental groups. With the exception of the pigs that had been restricted from birth to 8 weeks, the experimental animals generally were more difficult to harness, more noisy when isolated in the test room, and as can be seen in table 2, there were significantly more moves from one section to another during the 14-minute test period. The group restricted from birth to 8 weeks unfortunately had only three animals (one having died earlier), yet uniformly these three pigs and the six controls were easy to harness and were calm and quiet during the test period. The controls moved significantly less than three of the other groups (table 2). The 0 to 8 weeks-restricted group appeared to be intermediate in activity showing no significant difference from the controls and yet significantly fewer moves than the low protein 3 to 11 weeks group. Exploratory behavior as manifested by sniffing and licking the floor was seen only during the latter part of the test sessions and was exhibited primarily by the control and 0 to 8 weeks-restricted group.

The day following the spontaneous activity test described above, the animals were returned to the test room with the harness attached. On this occasion and for the succeeding 2 days the animals were subjected to a conditioned-avoidance procedure. The doorways between each of the 4 sections were now equipped with 30-cm-high wood hurdles. The protocol involved the administration of an initial shock when the animal was first isolated in the test room. There was then a 60-second interval followed by 10 seconds of continuous buzzer accompanied by intermittent (1 second) clicking signals. Accompanying the 10th signal and on the subsequent 20, 1-second interval signals, a controlled voltage shock was administered. The pig could interrupt the CS (conditioned stimulus) buzzer signals or the shocks by jumping the hurdle in either direction from one section of the room to the next. Automatic recordings were made of the number of avoidances during 9 tests in which the CS was given, the number of escapes after the US (unconditioned stimulus) had been initiated and the number of moves from one section to another during 10 intertrial periods of 60 seconds each (included 60 seconds before the first signal and after ninth signal). All animals either avoided or escaped the US. Table 3 which shows the results of this study gives only avoidance performance and

TABLE 2. SPONTANEOUS ACTIVITY IN A NEW ENVIRONMENT

Group designation[1]	Number of moves per pig		
	0-7 min[2]	8-14 min	total[3]
1. Restricted 3-11 wk (4)			55 ± 4.0
2. Low protein 3-11 wk (4)	50 ± 6.2[4]	22 ± 4.5	72 ± 5.7
3. Low protein 7-15 wk (4)			56 ± 6.5
4. Restricted 0-8 wk (3)	28 ± 4.4	21 ± 4.0	49 ± 3.8
5. Controls (6)	18 ± 0.8	15 ± 1.1	33 ± 1.1

[1] Number of pigs shown in parentheses.
[2] Record of movements at short intervals during the test session were unfortunately not made for all groups.
[3] Statistically significant differences for total moves: 5 vs. 1, $P < 0.01$; 5 vs. 2, $P < 0.001$; 5 vs. 3, $P < 0.025$; 5 vs. 4, N.S.; 2 vs. 4, $P < 0.05$.
[4] Mean ± SEM.

TABLE 3. CONDITIONED AVOIDANCE "ACQUISITION"

Group designation[1]	Avoidances in 9 trials per pig			Avoidance average for 3 days[2]	Intertrial jumps
	Day 1	Day 2	Day 3		
1. Restricted 3-11 wk (4)	5.2 ± 1.1[3]	7.0 ± 1.2	7.2 ± 1.1	6.5 ± 0.6	14 ± 1.3
2. Low protein 3-11 wk (4)	2.0 ± 0.4	5.5 ± 0.6	4.5 ± 1.5	4.0 ± 0.7	16 ± 1.1
3. Low protein 7-15 wk (3)	5.7 ± 0.4	8.3 ± 0.7	7.7 ± 0.4	7.2 ± 0.5	12 ± 0.6
4. Restricted 0-8 wk (3)	4.7 ± 0.9	7.7 ± 0.9	6.7 ± 0.4	6.4 ± 0.6	11 ± 2.7
5. Controls (6)	4.0 ± 0.4	6.9 ± 0.8	7.1 ± 0.6	6.0 ± 0.5	12 ± 1.8

[1] Number of pigs shown in parentheses.
[2] Controls (group 5) and low protein 3-11 wk (group 2) significantly different. For average of 3 days, $P < 0.005$. No other group differences were significant.
[3] Mean ± SEM.

numbers of intertrial jumps. It can be seen that group 2, the low protein 3 to 11 weeks group, performed more poorly than any of the other groups. However, because of small numbers in the experimental groups the only significant difference was between group 2 and the controls. Although no significant differences existed in the number of intertrial jumps it is interesting that group 2, low protein 3 to 11 weeks, showed the largest number of jumps.

The day following the third conditioned-avoidance session, an "extinction" test was run. The pigs were harnessed, placed in the test room and given an initial shock in the same manner used in the previous 3 days. However, in this session hurdles were removed so that there was only the 7.5-cm-high brace on the floor in each of the doorways. They were given three CS trials; following the 60-second interval after the third trial the CS buzzer signal started with 1-second clicks as in the previous sessions, but this time the CS continued for the entire 10-minute test period regardless of the pig's movements, yet no shocks were administered. The number of movements from one section to another was recorded for each of the 10 minutes of the test. For various reasons, although most commonly due to apparatus failure, a few pigs had to be dropped from this as well as other tests. As a result, three experimental groups and the controls were reduced in numbers by one pig each. Nevertheless, differences in extinction between controls and experimental groups were so large that by statistical analysis they were highly significant. As shown in table 4 the difference in movements was largely restricted to the second 5-minute period of extinction indicating that the initial level of excitement was not greatly different, but with continuing exposure to the buzzer signal (CS) the experimental groups were generally unable to inhibit the learned responses. The pattern of extinction performance is illustrated more clearly in figure 3 in which movements during each minute of the test are plotted against time. By this representation of data the experimental groups appear to divide into two classes, each differing widely from the controls. The continued high level of excitement of group 2 (low protein 3 to 11 weeks) is clearly seen in the graph. However, watching and listening to these animals (group 2) during the extinction test was far more

TABLE 4. CONDITIONED AVOIDANCE "EXTINCTION"

Group designation[1]	Number of moves per pig[2]		
	0-5 min	6-10 min	total
1. Restricted 3-11 wk (3)	27 ± 5.8[3]	15 ± 4.8	42 ± 4.0
2. Low protein 3-11 wk (4)	28 ± 6.7	24 ± 1.3	52 ± 2.5
3. Low protein 7-15 wk (3)	36 ± 6.9	15 ± 2.3	51 ± 9.2
4. Restricted 0-8 wk (3)	22 ± 7.2	13 ± 2.2	35 ± 9.0
5. Controls (5)	22 ± 5.2	4 ± 1.5	26 ± 5.1

[1] Number of pigs shown in parentheses.
[2] No significant differences during first 5 minutes. Significance of differences during second 5 minutes as follows: 5 vs. 1, $P < 0.001$; 5 vs. 2, $P < 0.001$; 5 vs. 3, $P < 0.001$; 5 vs. 4, $P < 0.001$; 2 vs. groups other than controls, N.S.
[3] Mean ± SEM.

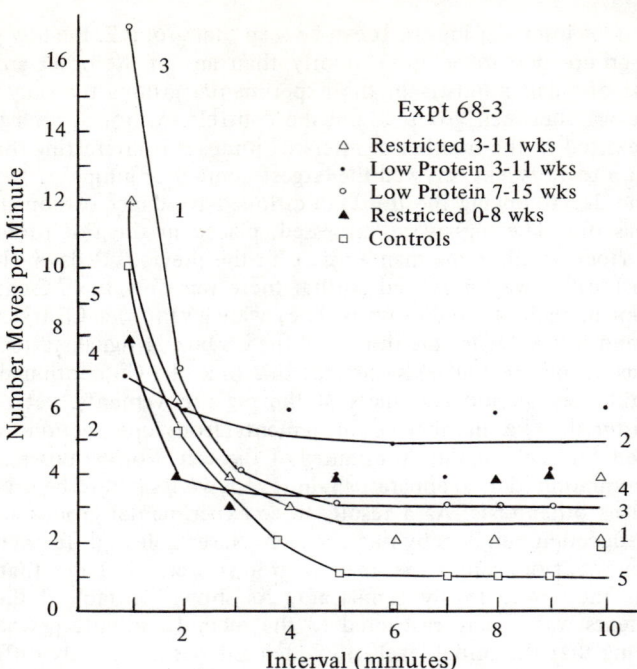

Fig. 3. Extinction of a conditioned response. Pattern of moves per minute for 10 minutes during which continuous conditioned stimulus (buzzer) was provided, but was not accompanied by unconditioned stimuli (electric shocks).

dramatic than the data indicate. They snorted and vocalized and continued active movement both between sections and within sections of the test room. They never reached a sufficiently calm state so that excitatory activity became exploratory activity. The control animals behaved in a completely different manner. During the first few minutes of exposure to the continuing buzzer signal they were highly excited, but this excitatory behavior rapidly declined and for the last 5 minutes of the test they were calmly sniffing and licking the floor and, in general, exhibiting exploratory behavior.

Discussion

An extremely interesting feature of these studies is the highly reproducible observation that the marked behavioral abnormalities, which develop as a consequence of a short period of malnutrition during early life, continue to be manifested after complete nutritional rehabilitation has been achieved and months after the initial nutritional insult was imposed. Furthermore, even though learning performance in certain tests may be impaired as a result of early malnutrition, the predominant behavioral characteristics observed in studies with pigs reported here, as well as in previous publications (2, 3, 8), appear to be related to fear of a new environment, elevated level of excitement under conditions of stress and inability to inhibit responses. An increased-hunger drive for food which has been observed in other studies was not seen. These behavioral changes might be categorized as overreaction or heightened emotionality in response to aversive stimuli. These characteristics could affect learning behavior by such mechanisms as altering the degree of reinforcement in operant testing or by increasing the level of distractions or frustrations. The behavioral responses reported above for previously malnourished pigs are remarkably similar to those of rats treated in a similar manner (5, 9).

Certain preliminary indications have emerged concerning the effect of the animal's age when malnutrition was imposed and the relative damaging effect of protein deficiency as compared with calorie deficiency on behavioral development. Although firm conclusions cannot be drawn from this study, two relationships are worthy of comment. First, a critical age in the pig when the initiation of malnutrition has its greatest effect upon behavioral development appears to be prior to 7 weeks. Second, protein deficiency, if initiated sufficiently early, would appear to have a greater effect upon behavioral development than calorie deficiency. A more thorough examination of these factors in future studies will be very important.

REFERENCES

1. Barnes, R.H., S.R. Cunnold, R.R. Zimmermann, H. Simmons, R.R. MacLeod and L. Krook 1966 Influence of nutritional deprivations in early life on learning behavior of rats as measured by performance in a water maze. *J. Nutr.* 89:399.

2. Barnes, R.H., A.U. Moore, I.M. Reid and W.G. Pond 1967 Learning behavior following nutritional deprivations in early life. *J. Amer. Diet. Ass.* 51:34.

3. Barnes, R.H., A.U. Moore, I.M. Reid and W.G. Pond 1968 Effect of food deprivations on behavioral patterns. In: *Malnutrition, Learning and Behavior*, ed., N.S. Scrimshaw and J.E. Gordon. M.I.T. Press, Cambridge, Mass., p. 203.

4. Barnes, R.H., C.S. Neely, E. Kwong, B.A. Labadan and S. Frankova 1968 Postnatal nutritional deprivations as determinants of adult behavior toward food, its consumption and utilization. *J. Nutr.* 96:467.

5. Frankova, S., and R.H. Barnes 1968 Influence of malnutrition in early life on exploratory behavior of rats. *J. Nutr.* 96:477.

6. Frankova, S., and R.H. Barnes 1968 Effect of malnutrition in early life on avoidance conditioning and behavior of adult rats. *J. Nutr.* 96:485.

7. Barnes, R.H., I.M. Reid, W.G. Pond and A.U. Moore 1968 The use of experimental animals in studying behavioral abnormalities following recovery from early malnutrition. In: *Calorie and Protein Deficiencies*, eds. R.A. McCance and E.M. Widdowson. Churchill Press, London, p. 277.

8. Barnes, R.H. 1967 Experimental animal approaches to the study of early malnutrition and mental development. *Federation Proc.* 26:144.

9. Levitsky, D.A., and R.H. Barnes 1970 Early malnutrition: effect on emotionality in the adult rat. *Nature.* In press.

ANALYSIS OF LABORATORY EXPERIMENT EXAMPLE

Behavioral Abnormalities in Young Adult Pigs Caused by Malnutrition in Early Life

Purpose of Study. To determine behavioral changes of malnourished pigs after nutritional rehabilitation had been achieved.

Hypotheses. Three null hypotheses, deduced from the discussion of results, are as follows:

1. There are no significant differences in learning behavior between early malnourished (experimental) and control pigs.

2. There are no significant differences in exploratory behavior between early malnourished (experimental) and control pigs.

3. There are no significant differences in excitatory behavior between early malnourished (experimental) and control pigs.

Components of Study.

Component #1 – Population to be Studied: This study was comprised of four experimental groups and one control group of pigs. The authors state that "insofar as possible, littermates were distributed evenly within the groups."

Component #2 – Independent Variable: Malnutrition (restricted protein or calorie intake).

Component #3 – Dependent Variable: Behavior:

1. Learning behavior
2. Exploratory behavior
3. Excitatory activity

The experimental and control groups were designated as follows:

Group #1 – Restricted (calorie deprivation) 3-11 weeks of age

Group #2 – Low Protein 3-11 weeks

Group #3 – Low Protein 7-15 weeks

Group #4 – Restricted 3 days-8 weeks

Group #5 – Control diet 3-11 weeks

The independent variable (malnutrition) was introduced to the four experimental groups and, following a three-month period of nutritional rehabilitation, the effect (in terms of behavior) of the malnutrition on the experimental groups was compared with the effect of the *absence* of this independent variable on the control group.

This effect (in terms of behavior) constituted the dependent variable. Examples of "operational definitions"* of behavior in this study were:

1. Learning behavior as measured by a pig's determining that raising the right-hand lid on a feeder box with the snout would cause food to be placed in the pan under the left-hand lid.

2. Exploratory behavior as manifested by sniffing and licking the floor when first isolated in a test room.

3. Excitatory behavior as measured in terms of number of moves per minute under conditions of stress (anticipation of buzzers and electric shocks).

---

*See chapter 3, page 49, for discussion of "operational or working definitions."

FABRIC SOILING BY AIR POLLUTION

HELEN FACER GOODRICH AND ELIZABETH FLOWERS THOMAS

Previous studies have been reported on such air pollutants as carbon monoxide, sulfur dioxide, oxides of nitrogen and ozone (1, 2). And the effect of pollutants on fabric deterioration and color changes has been investigated by Salvin (3), Peters and Saville (4) and others. But few studies have dealt with fabric soiling from pollutants; and pollutant tests generally have been distorted by the use of weathering tests that are affected by wind, rain, sunlight and other factors in addition to contaminants.

It was the purpose of this study to determine the effects of selected pollutants on the soiling of representative apparel fabrics by comparing spectrophotometric measurements before and after exposure.

Procedure

Experimental Fabrics. Five types of experimental fabrics were used — 100% cotton, 100% polyester, a 65/35 polyester/cotton blend, the same blend with a durable press (DP) finish and the same blend with both a DP and soil release (SR) finish. The first three fabrics were bleached and scoured but otherwise unfinished.

Forty-two 3x5 in. samples of each type of fabric were used. A table of random numbers was used to select the fabrics from the quantity of specimens possible from five-yard lengths of each fabric. A table of random numbers was also used to sort the samples for various contaminants, exposure levels and replications.

Contamination of Fabrics. The fabrics were exposed to nitrogen oxides and tobacco smoke in a type of gas chamber recommended for AATCC Test Method 23-1962 (5). . . .

The tobacco smoke was produced from a smoking device designed to deliver smoke at a constant rate. Cigarettes were held in a vertical glass tube slightly crimped at the bottom so that only ashes fell through. The tubing was inserted into a rubber stopper supported in a vacuum flask. Compressed air, which flowed through a tube connected at the neck of the flask, was controlled by a needle valve and monitored by a flowmeter at two cubic centimeters per minute. Nonfilter cigarettes were inserted into the glass tube and allowed to burn completely (15 per hour), producing a white smoke which was directed into the chamber.

A gas partitioner monitored the contaminants within the chamber. A vacuum pump pulled a sample of the air from the chamber into the gas partitioner from which gas chromatograms were produced by a recorder. Readings were made approximately every four hours. . . .

Exposure levels of 0.75, 1.5, 3, 6, 12 and 24 hours were selected as a result of a pilot study. There were three replications.

Reprinted with permission from *Textile Chemist and Colorist*, Journal of the American Association of Textile Chemists and Colorists, Vol. 2, No. 13, July 1, 1970, pp. 213-217.

Evaluation Of Soil. Reflectances of the original and exposed fabrics were determined by spectrophotometric measurements made on a recording spectrophotometer. The wavelengths of light utilized in making the measurements ranged from 350 to 760 nanometers — approximately the visible spectrum. The reflectance measurements were transferred to computer cards with a chart reader and an analog-hybrid computer.

The amount of soil on the fabrics was computed from the reflectance measurements by the Kubelka-Munk equation (6):

$$\frac{K}{S} = \frac{(1 - R)^2}{2R}$$

where K = absorbed light factor
    S = scattered light factor
    R = reflectance.

Statistical Analysis. Analysis of variance was used to determine statistical differences among contaminants, exposure levels, fabrics and the two sides of the fabrics. The significant differences among the fabrics were determined by the Newman-Keuls sequential range test (7).

Results And Discussion. The study was limited to the evaluation of the acceptance of the specified air-borne soils by the various experimental fabrics. No attempt was made to measure the soil retention or the soil release characteristics of the fabrics.

Appearance And Hand. The tobacco smoke left a very visible yellow-brown stain on all fabrics even after the first exposure level of 0.75 hour. . . . In addition to the discoloration, the contaminated samples exposed to 6, 12 and 24 hours of smoke felt gummy and easily soiled one's hand. After the samples were allowed to stand, the stickiness disappeared but the fabrics became quite stiff.

The oxides of nitrogen did not soil the fabrics as greatly as did the tobacco smoke. . . . Some visual soiling, however, was apparent on the fabrics after 6, 12 and 24 hours of exposure. Although the fabrics subjected to the three longest levels of exposure to nitrogen oxides were slightly yellowed, they were not sticky. The fabrics remained pliable.

Apparent Soil Computations. The apparent soil was computed from the reflectance measurements. The mean apparent soil for the different variables and combinations of variables was determined. The overall mean resulting from the exposure of the fabrics to tobacco smoke was 1.2296, which greatly exceeded the 0.0585 obtained from exposure to oxides of nitrogen.

The relationship of the amount of soiling by the two contaminants at various levels of exposure is presented in Table 1. The amount of soiling increased in direct proportion to the level of exposure. As the time of exposure doubled, the degree of soiling approximately doubled.

· The mean soiling produced by tobacco smoke was considerably higher than that of the soiling produced by the oxides of nitrogen at the corresponding levels of exposure. In fact, the mean apparent soil resulting from exposure to nitrogen at all levels except that of the greatest duration was less than the mean apparent soil resulting from 0.75 hour of exposure to tobacco smoke.

TABLE 1. APPARENT SOIL MEANS OF
CONTAMINANTS AND EXPOSURE LEVELS

Exposure Level (Hours)	Contaminants	
	Smoke	Oxides of Nitrogen
0.75	0.0990	0.0075
1.5	0.2728	0.0150
3	0.4706	0.0293
6	0.9509	0.0801
12	1.8165	0.0581
24	3.7679	0.1612

TABLE 2. APPARENT SOIL MEANS OF FABRICS

Fabric	Mean
100% Cotton	0.6785
100% Polyester	0.4641
65/35 Blend	0.6858
65/35 Blend, DP	0.7175
65/35 Blend, DP & SR	0.6745

TABLE 3. APPARENT SOIL MEANS OF
FABRICS AND CONTAMINANTS

Fabric	Contaminants	
	Smoke	Oxides of Nitrogen
100% Cotton	1.2742	0.0829
100% Polyester	0.8801	0.0481
65/35 Blend	1.3354	0.0362
65/35 Blend, DP	1.3631	0.0720
65/35 Blend, DP & SR	1.2954	0.0536

Table 2 shows that the 100% polyester fabric exhibited much less soiling than did the other four types of fabrics when exposed to all levels of exposure for both contaminants. Only small differences were shown in the mean overall soiling of the fabrics composed of polyester and cotton and of the 100% cotton fabric. The highest degree of soiling of all the tested fabrics was exhibited by the polyester/cotton blend with the durable press finish.

Table 3 shows that the relationship of the mean apparent soil on the various types of fabrics for all exposure levels to smoke was similar to that of the various types of fabrics after being subjected to the series of exposures of both types of contaminants. The 100% polyester fabric showed the least amount of soil, and the durable press polyester/cotton blend exhibited the greatest amount of soiling. The remaining fabrics showed slightly less soiling than did the fabric with the durable press finish.

When exposed to all levels of oxides of nitrogen, the polyester/cotton blend with no finish exhibited the least amount of soiling and the 100% polyester fabric was in second place. The 100% cotton fabric was soiled the most by nitrogen oxides.

The means of apparent soil exhibited by each type of fabric after each level of exposure to a contaminant are shown in Fig. 1 and 2. The increase in length of exposure increased the mean apparent soil on each type of fabric. A slight dip in the curve occurred for all tested fabrics exposed to oxides of nitrogen at the 12-hour exposure level. By applying the Newman-Keuls sequential range test, this dip was found not significant and was attributed to experimental error.

Analysis Of Variance. The analysis of variance results showed that there were several statistically significant variables within the research design. The two contaminants differed significantly in the amount of soil deposited on the fabrics. The mean apparent soil of exposure to smoke was 1.2296 in contrast to 0.0585, the mean apparent soil of nitrogen oxides. The chamber was filled with smoke throughout the testing period and partially obscured the fabric specimens. In contrast, the nitrogen oxides did not produce any visible haze in the chamber during the test period.

It was found that the various exposure levels were a significant factor in the testing procedure. As the time of exposure doubled, the amount of apparent soil approximately doubled.

There were also significant differences in the degree of soiling sustained by the various types of fabrics. The means of apparent soil of the 100% cotton fabric and the three blended fabrics were very close, ranging from 0.6745 to 0.7175. In contrast, the 100% polyester fabric attracted less soil — a mean of 0.4641.

The degree of soiling measured on the two sides of the fabric was not a significant factor in the experiment.

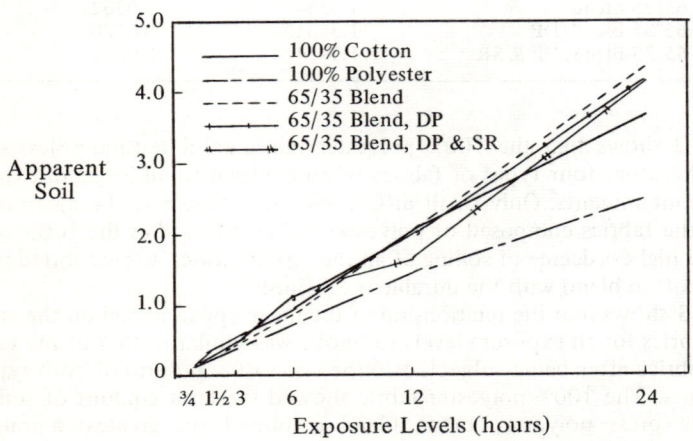

Fig. 1. Mean apparent soil of fabrics exposed to smoke.

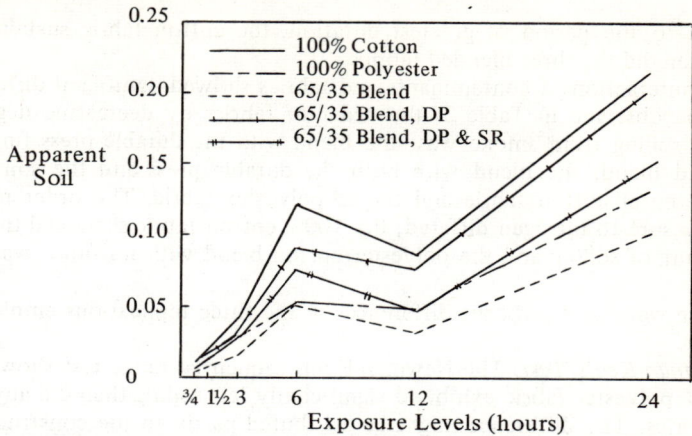

Fig. 2. Mean apparent soil of fabric exposed to oxides of nitrogen.

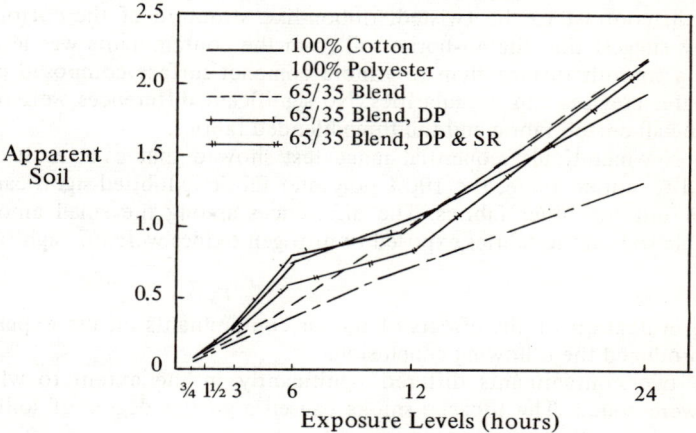

Fig. 3. Interaction of fabrics and exposure levels.

The interaction of the contaminants and the various exposure levels differed significantly. As the level of exposure increased (as shown in Table 1), the tobacco smoke soiled the fabrics at a much greater rate than did the oxides of nitrogen. The soiling by nitrogen oxides increased at a slower rate and never reached the soiling potential of the tobacco smoke.

Another significant factor was the interaction of the experimental fabrics and the various exposure levels. As indicated in Fig. 3, the five fabrics exhibited varying degrees of soiling when subjected to specific exposure levels. The all-cotton fabric showed relatively greater amounts of soiling at the low levels of exposure than was shown by the other fabrics. As the length of exposure increased to the period of greatest duration, the cotton fabric sustained less soiling than did the three blended fabrics.

The interaction of contaminants and fabrics showed significant differences. As can be observed in Table 3, the order of fabrics by decreasing degrees of apparent soiling from smoke was: the blend with the durable press finish, the unfinished blend, the blend with both the durable press and the soil release finishes, the all-cotton fabric and the all-polyester fabric. The order resulting from exposure to nitrogen differed; the 100% cotton fabric sustained the greatest amount of soiling and the polyester/cotton blend with no finish was soiled the least.

There were no significant differences in the three replications employed in the study.

Newman-Keuls Test. The Newman-Keuls sequential range test showed that the 100% polyester fabric exhibited significantly less soiling than did any of the other fabrics. The difference might be attributed partly to the construction of the fabric and the structure of the fibers. The 100% polyester fabric contained fewer yarns per inch than did the other fabrics, and the polyester fibers were smooth, in contrast to the twisted, ribbon-like structure of the cotton fibers. This may suggest that the air-borne soil from the contaminants was less apt to cling to a smooth surface than to a more compact surface composed of fibers with greater crevices and irregularities. No significant differences were obtained among the all-cotton fabric and the three blended fabrics.

The Newman-Keuls sequential range test showed that as a result of being subjected to smoke alone, the 100% polyester fabric exhibited significantly less soil than did the other fabrics. The differences among the small amounts of measurable soil on the fabrics exposed to nitrogen oxides were not significant.

Conclusions

The evaluation of the effects of the air contaminants on the experimental fabrics produced the following conclusions:

The two contaminants differed significantly in the extent to which the fabrics were soiled. The tobacco smoke caused a greater degree of soiling than did the oxides of nitrogen.

The six exposure levels, 0.75, 1.5, 3, 6, 12 and 24 hours, employed in the study provided significant differences in the degree of soiling. The amount of soiling increased with increased exposure time.

Among the five fabrics tested, the 100% polyester fabric was soiled significantly less than were the other fabrics composed of all-cotton and blends of polyester and cotton. This difference was attributed partly to the construction of the fabric and the structure of the fiber.

There were no significant differences in the soiling on the two sides of the fabrics.

Acknowledgements

This study was undertaken at Purdue University as partial fulfillment for the Master of Science degree by Helen F. Goodrich. Elizabeth F. Thomas directed the study.

The authors wish to acknowledge the helpful assistance and technical guidance of the following people at Purdue University: Virgil L. Anderson, Professor of Mathematical Sciences, Margaret M. Boyle, Head of the Department of Clothing and Textiles, Gerald L. Zachariah, Associate Professor of Agricultural Engineering, and Philip R. Goodrich, Doctoral Candidate in Agricultural Engineering.

REFERENCES

1. Jaffe, Louis S., *Journal of the Air Pollution Control Association*, Vol. 17, 1967, p375.

2. Middleton, John T., *Proceedings: The Third National Conference On Air Pollution*, Washington, D.C., December 12-14, 1966, U.S. Department of Health, Education and Welfare, Public Health Service Publication No. 1649, p45.

3. Salvin, Victor S., *Journal of the Air Pollution Control Association*, Vol. 13, 1963, p416.

4. Peters, Jane Spence and Saville, Dorothy, *American Dyestuff Reporter*, Vol. 56, 1967, p27.

5. American Association of Textile Chemists and Colorists, *Technical Manual*, Vol. 45, Research Triangle Park, N.C., 1969, Test Method 23-1962, p141.

6. Kubelka, P. and Munk, F., *Zeitschrift für Physikalische Chemie*, Vol. 12, 1931, p593

7. Anderson, Virgil L., "Designs and Optimum Techniques for Consulting Statisticians and Experimenters," Purdue University, Lafayette, Ind.

ANALYSIS OF LABORATORY EXPERIMENT EXAMPLE

Fabric Soiling by Air Pollution

Purpose of Study. To determine the effects of selected pollutants on the soiling of representative apparel fabrics by comparing spectrophotometric measurements before and after exposure.

Hypotheses. The following null hypotheses may be deduced from the discussion of results:

1. There are no significant differences in degree of soiling caused by tobacco smoke and soiling caused by oxides of nitrogen.

2. There are no significant differences in degree of soiling at different exposure levels.

3. There are no significant differences in degree of soiling sustained by various types of fabrics.

4. There are no significant differences in degree of soiling between the two sides of the fabrics.

Components of Study

Component #1 — Population to be Studied: Five types of experimental fabrics were used — 100% cotton, 100% polyester, a 65/35 polyester/cotton blend, the same blend with a durable press finish and the same blend with a durable press and soil release finish.

Component #2 — Independent Variable: Air pollutants:

1. nitrogen oxides
2. tobacco smoke

Component #3 — Dependent Variable: Soiling

EFFECTS OF ESTHETIC SURROUNDINGS: I. INITIAL EFFECTS OF THREE ESTHETIC CONDITIONS UPON PERCEIVING "ENERGY" AND "WELL-BEING" IN FACES [1]

A.H. MASLOW AND N.L. MINTZ

A. The Problem

Esthetically sensitive individuals together with city planners, art educators, and related workers have long been intuitively aware of the effects of esthetic surroundings. Yet as far as we know there have been no experimental studies published on the effects of beautiful and ugly environments upon people. Surveys of the experimental esthetics (1, 3), color (12), and art (5) literature show research to be centered on "formal" properties of rhythm, style, color, line, etc., color preference and personality studies, color-concept matching experiments, and projective technique and art therapy work. We have found research on the effects of music (9, 16, 17) and color (2, 4, 6, 7, 10, 11, 13, 14, 15, 18) to be focused on the behavioral consequences of different melodic styles or hues *per se*, but not on music or color as part of the complex esthetic environment. The present experiment was undertaken as an initial step in studying the effects of beauty and ugliness upon people. It tested the short-term effects of three visual-esthetic conditions: "beautiful," "average," and "ugly" rooms.

B. Method

Three rooms were used. The "beautiful" room (BR) impressed people as "attractive," "pretty," "comfortable," "pleasant." It was 11' x 14' x 10' and had two large windows, beige-colored walls, an indirect overhead light, and furnishings to give the impression of an attractive, comfortable study. Furnishings included a soft armchair, a mahogany desk and chair combination, two straight-backed chairs, a small table, a wooden bookcase, a large Navajo rug, drapes for the windows, paintings on the walls, and some sculpture and art

Reprinted with permission from *The Journal of Psychology*, 1956, Vol. 41, pp. 247-254. Copyright by The Journal Press.

[1] This research was supported by Brandeis University. We wish to express our thanks to R. Held and R.B. Morant for their helpful discussion and assistance, and J. Glick for his photography work. Another paper will present the more complex data obtained from subjects moving into a second esthetic condition.

objects on the desk and table. These were all chosen to harmonize as pleasantly as possible with the beige walls.[2] The "ugly" room (UR) evoked comments of "horrible," "disgusting," "ugly," "repulsive." It was 7′ x 12′ x 10′ and had two half-windows, battleship-gray walls, an overhead bulb with a dirty, torn, ill-fitting lampshade, and "furnishings" to give the impression of a janitor's store-room in disheveled condition. There were two straight-backed chairs, a small table, tin cans for ashtrays, and dirty, torn window shades. Near the bare walls on three sides were such things as pails, brooms, mops, cardboard boxes, dirty-looking trash cans, a bed-spring and uncovered mattress, and assorted refuse. The room was neither swept nor dusted and the ashtrays were not emptied. The "average" room (AR) was a professor's office 15′ x 17′ x 10′, with three windows, battleship-gray walls, and an indirect overhead light. Furnishings included two mahogany desk and chair combinations, two straight-backed chairs, a metal bookcase, window shades, a metal filing cabinet, and a cot with a pleasant-looking green bedspread. It gave the appearance of a clean, neat, "worked-in" office in no way outstanding enough to elicit any comments. To help restrict room differences to the visual mode, the experiment was done in the evening when the building was quiet; the S's chair in the three rooms was of the same type; the rooms were well-lit (though UR had direct, harsh light); and the windows were always open, preventing the dust and dirt in UR from developing a musty odor.

A six-point, two dimension rating scale was used to test the effects of the conditions upon an S's judgment of 10 negative-print photographs. The dimensions to be rated were "energy" and "well-being" for each photograph. The rating scale thus had 10 judgments per dimension, each judgment with a weight of from 1-6. Summing the dimensions separately would give two total scores, each having a possible range of from 10-60. These totals were averaged, giving an average "energy" and "well-being" score for each S. This average score could likewise range between 10 and 60. The 10 photographs were arranged alternately male and female, with two dummy extras[3] preceding and following this series. Duplicate series were used for the three rooms.

As each S was met by the interviewer (NLM), he was told approximately the following:

> We are conducting an experiment on facial stereotypy. You are familiar with Shakespeare's Cassius who had a lean and hungry look; this is an example of facial stereotypy. There cannot be any right or wrong answers as we are interested in the *impressions* faces give you.

At this point Köhler's expressive-line figures (8, p. 225) were demonstrated.

> In just the same way as these lines appeared to have particular concept characteristics, we think faces will have certain trait characteristics. You are going to see negative prints like this sample. By negative printing, and dressing the people in this unusual fashion, we minimized hairline, clothing,

---

[2] We wish to thank B. Maslow for her assistance in this.
[3] Used for purposes to be discussed in another paper.

and expression and emphasized bone structure and shape. We want you to give your impressions of these faces, similar to the way you gave impressions of the lines shown previously.

The BR and UR Ss were sent to their respective rooms to be tested by a naïve examiner who also thought the experiment was on facial stereotypy. The interviewer brought the AR Ss to their room and tested them. This elaborate prelude served two purposes. It insured the naïvete of the Ss and examiners (just one S guessed the purpose, and then only when thinking about the test a few days later), and it helped to reduce tension.

A test of visual-esthetic environment should emphasize spontaneity and informality or else task orientation or test anxiety may reduce the effects. This was demonstrated in a pilot study of similar design to this one,[4] which failed to show significant differences between conditions in part due to the Ss anxiety and task orientation; they hardly looked away from the test material. Therefore, as each S entered the room the examiner was called out on some pretext. The S was left in the room for two minutes, allowing him to "soak" in the visual field. When the examiner returned he engaged the S in a rambling discussion of "fatigue energy" and "displeasure/well-being" with the intention of getting the S to name the moods just discussed. By allowing the S to choose his own concepts instead of being given our concepts for the dimensions, we felt there was greater likelihood of achieving a common semantic process among the Ss. Assuming the S chose "weary/zestful" and "irritable/content," the examiner then continued:

> Now I would like you to tell me if this first face looks slightly, rather, or very weary, or slightly, rather, or very zestful. Then do the same for "irritable/content."

This was done for each of the 10 faces plus the four dummy extras. The S was encouraged to give any other impressions, and task-interrupting, idle conversation initiated by the examiner kept the atmosphere informal. The scores were marked on a scoresheet by the examiner. The S was in the room with the examiner at least 10 minutes additional to the time spent in the room alone.

Twenty-six male and 16 female undergraduate Brandeis University students volunteered for this experiment. They were recruited at large and simply told that we wanted them for "a study in faces and traits." Sixteen were for the BR group, 16 for the UR group, and 10 for the AR group. There were an even number of males and females in BR and UR, only males in AR. A naïve male and a naïve female were hired to examine the BR and UR Ss; one of the authors (NLM) examined the AR group.

The following controls were used with the BR and UR groups. Each experimenter tested eight Ss in the BR group and eight in the UR group, four of which were of one sex and four of the other. Half of the Ss in each group were asked to rate "energy" first and half to rate "well-being" first. After these groups were tested, the AR group was added to give additional information. Analysis of the BR and UR groups indicated these controls would be unneces-

---

[4] Conducted by B. Maslow and A.H. Maslow.

sary,[5] so all AR Ss were males, tested by a male examiner, and asked to rate "energy" first.

Our hypotheses were that scores obtained in the "beautiful" room would be higher (more "energy" and "well-being") than those in either the "average" or "ugly" rooms, and that scores in the "ugly" room would be lower (less "energy" and "well-being") than those in either the "average" or "beautiful" rooms.

C. Results

Table 1 gives the results of an analysis of variance on the differences in the scores obtained in the three rooms. The scores for the three rooms were significantly different, as shown by the F ratio. Since the variances were not significantly heterogeneous, the F indicates a significant difference in the means. Table 2 shows these differences. The average ratings for "energy" and "well-being" in BR were significantly higher (beyond the .001 level) than ratings in UR, and significantly higher (beyond the .05 level) than ratings in AR. The average ratings in AR were higher, but not significantly so, than ratings in UR.

TABLE 1. DIFFERENCES IN SCORES OBTAINED FOR THREE ROOM CONDITIONS BASED ON AN AVERAGE SCORE FOR EACH OF 42 Ss

Source of variation	df	Variance estimate	F	p
Between rooms	2	153.25	6.49	< .01
Within rooms	39	23.63		
Total	41			

TABLE 2. DIFFERENCES BETWEEN THE MEANS OF SCORES IN THREE ROOM CONDITIONS

Room	Mean	Compared to room	Mean difference	t*	p**
UR	31.81	AR	2.19	1.12	< .30
AR	34.00	BR	3.99	2.04	< .05
BR	37.99	UR	6.18	3.54	< .001

*The within rooms variance estimate of Table 1 was used as the estimate of the standard error of the difference.
**Since the standard error was based on 39 df, the t was entered as a CR in the normal probability table.

---

[5] A four-way classification analysis of variance was done on BR and UR for rooms, experimenters, sexes, and rating order. The scores for rooms were significantly different, but those for experimenters, sexes, and rating order were not, nor did the four variables interact significantly.

Since an average score below 35 would indicate the S generally rated the 10 faces as "fatigued" and "displeased," while one above 35 would indicate the S rated the faces as having "energy" and "well-being,"[6] Table 2 indicates a second result. It can be seen that the mean for the UR group is within the "fatigued" and "displeased" range; the mean for AR at the upper limit of the "fatigued" and "displeased" range; and the mean for the BR group within the "energy" and "well-being" range.

D. Discussion

We may summarize the results as follows. The Ss in our "beautiful" room gave significantly higher ratings (more "energy" and "well-being") than Ss in either the "average" or "ugly" rooms. Also, while the mean for the scores in the "beautiful" room fell in the "energy" and "well-being" range, the means for the other two groups fell in the "fatigued" and "displeased" range, indicating a qualitative difference in the group scores. We can be rather confident that the difference between the scores obtained in BR and UR is reliable. While the scores in AR are significantly lower than those in BR and somewhat higher than those in UR (results which are in the expected order), we cannot be as confident of where, between BR and UR, the AR group is placed. Recognizing the situational nature of our definitions of beauty, average and ugly, there still are interesting implications if our research would continue to find the effects of "average" surroundings to lie closer to those of "ugly" than to those of "beauty," rather than finding that effects of "average" lie midway between the two, or closer to "beauty." This, of course, would have immediate relevance for professors and their offices.

While many questions remain to be answered by research now in progress, certain points may be noted at the present time. We may begin by excluding the possibility that differences between groups resulted from suggestion or a "rôle-playing" attitude assumed by the examiners or the Ss. Indirect interviewing of the examiners after each day's testing, and each S after being tested, assured us that the examiners and Ss continued to be unaware of the experimental purpose. The controls for noise, odor, time of day, type of seating, examiners, etc., make us rather confident that the potent factor lay in the visual-esthetic qualities of the three rooms.

Regarding the effects obtained, a number of problems come to mind, some of which will be treated in later papers. Were these merely short-term effects; would the Ss adapt to the rooms with time and negate the initial differences obtained? How many individuals in each group were affected by the conditions? Were the Ss affected by the rooms *per se*? The possibility also exists that the results could have been obtained via the effect of conditions upon the examiners. This, of course, would not change the major implication of the findings; it would shift the emphasis from the rooms having a short-term effect

---

[6] A *rho* based on the 42 Ss for the separate dimension totals ("fatique/energy" and "displeasure/well-being") showed the dimensions to have a positive correlation of .79, significant beyond the .001 level.

directly upon the Ss to their having a long-term effect upon the examiners, which sufficiently affected the interpersonal relations between examiner and S so as to cause differences in group scores irrespective of which examiner was present.

In considering what may be the "potent" visual-esthetic aspects of the rooms, we may tentatively exclude as crucial in themselves the differences between room sizes, and neatness, orderliness, or cleanliness. Although UR was the smallest, AR was the largest; although UR was dirty and messy, AR was clean and neat. Both UR and AR had gray walls and cold colors in contrast to beige walls and warm colors in BR. While this may be important for understanding the difference between BR and AR scores, by itself it would not explain the possibly genuine difference between AR and UR scores. At present the most reasonable conclusion appears to be that all of these aspects were operating to produce three esthetically different-appearing rooms, which in the case of "beautiful" and "ugly" resulted in clear differences between Ss ratings of the "energy" and "well-being" of faces.

E. Summary

An experiment was conducted as an initial step in studying the effects of esthetic surroundings upon people. Three visual-esthetic conditions were used: "beautiful," "average," and "ugly" rooms. In each room, subjects unaware of the experimental purpose were asked to rate the "fatigue/energy" and "displeasure/well-being" of 10 negative-print photographs of faces. The results were: (a) the group in the "beautiful" room gave significantly higher ratings (more "energy" and "well-being") than groups in either the "average" or "ugly" rooms; (b) the "average" room group had somewhat higher ratings than the "ugly" room group; (c) the mean score for ratings in the "beautiful" room fell in the "energy" and "well-being" range, while the means for the ratings in the other two rooms fell within the "fatigued" and "displeased" range. Discussion pointed out that: (a) suggestion, "rôle-playing," or variables other than visual-esthetic ones did not account for the differences obtained; (b) there seems at present to be no single visual-esthetic quality that can account for the differences among all three groups. (c) the effects may possibly have been obtained by the rooms' affecting the subject-examiner relationship.

REFERENCES

1. Chandler, A.R., and Barnhart, E.N. A Bibliography of Psychological and Experimental Esthetics, 1864-1937. Berkeley: Univ. California Press, 1938.

2. Deutsch, F. Psycho-physical reactions of the vascular system to influences of light and to impressions gained through light. *Folia Clinica Orientalia*, 1937, 1, Facs. 3 and 4.

3. Drought, R.A. A survey of studies in experimental esthetics. *J. Educ. Res.*, 1929, 20, 97-102.

4. Ehrenwald, N. Referred to by Ellinger, F. The Biologic Fundamentals of Radiation Therapy. New York: Elsevier, 1941.

ANALYSIS OF LABORATORY EXPERIMENT EXAMPLE

Effects of Esthetic Surroundings: Initial Effects of Three Esthetic Conditions Upon Perceiving "Energy" and "Well-being" in Faces

Purpose of Study. To determine the effects of beautiful and ugly environments on people.

Hypothesis. The following null hypothesis may be deduced from the discussion of results of this study:

There are no significant differences among Ss in "beautiful," "average," or "ugly" rooms with respect to their perception of "energy" and "well-being" in faces.

The authors hypothesized that scores obtained in the "beautiful" room would be higher (more "energy" and "well-being") than those in either the "average" or "ugly" rooms, and that scores in the "ugly" room would be lower (less "energy" and "well-being") than those in either the "average" or "beautiful" rooms.

Components of Study.

Component #1 — Population to be Studied: Twenty-six male and 16 female undergraduate students, recruited at large, volunteered for the experiment. Sixteen were assigned to the BR group, 16 to the AR group, and 10 to the UR group.

Component #2 — Independent Variable: Esthetic environment

Component #3 — Dependent Variable: Perception of "energy" and "well-being" in faces

FIELD EXPERIMENTS

As we have seen, the purpose of laboratory experiments is to test hypotheses derived from theory by studying the precise interrelations of variables and their operation through controlling variance under research conditions that are uncontaminated by the operation of associated or extraneous variables. Kerlinger contrasts laboratory and field experiments in this way:

A field experiment is a research study in a realistic situation in which one or more independent variables are manipulated by the experimenter under as carefully controlled conditions as the situation will permit. The contrast between the laboratory experiment and the field experiment is not sharp: the differences are mostly matters of degree. Where the laboratory experiment has a maximum of control, most field studies must operate with less control, a factor that is often a severe handicap to the experiment. (Kerlinger, 1964, p. 382)

Description

The field experiment endeavors to make the research situation closely approximate the conditions of the laboratory experiment. Field experiments are suited to testing broad hypotheses. An example of such a hypothesis is the following: "The more cohesive the group, the more effectively it can influence its members." (Festinger, Schachter, and Back, 1950, p. 100) This is a broad hypothesis but one that is not difficult to put in operational terms and test in field experiments. Field experiments are generally flexible and applicable to a wide variety of problems.

The main weaknesses of field experiments are practical. Although the manipulation of an independent variable may be theoretically conceivable, it may not be possible or practical. Many variables cannot be manipulated, particularly in our society and in our schools. It is also sometimes difficult, especially in school situations, to randomize a sample. There may be an unwillingness to break up class groups or allow children to be assigned to experimental groups at random. Even if such randomization is permitted, the independent variable may be blurred because of the effects of other uncontrollable variables on the results. In realistic situations in schools and communities, extraneous independent variables tend to abound.

EXAMPLE AND ANALYSIS
OF FIELD EXPERIMENT

CONTROL OF AGGRESSION IN A
NURSERY SCHOOL CLASS[1, 2]

PAUL BROWN AND ROGERS ELLIOTT

The aim of the present study was to add to the data of the field of social learning theory (Bandura and Walters, 1963), at several points. First, among the techniques of controlling operant social behavior, simple extinction (Williams, 1959), simple reinforcement (Azrin and Lindsley, 1956), or both of them in combination (Zimmerman and Zimmerman, 1962; Ayllon and Michael, 1960; Baer, Harris, and Wolf, 1963) have been employed frequently with children. Second, the use of explicit learning techniques has been shown effective in young nursery school subjects (Ss) in two recent papers (Baer *et al.*, 1963; Homme, de Baca, Devine, Steinhorst, and Rickert, 1963). Finally, antisocial acts of the assertive-aggressive kind are known to have operant components which are extinguishable (Williams, 1959) and reinforcible (Cowan and Walters, 1963).

With the above as background, we took seriously the following:

> Theorizing and experimentation on the inhibition of aggression have focused exclusively on the inhibitory influence of anxiety or guilt, on the assumption that response inhibition is necessarily a consequence of pairing responses with some form of aversive stimulation. The development of aggression inhibition through the strengthening of incompatible positive responses, on the other hand, has been entirely ignored, despite the fact that the social control of aggression is probably achieved to a greater extent on this basis than by means of aversive stimulation (Bandura and Walters, 1963, p. 130).

We set out to control the aggressive behavior of all of the boys in an entire nursery school class, by using as techniques the removal of positive generalized reinforcement (attention) for aggressive acts, while giving attention to cooperative acts.

Method

Subjects. The subjects were the 27 males in the younger (3- to 4-year-old) of the two groups at the Hanover Nursery School. Observation and teachers'

Reprinted with permission from *Journal of Experimental Child Psychology*, Vol. 2, pp. 103-107, 1965.

[1] This is a report of work done by the first author, under the direction of the second, in partial fulfillment of the requirements of the senior courses in independent research at Dartmouth.

[2] The authors thank Edith Hazard, director, and the members of the staff of the Hanover Nursery School. Not only did they make this study possible, they made it very enjoyable.

reports made it clear that the younger boys were more aggressive than any other age-sex subgroup.

Ratings. Aggressive responses were defined by enumeration of the categories of the scale devised by Walters, Pearce, and Dahms (1957). The scale has two major subcategories — physical aggression and verbal aggression. Each of these is subdivided into more concrete categories; e.g., under physical aggression are categories labeled "pushes, pulls, holds"; "hits, strikes,"; "annoys, teases, interferes"; and there are similar specific descriptions (e.g., "disparages"; "threatens") under the verbal category.

The observations of the behavior were made by two raters, both undergraduates at Dartmouth.[3] They were trained in the use of the scale, and given practice in observing the class during the free-play hour from 9:20 to 10:20 in the morning. Such observation was possible because the rater could stand in a large opening connecting the two spacious play areas. The rating scale had the categories of aggressive behavior as its rows, and 12 five-minute intervals as its columns. The raters simply checked any occurrence of a defined behavior in the appropriate cell.

One rater observed on Monday, Wednesday, and Friday mornings; the other observed on Tuesday and Thursday. On two of the four observed Wednesday sessions, both raters observed, so that interrater reliability could be estimated. At the conclusion of the study, the raters were interviewed to determine what changes, if any, they had observed in the behavior of teachers and children, and whether they had surmised the research hypothesis.

Procedure. The pre-treatment period was simply a one-week set of observations of aggressive responses by the younger boys, to furnish a reference response rate. Two weeks later the first treatment period was initiated by the teachers and the first author (see below) and it lasted for two weeks. Ratings were taken during the second week of this period. The teachers were then told that the experiment was over, and that they were no longer constrained in their behavior toward aggressive acts. Three weeks after this another set of ratings was taken to assess the durability of the treatment effect. Finally, two weeks after this follow-up observation, the treatment was reinstituted for two weeks, and, again, observations were made in the second of these weeks.

The teachers were the agents of treatment (along with the first author) and they were instructed verbally, with reference to a typed handout, which read in part as follows:

> There are many theories which try to explain aggression in young children. Probably most are partly true and perhaps the simplest is the best. One simple one is that many fights, etc. occur because they bring with them a great deal of fuss and attention from some adult. If we remember that just 3 or 4 short years ago these children would have literally died if they were not able to command (usually by crying) attentive responses from some adult, we can see how just attending to a child could be rewarding. On the other hand, when a child is playing quietly most parents are thankful for the

[3] We thank James Miller and James Markworth for their assistance.

peace and leave well enough alone. Unfortunately, if attention and praise is really rewarding, the child is not rewarded when he should be. Thus, many parents unwittingly encourage aggressive, attention-getting behavior since this is the only way the child gets some form of reward. Of course this is an extreme example but it would be interesting to see if this matter of attention is really the issue, and the important issue especially in a setting where punishment of behavior is not a real option.

At the school I have noticed that whenever it has been possible cooperative and non-aggressive acts are attended to and praised by teachers. During the intervening week we would like to exaggerate this behavior and play down the attention given to aggressive acts. I hope to concentrate on the boys, but if a boy and girl are concerned that is perfectly all right.

Briefly, we will try to ignore aggression and reward cooperative and peaceful behavior. Of course if someone is using a hammer on another's head we would step in, but just to separate the two and leave. It will be difficult at first because we tend to watch and be quiet when nothing bad is happening, and now our attention will *as much as possible* be directed toward cooperative, or non-aggressive behavior. It would be good to let the most aggressive boys see that the others are getting the attention if it is possible. A pat on the head, 'That's good Mike,' 'Hello Chris and Mark, how are you today?' 'Look what Eric made,' etc. may have more rewarding power than we think. On the other hand, it is just as important during this week to have no reprimands, no 'Say you're sorry,' 'Aren't you sorry?' Not that these aren't useful ways of teaching proper behavior, but they will only cloud the effects of our other manner of treatment. It would be best not even to look at a shove or small fight if we are sure no harm is being done; as I mentioned before, if it is necessary we should just separate the children and leave.

Results and Discussion

The Raters. The correlation between the raters of total aggressive responses checked in each of 24 five-minute periods was 0.97. This is higher than the average interrater correlation of 0.85 reported by Walters, *et al.* (1957), but their raters were working with a one-minute, rather than a five-minute observation period.

When interviewed, one rater said that the only change he saw in the children was in the two "most troublesome" boys, who at the end (the fourth-rating period) seemed less troublesome. The other noticed no change in any of the children, even though his ratings described the changes shown in Table 1. One rater had noticed, again during the fourth-rating period, that the first author was being "especially complimentary" to one of the troublesome boys, and the other rater did not notice any change in the behavior of any adult.

Aggressive Responses. Table 1 presents the average daily number of physical, verbal, and overall aggressive responses in each of the four periods of observation. Analyses of variance of the daily scores as a function of treatments yielded F ratios ($df = 3$, 16) of 6.16 for physical aggression ($p < 0.01$), 5.71 for verbal aggression ($p < 0.01$), and 25.43 for overall aggression.

TABLE 1. AVERAGE NUMBER OF RESPONSES IN THE
VARIOUS RATED CATEGORIES OF AGGRESSION

	Categories of Aggression		
Times of observation	Physical	Verbal	Total
Pre-treatment	41.2	22.8	64.0
First treatment	26.0	17.4	43.4
Follow-up	37.8	13.8	51.6
Second treatment	21.0	4.6	25.6

There seems little doubt that ignoring aggressive responses and attending cooperative ones had reliable and significant effects upon the behavior of the children.

Verbal aggression did not recover after the first treatment, while physical aggression did. Since we were rating children, not teachers, we offer the following speculation with only casual evidence. We believe the teachers find it harder to ignore fighting than to ignore verbal threats or insults. It is certainly true that the teachers (all females) found aggression in any form fairly difficult to ignore. During treatment periods, they would frequently look to the first author as if asking whether they should step in and stop a fight, and they often had the expression and behavior of conflict when aggressive, especially physically aggressive, behavior occurred — i.e., they would often, almost automatically, move slightly toward the disturbance, then check themselves, then look at the first author. The more raucous scenes were tense, with the teachers waiting, alert and ready for the first bit of calm and cooperative behavior to appear and allow them to administer attention. The teachers, incidentally, were skeptical of the success of the method when it was first proposed, though they came ultimately to be convinced of it. What made its success dramatic to them was the effect upon two very aggressive boys, both of whom became friendly and cooperative to a degree not thought possible. The most aggressive boys tended to be reinforced for cooperative acts on a lower variable ratio than the others, because teachers were especially watchful of any sign of cooperation on their parts.

Conclusion. As Allen, Hart, Buell, Harris, and Wolf (1964) have pointed out recently, the principles involved in the present application of controlling techniques are simple. What makes this and other demonstrations of them successful in a real-life setting is systematic observation, systematic application, and systematic evaluation.

REFERENCES

Allen, Eileen K., Hart, Betty, Buell, Joan S., Harris, Florence R., and Wolf, M.M. Effects of social reinforcement on the isolate behavior of a nursery school child. *Child Develpm.*, 1964, 35, 511-518.

Ayllon, T., and Michael, J. The psychiatric nurse as a behavioral engineer. *J. exp. anal. Behav.*, 1959, 2, 323-334.

Azrin, N.H., and Lindsley, O.R. The reinforcement of cooperation between children. *J. abnorm. soc. Psychol.*, 1956, 52, 100-102.

Baer, D.M., Harris, Florence R., and Wolf, M.M. Control of nursery school children's behavior by programming social reinforcement from their teachers. *Amer. Psychologist*, 1963, 18, 343. (Abstract.)

Bandura, A., and Walters, R.H. *Social learning and personality development.* New York: Holt, 1963.

Cowan, P.A., and Walters, R.H. Studies of reinforcement of aggression. I. Effects of scheduling. *Child Develpm.*, 1963, 34, 543-551.

Homme, L.E., de Baca, P.C., Devine, J.V., Steinhorst, R., and Rickert, E.J. Use of the Premack principle in controlling the behavior of nursery school children. *J. exp. anal. Behav.*, 1963, 6, 544.

Walters, J.C., Pearce, Doris, and Dahms, Lucille. Affectional and aggressive behavior of preschool children. *Child Develpm.*, 1957, 28, 15-26.

Williams, C.D. The elimination of tantrum behavior by extinction procedures. *J. abnorm. soc. Psychol.*, 1959, 59, 269.

Zimmerman, Elaine H., and Zimmerman, J. The alteration of behavior in a special classroom situation. *J. exp. anal. Behav.*, 1962, 5, 59-60.

ANALYSIS OF FIELD EXPERIMENT EXAMPLE

Control of Aggression in a Nursery School Class

Purpose of Study. This experiment was conducted in a real-life setting, thereby qualifying as an example of a field experiment. Its purpose was to control the aggressive behavior of all of the boys in an entire nursery school class by removal of positive generalized reinforcement (attention) for aggressive acts, while giving attention to cooperative acts.

Hypothesis. The following null hypotheses are deduced from discussion of results:

1. There are no significant differences in children's physical aggressive responses with removal by teachers of attention to aggressive acts while giving attention to responsive acts.

2. There are no significant differences in children's verbal aggressive responses with removal by teachers of attention to aggressive acts while giving attention to responsive acts.

3. There are no significant differences in children's overall aggressive responses with removal by teachers of attention to aggressive acts while giving attention to responsive acts.

Components of Study.

Component #1 — Population to be Studied: The subjects were the 27 males in the 3- to 4-year-old group at a nursery school. The study was a before-after experiment, with the Ss serving as their own controls.

Component #2 — Independent Variable: Selective reinforcement (Ignoring aggression and attending to cooperative acts)

Component #3 — Dependent Variable: Aggressive responses

A pre-treatment period was a one-week set of observations of aggressive responses by the boys to furnish a reference response rate ("before" measure). Two weeks later the first treatment period was initiated and lasted two weeks, after which ratings were taken ("after" measure). Three weeks later another set of ratings was taken to assess durability. Treatment was then re-instituted for another two weeks followed by more observations.

CHAPTER 7

Survey Research

Surveys have become so common that they are frequently held in disrepute. Nevertheless, purposeful surveys which are well-planned and analyzed have an important place in home economics research. Their principal contribution is in describing current practices or beliefs with the intent of making intelligent plans for improving conditions or processes in a particular local situation.

SURVEY RESEARCH DEFINED

The dictionary definition of a *survey* is:

> A critical examination or inspection, often of an official character, for an implied or specified purpose; an ascertaining of facts regarding condition or conditions, to provide exact information, esp. to those responsible or interested; often, a study of a given area with respect to a certain condition, or its prevalence; as, a *survey* of a ship's stores, a state's roads, or the schools of a district; the social trends or unemployment *surveys* of 1932; also, a report, study or document presenting the results of such an examination. (Webster, 1957)

This definition indicates fact-gathering and describing the status quo. Such a purely descriptive survey method has been criticized for not being a forward looking approach to the solution of problems:

> This type of study, so firmly entrenched in the educational mind, is not scientific. . . . To ferret out pupil-teacher ratios, bonded indebtedness, curricular practices, and the like is basically routine fact-gathering and has little resemblance to scientific behavioral research. (Kerlinger, 1964, p. 392)

Much of the research related to home economics could be criticized for being largely of this *descriptive survey* type, setting forth facts and observations without seeking causes and analyzing interrelations among variables. The purely fact-gathering type of survey will not be discussed in this book.

Survey research in the social scientific sense is a development of the twentieth century. It is explanatory or analytical in nature. In this type of survey research, inferences can be drawn from samples to the whole population regarding the prevalence, distribution, and interrelations of economic, sociological, and psychological variables. Survey research is probably most commonly used to obtain the opinions and attitudes of individuals and to study social structure. (Kerlinger, 1964)

CONDUCTING A SURVEY

The six basic steps of survey work are similar to those taken in other types of research. Although the following sequence usually is followed, the six steps are not independent of one another. Actually, decisions at each point should be made in relation to previous and subsequent steps in the process.

1. *General Objectives.* Ordinarily, the general objectives or purposes of a survey are stated in broad terms, indicating the necessity of the study and its scope. The researcher should ask himself whether a survey is the best way to obtain the desired information. Also, he should consider whether it is likely or even possible that changes could be made if recommended as a result of his proposed study.

2. *Specific Objectives.* At this stage the specific questions to be answered by the study are enumerated. (See discussion of "Statement of the Problem" in Chapter 3.) Hypotheses to be tested should be specified at this time.

3. *Sampling Plan.* Since a survey requires responses from other people, the researcher should be sure he is likely to be able to find persons who are qualified and interested in his study. Do the respondents know the information sought? Is it reasonable to ask them to provide the kinds of information needed?

Probably one of the most important contributions made by survey researchers to the social sciences has been rigorous sampling procedures. In its simplest terms, sampling in a survey involves deciding how many and which people to observe or question. Size and representativeness are two key factors in a sampling plan.

Housewives are often surveyed regarding their opinions of various consumer products. Obviously it would be almost impossible to question all the people in many communities. Moreover, it has been demonstrated mathematically that we can approximate the characteristics of all the people (including the opinions of housewives) by studying some of the people (a sampling). Types of sampling are discussed in Chapter 9.

4. *Data Collection.* Information for a survey is usually obtained by mailed questionnaire, personal interview, or direct observation. Of these methods, the personal interview is often the most useful and powerful for survey research. Choice should be based upon the validity and reliability of the data that can be obtained within the limits of time and other available resources. (See Chapter 10 regarding validity and reliability.)

A questionnaire, interview schedule, or observation guide must be constructed prior to contacting the people selected (hopefully at random) for a study. Often graduate students (and unfortunately some experienced researchers) hurriedly construct questionnaires that give the impression of having been accomplished during a short break between classes. "Throwing together" such questionnaires, in the name of survey research, to administer to a group of people conveniently selected by the researcher probably accounts for the lack of esteem often afforded to this research method. In addition to knowledge of sampling theory, a competent survey researcher must be trained in questionnaire construction or interview and observation techniques. These topics will be discussed in more detail in Part IV (Methods of Data Collection).

Before using a questionnaire or interview schedule in the actual survey, it should be pretested to determine whether it is easily understood and elicits the information desired. Someone who lacks the researcher's familiarity with his problem can point out ambiguous and pointless questions. A pilot study, conducted on a small scale with a group similar to those who will be in the major study, can give valuable suggestions for dropping or revising questions as well as for adding important items that might have been overlooked.

When personal interviews are to be conducted, interviewers must be trained to gather information correctly. They should be provided an instruction manual explaining the objectives of the study. Provision should be made for their supervision.

5. *Data Analysis.* Plans for analyzing the data should be made at the time the questionnaire or other technique is designed, keeping in mind at all times the hypotheses to be tested through the survey.

The data are prepared for analysis by coding. This is accomplished essentially by organizing questionnaire responses into numerical categories. Categorizing is a useful technique for reducing the number of items to be studied, for revealing similarities among responses, and for laying the basis for generalizing from the data. Categories should be small enough to insure the homogeneity of the cases falling within a single category, yet large enough to permit an observer to differentiate between the cases in various subgroups.

After coding, data are transferred generally to machine-punched data cards through which tabulations are made. Machine tabulations provide exact and rapid counts of responses. Of course, if the researcher has a small amount of data from a small sample and does not have access to data processing equipment, responses can be hand tabulated.

Since a questionnaire may contain 50, 100, or more questions, a tabulation of the relationship between responses given to each question would be impractical. A determination must be made regarding the most worthy relationships between factors. The questionnaire items or responses to be compared should be determined by the hypotheses to be tested in the survey.

Specific methods of presenting and analyzing data are discussed in Chapters 15 and 16.

6. *Reporting.* Following analysis and interpretation of the data, a report should be presented to the public in the form of a graduate thesis and/or journal

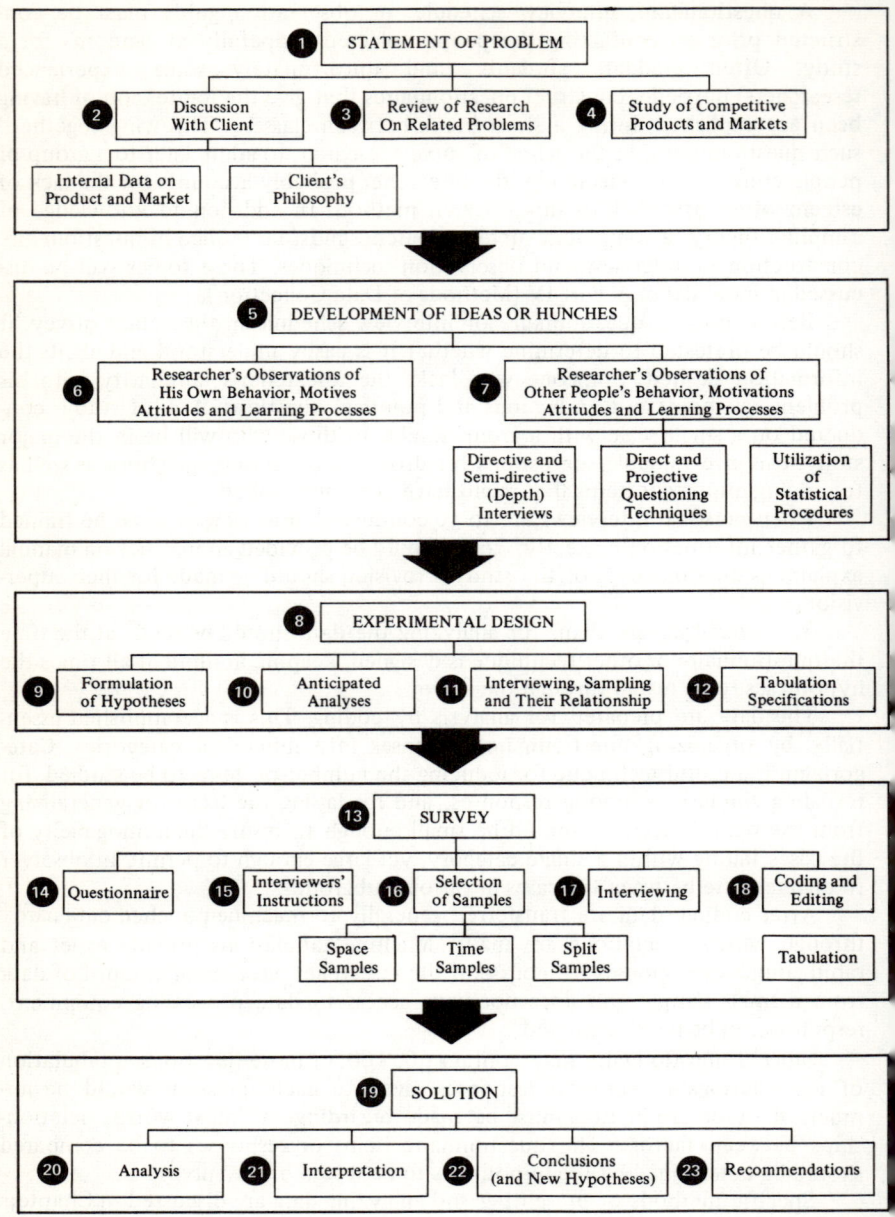

Figure 17. How to Solve a Typical Consumer Research Problem. Reprinted with permission from *Research Methods in Economics and Business,* Ferber and Verdoorn, Macmillan, 1962, p. 30.

articles. Many times the individuals who responded to the questionnaire or inter-view are interested in receiving an abstract of the findings.

Figure 17 provides a diagrammatic scheme for solving a "Typical Consumer Research Problem." This scheme is similar in process to that described in the steps enumerated above.

LIMITATIONS OF SURVEY STUDIES

A few possible limitations of survey studies should be emphasized. Surveys are dependent on the cooperation of respondents. If the procedure seems too tedious or unimportant, the percentage of respondents may be reduced and those responses which are given may be careless and/or insincere.

Information not known to the respondents cannot be obtained in a survey. For example, an exact determination of amounts saved by individual families would require knowledge of annual increases in value of their life insurance reserves and of the amounts of depreciation on houses, autos, and other large items owned. Also, most people have not given much thought to the amount of money spent on food and clothing over a year.

Requesting information considered secret and asking questions that appear to check upon honesty of the respondent are not likely to evoke accurate answers and should therefore be avoided. Respondents are likely to overestimate those characteristics that will make them look good and to minimize those for which society has low esteem.

Information obtained from a single survey is less reliable than trend data derived from two or more surveys made by the same methods.

Surveys cannot be aimed at obtaining exact quantitative forecasts of things to come, e.g., plans to purchase houses during the next twelve months. Only a relatively short, specific period of time can be covered by survey reporting.

EXAMPLE AND ANALYSIS OF SURVEY RESEARCH

The analysis of the following example of a survey research study is in accord with the format discussed in this chapter relative to steps to be taken in conducting a survey.

DIET AND NUTRITURE OF PRESCHOOL CHILDREN IN HONOLULU (Survey of Low- and Middle-Income Families)[1]

MYRTLE L. BROWN, DORIS S. SMITH, JAMES L. MERTZ, SADYE F. ADELSON

This report is one phase of a study of diet and nutriture of two- and three-year-old children of low- and middle-income families in Honolulu. The study was undertaken because, until recently, there has been a dearth of quantitative data available on dietary intake and nutritional status of preschool children in the United States and, more specifically, no such information was available for children in Hawaii. Previous surveys in Hawaii have dealt with the diets of low-income families (1-3), hospital diets (4), and diets of pregnant women of low- to lower-middle-income status (5).

In this study, we concentrated our efforts on children of low-income families and included those of middle-income families for comparative purposes, to determine the relationship of family economic level to diet and nutriture of young children. Dietary, biochemical, and clinical methods were used for evaluation.

Sample

Families with children two (twenty-four to thirty-five months) and three (thirty-six to forty-seven months) years old and living within five major areas in the city of Honolulu were identified from birth records. Obviously high-income families were eliminated on the basis of the father's occupation. The final sample of low- and middle-income families was randomly drawn from the remaining

Reprinted with permission from *Journal of the American Dietetic Association*, Vol. 57, No. 1, pp. 22-28, July, 1970.

[1] Supported by U.S. Department of Agriculture Cooperative Agreement No. 12-14-1000-8438 (62) from the Consumer and Food Economics Research and the Human Nutrition Research Divisons, Agricultural Research Service. Accepted for publication March 5, 1970.

[2] The authors wish to express their appreciation to Hilda Freitas, Leimomi Sills, Vivian Shinmoto, and Mary Maertens who interviewed the mothers; and to Mrs. Maertens, Elsie M. Kawakone, and Rhoda Yoshino, who coded dietary data for computer analysis. The authors are further indebted to Judith Mendelson for assistance in laboratory analyses; to Walter Yee, Assistant Director, University of Hawaii Computer Center, for programming dietary data for the IBM 360 computer; and to Carol A. Pearson and Miss Yoshino for statistical analysis of data.

records. Because too few low-income families could be drawn from these areas of the city, two adjoining housing projects were also sampled.

The low-income groups comprised families with incomes that, for family size, would qualify them for the Food Stamp Program. The low and middle incomes represented distinctly different income levels. For example, for a family of three, low income was designated as $180 to $210 per month, the middle-income range as $415 to $665. As family size increased, income designated as low and middle also increased. For a family of six, the low-income range was $285 to $325, for the middle-income group, the range was $500 to $750 monthly.

The final sample comprised 281 children (of 249 mothers) and represented roughly one-third of contacts made. Of 730 eligible families, 351 refused to cooperate and 130 had to be dropped from the study for various reasons, most often illness of child or parent or failure to complete tests. Descriptive data on the children and their families are shown for the two income groups in Table 1. Nineteen pairs of siblings were included in the low-income group and thirteen in the middle-income. Low-income families were larger than middle-income families. Fewer fathers and mothers of the low-income group were employed. Low-income parents were, on the average, less well educated; 7 per cent of low-income mothers and 11 per cent of low-income fathers had had training

TABLE 1. DESCRIPTION OF SAMPLE BY INCOME

DESCRIPTOR	LOW-INCOME	MIDDLE-INCOME
Mother interviewed	128	121
Children in sample	147	134
Persons living in household (mean)	$6.4 \pm 2.5°†$	$4.7 \pm 1.5°$
Persons living on family income (mean)	$6.2 \pm 2.1°$	$4.6 \pm 1.4°$
Families headed by women (%)	15	1
Mother employed (%)	2	17
Father employed (% in intact households)	75	98
Mother's educational level (mean yr.)	$10.6 \pm 1.6°$	$12.8 \pm 2.0°$
Father's educational level (mean yr.)	$10.0 \pm 2.9°$	$12.8 \pm 2.1°$
Mother's age (mean yr.)	28.4 ± 5.8	29.0 ± 5.8
Father's age (mean yr.)	33.9 ± 9.8	32.1 ± 6.8
Age and sex		
Two-year-old boys	38	31
Two-year-old girls	27	29
Three-year-old boys	38	38
Three-year-old girls	44	36
Ethnic group		
Hawaiian (and part-Hawaiian)	76	42
Japanese	1	60
Caucasian	12	4
Other	58	28

°Significant difference, p = 0.001.
†Standard deviation.

beyond high school as compared with 40 per cent of middle-income mothers and fathers. Mean ages of mothers and fathers of both income groups were similar. Only seven mothers, all low-income, were below twenty years of age.

Procedures

Dietary data were obtained from the mother by four interviewers trained specifically for the study. All interviews were conducted in the home. Dietary intake for a three-day period, including one week-end day, was obtained by mother's recall of the child's food intake for the previous day and time prior to interview, and by records kept by the mother for the remainder of the three-day period. Dietary records were coded and intake calculated by computer, using food composition data for computer use obtained from the Consumer and Food Economics Research Division, U.S. Department of Agriculture (unpublished data). For some local foods and food combinations, nutrient values were obtained from other sources (6-9).

The majority of the children were subsequently examined in a clinic by one pediatrician; forty-one children were examined by a second physician when the usual pediatrician was absent from the clinic. Height and weight measurements were taken with the subjects barefoot and wearing lightweight clothing, using standard clinical scales and calibrated steel rod and horizontal crossbar attached to the scale. Blood was collected by finger tip prick and analyzed for hemo-globin[3], hematocrit[4], and plasma amino acid ratio[5] (10). A single random urine sample was collected for determination of creatinine (11), urea nitrogen (12), thiamine (13), and N-methyl nicotinamide (13). Clinical examinations and blood and urine collections were made for the most part within two weeks after the dietary record was made. The intervening period was never greater than one month.

Results

Nutrient Intake. The results of chemical analyses were available before the coding of dietary data could be completed, and it became apparent very early that, for many subjects, urinary excretion of thiamine and N-methyl nicotin-amide was far in excess of levels normally excreted by well-nourished young children (13). Because unusually high excretion levels were observed primarily among those children known to be taking vitamin supplements, intakes from food were calculated separately from nutrients provided by supplements, on the hypothesis that food intake alone might well supply sufficient nutrients for many of the children. Nutrient intakes presented in Table 2, therefore, represent nutrients supplied by food alone. The Recommended Dietary Allowances (14) also are shown.

Mean intakes of calcium, riboflavin, and ascorbic acid were significantly higher for middle-income children than those of low-income families. Mean

---

[3] Hycel, Inc., Houston; cyanmethemoglobin determination, 1959.
[4] Seventy-five mm. capillary tubes centrifuged for 3 min. at 12,300 r.p.m.
[5] Nonessential amino acids:essential amino acids.

TABLE 2. CALCULATED NUTRIENT INTAKE FROM
FOOD INTAKE OF PRESCHOOL CHILDREN

INCOME GROUP	NUMBER OF SUBJECTS	ENERGY	PROTEIN	CALCIUM	IRON	VITAMIN A	THIAMINE	RIBO-FLAVIN	NIACIN	ASCOR-BIC ACID
				Two-Year-Olds						
		calories	*gm.*	*mg.*	*mg.*	*I.U.*	*mg.*	*mg.*	*mg.*	*mg.*
Low-income	65	1,186±430°†	46.6±20.1	602±363°°	6.3±3.9	2,510±2,960	0.58±0.29°	1.15±0.61°°	7.7±4.3	33±39°°
Middle-income	60	1,305±607°	48.3±18.9	702±372°°	6.1±3.3	2,920±2,060	0.64±0.32°	1.33±0.60°°	8.0±4.2	62±75°°
Recommended allowance . . .		1,300	40	800	15	2,000	0.6	0.7	6‡	40
				Three-Year-Olds						
Low-income	82	1,386±495	51.6±21.6	631±382°°	7.6±4.1	3,000±3,660	0.68±0.34	1.22±0.63°	8.7±4.5°	41±46°°
Middle-income	74	1,357±420	52.4±20.5	742±407°°	6.8±3.7	3,410±3,370	0.65±0.28	1.37±0.65°	7.9±3.6°	52±42°°
Recommended allowance . . .		1,600	50	800	10	2,500	0.7	0.8	8‡	40

°Significant at 5% level.
°°Significant at 1% level.
†Standard deviation.
‡Mg. equivalents.

caloric intake of middle-income two-year-olds also was significantly higher. On the basis of body weight, energy intakes were 88 and 100 calories per kilogram for low- and middle-income two-year-olds and 90 and 88 calories per kilogram for the three-year-olds respectively.

Niacin intake was significantly higher for three-year-old children of low-income families than those of middle income. However, mean intake of pre-formed niacin for all groups approached the recommended allowance of 8 mg. equivalents and, on the basis of average protein intake, actual niacin supply (including niacin from tryptophan) was estimated to be roughly twice the mean intake of preformed niacin.

Because variation was great, as indicated by the high standard deviations, it seemed of interest to evaluate individual nutrient intakes to determine the relative level of intakes according to income level. For this purpose, we ranked nutrient intakes according to whether they met or exceeded two-thirds of the recommended allowances or were below two-thirds of this level (recognizing that the arbitrary rating does not necessarily reflect dietary adequacy or inadequacy). As shown in Table 3, a higher percentage of low-income children had low intakes of calcium, vitamin A, and ascorbic acid, while low intakes of other nutrients is roughly the same for both income levels (Table 3).

Extremely low intakes were not observed to any significant degree except for calcium, iron, and ascorbic acid. Twelve per cent of low-income and 6 per cent of middle-income diets were calculated to contain less than 300 mg. calcium. Iron intakes below 5 mg. per day were recorded for roughly 15 per cent of all children. Ascorbic acid intakes below 13 mg. were noted for 19 and 6 per cent of low- and middle-income children, respectively.

Nutrient Supplements. Of the 147 low-income children, 50 (34 per cent) were taking a vitamin preparation; 103 (77 per cent) of the middle-income group were taking a supplement. Not all children were taking supplements daily, and fewer children were taking iron supplements than vitamin preparations (27 low-income children and 17 children of middle-income families).

In general, vitamin intakes from food were similar for middle-income children taking supplements and for those who were not (Table 4). Vitamin

TABLE 3. PER CENT OF DIETS BELOW TWO-THIRDS OF
RECOMMENDED ALLOWANCES (14)

NUTRIENT	DIETS BELOW 2/3 OF RECOMMENDATION	
	Low-income	Middle-income
	%	%
Protein	0	1
Calcium	41	21
Iron	69	76
Vitamin A	24	10
Thiamine	21	18
Riboflavin	5	2
Ascorbic acid	47	20

TABLE 4. CALCULATED VITAMIN INTAKE OF PRESCHOOL CHILDREN FROM FOOD AND VITAMIN SUPPLEMENTS

INCOME GROUP	NUMBER OF CHILDREN	VITAMIN A	THIAMINE	RIBOFLAVIN	NIACIN	ASCORBIC ACID
		I.U.	*mg.*	*mg.*	*mg.*	*mg.*
Two-Year-Olds						
Low-income						
Unsupplemented	43	2,150 ± 1,370°	0.57 ± 0.24	1.07 ± 0.50	7.3 ± 3.5	25 ± 20
Supplemented	23					
Food only		2,780 ± 1,840	0.61 ± 0.17	1.33 ± 0.41	7.3 ± 2.1	31 ± 22
Food + supplement		6,280 ± 1,950	2.46 ± 0.80	3.27 ± 0.83	22.4 ± 6.7	70 ± 21
Middle-income						
Unsupplemented	14	3,280 ± 1,660	0.70 ± 0.20	1.34 ± 0.48	8.0 ± 3.1	42 ± 26
Supplemented	46					
Food only		2,810 ± 1 370	0.63 ± 0.26	1.33 ± 0.48	7.1 ± 2.8	44 ± 25
Food + supplement		6,290 ± 1,870	1.88 ± 0.76	2.71 ± 0.86	17.8 ± 7.0	46 ± 34
Recommended allowance (14)....		2,000	0.6	0.7	6	40
Three-Year-Olds						
Low-income						
Unsupplemented	54	2,610 ± 1,590	0.66 ± 0.25	1.18 ± 0.51	8.4 ± 3.1	32 ± 22
Supplemented	28					
Food only		3,030 ± 1,680	0.71 ± 0.28	1.28 ± 0.53	9.2 ± 3.2	39 ± 24
Food + supplement		5,490 ± 3,220	2.58 ± 0.82	3.52 ± 1.02	27.1 ± 7.8	51 ± 32
Middle-income						
Unsupplemented	16	3,310 ± 990	0.65 ± 0.11	1.32 ± 0.34	7.9 ± 2.0	44 ± 20
Supplemented	57					
Food only		3,090 ± 1,820	0.66 ± 0.24	1.38 ± 0.62	7.9 ± 2.9	42 ± 24
Food + supplement		6,350 ± 1,970	1.93 ± 0.57	2.88 ± 0.88	19.5 ± 6.7	52 ± 31
Recommended allowance (14)....		2,500	0.7	0.8	8	40

° Standard deviation.

intakes of low-income children receiving supplements appeared somewhat superior to those of children who did not, but the differences were not statistically significant. These minor differences in vitamin intake were confirmed when unsupplemented and supplemented diets were compared with the recommended allowances. Fewer low-income children who were taking supplements consumed less than two-thirds the recommended intakes for iron and vitamins (Table 5) and, although the differences between unsupplemented and supplemented diets were not significant by the chi square test, the trend was consistent. No consistent differences or trends were observed in the data for middle-income children.

Supplementation increased vitamin intakes to two to four times the recommended allowances (Table 5).

Medical History and Clinical Examination. A brief medical history taken by the pediatrician revealed a somewhat higher reported incidence of measles, mumps, diarrheal episodes, and ear infections among the low-income children. More in this group had also been hospitalized for various ailments than the middle-income children. History of respiratory illness was reported with the same frequency for both groups, and patterns of sleep and daytime rest also were similar.

Clinical examination revealed no evidence of specific nutritional deficiencies. However, some possibly related conditions were observed. Muscle tone was judged by the physican to be fair or poor in 35 per cent of low-income children as compared with 18 per cent of middle-income. Pallor and apathy were recorded for approximately 10 per cent of low-income children and 5 per cent of the middle-income group.

Height and Weight. Height and weight of the children in the two groups were not significantly different (Table 6). Comparison of our sample with the sex-specific weight-for-age and height-for-age percentiles developed by the Fels Research Institute on Ohio-born children (15) indicated that the Honolulu children were comparable in terms of weight but were short in comparison with

TABLE 5. PER CENT OF SUPPLEMENTED AND UNSUPPLEMENTED
DIETS BELOW TWO-THIRDS OF RECOMMENDED ALLOWANCES
(14) FOR IRON AND FOUR VITAMINS

NUTRIENT	PER CENT OF DIETS BELOW 2/3 RECOMMENDATION				Total Sample
	Low-income group		Middle-income group		
	Unsupplemented (N = 90)	Supplemented (N = 57)	Unsupplemented (N = 30)	Supplemented (N = 104)	
Iron	72	63°	67	79†	72
Vitamin A	27	19	3	13	17
Thiamine	23	18	10	20	20
Riboflavin	7	2	0	3	4
Ascorbic acid	52	39	23	19	34

°Only 27 children receiving iron-containing supplement.
†Only 17 children receiving iron-containing supplement.

TABLE 6. HEIGHT AND WEIGHT OF TWO- AND THREE-YEAR-OLDS FROM LOW- AND MIDDLE-INCOME FAMILIES

AGE	LOW-INCOME GROUP			MIDDLE-INCOME GROUP		
	Number of children	Height	Weight	Number of children	Height	Weight
		in.	*lb.*		*in.*	*lb.*
Two-year-olds	64	35.10±1.53°	29.80±3.65	58	34.89±1.52	28.80±3.98
Three-year-olds	80	38.22±1.74	34.09±4.59	73	38.18±1.79	34.25±5.02

° Standard deviation.

the Fels norms. The majority fell between the 25th and 75th percentiles in the weight-for-age classification; 9 per cent were below the 5th percentile and 7 per cent were above the 95th percentile. In the height-for-age classification, 26 per cent were below the 5th percentile and 36 per cent below the 10th percentile. No child was above the 95th percentile for height, and only 8 per cent were above the 75th percentile. These data on height and weight will be reported in detail in a separate publication (16).

Biochemical Evaluation. Mean values for biochemical measurements were tabulated in relation to family income (Table 7), and results for children who received supplements are reported separately. Hemoglobin and hematocrit levels were somewhat lower for low-income children as compared with those of the middle-income group. The differences were statistically significant only for children whose diets were supplemented. The mean ratio of plasma amino acids of low-income children not given supplements was higher than for middle-income children. However, mean ratios for both income groups were within normal limits (10). Excretion of thiamine and niacin was twofold greater among children whose diets were supplemented. Vitamin excretion levels for all groups, however, were well above those suggested as indicative of adequate vitamin status (13).

There was considerable variation among the sample, but the degree of variation was similar for both income groups as indicated by similar standard deviations. Four per cent of the children had hemoglobin levels below 10 gm. per 100 ml. and 1 per cent of hematocrit levels were below 30 per cent. Six per cent of children excreted fairly low levels of urea nitrogen, below 6.9 mg. per gram. However, plasma amino acids were below 3.0 for all children, and thiamine and niacin excretions were uniformly high.

Calculation of correlations between dietary, biochemical, and clinical data yielded unexpected results. For example, protein intake was not significantly correlated with levels of plasma amino acid ratios or urea nitrogen:creatinine ratios (although these two measures of protein nutrition yielded a negative correlation significant at the 1 per cent level). However, a highly significant correlation was found between calcium intake and levels of these two measures of protein nutriture. Similarly, neither iron nor protein intake correlated with

TABLE 7. BIOCHEMICAL DATA BY INCOME AND SUPPLEMENTATION

SUBJECTS	NUMBER OF CHILDREN	HEMOGLOBIN	HEMATOCRIT	PLASMA AMINO ACID RATIO	UREA NITROGEN: CREATININE RATIO	THIAMINE: CREATININE RATIO	NIACIN: CREATININE RATIO
				Low-Income Group			
		gm./100 ml.	*%*		*mg./gm.*	*mcg./gm.*	*mcg./gm.*
All children	146†	11.7 ± 1.17 ‡	36.0 ± 2.52	1.56 ± 0.40	13.63 ± 4.56	1,195 ± 1,511	16.6 ± 19.9
Unsupplemented diet	96	11.7 ± 1.24	36.0 ± 2.61	1.61 ± 0.43°°	13.13 ± 4.56	823 ± 760	12.8 ± 6.9
Supplemented diet	50	11.8 ± 1.06°	36.0 ± 2.41	1.47 ± 0.34	14.44 ± 4.48	1,793 ± 2,122	22.7 ± 30.0
				Middle Income Group			
All children	132#	12.2 ± 1.20	36.9 ± 2.27	1.50 ± 0.37	14.87 ± 5.73	1,960 ± 2,340	23.0 ± 30.6
Unsupplemented diet	29	12.1 ± 1.41	36.1 ± 2.70	1.52 ± 0.32°°	14.46 ± 4.63	878 ± 542	12.6 ± 4.9
Supplemented diet	103	12.2 ± 1.08°	37.1 ± 2.12	1.50 ± 0.39	14.97 ± 6.07	2,268 ± 2,569	26.2 ± 34.2

°Significant at 5% level.
°°Significant at 1% level.
†Data missing for 1 child
‡Standard deviation.
#Data missing for 2 children.

hemoglobin or hematocrit levels, but there was a correlation significant at the 5 per cent level between calcium intake and hemoglobin. Correlations between vitamin intakes and excretions were attempted only for children not taking vitamin supplements. Among these subjects, no significant correlations were observed. Energy supply of the diets and intakes of fat, protein, and niacin, however, were inversely correlated with thiamine excretion.

Although clinical examination yielded no specific evidence of deficiency disease, the physician's subjective rating of pallor coincided with low hemoglobin and hematocrit levels. Hemoglobin of children so rated was significantly lower (5 per cent by t test) than the other children, 10.6 as compared with 11.8 gm. per 100 ml. Hematocrit levels also were lower among children receiving a clinical rating of apathy, 33.6 compared with 36.3 per cent; this difference was significant at the 2 per cent level.

Comments

The sample in this study represents roughly 30 per cent of the families contacted. The ethnic distribution suggests that the group is representative of the Honolulu population within the given income levels. However, the high refusal rate indicates that whatever factors influenced the willingness of families to cooperate conceivably may also have influenced the findings. A large number of those who refused to cooperate objected to the clinic visit, even though transportation was provided. According to the interviewers' observations, mothers who participated for the most part appeared to be highly motivated and interested in the welfare of their children and, further, had few interests outside the home and mother-role. While this is a subjective observation, it may be of some significance. Although we believe that our sample was fairly representative of the total population within the income levels studied in terms of physical characteristics, we suspect that there may have been subtle sociologic and even personal differences that are not easily defined. Further, we believe that these sociologic and personal differences may occur more commonly in collecting survey data than is generally recognized.

Both income levels were fairly low in comparison with income levels and cost of living in Hawaii; indeed, the similarities between data on children of the low- and middle-income groups are greater than the differences. The fact that heights and weights of both groups were nearly identical suggests that nutritional histories of the two groups were not widely different. Both groups, however, were short in comparison with the Ohio-born children who provided data for the Fels norms, a finding also reported recently for Mississippi children of low-income families (17). We have considered that the racial composition of our sample may account in part for the short stature of the children, but we cannot rule out some degree of present or previous undernutrition as a possible contributing factor. Energy intakes of the Honolulu children, for example, tended to be lower than those reported by Beal (18) for upper-middle class, Mainland children and are more like figures reported for the Mississippi low-income, preschool children (17), who also were reported to be short for their age.

Calculated protein intakes were uniformly high and accordingly, niacin intakes appeared to be generally satisfactory. Calcium, riboflavin, and ascorbic acid levels were lower for low-income children than those of middle-income families. Since mean levels of riboflavin were high and fewer than 5 per cent of children's diets contained less than two-thirds of the recommended allowance, it would seem that inadequacy of this nutrient is not likely a significant problem in this sample. The higher incidence of low intakes of calcium, ascorbic acid, and vitamin A among low-income families suggests that the possibility of inadequate intakes of these nutrients may be greater for the children at this income level. The difference between the two groups in intake of these nutrients was associated with a lower consumption of milk and fruit and fruit juices of high ascorbic acid content by low-income children.

Calculated intakes of iron were somewhat higher among low-income children, as was the consumption of cereal grains. It was not surprising that iron intakes compared unfavorably with recommended levels, since it is generally conceded that the higher levels now recommended are difficult if not impossible to supply in the diet on a continuing basis except by the use of highly fortified foods (or by supplementation). The fact that calculated iron intakes of nearly a fourth of the children (both groups) were below 5 mg. daily suggests that attention should be paid to ways of increasing iron intake for children of this age whose diets are still dominated by milk. However, the incidence of hemoglobin levels below 10 gm. per 100 ml. (4 per cent) was lower than that reported for Mainland children of low-income families — 15 per cent (17) and 22 percent (19) among Mississippi and New York preschool children, respectively, and an even higher incidence reported for some areas of the country (20).

The failure to find a significant correlation between nutrient intakes and blood and urine analyses is not uncommon, possible reasons having been enumerated recently by Owen *et al.* (17). It seems likely that the most significant factors are related to the errors inherent in dietary calculations and possibly the time between dietary observations and collection of blood and urine samples. With some exceptions, nutrient levels in blood and urine reflect fairly recent dietary intakes. The majority of clinic visits were made within two weeks of dietary interviews, and never more than one month. Undoubtedly, less time lag between dietary and biochemical data would have been preferable.

These findings suggest that, although there is apparently little serious malnutrition among preschool children in Honolulu, calcium and ascorbic acid and possibly vitamin A intakes may be inadequate for some children, particularly those of low-income groups. Similar data were reported for low-income, preschool children in Mississippi (17), where incidence of low intakes was considerably higher, and family income was less than half that of the Honolulu children. Low intakes of vitamin A appeared to be more prevalent in Honolulu than in Mississippi, probably due to high consumption of the green leafy vegetables known to be habitual in the South.

The significance of low dietary levels of calcium to health must be interpreted with caution, since calcium requirements remain a matter of controversy (21). Intakes of 13 mg. ascorbic acid per day are considered borderline, however, by most interpreters of dietary standards (22).

Dietary intakes of iron by preschool children appear to be unrelated to income level, suggesting that attention be given to insure adequate intakes of this nutrient for all young children.

Summary

A nutritional survey was made of 281 two- and three-year-old children of low- and middle-income families in Honolulu, using dietary, biochemical, and clinical methods of evaluation. Analysis of individual diets indicated that low-income children were more likely to have low (and possibly inadequate) intakes of calcium, ascorbic acid, and to a lesser extent, vitamin A. Calculated caloric intakes tended to be somewhat low for the sample as a whole, and about one-fourth of the children of both income groups consumed diets that could be presumed to be inadequate in iron.

Honolulu children were short in comparison with norms developed on Ohio-born children; weight of Honolulu children was more similar to the Mainland norms. No difference between height, weight, or biochemical measurements was observed between the two groups. Clinical examination revealed no overt symptoms of nutritional disease, but some possibly related conditions were noted which were somewhat more prevalent among low-income children.

REFERENCES

1.   Miller, C.D.: A Study of the Dietary and Value of Living of Forty-Four Japanese Families in Hawaii. Univ. Hawaii Research Pub. No. 18, 1938.

2.   Potgieter, M.: The Adequacy of Diets of Thirty-eight Honolulu Families on Relief. Hawaii. Agric. Exper. Sta. Bull. No. 91, June 1944.

3.   Potgieter, M., and Nakatani, K.: Diet and Health in Rural Hawaii. Hawaii Agric. Exper. Sta. Tech. Bull. No. 21, Feb. 1954.

4.   Walker, M., Wenkam, N.S., and Miller, C.D.: Fat, protein, sodium and calories in diets in Hawaii. J. Am. Dietet. A. 35: 122, 1959.

5.   Huenemann, R.L., French, F.E., and Bierman, J.M.: Diets of pregnant women in Kauai, Hawaii. Two dietary survey methods compared. J. Am. Dietet. A. 39: 569, 1961.

6.   Miller, C.D., and Branthoover, B.: Nutritive Value of Some Hawaii Foods. Hawaii Agric. Exper. Sta. Circ. 52, 1957.

7.   Church, C.F., and Church, H.N.: Bowes and Church Food Values of Portions Commonly Used. 10th ed. Philadelphia: J.B. Lippincott Co., 1966.

8.   Food & Nutr. Research Center: Food Composition Table Recommended for Use in the Philippines. Rev. Manila: Natl. Inst. Sci. & Tech., 1964.

9.   Tables of Food Composition in Japan. Rev. ed. Tokyo: Natl. Inst. Nutr. 1967.

10.   Whitehead, R.G.: Rapid determination of some plasma amino acids in subclinical kwashiorkor. Lancet 1: 250, 1964.

11.   Clark, L.C., Jr., and Thompson, H.L.: Determination of creatine and creatine in urine. Anal. Chem. 21: 1218, 1949.

12.   Karr, W.G.: A method for the determination of blood urea nitrogen. J. Lab. Clin. Med. 9: 329, 1924.

13.   Interdepartmental Comm. on Nutr. for Natl. Defense: Manual for Nutrition Surveys. Rev. ed. Bethesda, Md.: Natl. Inst. of Health, 1963.

14.   Food & Nutr. Bd.: Recommended Dietary Allowances. Seventh Revised Edition, 1968. Natl. Acad. Sci. Pub. No. 1694, 1968.
15.   Suggested Guidelines for Evaluation of Nutritional Status of Preschool Children. Rev. Washington, D.C.: U.S. Children's Bureau, 1967.
16.   Smith, D.S., and Brown, M.L.: Anthropometry in Hawaii preschool children. Amer. J. Clin. Nutr. in press.
17.   Owen, G.M., Garry, P.J., Kram, K.M., Nelsen, C.E., and Montalvo, J.M.: Nutritional status of Mississippi preschool children. Amer. J. Clin. Nutr. 22: 1444, 1969.
18.   Beal, V.A.: Nutritional intake of children. 1. Calories, carbohydrate, fat and protein. J. Nutr. 50: 223, 1953.
19.   Haughton, J.G.: Nutritional anemia of infancy and childhood. Amer. J. Pub. Health 53: 1121, 1963.
20.   Prevention of Iron-Deficiency Anemia in Infants and Children of Preschool Age, 1967. Washington, D.C.: U.S. Children's Bureau, 1967.
21.   Council on Foods & Nutr.: Symposium on human calcium requirements. J.A.M.A. 185: 588, 1963.
22.   Young, E.G.: Dietary standards. In Beaton, G.H., and Mellemy, E.W., eds: Nutrition, An Advanced Treatise. Vol. II. N.Y.: Academic Press, 1961.

ANALYSIS OF SURVEY RESEARCH EXAMPLE

Diet and Nutriture of Preschool Children in Honolulu

General Objectives. The study was undertaken because, until recently, there has been a dearth of quantitative data available on dietary intake and nutritional status of preschool children in the United States and, more specifically, no such information was available for children in Hawaii. Previous surveys in Hawaii have dealt with the diets of low-income families, hospital diets, and diets of pregnant women of low- to lower-middle-income status.

In this study, efforts were concentrated on children of low-income families and included those of middle-income families for comparative purposes, to determine the relationship of family economic level to diet and nutriture of young children. Dietary, biochemical, and clinical methods were used for evaluation.

Specific Objectives (Hypotheses). Specific objectives and hypotheses were not stated in this research article. However, several null hypotheses can be deduced from the discussion of the results of the study, as follows:

1.   There are no significant differences in mean intakes of calcium, niacin, riboflavin, and ascorbic acid between children from middle-income and low-income families.

2.   There are no significant differences in vitamin supplement intake between children from middle-income and low-income families.

3.   There are no significant differences in vitamin intake from food between middle-income children taking supplements and those who were not.

4. There are no significant differences in incidence of measles, mumps, diarrheal episodes, and ear infections between children from middle-income and low-income families.

5. There are no significant differences in height and weight between children from middle-income and low-income families.

6. There are no significant differences in biochemical measurements (hemoglobin and hematocrit levels; plasma amino acids; excretion of vitamins).

7. There is no significant relationship between dietary, biochemical, and clinical data.

Sample. The sample of 281 children in this study represented about 30% of families contacted. The "obviously high-income families" were eliminated on the basis of the father's occupation. The final sample of low-income and middle-income families was randomly drawn from birth records of families with children two and three years old living within five major areas in the city of Honolulu. The authors state that the ethnic distribution suggests that the group is representative of the Honolulu population within the income levels studied.

However, they also emphasize that the high refusal rate indicates that whatever factors influenced the willingness of families to cooperate conceivably may also have influenced the findings. They further stated "that these sociologic and personal differences [between those who participate and those who don't] may occur more commonly in collecting survey data than is generally recognized."

Data Collection. The dietary data were obtained from mothers in their homes by four interviewers trained specifically for the study. Dietary intake for a three-day period was obtained by mothers' recall and by records kept by the mother. The majority of children were subsequently examined in a clinic by a pediatrician.

Analysis of Data. Dietary records were coded and intake calculated by computer, using food composition data for computer use obtained from the U.S. Department of Agriculture. Hypotheses were tested by appropriate statistical techniques.

CHAPTER 8

Field Study

Complex problems of human relationships can be tackled through field study. In this chapter some of the possible kinds of studies will be presented and field study approaches will be compared with those of other kinds of research.

FIELD STUDY DEFINED

"Field studies are ex post facto scientific inquiries aimed at discovering the relations and interactions among sociological, psychological, and educational variables in real social structures." (Kerlinger, 1964, p. 387). The field researcher ordinarily manipulates no independent variables. He observes life as it takes place in a natural setting. This natural setting may be in a community, school, factory, or other organization.

Field studies are employed to a great extent by the anthropologist. While formerly there appeared to be a conflict between the traditional, qualitative anthropological approach and quantitative approaches, today anthropological field studies range from the extreme of interpretative descriptions of primitive societies to investigations employing standardized quantification of data in support of hypotheses. A methodological weakness in anthropological field work has been too great a reliance upon relatively few informants to obtain a picture of a society or culture. Anthropologists are not in agreement that the trend toward a more quantitative status for the discipline is altogether a benefit. One anthropologist reported that students from sociology and psychology being trained in anthropology have to learn to "listen to the data" until a pattern emerges rather than to set up preconceived categories.

RELATION OF FIELD STUDY TO OTHER
RESEARCH METHODS

It is not always easy to distinguish a field study from several other kinds of research. For example, field study may involve survey techniques. Also, field research may have historical aspects. There are also resemblances between exploratory field study and laboratory or experimental field research. Each of these will be discussed more fully in this section.

In field studies data may be collected through the use of observations, interviews, personal documents, and/or case studies.

Survey and Field Study

Field studies differ from surveys with respect to the greater scope of surveys and the greater depth of field studies. A surveyor is in touch with more people but his contacts are more formal and impersonal than those of the field researcher.

The tasks for the field researcher are more varied and often more difficult than those for the interviewers in a survey. Not only must the support of groups to be studied be obtained for the investigator to spend weeks or months in a community gaining access to privileged information but much of the interviewing must be with top leaders of the community. More of their time may be required for in-depth interviews and possibly for reinterviews.

The *extensive* survey research method can be a good adjunct to *intensive* field studies. Through this method, major hypotheses of the studies, particularly those involving observed attitudes and behavioral patterns, could be checked by using a standard stimulus applied to a carefully selected sample of people to ensure that the attitudes and behaviors were representative of the entire group studied.

Glock expressed well the complementary uses of survey and field techniques in anthropology:

> If anthropology has a message for survey research, it is this: delay the construction of schedules of all kinds until something is known about the cultural context of the phenomenon under study; do not assume that all slices of social actuality are always identically responsive to theoretical constructs; remember that all such constructs are, in the last analysis, human conceptions of the social situation at one place and time, and their relevance to a new situation must always be a problem for investigation.
>
> If survey research has a message for anthropology, it is this: first, often context can be known in general terms, known sufficiently well to permit the use of instruments which will materially aid in the checking of particular hypotheses, or hasten the collection of certain types of data. It is not always necessary to know the culture in detail; the intelligent and well-educated observer can operate on the basis of our growing comparative knowledge of cultures and social systems. Second, whenever specific hypotheses are to be tested in fieldwork, the anthropologist has an obligation to construct and

utilize instruments which will adequately represent the population under study. (Glock, 1967, pp. 302-303)

A survey is made with a sample, hopefully, that is representative of a larger population. As mentioned earlier, the survey research method can be a good adjunct to field studies. In this respect, the analysis of data can become quantitative. Malinowski (1922, p. 17), for example, referred to such quantification as "method of statistic documentation of concrete evidence." This method includes using census data and other lists to describe village life (e.g., number and type of dwellings, household composition, occupations of the people, etc.)

Hillway made the following observation about how the case study methods and surveys can supplement each other:

> When human beings constitute the subject matter of a study, actual examples of the experiences and the development of individual histories add reality to the picture. Quantitative data tend generally to make the description abstract; case histories can make it human. (Hillway, 1964, pp. 238-239)

Case Study and Genetic Study

A *case study* is "a comprehensive study of a social unit — be that unit a person, a group, a social institution, a district, or a community." (Young, 1966, p. 247) Data for a case study can be gathered during an entire life span or for a portion of it. Behavior is studied in such precise detail that the case study method has been called "the social microscope."

The following outline of criteria for the life or case history has been adapted from Dollard:

1. The subject must be viewed in a cultural series. That is, even though he is singled out for individual study, he must be regarded as a member of a culture group or community. Community values, standards, and way of life can be studied only through life histories of persons. (See, for example, W.L. Warner et al., Yankee City Series)

2. Behavior of individuals must be viewed as socially relevant. That is, behavior should be seen as arising in response to definite social stimulations.

3. The family of the subject of study must be viewed in its role of transmitting the culture and way of life of the group through its individual members.

4. The specific method of elaboration of organic materials into social behavior must be shown.

5. The continuous related character of experience from childhood through adulthood should be stressed.

6. The social situation must be studied in order to learn the kind and degree of social pressures, social forces, social participation or abstention, exercised by the subject.

7. The life history material must be organized and conceptualized. (Dollard, 1949, pp. 8-36)

Caution must be exercised not to generalize about a single case. Important information for advancing human knowledge and for determining courses of action can grow out of many replications of case studies.

The principal difference between a case study and *genetic research* is in the direction of the study. A case study is ex post facto, looking back to gain understanding of the individual's or unit's development. On the other hand, genetic research is forward-looking, following the growth as it occurs. This is known as longitudinal research, where the same individuals are studied over a long period of time.

A classic illustration of a genetic study may be found in Terman's comprehensive report on gifted children and their development. He studied a large number of cases and included a variety of characteristics. A later investigation followed these same individuals into their adult lives. (Terman et al., 1925 and 1947)

Other examples of long-term studies include the work of biologists on the life cycle of small organisms, Gesell's studies of young children's behavior development, and Piaget's study of mental processes.

One of the major problems in doing a genetic study is that many of the subjects move and it is difficult, perhaps very costly, to contact them in person through several years. For this reason, the initial group on whom data are gathered must be larger than the number the researcher hopes to have in the final part of the study.

Other problems affecting genetic studies center around the tests or scales that might be used. Are the psychological tests used at different age levels, perhaps from childhood through adulthood, really equivalent? Are the individuals likely to lose some of their interest in cooperating and their motivation to perform well as they are tested repeatedly?

To alleviate such problems, a longitudinal study is often combined with a cross-sectional (survey) study. While initial measurements are made with a younger group (the beginning of a longitudinal study), data are gathered from an older group of the same age the younger ones will be when they are retested.

Field Study and Field Experiment

Field experiments, which were discussed in Chapter 6, are planned carefully to test specific hypotheses. In some instances, hypotheses may be developed prior to a field study, but they are often suggested during the preliminary or "scouting expedition."

The field researcher ordinarily manipulates no independent variables. He observes life as it takes place, in its natural setting. Needless to say, it is difficult for the researcher to separate and study the variables relating to the problems he is studying in the field situation. Such variables are multiple and complex.

Festinger contrasted exploratory studies with hypothesis-testing research. It might be helpful to think of a field study as similar to the exploratory research which "attempts to see what is there rather than to predict the relationships that will be found." (Festinger and Katz, 1953, p. 74)

Field Study in Historical Perspective

The sources of information and the techniques used in a field study resemble those in documentary or historical research. They might include personal interviews, observations, personal documents such as diaries and letters, newspaper records, and records from community agencies. Through sources such as these, information might be obtained about an individual's home and family background, habits and interests, the neighborhood, test scores, etc. The emphasis is the individual or a unit. The result is a description and explanation of the principal factors which have contributed to his present status.

The following two illustrations of well-known field studies show the same care in handling sources of information as would be shown in documentary research. They also involve some approaches used in survey studies.

1. Thomas was the first sociologist to introduce detailed field studies of total social situations and their basic preceding elements. In his *Source Book of Social Origins* (1909) he examined behavioral patterns of simple societies in an attempt to understand the more complex development of modern complex societies. In cooperation with the Polish sociologist, Florian Znaniecki, he conducted field studies which resulted in the comprehensive two-volume publication, *The Polish Peasant in Europe and America* (1927). Extensive data on personality dynamics, attitudes, and emotional life were accumulated through personal documents, introducing what was later known as the life history or case study technique.

As expressed by Young (1966, p. 40):

> The *Polish Peasant* represents a turning point in the development of social science method. It was the first field study of any magnitude which concerned itself with selective subject matter and with methodology as well. It stressed field research as a method of discovering, specifically and realistically, what actually is, and not what is assumed to be, a method aimed at ascertaining, intimately and concretely, social attitudes, social values, and other forces which motivate the person and the group. Thomas and Znaniecki conceived research as a method of depicting society as an organic social process – a process interwoven with the cultural setting, the social institutions, the community, and the person.
>
> The personal document, especially the diary, autobiography, and the personal letter, assumed considerable significance as a research tool which facilitated the study of the inner life of the family and its members. Life-history documents came into immediate and widespread use in a variety of research studies.

Spurred by Thomas's field research, most of the sociological studies which rapidly followed were interdisciplinary studies by sociologists, anthropologists, psychologists, political scientists, and economists.

2. *Middletown* and *Middletown in Transition* are regarded as classics in the study of community life. Following is a condensed form of Lynd's field workers' approach in Middletown. (Lynd, 1929 and 1937)

Researchers came to Middletown "to study the growth of the city." Middletown was a midwestern city with a population of approximately 35,000. It was chosen for this study because it had two major characteristics considered desirable for a study of cultural change: that it be representative of contemporary American life and that it be compact and homeogeneous enough to be manageable in a total-situation study. Middletown had an industrial culture, but the city was not dominated by a single industry. Glass, metal, and automobile industries predominated. It was known as "a good music town," and its civic and women's clubs were strong. Nearly 85 per cent of the population was native white of native parentage. The city was studied in terms of six main life activities: getting a living, making a home, training the young, using leisure, engaging in religious practices, and engaging in community activities..

At the commencement of the study no fixed schedules were drawn up. The people were observed in terms of the six activities and an attempt was made to determine the trends of change exhibited over the preceding 35 years. Half of the study was narrowed as the study progressed by concentrating on the years 1900 and 1924. It was further narrowed by concentrating upon certain business and working class groups.

Although the study was comprehensive, some subjective selection of data to be collected was inevitable. The criterion of selection in general was that institutions would not be studied for their own sake but with reference to the life activities which they serve. Therefore, some behavior which would have been of interest to the study of a given institution became less relevant to this study. The following techniques were included in collecting data:

Participation in the local life. The research workers shared in every way possible the life of the city by living in apartments or in private households, and by assuming obligations similar to those of other residents of Middletown. The researchers attended churches, school assemblies and classes, court sessions, political rallies, civic club lunches, lectures, annual dinners, card parties, etc.

Data were collected from meetings, individual interviews, or casual conversations by taking inconspicuous notes during the meeting or interview and transcribing them in detail immediately following such discussions according to the standardized form adopted. If conditions prevented taking notes at the time, the record was made immediately after, from memory.

Examination of documentary material. Whenever available, documentary materials in the form of census data, city and county records, court files, school records, and detailed diaries of leading citizens were used.

Compilation of statistics. In cases where statistical material was not already available, data were sometimes compiled from sources in the city, at the state capital, etc. Such data included wages, club memberships, church memberships, attendance at movie theaters, ownership of automobiles, etc.

Interviews. Interviews conducted in the study varied from the most casual conversations with streetcar conductors, barbers, etc., to carefully planned interviews with people especially qualified to give information on particular aspects of community life. During the course of the study it seemed desirable to test individual families with respect to certain hypotheses regarding trends observed in the behavior of the community. Therefore, schedules were drawn up on the basis of these observed characteristics and a group of 124 families of the working class and 40 families of the business class were interviewed. The total of the families interviewed in any one section of the city was roughly proportional to the working class population of that section. The working class families selected were believed to be a representative sample of those employed in the manufacturing and mechanical industries dominating Middletown.

Questionnaires. Questionnaires were used at some points in the study to serve as extensions of the interview. Data secured from the questionnaires included club memberships and activities, life of the high school population, etc. In the foreword to *Middletown*, Wissler, of the American Museum of Natural History, stated:

> So this volume needs no defense; it is put forth for what it is, a pioneer attempt to deal with a sample American community after the manner of social anthropology. . . . This volume is a contribution to history, not the usual kind of history, but the kind that is coming more and more into demand, a cross-section of the activities of a community today as projected from the background of yesterday, and the authors are to be commended for their foresight in revealing the Middletown of 1890 as a genesis of the Middletown of today, not as its contrast.

He further stated that this study shows clearly the changes each decade has brought and the imperfect way in which our communities, of which this is a sample, have met the new conditions under which they must function. (Wissler, in Lynd, 1929)

CARRYING OUT A FIELD STUDY

Since there are many variations in the procedures that might be employed in field study, it may not be possible to follow any particular steps exactly. A field investigator must be very sensitive and personal so he can become a part of the community or group he is studying. He must be flexible in adapting the following steps.

1. *Objectives.* In the preliminary planning for a field study, the scope of the study and general objectives should be determined first. However, in contrast to the experiment and survey, the information sought in a field study is not highly structured and limited by a rigid theoretical framework developed in advance. The major objective in field study is "a respect for cultural context." (Glock, 1967)

> In the anthropological sense used here, "culture" has a broad meaning: Culture includes all of man's acquired power of control over nature and himself. It includes therefore, on the one hand, the whole of man's material civilization, tools, weapons, clothing, shelter, machines, and even systems of industry, and, on the other hand, all of non-material or spiritual civilization, such as language, literature, art, religion, morality, law and government. (Ellwood, 1927, p. 9)

The noted anthropologist, Margaret Mead, tested G. Stanley Hall's general theory that the stressful period of adolescent behavior is an inevitable phase of human development and therefore a fundamental biological trait of all adolescents. Dr. Mead questioned this theory and hypothesized that, to the contrary, adolescent behavior is conditioned by cultural values and attitudes. Her intensive field study, *Coming of Age in Samoa*, was conducted to test her hypothesis. In Samoa she did not find a stressful period of adolescent behavior and she related such absence of stress to the socially approved means of dealing with sex tensions that she observed among the Samoan people. (Mead, 1953)

2. *The Scouting Expedition.* This stage is exploratory and informal in nature. The field researcher makes contact with the group to be studied either by observing it on frequent visits or living and participating in the group. During this period, the researcher should gain some understanding of the important variables in the situation, forming a basis for systematic observation and other methods of data collection that the field study may require.

Since the main objective in field studies is "a respect for cultural context," the following variables may be useful. They are similar to those which psychologists and sociologists are finding important in understanding the specifics of group behavior.

a.   *The material culture* (artifacts or man-made products)

This material culture includes man's crafts, tools, weapons, buildings, his textiles and clothing, etc. Observations should be made regarding the production of these materials, the use people in a given cultural group make of these materials, the influence they have on their social and economic organization, on the personality of the individual, etc.

b.   *Origins and cultural changes*

Every group has a social heritage — attitudes and values with their accompanying practices that are brought by a cultural group when they immigrate to a new land. These heritages affect the way of the group in the new land and of their ancestors. Cultural changes should be observed in relation to these heritages.

c.   *Social organization*

The total structure of the group being studied with respect to the major social groups and subgroups should be described.

d.   *Family organization*

The family should be observed with respect to the form of family life; its degree of stability; status and roles of men, women, and children; sources of family income; educational practices, including attitudes toward sexual experience, etc.

e.   *Religious organization*

The primary beliefs of the group should be determined, as well as the place of religion in the lives of the people.

f.   *Value systems and goals of major social groups and subgroups*

g.   *Group cooperation*

h.   *Group conflicts and tension*

3.   *Research Design and Methods of Data Collection.* The research design should be formulated during the scouting stage as the researcher begins to see relationships between variables in the field situation and the theoretical literature.

The field study lends itself to combining several data collection techniques. Prior to, or in conjunction with field research, a library survey should be conducted. Clyde Kluckhohn, an eminent field researcher, maintained that "unless a greater proportion of available source materials are collated and synthesized, field research will suffer materially, for the right questions will not be asked." (Kluckhohn, 1945, p. 146)

The field study is concerned with the unique qualities of the population or individual being studied, rather than with the presentation of standardized stimuli to a population selected on the basis of clearly defined criteria. Data collection is exploratory, with the movements of the researcher adjusted to the rhythms of everyday life of the people rather than to the requirements of a structured research instrument. Among his data collection techniques can be observation, interviewing, visiting events and people, photographing and sound recording, reviewing personal documents such as diaries, developing case studies, etc.

4. *Full-Scale Field Study.* "The field researcher needs to be salesman, administrator, and entrepreneur, as well as investigator." (Kerlinger, 1964, p. 391) The field study usually continues over a period of time, permitting continued observation of social interaction and relationships. The field researcher is concerned with establishing personal relationships with his subjects. His individual subjects are viewed as persons and not simply as a "population" or "sample." He is concerned with many complex variables, with individuals behaving in a cultural context. Group support is essential because he may spend weeks or months in the community seeking access to privileged information, attending all types of meetings, and often reinterviewing people.

Ideally, most of the problems of research design and data collection should be solved before the field operation. However, in actual practice the observations made in the scouting expedition and the content of a pretested research instrument may assume new meaning when applied to events or situations which may have suddenly changed. The researcher or research team should therefore maintain a balance between preserving the original research objectives and design and providing soundness of judgment in determining changes in procedure which may be desirable during the progress of the field work.

5. *Data Analysis.* Voluminous data are usually collected in field studies. For purposes of analysis, they must be combined and many interesting but extraneous observations neglected. In this respect, the researcher sometimes cannot see the forest for the trees. Because of his personal involvement, he may become so intimately involved with "side issues" that he loses sight of his research objectives and hypotheses.

6. *Reporting.* As for other types of research, following the analysis and interpretation of the data, a description of the study and its results should be communicated to the public in the form of a thesis and/or research journal article. Field studies also lend themselves to more popular writing in the form of books and magazine articles. Care should be taken, however, in writing a research report of such a study to concentrate on the objectives and hypotheses of the study and avoid a temptation to make it resemble a novel, which may be entertaining but not scientific.

Writing up a case study should be considered as carefully as writing up a laboratory experiment. Carefully selected data recorded uniformly may provide a basis for comparisons among people and groups which could lead to the development of scientific generalizations. Such a result could be achieved more easily if both the case study and statistical methods are used. Young stated that in many aspects the case study method is not unlike statistics:

> There is, of course, a recognition of a set of specific and general factors to be studied. The more careful case histories also recognize the problem of sampling, since the aim is to avoid the temptation to generalize from one case. So, too, references are frequently made to typical cases, which is a way of referring to some central tendency. Likewise, attention is given to the divergent instance, which is but an informal way of stating facts about variability. Finally, the worker with these data may compare his findings with those of other samples, and in order to expose dynamic relations he may indicate in qualitative terms covariation and correlation between selected factors and situations. (Young, 1940, pp. 250-251)

EXAMPLES AND ANALYSES
OF FIELD STUDY

BARK CLOTH OR TAPA: ITS PAST AND PRESENT-DAY USES IN SELECTED AREAS OF THE PACIFIC AS RELATED TO SOCIAL CHANGE

BARBARA CHRISTENSEN

My decision to conduct a field study in the islands of the Pacific for my doctoral dissertation grew out of seven years' experience working in Hawaii with Polynesian people from many of the islands, and from the lack of printed information on tapa in the Pacific area. The islands included in my study were Fiji, Hawaii, American Samoa, Western Samoa, Tahiti, and Tonga. Before traveling to the islands for the field portion of my study, it was necessary to make some preliminary preparations so the data could be collected as efficiently and objectively as possible. A questionnaire was developed from information accumulated from my readings and from former experiences with Polynesian people. A pilot study was conducted to help determine the applicability and clarity of the questions. Subjects for the pilot study included people who had spent a year or more in different areas of the Pacific in which the final study was to be conducted, or who were indigenous to these areas. These subjects were requested to suggest other people in the United States or in the Pacific area who might know about tapa and/or who might be able to refer me to people who did have such knowledge. Counselors of foreign students at Utah State University, the University of Utah, and Brigham Young University were contacted for Polynesian students in their schools. From these a list of possible informants was started, with one or more pages for each country with the name of the person, his address, and the name of the person who had suggested the informant. Often the person contacted asked who had suggested him.

From interviews, the questionnaire was restructured and an answer sheet was developed from the finished form of the questionnaire. As many anticipated replies as possible were listed to facilitate the problem of rapidly recording the answers.

The questionnaire was administered through personal and group interviews in the field to:

1. Individuals suggested in the pilot study.
2. Older individuals, since they might know more about the past.
3. The chiefs who direct ceremonies and determine what should be worn.
4. Individuals in as many different villages and islands as possible within each culture to give a broad base for the survey rather than a confined or regional viewpoint.

Reprinted with permission from Barbara Christensen. Proceedings, National Textiles and Clothing Meeting, Minneapolis, June 19-22, 1968. See also "Berk Cloth or Tapa: Its Past and Present-day Uses in Selected Areas of the Pacific as related to Social Change." Doctoral dissertation, on which report was based, conducted at Utah State University (1968) under the direction of Norma H. Compton.

Language was a problem since so many areas were to be included in the study, each with its own language. It would have been impossible for me to learn all of these languages well enough to understand both the vocal and the subvocal communications, so well qualified translators were used. There is always the possibility that the translators may have refrained from translating material that they would prefer not to discuss. However, this problem did not appear to exist in this case, inasmuch as there were great similarities in the answers that were received from the various translators in the several areas.

In most of the areas I lived with friends. This was extremely helpful, in that they could tell me how to address persons of high status in their country, and the proper etiquette to avoid offending those I was interviewing. For example, when sitting in a grass house (fale) one should sit on the floor with legs crossed, never straight out in front or pointed toward anyone. When my legs got numb I would fold them so they went out to the side and behind, but never sticking straight out in front. Also, I always wore a dress and never slacks or shorts. Slacks and shorts are not worn by the natives of the Pacific islands visited. I wanted to represent myself, the University, and my country in the best possible manner.

In Fiji I worked through the Fijian Affairs Board, who approved the study in Fiji and supplied an open letter to the chiefs requesting their assistance with this project in any way possible, and informing them that the study had been approved by the board.

Tapa is produced in Fiji only in certain areas where the soil conditions and climate are favorable. From a fact sheet compiled by the Fiji Visitors Bureau, it was found that in the past tapa had been made in the Ra Province on Viti Levu, in Macuata Province, Cakaudrove Province, the Lau group of islands, and on Vatulele, but it was not known whether tapa was still being made in these places. Therefore, the research was started with those areas that were known to produce tapa, while the Fijian Affairs Board checked the other areas.

A tape recorder was taken on the research trip, but was used sparingly because it was found that it frightened some of the interviewees even though permission was always asked before it was used. I could not afford to lose an interviewee once a good one had been found.

Transportation between the islands varied considerably. Passage by a copra boat was taken through the Lau Island group since this is just about the only way, except by chartering a private yacht, that these islands could be reached at the time this study was conducted.

Since there are no hotels, cafes or other facilities for visitors throughout the Lau Islands, group interviews were conducted with the women assembled at each of the various islands. This arrangement appeared to be satisfactory, inasmuch as the Fiji Broadcasting System requested the people to assemble before arrival of the ship. In one village the chief read the letter from the Fijian Affairs Board and summoned the villagers together by blowing the shell horn. He translated each question to the assembled group of women, waited while they discussed their answer, and then translated the answer to me. There was good interchange; there seemed to be a wide variety of likes for color and design — and no specific individual seemed to dominate the answering of the questions. The trip through the Lau Islands was undertaken during the school holidays, so there was always a school teacher who could translate the questionnaire from English to Fijian.

On several islands the women had preparations for formal receptions waiting on the beach, with demonstrations of how the tapa is made in their islands. On one of the islands an old photographic album was borrowed, showing the use of bark cloth. Duplicates were made of the pictures in the album. Prints of pictures taken of ceremonial functions over the past 80 years were reviewed in the two photographic studios and the Public Relations office in Fiji, and copies of applicable pictures made.

Since there was just one truck and one jeep which belonged to government maintenance and possibly one or two motorcycles on the island of Ta'u in Samoa, I walked everywhere, except to one village seven miles away. This village was reached by riding in the maintenance truck on one of its regular trips. As usual there were no telephones, so I just went and waited to interview those who were suggested. Patience is a prime quality needed for this type of research.

Only in Manu'a did one person suggest payment for information. She said that many researchers had come in, asked the villagers what they knew, and then made a fortune on a book, none of which was ever returned to the people. Others made similar comments, but did not ask to be paid. The problem of misrepresentation of a culture was expressed by one of the interviewees in Hawaii. The Hawaiians feel that some authors, who have written about ancient Hawaii, do not grasp the entire scope of the culture, and therefore misrepresent it. Therefore some of the residents asked me why I wanted the information. When authors misconstrue the facts, according to the informant, the interviewees who gave the information lose status among their fellow Hawaiians. Therefore, the type of information we as researchers write often influences the possibilities of others doing research in the same area. I hope to have people who are well educated in each area comment before I print the findings. This will guarantee nothing; the comments may never be returned; but at least they will have had the opportunity to correct anything they feel strongly about. I would like to return the findings to an authority on the subject in each area, but in many areas there no longer are any authorities. There is no public library in Tonga. Therefore, any information preserved must be passed on from parent to child.

The use of statistics in the Pacific area does not have a long history, so figures are available only for recent years in some areas. Even more important, when the figures are available they often may not be completely accurate. According to the Department of Immigration in Tonga, figures are available for only the past six years.

In addition to direct interviews in the field, the accuracy of responses and gaps in information were checked wherever possible by visits to libraries and museums. Tapa collections were also photographed at these sources. Pictures were taken of the bark cloth and displays in the Fiji Museum in Suva. The Suva city library, the Sir Alport Barker Library, and the archives were surveyed for information concerning the study, particularly for sources which might not be found elsewhere.

At Sydney, Australia, photographs were taken of the bark cloth in the

Australian National Museum. The pertinent references in the Mitchell Library were also consulted. At Auckland, New Zealand, all except the white pieces and a few repetitions of patterns of bark cloth were photographed at the Auckland War Memorial Museum. A Master's thesis by Tamahori (1963) was consulted at the Auckland University Library.

The libraries in both Western Samoa and American Samoa were used with assistance from the librarians regarding the best sources for interpretation of the culture of Samoa. The museum and its library were consulted at Papeete, Tahiti. At the University of Hawaii Library and the Bishop Museum, additional library research was undertaken. Special permission was granted for study of the tapa collection at the Bishop Museum.

To illustrate my work I will state some of the hypotheses and give some of the findings.

Hypothesis: The present-day designs will reflect some of the cultural changes that have occurred within the cultures studied.

The meaning of the designs was determined by questioning those who made or make the tapa or who know about the designs. The explanations were sufficient for some of the designs, but for others the history and cultural background were studied in the literature and the museums to determine if the designs had been inspired by specific incidents. Since symbolism is related to meaning, the information was further studied to determine whether symbolism existed.

Following are a few examples of evidence that I found in support of this hypothesis. A wreath of chestnut leaves either surrounding the crown of Tonga or used separately represents the wreath of ifi leaves that an individual wore when he went before the king or chief to ask for forgiveness. It is symbolic of humility and submission.

The word "sisi" means a waistband made from sweet smelling flowers, seeds, leaves, and/or other materials. Some of these sisis are designed for specific chiefs, and some are also design elements of tapas called ngatus in Tonga. Often they are accompanied by a description in block letters telling whose sisi is depicted. It is a great compliment to a noble to have a kupesi or design tablet made with a design dedicated to him, and an even greater compliment to be presented a ngatu with his design on it.

Queen Salote of Tonga is said to have made the comment that the history of Tonga is recorded in its tapas and mats. Many of the designs on the Tongan tapas today are graphic and pictorial rather than geometric. Queen Salote gave to the museum of Tuloa College one design tablet that shows the first bandstand for the first brass band in Tonga. Another design tablet noted by Koch depicts the airplane that the Tongans purchased and gave to England during the Second World War.

Not only do the tapas record the history and the culture, but frequently the area where the ngatu was made can be determined by the designs. The kupesi makers use the famous landmarks in their area as inspiration for their design tablets. Thus, those tapas from Houma depict the blowholes, those from Kolovai show the sacred bats that live only in that area, and those from Haketa picture the Ha'amonga.

In Fiji some of the older designs were identified by the designs shown on an 1840 tapa in the Fiji Museum. One design is that of a cannibal fork used to eat human flesh. Usually the Fijian ate with his fingers, but human flesh he ate with a fork, the only eating utensil he had.

Designs influenced by the ships and the early missionaries are those taken from the ship's compass and from the lace on the dresses of the wives of the early missionaries. Some of the newer tapas are being designed with such items as a Fijian bure (house), a shell, or a turtle in the center of a cloth with paintings of traditional Fijian designs around the edge. It is thought these changes are being instituted for greater salability of the bark cloth to the tourists. Newer designs are inspired by such things as the tread on the tires of trucks and cars imported into Fiji, razor blades, clothes pegs, barbed wire, and rabbit ears.

Tovey says that it is probable that some of the bark cloth designs in Samoa came from tattoo designs. Taylor states that many of the geometric designs on bark cloth from Samoa as well as most of the other Polynesian islands have been shown to originate from weaving, plaiting, and decorative sennit lashing on houses, canoes, and other places where lashing is used. Occasionally these were copied so carefully that the irregularities in the plaiting appeared in the designs on the bark cloth.

In summary, Tongan and Fijian bark cloth designs definitely reflect some of the cultural changes that have occurred, while Samoan bark cloth is less changed. The designs used on the small amount of tapa made in Hawaii today are definitely traditional. No designed bark cloth is made in Tahiti today.

Hypothesis: Tapa for ceremonial purposes and costumes for holidays will be used after the use of tapa for other functions has ceased.

A questionnaire was given to representatives from various social strata in each area to determine the purposes for which tapa is still used. I attended as many festivals, ceremonials, or holidays as time permitted. Written accounts of such occasions over the past several years were read to supplement the firsthand information.

In Hawaii, where tapa is a very precious item and is either treasured as a family heirloom or stored in the Bishop Museum, very little if any real tapa is used for costumes for ceremonial occasions. One person reported that tapa costumes had been used one time to her knowledge, but this was the only report of this kind from all those questioned. However, woven fabrics with stenciled or printed tapa patterns are used for costumes for such occasions as Aloha Week and Kamehameha Days, in school pageants, and other ceremonies.

In the three countries where tapa is still made, the findings are quite different. Every respondent in Fiji mentioned that tapa still was used at ceremonial occasions. A dance troupe that appears at the Grand Pacific Hotel each Saturday night wears bark cloth costumes. When the Duke and Duchess of Kent visited Fiji after the coronation in Tonga, they were honored with the traditional presentation of the tabua (whale's tooth) and yaqona (kava) ceremony. All participants were dressed in traditional costumes, and all those who danced were costumed in bark cloth. This was also true of Queen Elizabeth's visit in December, 1953.

The Tui Naiau was one of the paramount chiefs of Fiji. When he died all of the people of the Lau Islands dressed in black for six months, and the family wore black for a year. For such an important person, the people from all over the Lau Islands, and from many of the other areas of Fiji, came bringing ceremonial gifts of bark cloth, food, tabua, tins of kerosene, and other goods of value. A statue representing the deceased constructed of sennit, which is coconut fiber braided into rope, was erected and draped in bark cloth, and the gifts were laid in front of the statue. There were traditional feasts presented by the family of the deceased, and gifts of bark cloth, and other goods were presented to those who came to celebrate the lifting of mourning.

Hypothesis: Clothing has been used to designate specific social roles such as age, sex, and religion.

An interview questionnaire was given to representatives from various social strata in each area studied. Questions concerning the use of clothing, design, and color on tapa to express social roles of age, sex, and religion were included in the questionnaire. Written references were used to supplement the answers to the questionnaire or to find answers not available from respondents.

The relationship of wealth to quantity is illustrated by a chief in Fiji shown wearing 600 feet of bark cloth (Ciba Review, 1940) and Kamamalu, one of the Hawaiian queens, rolled up in 70 thicknesses of tapa. She actually lay down on the ground and rolled to wind this amount of tapa around her, and did the same in reverse to undress.

Since no books are available on the clothing of the different areas of Fiji, I had to obtain as much information as possible and compare it with the references from early explorers, missionaries, and traders.

Nowhere is the divergence in costume more obvious than in the clothing that could be worn only by the chief. The chief received the best tapa that was made; only the chiefs were able to wear the smoked bark cloth. Williams says the dress of Fijian men was white, brown, or figured tapa, from 3 to 100 yards in length. After the sulu or skirt of bark cloth came the sash or thin white or brown masi several yards long, which was tied in a bow below the waist in the back. Then came the train of the thinnest and whitest masi, which girded the loins with a sufficient length to trail behind. In Bau only the chief could use the train. Everyone stayed away from this train, for to step on it or touch it meant certain death. The length of the loin cloth in the front was sometimes very inconvenient for walking, and so was thrown over the shoulder to get it out of the way. Although not reported anywhere, this may have evolved to the use of the diagonal strip of masi used to denote chiefly rank today.

Ratu Kini Dimuri indicates that the present costume worn by the servers of the yaqona ceremony is similar to the costume worn by the warriors in the past, particularly when black is used around the eyes, on the face, and on the body of the yaqona server.

In Lau, when a couple were married the man went several times to the woman's house wrapped in bark cloth and mats, took them off and left them for the family of the bride. The bride did likewise to the groom's family. Whenever possible, only Fijian masi kesas were used because the Fijians felt that they were more noble. It may be from this custom that the present costumes of the bride and groom were evolved.

In summary, the main prerequisite of this type of research was careful preplanning and then adaptability to the situation at hand.

It was found that the countries with the least amount of contact with the rest of the world had the greatest amount of change of design; the design change obviously reflecting the contact. The areas with the greatest amount of world contact appeared to have the least design change, but the production of tapa had diminished.

Tapa was used for ceremonial occasions after its use for other functions had ceased. It was used, along with other items, to denote the rank and the status of social position and was used extensively in rites of passage. Those items of attire which took the longest to produce or were the least in supply and the greatest in demand were the items used to denote the highest social positions in the status systems. In areas where the colors of the tapa had been more extensively developed, color was used with other items to denote the differences in status. In other areas, designs, the quantity of tapa worn, and the way the garments were worn denoted the status. Tapa in the past was used in much the same way as woven fabric would be used today and for many of the same uses.

ANALYSIS OF FIELD STUDY EXAMPLE

Bark Cloth or Tapa: Its Past and Present-Day Uses in Selected Areas of the Pacific as Related to Social Change

In Christensen's field study, she followed the steps suggested in this chapter for conducting a field study.

Objective. As indicated previously, the major objective of a field study is "a respect for cultural context." That the objectives of Christensen's study followed this pattern is evidenced by the following six objectives which were given in Chapter 1 of her dissertation.

To determine whether or not:

1. The making of bark cloth or tapa is related to the social and economic changes which have occurred in the islands of the Pacific area.

2. The social and economic changes have had any influence on the symbolism of the designs and colors used on the bark cloth.

3. The amount of contact with other countries has influenced the amount of tapa made and the designs and colors used.

4. The original tapa designs printed on fabrics imported into the selected countries would be more readily sold than designs not indigenous to their area.

5. Any specific functions for tapa outlive others, and which functions are still prevalent in the different areas of the Pacific area being studied.

6. The designs and colors used on tapa designate specific social functions such as age, sex, social status, or religious, social, or service functions.

The Scouting Expedition (in this case, a pilot study). Before traveling to the Pacific islands for the actual field study, Christensen did some exploratory work in this country. Based upon her readings and former experiences with Polynesian people, she designed a questionnaire and conducted a pilot study with subjects who had spent a year or more in different areas of the Pacific in which the final study was to be conducted, or who were indigenous to those areas.

A list of possible informants was also started at this stage of the investigation.

Based upon the pilot study, the questionnaire was restructured and an answer sheet developed.

Research Design and Methods of Data Collection. Prior to and in conjunction with the field research, library surveys were conducted and museums visited. Photographs were taken of many of the tapa displays. Documents were searched for statistics bearing on the research. Observations and direct interviews were conducted in the field. A camera and tape recorder were taken on the research trip.

Among the hypotheses included in the dissertation were:

1. The present-day designs will reflect some of the cultural changes that have occurred within the cultures studied.

2. Tapa for ceremonial purposes and costumes for holidays will be used after the use of tapa for other functions has ceased.

3. Clothing has been used to designate specific social roles such as age, sex, and religion.

Full Scale Field Study. Emphasis has been placed upon the need for gaining group support and establishing personal relationships with subjects in a field study.

Since Christensen had personal contacts on the islands, she lived with friends in most areas. Language was a problem in conducting interviews, however, so translators had to be used.

People in the Fiji Broadcasting System and the Fijian Affairs Board, etc., assisted in gaining support of groups to interview on the islands.

Data Analysis. Voluminous data were collected in this study. They were analyzed in relation to the original hypotheses. See Christensen's doctoral dissertation or her research article analyzed here for evidence presented in support of hypotheses.

THE FAMILY AS ENVIRONMENT FOR EDUCABILITY IN COSTA RICA

GEORGIANNE BAKER, BEATRICE PAOLUCCI

Organizing resources for goal achievement is a process examined in home management as well as in many social science areas concerned with education, change, and development. This capacity for arranging means to meet needs, when it operates within the family where the ends sought affect individual growth and potential, may play a significant intervening role in societal change. Hagen suggested that, viewed over long periods of time, families in their managerial-developmental capacities may add impulse or impediment to national social and economic goals (1). For this reason there is need for increased scientific understanding and prediction of, and application of knowledge about, resource organization at the family level in both developing countries and among subcultural groups in industrialized countries.

Home management focuses on how families organize resources to mediate values and attain specific goals. It

> ... deals with husbanding resources so that the more intangible as well as tangible goals of the family are reached. Recognition that child-rearing practices result in different personality types and that possibilities for growth are enhanced if one acquires skills, knowledge, and attitudes valued by a particular culture, obligates adults to so arrange the home environment for children that it offers the best chances for optimum growth (2).

The authors focus on this orientation in an area of wide concern, that of family environmental influences upon children's successful participation in the education system. The family is viewed as an environment that can be managed to shape the development of individuals. According to Bloom,

> Variations in the environment have greatest quantitative effect on a characteristic at its most rapid period of change and least effect on the characteristic during the least rapid period of change (3).

Following this thesis, the family might be considered as an environment which represents a set of powerful persisting forces affecting a human characteristic, such as the child's educability (4, 5) which is undergoing rapid development at a particular period, in this case at the preschool age. Then, located within the home, the neighborhood, and the community in which the young child carries out his activities would be found the resources or means for helping him to learn new concepts or discriminations preparatory to school experience. Operationally the environment would be bounded by the child's direct and indirect involvement with these resources, whether they be persons, activities, or objects.

Reprinted with permission from *Journal of Home Economics*, Vol. 63, pp. 161-167, March, 1971. Copyright by the American Home Economics Association, Washington, D.C.

This theoretic orientation combines a managerial and developmental point of view in support of the philosophy that optimal human development should be the criterion for family management and that individual family members actively participate in family managerial efforts. When the family environment is unsupportive of human development, imaginative solutions may be required. However, in order to suggest action, increased ecological understanding of the "mutually sustaining relationships that couple man with his environment" (6) is needed. The purpose of the discussion which follows, based on recent research in Costa Rica (7), is to describe the resourcefulness of a family as it relates to a specific family and societal goal — educability of the preschool child.

First, terrain, socioeconomic conditions, and education in Costa Rica are described because of the importance of understanding the cultural and geographic space of the wider environment and therefore the constraints ultimately placed on family resource availability and use. Next, the Arias-Salazar family is introduced, and their resources are described in relation to activities of Oscar, a preschool child in the family.[1] These data are summarized into a profile of family resourcefulness to suggest a tentative descriptive tool for specifying family as environment for educability.

Geographic Location of Study Families

The Meseta Central of Costa Rica, where the 89 families who participated in the research[2] live, is a tropical valley 60 miles long and 30 miles wide. It is identified as the most important and most developed region of the country, although accounting for only one-tenth of the total land area. Heights above sea level range from 1900 to 6500 feet, and the valley is ringed by mountains and volcanic peaks. It is a productive agricultural zone with large and small farms producing principally coffee and sugar cane but also milk, beans, corn, vegetables, and fruits (8).

As the most densely populated region of the country, it contains seven-tenths of the total population. San José, the capital, has about 71 per cent of the urban population (9). Some 40 per cent of San José's citizens have been estimated to be middle class, with the rural middle class of the Meseta probably not more than 1 to 3 per cent of the population (10). In this valley are relatively few isolated communities; however, in rural areas the roads are dirt and difficult to traverse by ordinary means of transportation, especially in the rainy season.

Socioeconomic Conditions

The country is the fourth smallest Latin American nation in territory, and second smallest in population, with about one and three-fourths million people.

---

[1] Names used in this study are fictitious.

[2] Families were selected from among those who participated in a 1966 nutrition survey conducted under the leadership of the Institute of Nutrition for Central America and Panama in Guatemala City, Guatemala. This 1966 research was supported by the Advanced Research Projects Agency (Project AGILE) and was monitored by the Nutrition Section, Office of International Research, National Institutes of Health, under ARPA Order No. 580, Program Plan No. 298.

Ethnic composition is about 97 per cent white or mixed, about 2 per cent Negro, and less than 1 per cent Indian (11). Population has been increasing in recent years at an annual rate of about 3.6 per cent, among the highest rates in the world. The death rate is relatively low and life expectancy high. Urban communities (2000 persons or more) account for one-third of the people, and these centers are growing at a yearly rate more than twice that of rural areas (12). As early as 1950, 22 per cent of the population was estimated as middle class (13). Income per capita has been higher than in the rest of Central America; in 1960 it was $341, increasing to $385 by 1968 (14).

Agriculture is the most important part of the economy; however, industrial growth is being encouraged by market developments both within and without the Central American common market area. Almost half of the economically active population works in agriculture. With a government traditionally sensitive to farm problems, Costa Rica has undertaken legislation and programs to develop this sector. However, until very recently the majority of farm land was devoted to subsistence needs (9).

Education: A National Goal

In Latin America education is considered a crucial element of economic and social development and nation-building. The individual perceives education as the surest means to personal advancement (15). Costa Rica's basic education code reflects the idea that all persons have the right to an education, and the state is obligated to provide it in an adequate manner (16). To stimulate and guide personality development of children, to provide basic knowledge and activities which favor intellectual development and habits needed to act efficiently in society, and to instill abilities to live healthfully, to view the universe rationally, to prepare for work, to appreciate and create beauty, and to cultivate Christian customs are stated goals of primary education. Parents are responsible by law to cooperate. The schools, in turn, must provide the opportunity to link families with the education process. Among other obligations, parents must be concerned about children's conduct in and out of school and try to create adequate home conditions for their development.

A 1965 study indicated the Costa Ricans place high confidence in formal education institutions (17). Their perceptions of the future are favorable and relevant to modernity in that they have high educational aspirations for their children (47% hoped for university-level achievement) and they are optimistic about reaching these aspirations. Children 5 to 14 years of age make up 20 per cent of the population, and in 1968 80 per cent of them were in school. In that year the government, which gives high financial priority to education, allocated 30 per cent of total national expenditures to education (9).

The Arias-Salazar Family and Resources for Oscar's Educability

The head of the family, José Alberto, his wife, Clara Luz, and their children live in an agricultural workers' community on a large coffee finca, or farm, an hour's bus ride from San José. It is a mixed occupation family. José Alberto works as a jornalero, or contracted day laborer, on the farm; his son Manuel works with him. Another son, Rafael, works in a factory in town. Other children contribute to family income by working during coffee harvest. In a recent year total family income was $1000; with 14 members at home then income amounted to about $75 per person for the year.

José Alberto never attended school; Clara Luz completed one year. Of the older children, Rafael finished six years of primary school on the farm where they live. Although the family has relatives on the same and other nearby farms, they do not see them very often. There is a new baby in the family; also three children in the three-to-six-year-old preschool category (another who would have been in this age group died recently). Oscar, the child selected for purposes of the study, is four and a half years of age.

Space, Child's Movement, Care, and Appearance. The family lives in one of a row of workers' homes. There are seven "rooms," including a covered front porch and large covered patio, both with cement floors, and complete bath attached to the house. Oscar has his own bed in a bedroom where his parents and four others sleep in two beds. Six other children sleep in the other bedroom and two others sleep in the living room. The long kitchen across the back of the house contains running water at the sink, a wood-burning stove, several benches and tables where the children do homework after school, clotheslines, a cabinet for dishes, a radio, and a large two-wheel bicycle. The four windows all have glass and curtains, and there is an electric light bulb in each room.

Oscar is free to move in and about the home and neighborhood with safety and supervision. He can play on all sides of the house or at a friend's house. The street in front presents no dangers because it is a private road inside the farm; there is little traffic and the drivers are careful. By himself, Oscar can go only as far as the store a block away, but older brothers take him bicycle riding or by bus to neighboring towns.

Oscar does not drink milk, and he eats meat perhaps one to three times per week, usually in soup. He eats fruits and vegetables about once a week. His daily meals are usually rice and beans at 11 a.m. and soup at 6 p.m. He has sweetened coffee early in the morning and again at 2 p.m. He wears the same clothes day and night (short pants, undershirt, worn shirt, and no shoes). His clothes are changed if someone gives him other clothes to wear; if he is very soiled one of his sisters will wash his clothes. His mother also wears the same clothes every day, sometimes with shoes, but changes her apron. An older sister bathes the child about twice a week and washes him if he is soiled or is going somewhere. Oscar does not brush his teeth. He regularly sleeps well at night for about 11 hours.

Child's Play, Work, and Learning; Family Learning. The child likes very much to play with small cars, making roads of mud and pieces of wood. He also plays house with the other children, using their dishes and play stove, pretending that he is papa. Indoors he usually cuts out pictures of cars from old magazines. Oscar can eat, wash, and dress by himself, although he may put on clothes backwards. Clara Luz helps him dress, and a sister finishes the washing. He may go with José Alberto or an older brother to carry firewood, but doesn't do any other tasks.

When he sees the older children doing their homework he tries to write and count. He looks for cars in magazines almost every afternoon when it is raining and he cannot go outside. No one reads to him, but he listens to music on the radio every day and often goes to see television at a neighbor's, and at the farm store every Sunday.

One of Oscar's older sisters reads novels if a friend sends one to her, but she receives a book less often than monthly. Some of the older children like the stories on radio or television during the week. Some went once to the museum with their school classes. José Alberto and two of his older sons went once about six years ago to a coast town. Clara Luz only goes to San José if one of the children becomes sick and needs hospital care.

Child's and Family's Contacts. Oscar spends his days with smaller children and those of his own age. He has no contacts with adults who are not family members, and he rarely participates in any large group activities. José Alberto and the older children go to church on Sunday. The older ones like to visit their friends, and Clara Luz has friends who come to see her almost every day. At present they have no other community contacts or participation not related to the church, and none with extended family kin.

Clara Luz's comments revealed a perception that Oscar's opportunities for social contacts and his involvement with play and learning objects and activities could influence his later successful or nonsuccessful participation in school. She perceives little, no, or negative relationship between other resources and activities (such as tasks, physical care, and appearance) and his educability, or preparation for school.

Conceptual Framework

In presenting evidence of the resourcefulness of the Arias-Salazar family, three groupings of resources were used. Each group contained resources considered necessary to operationalize one or another of three environmental properties of importance relative to educability at the preschool age (18, 19). These properties are (a) *physical-spatial constriction* which refers to crowding, restriction on mobility, problems of regularity of physical routines, and variety in these elements and their use, all or any of which might interfere with either learning and attention, or activity and manipulative experiences of a child like Oscar; (b) cognitive *stimulation* which refers to preparatory experiences and skills for later learning (problem-solving tasks, dramatic play, culturally relevant knowledge, adult guidance) and opportunities for listening, remembering, and copying on Oscar's part, or that of other family members; and (c) *interaction*, which in the social-emotional or interpersonal realm refers to general non-cognitive experiences and exchanges which would provide Oscar (or his family) with opportunities for attention, feedback, and encouragement from adults, older children, and peers.

Development of a preschool child is enhanced or impeded by these resources (objects, events, activities, or persons) within the child's home environment that are available and that might be used to achieve the goal of educability for him. Resource categories and the properties they operationalized are summarized below.

RESOURCE CATEGORIES	PROPERTIES
Space, child's movement, care and appearance	Constriction
Child's play, child's task and work, child's learning, family learning	Stimulation
Child's contacts, family contacts	Interaction

Seven of the nine resource categories pertain to the child himself; two (family learning and family contacts) pertain to other family members, following a distinction discussed by Wolf who suggested dividing environment into *specific* forces affecting a particular individual (in this example, Oscar) and more *pervasive* forces affecting all persons within it (20).

The level of relation of each resource category to the goal of educability was determined by scoring the resource data on each dimension of resourcefulness: (a) availability-quantity, (b) availability-quality, (c) use-quantity, and (d) use-quality. Scores were translated into comparable ratings. These ratings ranged from a high of 8 to a low of 0. A high rating, 6 to 8, indicated that the resource category was highly related and directed toward the goal of educability; a middle rating, 3 to 5, indicated intermediate relation and direction; a low rating, 0 to 2, indicated low relationship and direction (21). A profile showing the level of relation of resources to the goal of educability is shown in the accompanying figure.

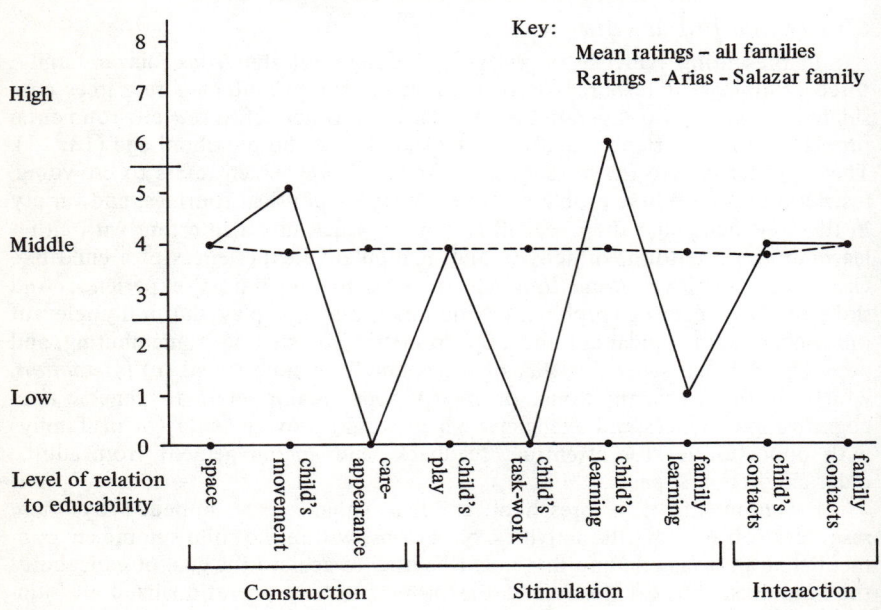

Profile of family resourcefulness for educability

RESOURCES

Discussion

The Arias-Salazar family, with a *high range* of ratings, from 0 to 6, and an *average total* rating of 28 (computed by summing all ratings), is representative of 43 per cent of the sample families. Peaks and troughs in the profile illustrate consistency, or lack of it, among the resource ratings. Three resources fall in the area of low relation to educability, five in the middle area, and one in the top area. The rating is lowest for care and appearance, and task and work, and highest for the child's learning resources category. Two environmental properties, constriction and stimulation, appear most affected by high inconsistency. Only the social interaction property, indicated by ratings on child and family contacts, presents an appearance of consistency, even though only the middle level of relation to educability is reached.

That there is physical constriction present in Oscar's environment is evident from the extreme rating (compared with other families of the sample) on care and appearance. Lack of stimulation is suggested in the extreme rating (again compared to other families) for doing things for himself and helping with little tasks at home. Influencing factors might be found in the pattern of family characteristics; for example, rural residence and very low family income and educational attainment of Oscar's parents. Others might be family size or number of similar-age siblings. It could be hypothesized that Oscar experiences competition with others for limited resources because of this particular pattern of family status and structure constraints. One result of such competition could be nonspecific, diffused attention (or nonattention) to such a nontraditional goal as educability which, after all, does not give Oscar's family immediate recognizable rewards.

In some ways, Oscar fares better than other children of the sample. He experiences only moderate physical constriction as far as household space and his own movements are concerned. He also experiences moderate amounts of stimulation through play, and social interaction through contacts with others. The profile suggests that Oscar's family environment for educability varies from low to moderately powerful and pervasive, in Bloom's terms, in its possible consequences for educability (22). The pattern of resources is shown to be neither completely supportive nor consistently negative in relation to the suggested goal.

Environmental effects upon the child might possibly be controlled or at least mediated by improvement in family status levels, by direct efforts in relation to low and moderately rated resource categories, or by efforts with Oscar himself but totally outside of the family, or by a combination of methods. Status characteristics of most influence, and possibly amenable to alteration, might be parental education or family income. Some resources could be examined for change possibilities, such as care and appearance for physical constriction, and either task and work or family learning for stimulation.

Even though education is a strong societal goal in Costa Rica, the level of attainment may be problematical due to such factors as population pressures, terrain, and competition for economic funds. The goal and the constraints are reflected at the family level, when family is viewed as environment for educability. Sussman suggests that cooperation, or reciprocity between family and society, ought to be the guiding principle for these linkages to be mutually reinforcing (23). Intervention, change, or education is probably needed at all levels and between levels — societal, family, and individual. If educability is a viable part of an important societal goal in a country like Costa Rica, then perhaps efforts in relation to it should be explored by national education planners, teachers, and extension workers. Further study could uncover some guidelines for action programs aimed at development of managerial competence of family members, especially in relation to guiding educability within the family. An outcome of this type would benefit families and the society.

REFERENCES

1. Hagen, E.E. *On the Theory of Social Change: How Economic Growth Begins.* Homewood, Illinois: The Dorsey Press, 1962.

2. Paolucci, B. Home Management Education. Paper presented at Fourteenth International Conference of the Family, International Union of Family Organizations, Rio de Janeiro, Brazil, July 1963, pp. 5-6 (Mimeographed).

3. Bloom, B.S. *Stability and Change in Human Characteristics.* New York: John Wiley and Sons, Inc., 1964, p. vii.

4. Hess, R.D., Shipman, V.C., and Jackson, D. Early experience and the socialization of cognitive modes in children. *Child Devel.*, Vol. 36, No. 4 (Dec. 1965), pp. 869-886.

5. Hess, R.D., Shipman, V.C., Brophy, J.E., and Bear, R.M. *The Cognitive Environments of Urban Preschool Children.* Chicago: Graduate School of Education, University of Chicago, 1968.

6. Hook, N.C., and Paolucci, B. The family as an ecosystem. *J. Home Econ.*, Vol. 62, No. 5 (May 1970), p. 315.

7. Baker, G.R. Patterning of Family Resources for Educability: Conceptualization and Measurement in Costa Rican Families. Unpublished Ph.D. dissertation, Michigan State University, 1970.

8. Lombardo, H.A. Analisis de una Economia Agricola dentro de la Meseta Central de Costa Rica. Serie Planeamiento No. 4. San José, Costa Rica: Instituto Interamericano de Ciencias Agricolas de la OEA, 1965, p. 15.

9. Inter-American Development Bank. Social Progress Trust Fund Eighth Annual Report. *Socio-Economic Progress in Latin America.* Washington, D.C.: Inter-American Development Bank, 1968, pp. 125-136.

10. Williamson, R.C. Some variables of middle and lower class in two Central American cities. *Soc. Forces*, Vol. 41 (Dec. 1962), p. 196.

11. Roy, P., Waisanen, F.B., and Rogers, E.M. *The Impact of Communication on Rural Development.* Paris: UNESCO, and India: National Institute of Community Development, 1969, pp. 19-20.

12. Inter-American Committee for Agricultural Development. *Inventario de la Información Basica para la Programación del Desarrollo Agricola en la América Latina: Centroamérica.* Washington, D.C.: Pan American Union, 1965, pp. 51-59.

13. United Nations, Economic Commission for Latin America. *Education, Human Resources and Development in Latin America.* New York: United Nations (E/CN.12/800), 1968, p. 108.

14. International Monetary Fund. Statistics Bureau. *International Financial Statistics.* Vol. 23 (May 1970), p. 92.

15. Céspedes, F.S. The Contemporary Educational Scene in Latin America. Report of Eastern Regional Conference of Comparative Education Society. Challenges and Achievements of Education in Latin America. Pan American Union, Washington, D.C., May 7-9, 1964, p. 42.

16. Chacón Jinesta, O. *Codigo de Educación: Leyes Anexas y Ley Fundamentals de Educación.* San José, Costa Rica: Imprenta Trejos Hermanos, 1965, pp. 313-336.

17. Waisanen, F.B., and Durlak, J.A. *Estudio sobre Actitudes hacia la Dinamica de Población.* Programa Inter-Americano de Información Popular. San José, Costa Rica: American International Association for Economic and Social Development, 1966.

18. Hess, R.D., and Baer, R.M. (Editors). *Early Education: Current Theory, Research, and Practice.* Chicago: Aldine Publishing Company, 1968.

19. Grotberg, E. (Editor). *Proceedings of Research Seminars: Critical Issues in Research Related to Disadvantaged Children.* Office of Economic Opportunity, Washington, D.C., 1968-69. Princeton, New Jersey: Educational Testing Service, 1969.

20. Wolf, R.M. The Identification and Measurement of Environmental Process Variables Related to Intelligence. Unpublished Ph.D. dissertation, University of Chicago, 1963.

21. Baker, *op. cit.*, pp. 218-251.

22. Bloom, *op. cit.*, pp. 194-195, 211-212.

23. Sussman, M.B. Some Conceptual Issues in Family-Organizational Linkages. Paper presented at family bureaucracy session, 64th meeting of the American Sociological Association, San Francisco, California, November 1969.

ANALYSIS OF FIELD STUDY EXAMPLE

The Family as Environment for Educability in Costa Rica

This research article presents a case study of an individual family in the context of a particular region in Costa Rica and of the larger republic.

Eighty-nine families participated in the research project from which the case study was drawn. The 89 families were selected from among those who participated in a nutrition survey in that country.

Referring to the criteria for the case history outlined on page 161, it can be noted that Baker and Paolucci's research singles out a subject (Oscar in the Arias-Salazar family) for individual study but regards him as a member of a cultural group. Community values, standards, and way of life are studied through the life history of Oscar. The data about Oscar and his family are organized to describe the resourcefulness of a family as it relates to a specific family and societal goal — educability of the preschool child.

Three groupings of family resources considered of importance relative to educability at the preschool age were used in presenting evidence of the resourcefulness of the Arias-Salazar family: physical-spatial constriction, cognitive stimulation, and social interaction. Quantitative ratings for each of these resources were computed for the Arias-Salazar family in relation to all families in the study. Results showed the presence of physical constriction in Oscar's environment as evidenced by the extreme rating on care and appearance of his family compared to other families in the sample. In other aspects of the environment, Oscar fared better than children in other families. "The profile suggests that Oscar's family environment for educability varies from low to moderately powerful and pervasive, in Bloom's terms, in its possible consequences for educability."

PART **III**

Sampling and Measurement

R*esearch usually involves selection of a sample to represent a larger group of people or objects. The ability to generalize from the sample to the total population depends on the quality of the sample. Various sampling techniques are discussed in this section, with particular emphasis being given to random sampling in which each element of the population has an equal opportunity to be selected.*

In addition to good research design, the quality of research depends on the adequacy of the measurement procedures used. "In its broadest sense measurement is the assignment of numerals to objects or events according to rules." (Stevens, 1951, p. 1) Measurement procedures comprise the "working or operational definitions" of the concepts being used in a study. Therefore, specification of what is to be measured and the sample to be measured are prerequisites to deciding how to measure. In an ideal measuring situation, all the differences in scores among individuals would be due to their differences in the characteristics being measured and these measurements would be dependable or reliable.

CHAPTER 9

Sampling

"Population" refers to a specified group of individuals or objects having a common, measurable characteristic. These characteristics could include events, test items, objects, attributes, or fabrics, as well as human beings. Often a population is too extensive to be enumerated. Even if it were possible to identify each of its elements, to study a whole population might be very costly and time-consuming. Therefore, most studies are based on a sample, or a portion of the population. When a sample is a good one, it is representative of the population and certain things can be predicted about the population from which it was drawn. This is known as statistical inference.

BENEFITS OF SAMPLING

Parten discussed the following advantages of sampling:

1. An estimate of the characteristics of the total population can be secured in a much shorter time than would be possible otherwise. In certain types of studies the time-saving is particularly helpful in making possible the analysis of data before they become outdated.

2. Properly designed samples may reduce the cost of a study by requiring fewer persons to gather and process the data and by reducing the necessary space and equipment.

3. The money saved by sampling can be used to study the same cases more intensively, extend the study to other groups, or repeat the study in the same area at a later time.

4. More attention can be given to each return, thus increasing the accuracy of analysis and trustworthiness of the results. (Parten, 1950, pp. 109-110)

PRINCIPLES IN DESIGNING A SAMPLE

Sample design is concerned with determining which elements of the population to study. Several questions must be answered prior to selecting the individuals:

1.   What is the *purpose* of the study? Sampling is no problem if the purpose is to study a particular class in Sun Valley School or a group of residents in the Sunnyvale housing tract. On the other hand, if the purpose is to generalize and determine a procedure suitable to apply with a larger group, sampling is important. Many statistical techniques assume a random sample was used as a basis for testing the significance of results.

2.   What is the *population* to be studied? A researcher may define his population as a fairly small group which can be studied in its entirety. Or, he may wish to sample a population such as the customers of a given store to determine their attitudes toward shopping in that store. On a still larger basis, he may be interested in the acceptability of a particular food product used nationwide.

3.   Is a complete list of the *individual elements* of the population available?

4.   What *type of sampling* will be most appropriate? Various types are discussed later in this chapter.

5.   What *size sample* is desired? Further details on size are presented in the following section.

6.   Is the plan *economically feasible*? Sample design requires a blending of sample theory with the resources available. How widely scattered is the population? What means of communication will be used? Will highly trained field workers be gathering the data? Do the administrators of cooperating programs understand research methodology?

SAMPLE SIZE

Other things being equal, large samples are more accurate than small samples. Therefore, it is advisable to use as large a sample as is practical. However, a sample representative of its population is more important than the size of the sample.

Ideally, a sample is a replica of the population. In reality, each sample drawn differs from other possible samples and from the population. Imagine drawing sample after sample. As the number of samples increases, the characteristics of the distribution of those samples resemble a normal curve. The mean (arithmetical average) of this distribution of sampling estimates should be very close to the actual mean of the whole population.

To illustrate the importance of sample size in terms of representation, Table 1 shows 10 sets of two IQs selected at random (using a table of random numbers) from a population of 293 IQs. Note that the means of each of the 10 sets of IQs range from 84.5 to 108.5, or 24.0 IQ points. The mean (or average of the means) for the total of 20 scores is 93.5. The mean of the entire population of 293 IQs was 95.0. Thus, with very small samples, *one* mean is undependable as an estimate of the population value.

TABLE 1. SAMPLES (n=2) OF IQs FROM A POPULATION OF 293 IQs OF FOURTH-GRADE CHILDREN

				Samples					
117	85	84	92	83	82	83	96	93	101
75	84	107	103	87	96	100	121	103	79
Mean: 96.0	84.5	95.5	97.5	85.0	89.0	91.5	108.5	98.0	90.0

Total mean = 93.55

Table 4.5, p. 62, from *Foundations of Behavioral Research Inquiry* by Fred N. Kerlinger. Copyright (©) 1964 by Holt, Rinehart and Winston, Inc. Reprinted by permission of Holt, Rinehart and Winston, Inc.

If the population is homogeneous, there is less tendency for samples to vary from the population than when samples are drawn from heterogeneous groups. For example, a sample of 10 interior designers may be representative of a population of interior designers employed in a small city. However, a sample of 10 artists probably would not be representative of all the various fields in which artists are employed in that same city. For a given degree of precision then, a smaller number of cases is required from a homogeneous than from a heterogeneous group.

Slonin summarized the factors that determine the sample size required: "degree of precision desired, variability of the data being sampled, sampling method used, and estimating procedure employed." (Slonin, 1960, p. 72)

Parten showed ways of computing necessary sample size and permissible errors of tolerance in sampling. (Parten, 1950, pp. 304-309) Usually it is desirable to determine the size of sample necessary and then draw a slightly larger one to allow a margin of safety. Riley cautioned that:

> *Bias is not affected by the sample size.* Large samples are no more successful than small samples in (1) overcoming distortion in the designation of the frame . . ., (2) offsetting the tendency of interviewers (if left to their own devices) to select only certain types of respondents, or (3) counteracting the greater readiness of certain respondents to reply (if respondents are allowed to select themselves). (Riley, 1963, p. 291)

At some point the statistical advantages of a larger sample must be weighed against the additional costs of gathering data. A larger sample is necessary when the population is to be divided into subgroups for a comparison of various characteristics. Also, a larger sample helps to ensure that uncontrolled variables will be operating randomly. On the other hand, a depth study of a small sample might make a greater contribution than a shallow study of a larger group. When time-consuming techniques (such as depth interviews and projective tests) are employed, a small sample is probably more feasible.

One of the major problems confronting a researcher is that of the non-respondent. He may draw a large, random sample but obtain a low percentage of response. In effect, the respondents are volunteers whose characteristics may differ from those of the nonrespondents. Perhaps they are more willing to reveal the kind of information requested (e.g., their income is high enough that they would not be embarrassed to reveal it). They may be more highly motivated toward achievement. Careful thought should be given to the questions to be asked in an effort to encourage a high percentage of response. If interviews are conducted, the time of day is important. Following up questionnaire nonrespondents and calling back to interview those who were not at home may help to make the sample more representative of the total population by eliciting a higher per cent of response.

TYPES OF SAMPLING

In general, sampling data in themselves are not very important. Their value lies in the information they yield about the total population. Sample design is concerned not only with the selection of a sample but also with the process of estimating population values. From this standpoint, probability sampling provides more meaningful data than nonprobability sampling.

Probability Sampling

Probability sampling means that every member of a population has an equal probability or chance of being selected as a sample of that population. Therefore, probability sampling provides the greatest insurance that a sample is representative of the population or universe from which it is taken — that the sample values do not differ more than a certain amount from the true population values.

Simple Random Sampling. This type of sampling is the basic probability sampling design. Through this technique, each element or item in the total population (whether the population consists of consumers, bread, children, or houses) has an equal probability or chance of being included as a sample of that population. To illustrate this *principle*, with an unrealistic number of cases for a study, assume that a simple random sample of two spools of thread is desired from a population of five spools of thread. Each of the five spools of thread could be labeled: 1, 2, 3, 4, 5. From this population there would be ten possible pairs of cases: 1-2, 1-3, 1-4, 1-5, 2-3, 2-4, 2-5, 3-4, 3-5, and 4-5. Write each of these combinations on a slip of paper, put the slips of paper in a hat, stir them thoroughly, and have someone select one blindly. The two numbers on the slip of paper selected, representing two of the five spools, constitute the simple random sample of spools. This same procedure could be repeated for a desired three samples. In both cases, the number of possible combinations would remain the same.

This same principle could be applied to a population of any size, but think of the hours involved in "playing this game" of making all possible combinations for a large group. The method can be simplified by selecting each case individually with a list of random numbers, to be found in most statistics books (see Table 2). The first step in this procedure is to number all items in the population to be studied. If the population contained 100 spools of thread, a number would

TABLE 2. TABLE OF RANDOM NUMBERS (8,000 NUMBERS)

	1-4	5-8	9-12	13-16	17-20	21-24	25-28	29-32	33-36	37-40
					First Thousand					
1	23 15	75 48	59 01	83 72	59 93	76 24	97 08	86 95	23 03	67 44
2	05 54	55 50	43 10	53 74	35 08	90 61	18 37	44 10	96 22	13 43
3	14 87	16 03	50 32	40 43	62 23	50 05	10 03	22 11	54 38	08 34
4	38 97	67 49	51 94	05 17	58 53	78 80	59 01	94 32	42 87	16 95
5	97 31	26 17	18 99	75 53	08 70	94 25	12 58	41 54	88 21	05 13
6	11 74	26 93	81 44	33 93	08 72	32 79	73 31	18 22	64 70	68 50
7	43 36	12 88	59 11	01 64	56 23	93 00	90 04	99 43	64 07	40 36
8	93 80	62 04	78 38	26 80	44 91	55 75	11 89	32 58	47 55	25 71
9	49 54	01 31	81 08	42 98	41 87	69 53	82 96	61 77	73 80	95 27
10	36 76	87 26	33 37	94 82	15 69	41 95	96 86	70 45	27 48	38 80
11	07 09	25 23	92 24	62 71	26 07	06 55	84 53	44 67	33 84	53 20
12	43 31	00 10	81 44	86 38	03 07	52 55	51 61	48 89	74 29	46 47
13	61 57	00 63	60 06	17 36	37 75	63 14	89 51	23 35	01 74	69 93
14	31 35	28 37	99 10	77 91	89 41	31 57	97 64	48 62	58 48	69 19
15	57 04	88 65	26 27	79 59	36 82	90 52	95 65	46 35	06 53	22 54
16	09 24	34 42	00 68	72 10	71 37	30 72	97 57	56 09	29 82	76 50
17	97 95	53 50	18 40	89 48	83 29	52 23	08 25	21 22	53 26	15 87
18	93 73	25 95	70 43	78 19	88 85	56 67	16 68	26 95	99 64	45 69
19	72 62	11 12	25 00	92 26	82 64	35 66	65 94	34 71	68 75	18 67
20	61 02	07 44	18 45	37 12	07 94	95 91	73 78	66 99	53 61	93 78
21	97 83	98 54	74 33	05 59	17 18	45 47	35 41	44 22	03 42	30 00
22	89 16	09 71	92 22	23 29	06 37	35 05	54 54	89 88	43 81	63 61
23	25 96	68 82	20 62	87 17	92 65	02 82	35 28	62 84	91 95	48 83
24	81 44	33 17	19 05	04 95	48 06	74 69	00 75	67 65	01 71	65 45
25	11 32	25 49	32 42	36 23	43 86	08 62	49 76	67 42	24 52	32 45

be assigned to each of the spools. Then the table of random numbers would be entered at some random point. Whether to move horizontally or vertically from the entry point would be predetermined. The numbers which are touched as one moves in that direction are included in the sample until the selected size sample is obtained. Each number is chosen from the still unselected cases, thereby eliminating any number that appears on the list more than once. Through this process, each one of the 100 spools has an equal chance of being chosen as part of the sample. The selection is therefore random.

When properly carried out, a sufficiently large random sample is likely to be representative of the population. Systematic differences between the sample and population tend to cancel each other out. Statistical procedures have been developed for estimating the required sample size and for judging the reliability of data based upon sample estimates. It is relatively easy to obtain a random sample, since it is not necessary to have knowledge of the characteristics of the population that might be important to a particular study. Many of the statistics that are widely used, such as the mean, standard deviation, and analysis of variance, assume that a random sample was used.

Among the difficulties that may be encountered in selecting a random sample are:

1.   A complete listing of the universe may not be available.

2.   Duplications on the list of the population need to be eliminated (e.g., adults in a continuing education program may be enrolled in two or more courses).

3.   Selecting a large random sample may be a laborious task.

4.   The sample may be widely scattered geographically, increasing the costs of an interview study.

5.   A poor or misleading sample might be obtained. For example, the mean of a sample might differ significantly from the mean of the population. Fortunately, such deviations occur infrequently.

6.   A random sample may not provide sufficient cases for analyzing data from special subgroups.

Stratified Random Sampling. In stratified (or representative) sampling, the population is divided into subpopulations, called strata, and a simple random sample is selected within each strata. These subsamples are then joined to form the total sample. This method takes into account parts of the population which are known to be different before the sample is selected. If the differences between classes (e.g., between males and females) are large compared to variation within classes (e.g., among the males and among the females), stratification contributed to the efficiency of sampling.

Cities are often stratified into socioeconomic levels before a sample is selected from each strata. Other variables that are sometimes used include age and education. Each individual or unit can be placed in only one of the strata. If the characteristic used for the stratification is based upon the anticipated outcome of the study, one should be able to obtain greater accuracy with a smaller sample size than if the population were not stratified.

In *proportional* stratification, the characteristics of the sample are drawn in the same proportion as they are represented in the universe. For example, a study of teenagers enrolled in community recreation programs starts with separate lists of boys and girls. A 10 per cent sample, drawn at random from each group, would maintain the same proportion of girls as in the total population.

Disproportional stratification means that an equal number of cases is drawn from each subgroup regardless of the proportions in the population. For the type of study described in the preceding paragraph, the same number of boys and girls would be selected even though the population might have more girls than boys. The advantages of disproportional sampling lie primarily in the economy of gathering data from a small group and in the ease of comparing data when the subgroups are of equal size. In reality, some of the strata may have too few persons to provide even the minimum number needed for the sample, or some of those who were chosen may not respond. The result often is inequality in numbers. The sample then "has the combined disadvantages of unequal numbers of cases, smallness, and nonrepresentativeness." (Parten, 1950, p. 229)

Stratified sampling helps to insure the inclusion of each essential group in the sample. Another advantage is that it is not necessary to have a complete list of the population. When the population is homogeneous and the data for stratifying are accurate, greater precision may be achieved with fewer cases than would be possible with a random sample. A further advantage is that the statistics which are applicable to random samples may be applied when the individual cases selected for each strata have been chosen at random.

One of the possible difficulties that might be encountered is in choosing the strata significant to the study. It is important to know which factors to select as well as their relative frequency in the population. If a sample is to be stratified on several factors, it may be difficult to find enough cases to meet the specifications. Since cases are selected at random within each stratum, it is possible to obtain a poor representation.

Selltiz indicated that the:

> ... procedure of drawing a simple random sample and then dividing it into strata is equivalent to having drawn a *stratified* random sample using, as the sampling fraction within each stratum, the proportion of that stratum that turned up in our simple random sample. Thus, even though we were not in a position to stratify in advance, we can take advantage of the increased efficiency of stratified sampling. (Selltiz, 1959, p. 534)

Cluster Sampling. Sometimes groups are selected as the sampling unit because of reduced transportation costs and greater ease in identifying groups rather than individuals. When a complete listing of the population would be impossible, as in a study of the consumers who use a certain food product, cluster sampling might be used. This method consists of a sample within a sample, moving through a series of stages.

The term "cluster" is used with reference to various groups, such as schools, classes, households, work sections, and geographic areas. When this approach is used to select a sample of individuals who reside in a specific area, the method is called *area sampling*. For example, to survey a group of urban households, a sample may be taken of cities. A list of cities could be prepared and a simple or stratified random sample taken from the list. From each city selected, a random sample of districts could be taken, and within each selected district, a random sample of households.

A possible disadvantage of cluster sampling is that "natural stratification" might exist. Persons who live or work together might tend to be homogeneous in race, background, education, income, or other factors. To reduce the effects of other sources of differences when conducting an experiment, it is important for both experimental and control groups (or both forms of treatment) to be tested in each area or cluster that is used.

Systematic Sampling. When a complete list of the elements of a population is available, it may be easier to select a sample directly from that list rather than go through the process of numbering each item and drawing random numbers. Systematic or serial sampling can provide an equal opportunity for all units to be drawn if the first item is selected at random. This can be done by deciding what size sample is wanted, dividing the total number in the population by the desired sample size, and using this number as the basis for systematic selection. For example, if there are 400 schools from which to draw a systematic sample of 50 schools, eight is the size of the interval to be used. Start by drawing at random a number between one and eight, and use this as the first unit of the sample. Then continue, taking every eighth one on the list until the sample of 50 is completed.

How effective this sampling plan is depends on the type of list used. An alphabetical list probably is not random, since members of the same family and of certain ethnic groups may be clustered. If families are grouped by income and placed in rank order within each group, a sample that included families 1, 11, 21, etc., would have a higher income average than any other possible sample drawn from that group.

Nonprobability Sampling

In nonprobability sampling, there is no assurance that every element has an equal chance of being included.

Accidental Sampling. Accidental sampling consists of simply taking the cases that are available and continuing the process until a designated sample size is reached. The first 50 customers entering a store on a given day could be studied this way or a college professor could study the students in his classes. If one wishes to generalize to the larger population, he would have to assume that these customers are representative of all customers in the population being considered or that the college students represent college students in general. Otherwise, the conclusions would be limited to the 50 customers in the given store or to the students in these specific classes. The results would have narrower applications in such instances.

Quota Sampling. Through this method, one would sample elements of a population in the same proportions in which they occur in the population or have enough cases from each stratum to make an estimate of the proportion of each stratum in the total population.

If a population is known to have an equal number of males and females, the interviewers should sample equal numbers. If 10 per cent of a population of college professors are sixty years of age, then approximately 10 per cent of a sample representing the population of college professors should be sixty years of age or a correction for disproportions in the sample must be made.

This technique is widely used in opinion and attitude surveys. Interviewers must be carefully instructed as to what characteristics and in what proportion they should seek. Even with training, they may resort to easier methods such as selecting people who are gathered in one spot. Interviewers must have clear, simple, practical, and complete instructions as to how to fill the quotas.

Purposive Sampling. Purposive (or judgment) sampling is based on hand-picking the individual elements in keeping with one's needs. Judgment samples have an unknown possibility of error. As with other nonrandom methods of sampling, the usual procedures of statistical analysis are not applicable because the sample cannot be considered representative of any known population. Nevertheless, if good judgment is used in drawing a sample, useful information can be obtained about a group which may suggest significant problems and hypotheses for study with a more extended population from which generalizations can be made. Cornell listed several examples of purposive samples:

1. Sample of convenience, such as using a class that is handy.

2. Canvas of experts, such as mailing a questionnaire to carefully chosen, *informed* persons.

3. Sample based on an absolute list not adequately covering the population, such as a telephone directory for use in sampling the adult population of a city.

4. Sample with a high degree of nonresponse, which might be the result when a questionnaire is mailed to individuals.

5. Pinpoint or representative-area sampling, such as the purposive selection of a *typical* school, classroom, or community. (Cornell, 1960, pp. 1181-83)

This chapter can only sensitize students to some of the sampling problems. For further details and possible solutions, more comprehensive books should be consulted.

CHAPTER 10

Measurement

Measurement is a process of finding out *how much*. The first and very important step in measurement is to define the objectives — determine exactly *what* is to be measured. Another part of the measurement process is to decide *how* to do the measuring — to select or develop an instrument that will best perform the task. Finally, consideration should be given to *why* the measurements are to be obtained — measurement data are simply a means to an end rather than ends in themselves.

Even though measuring tools are indispensable, they are often imperfect. Researchers are constantly challenged to use their ingenuity to improve the instruments now being used and to develop new ways of going beyond present capabilities. Parts IV and V of this book give examples and further information pertinent to gathering and analyzing data.

SCALING TECHNIQUES

Effectiveness in daily life depends upon the ability to distinguish among objects and make differential responses to them. Some of these distinctions are simple and clear-cut whereas others are complicated and qualitative in nature. Therefore, scales have been used to assist people to make differentiations.

Several kinds of scales have been classified in ascending order of their precision, so that each succeeding type of scale presupposes the ability to perform all of the operations of the earlier scales. These scaling levels include: nominal, ordinal, interval, and ratio.

Nominal Scales

At the nominal (or classificatory) level, objects or individuals are classified into distinguishable, named categories with no implication of "more" or "less."

Examples of such scales are the classification of people by religion, nationality, occupation, sex, disease, or any other classification by which groups may be distinguished from one another by name. Objects can be classified nominally also (e.g., type of architecture, acid or alkaline solution, synthetic or natural fibers).

Two or more categories may be used. The members of any one classification must possess the property or characteristic being scaled and they must differ from members of another classification. Since there is no indication that they represent "more" or "less" of the characteristic involved, the members within a category are equated. Statistical operations are limited to those appropriate to counting (such as the mode). There is no way of knowing about other differences that might exist between various categories.

Ordinal Scales

In ordinal (or ranking) scales, objects or individuals in one category not only differ from those in other categories but they stand in some kind of relation to one another, with no indication of the distance between the categories. The difference of "more" or "less" between categories enables each individual to be placed in some order as: greater than, equal to, or less than each of the others (e.g., sergeant, corporal, private).

Ordinal scales are described as an elastic yardstick that is stretched unevenly. There is no indication that the distance between two points would be equal to that between two other points. Neither is there any way of knowing how high the group as a whole performs or how variable the group is. For example, does the group consist of six geniuses or six moderately capable students? How much better is the first one than the last one in the group? Appropriate statistics include the use of medians, percentiles, and rank-order correlations (see Chapter 15).

Interval Scales

In addition to the properties of the nominal and ordinal scales, an interval scale has the characteristic of equal distances between any two numbers on the scale. This is a quantitative scale with distances of known size, as in temperature measurement. Most test scores are treated as though they are interval scales.

Most of the commonly used statistical methods are applicable with interval scales. Scores can be compared by adding or subtracting (e.g., Bob's score is 16 points lower than John's). Multiplication and division are meaningless since the relationship between points is in terms of distance but the zero point is arbitrary (e.g., one could not state that 90°F is twice as warm as 45°F).

Ratio Scales

A ratio scale (or fundamental measurement) combines all the characteristics of the previous scales and, in addition, it has a true zero point as its origin (i.e., mass or weight). All common physical measurements are of this type: weight, height, time, volume, money. For example, a six-pound roast is four pounds heavier than a two-pound roast and it is also three times as heavy. Examples of psychological measurements include the number of trials required to learn a task, length of time to respond to a visual stimulus, and measures of loudness.

All statistical operations can be applied since one score can be multiplied or divided by another. Avoid making the mistake, though, of assuming that all measures are ratio scales. It is not possible, for example, to consider one person twice as handsome as another or one child twice as bright as another. (What would zero IQ mean?)

The social sciences often must depend on crude measurements that impose certain limitations on the data. Of course, when it is possible to use a ratio scale, it is the highest level and should be used. Since numbers do not always represent what the researcher means, it is important to specify the type of scale that was used.

VALIDITY OF MEASUREMENT

To determine the validity of measurement, ask the question: "Are we measuring what we think we are measuring?" It is not possible to study validity without inquiring into the nature and meaning of one's variables. Validity is no great problem when measuring certain physical properties, such as the length and weight of an object. In this case, there is often a direct and close relationship between the nature of the object being measured and the measuring instrument. On the other hand, if the researcher wishes to study the relations between personality characteristics and the decision-making processes of a consumer, there are no rulers or scales to weigh accurately the degree of a personality characteristic possessed or a decision-making process. In such cases as these, it is necessary to develop indirect means to measure these nonphysical properties. These means are often so indirect that their validity may be questioned.

When choosing a test or other measuring device, the most important factor is its validity — its ability to do what the user is trying to accomplish. Validity is concerned with *what* the test measures and *how well* it fulfills its function. It is not possible to answer the question, "Is this a valid test?" Rather the researcher's concern should be how valid this test is for the decision he wishes to make.

The American Psychological Association defined three types of validity, each of which is involved in making a different kind of judgment: (American Psychological Association, 1966, pp. 12-14)

Content Validity

Content validity is used to determine how an individual would perform at the present time in a given universe of situations of which the test constitutes a sample. The questions or situations included in the test must represent the content areas or behavioral patterns to be assessed. They must be appropriate for the individuals under study and for the circumstances in which they are being used. Content validity is determined by a logical process, by examining the representativeness of the test content. Representativeness or sampling adequacy of the content of a measuring instrument is determined by analyzing the substance, matter, and topics covered. Does it adequately measure what it is supposed to measure? The American Psychological Association (1954) suggested that four factors determine content validity of a test: (1) item selection, (2) item description, (3) range and balance of items, and (4) manner of item presentation.

If a home management professor prepares an objective-type test for a course in which she focused on the decision-making process, and she wishes to determine its validity, she should examine each item on the test for its relevancy to measuring a student's understanding of the principles of decision making. Ideally, if her test is to be high in content validity, it should have a random sample of *all* items which could possibly be included in a test to measure decision making. Unfortunately, a random sample of items from a universe or population of test content is not possible. Thus, the content validity of collections of test items is based upon judgments. The professor, either by herself or with the assistance of others, judges the representativeness of each item as a measure of students' understanding of the decision-making process. In this respect, some types of items are easier to judge than others. If judges are given specific directions for making judgments regarding the kind of measurements to be made on a test instrument, then some method of pooling independent recommendations of the judges can be made.

Predictive Validity

Predictive validity is used to estimate success or future behavior from the results of a present measurement. This form of validity is useful when hiring job applicants to predict their success in a particular job on the basis of a test battery. Also, it is used in selecting students for admission to college and professional schools. The method involves administering the test, waiting for the events the test is attempting to predict to occur, and then correlating the test scores with some measure of performance appropriate to the event. Academic achievement, performance in specialized training, and on-the-job performance are among the criteria for validating scores on a predictor (such as a scholastic aptitude test or a test battery).

The greatest difficulty of predictive validation is the criteria. In some cases it may be difficult to obtain possible criteria and in other cases their validity may be doubtful. For example, aptitude tests predict future achievement. Yet, what criterion can one use to test the predictive validity of an artistic or musical aptitude test? What criterion can be used to validate a measure of teacher effectiveness?

The *Gordon Personal Profile* (Gordon, 1965) is an example of an instrument that has been studied in relation to its predictive validity. It is a brief self-administering questionnaire, comprised of 18 items designed to measure four personality traits: *ascendancy* ("takes the lead in group discussions," "able to make important decisions without help"); *responsibility* ("sees a job through despite difficulties," "thorough in any work undertaken"); *emotional stability* ("calm and easygoing in manner," "free from care"); and *sociability* ("enjoys having lots of people around," "a good mixer socially"). The individual taking the test is asked to select the statements "most" and "least" like himself from each group of items presented to him.

Several determinations have been made of the predictive validity of this instrument. Moderate correlations were found between individuals' scores on these four measures and the ratings of their behavior made by counselors and their peers. A close relationship was also found between individuals' scores on the instrument and indices of performance adequacy in industrial situations. A reviewer of the instrument has stated that "generally the validity of the Gordon Personal Profile seems as good as usually found in the better inventories of this type." (Dicken, in Buros, Ed., 1965, p. 103)

Construct Validity

A construct is a theoretical, imaginary mechanism or theory to account for behavior as it is observed. Construct validity focuses more on the property being measured than on the test itself. To know why a relationship exists between two measures, one must know the meaning of the constructs entering the relation. The theory behind the test must be validated. Actually, whenever hypotheses are tested, construct validity is involved.

Construct validity is valuable for scientific purposes rather than immediately practical purposes. It is more complex than the other types, since it involves developing a theory about what a score means psychologically and what causes a person to get a certain score. Construct validity is important in measuring abilities, attitudes, personality characteristics, and complex behavior patterns.

Following are some actual examples of construct validations:

1. Sarason et al., (Sarason, 1960, pp. 125-128) determined the validity of their Test Anxiety Scale for Children (TASC). One of their validity tests was to correlate the TASC with teacher ratings of children's anxiety. The TASC was administered to over 2,200 second through fifth grade pupils, who were also rated by their teachers on a 17-item anxiety rating scale. The correlations between the TASC and the ratings were low. However, since they were for the most part statistically significant, they yielded evidence of the validity of the TASC. The relations between the TASC and intelligence and achievement were also tested by Sarason and his colleagues. As predicted, the correlations were low and negative.* The important relation between general anxiety and test anxiety also supported Sarason's expectations, adding further evidence to his confidence in the construct validity of the TASC.

2. Another method illustrating construct validity and construct validation is the technique of correlating test items with total scores. Since the total test score of any individual is assumed to be valid, to the extent that any item measures the same thing the total score does, the item is valid.

In order to study the construct validity of any measure, it is advisable to

_____

*The correlation technique is discussed in Chapter 15. This technique uses scores or measures for two variables for each individual in a group to determine whether there is a relationship between the variables. A negative correlation indicates that, as the measure for one variable goes up, the other goes down.

correlate the measure with a large number of other measures. There are statistical tools available for doing this. Such a tool, called *factor analysis*, in effect tells what measures the same thing and to what extent they measure what they measure. "In fact, factor analysis may almost be called the most important of construct validity tools." (Kerlinger, 1964, p. 454)

RELIABILITY OF MEASUREMENT

Reliability of measurement indicates the consistency of independent but comparable measures of the same individual, group, or situation. There are three possible sources of variation affecting an individual's scores: variation arising from the measurement itself, changes within the individual over a period of time, and differences in the samples of tasks covered by the instrument. Several methods have been developed to control these variations and obtain estimates of reliability:

1. *Comparisons over time (or stability)*. Stability refers to the consistency of measures on repeated applications. If the measuring instrument is based upon observations, numerous repeated observations may be made. With the use of interviews, questionnaires, or projective tests, usually two administrations of the instruments are made. This method is often called the test-retest procedure. Two weeks to one month is usually considered a suitable interval between two administrations of many psychological tests. The common practice is to compromise between waiting long enough for the effects of the first testing to wear off but not long enough for a significant amount of real change to take place. (Selltiz et al., 1966, p. 171)

An example of testing for stability of measurements over a period of time is found in Compton's development of an instrument to determine women's preferences for color and design in clothing fabrics. (Compton, 1962, 1965 a and b, 1966) The primary function of the Compton Fabric Preference Test is to determine relationships between such clothing fabric preferences as measured on this instrument and social and personality characteristics of the individual. In 1962 the instrument was administered twice to a group of 30 students at a two-weeks' interval to establish test-retest reliability and to control the influence of momentary mood on the preferences. The correlation coefficients in Table 3 were calculated from the scores of these students on the two administrations of the instrument. These correlation coefficients show a high degree of consistency of preferences on the two test administrations, indicating high reliability for all parts of the test. (See Chapter 15 for a description of the correlation statistical technique.) Since its development, the Compton Fabric Preference Test has been used many times by graduate students and other researchers throughout the country.

2. *Comparability of forms (or equivalence)*. Equivalence involves arriving at consistent results from two parallel measurements used with the same individuals at approximately the same time. Parallel forms are similar in content and difficulty. When the measuring device requires observations, two different observers might use the instrument to measure the same individuals at the same

TABLE 3. TEST-RETEST RELIABILITY COEFFICIENTS
FOR COMPTON FABRIC PREFERENCE TEST (COMPTON, 1962)

Saturated Colors	.92
Tints	.81
Shades	.87
Strong Contrasts	.87
Weak Contrasts	.87
Large Designs	.88
Small Designs	.88

time. When individual subjects respond to tests or scales, two parallel forms of the test are applied with the same individuals at the same sitting or at two different times. The coefficient of equivalence is determined by correlating the scores or ratings resulting from the two forms. When two (or more) observers are used, the correlations are based on independent ratings given by the two investigators.

3. *Internal consistency (or split-half method).* Based upon a single administration of a test or other instrument, two scores can be obtained for each individual by dividing the test into equivalent halves. Usually this involves a score based on the odd-numbered items and another score based on the even-numbered items. The correlation between these scores is used to estimate the reliability that would result from a full-length test. Sometimes an analysis of variance method is used (Kuder-Richardson technique).

In general, the reliability of a test can be increased by increasing its length, provided the additional items are similar in difficulty and discrimination to those included on the shorter test. Practical limitations must be considered, however, so fatigue and boredom will not distort the scores. Also, clarity in the wording of items, in the directions for responding, and in scoring procedures can boost reliability. Reducing the possibility of getting correct answers merely by guessing and providing an inflexible scoring key (one which lists all acceptable answers) make the scoring more accurate and objective, thereby increasing reliability.

Validity and reliability are closely related in that a valid test must be reliable. Nevertheless, a test can be reliable without being valid. Reliability is concerned with the *precision* of measurement. To be reliable, the test must give accurate and consistent results, regardless of what it measures.

PART IV

Methods of Data Collection

*G*raduate students appear to concentrate on two or three methods of collecting data. As a result, the research scope and sophistication tend to be narrow.

The next four chapters are not conclusive but are designed to acquaint students with a wide range of methods that can be employed in collecting data for home economics research projects. Such methods can be classified in terms of their degree of directness. They vary from the direct method used in questionnaires and interviews, in which subjects are asked directly for information about themselves or their attitudes about a topic, to the indirect method in which subjects respond to a vague, unstructured stimulus such as an inkblot. The indirect approach assumes that the subject will provide the information needed without realizing he is giving it.

CHAPTER 11

Observational Methods

Direct, systematic observation often bridges the gap between what people say or believe they would do in a specific situation and what they actually do. Overt behavior may be observed in its natural setting or in situations that are created especially for the study of certain factors. The observer may be inconspicuous, his presence may be obvious to the group though drawing as little attention as possible, or he may be an active participant in the group he is observing. The latter situation, where a person is a participant-observer, enables him to be accepted as a member of the group, and the group behavior is least likely to be affected by his presence.

OBSERVATION WITH SCIENTIFIC INSTRUMENTS

Direct observation is relied upon as the method of data collection in experimental laboratory and field research settings. It is also employed in field studies, often in conjunction with other methods. It has been the basic method in astronomy and the earth sciences, biology, anthropology, and sociology.

Observations may be made by the researcher with or without the assistance of scientific instruments. In observing a visual object, the scientist may have magnifying glasses, microscopes, cameras, and other devices to aid him mechanically. To assist in observing and recording sound, he may have amplifying tubes, recording machines, etc.

Of course, some scientific instruments, when properly used, automatically record observations with little judgment required of the researcher, i.e., an Instron machine to measure the strength of a textile fabric in terms of grams required to break the yarns, various laboratory scales, a colorimeter for measuring small differences in color between samples that are nearly alike. With routine calibration checks of the instruments and careful transfer of data from the recording instrument for tabulation by the researcher, precision can be safe-guarded.

OBSERVATION OF HUMAN BEHAVIOR

Observation is the basic means of learning. People are constantly observing activities and behavior in progress around them. However, accounts of witnesses to crimes and other events reveal that two observers may interpret an incident quite differently and often inaccurately. Such everyday observations are far from scientific. An observation technique becomes scientific to the extent that it: "(1) serves a formulated research purpose, (2) is planned systematically, (3) is recorded systematically and related to more general propositions rather than being presented as a set of interesting curiosa, and (4) is subjected to checks and controls on validity and reliability." (Selltiz et al., 1969, p. 200)

The observational method makes it possible to record behavior as it occurs, either in a laboratory or real-life situation. It rules out the disadvantage of depending upon someone else's memory and interpretation of an event.

In exploratory studies, observation is likely to be unstructured and broad in content because one may not know in advance the most relevant behaviors to observe. However, once observations can be structured, clearly defined behaviors should be observed and recorded. It is not possible to record all details of all behavior that occurs; observations must be selective.

When planning observational studies, the following factors should be considered: the participants, setting, content, sampling of behavior, recording instruments, and the observer.

The Participants

An appropriate group of subjects must be selected to observe. Observation probably has had its widest application in the study of young children. This is to be expected because of their limited ability to express their feelings in words. Their behavior is genuine and not so likely to be influenced by the presence of an observer. Observation is particularly useful also in studies of intercultural understanding, mentally ill persons, or other groups who lack facility in verbal communication.

In "participant observation," the observer or researcher takes part in the activities of the group being observed. He is a participant and his role as an observer may or may not be known to the group. He may live in the same community with the subjects and get the "feel" of the meaning of the activities to the regular participants. Therefore, he plays a dual role and must be objective at the same time he participates. Through such direct participation, he can often probe more deeply than an outside observer into behavioral processes and gain greater understanding for analysis of the problems under study.

A nonparticipant, or outside observer, must take a position in relation to the participants being observed where his presence will not disturb the usual functioning and behavior of the group.

An individual may observe himself by keeping track of what he does for a certain period of time with respect to a specific behavior or by looking back on situations in which he manifested certain behavior. For example, Paolucci asked 24 beginning teachers to keep a log for two weeks indicating their decisions regarding management. This part of her study involved a planned self-report where the teachers were asked to keep their own records on a specific topic for a given length of time. She supplemented the teachers' self-reports by visiting each teacher to see her at work and interview her after the logs had been completed. (Paolucci, 1956)

Setting

A researcher may observe behavior in a structured laboratory situation where variables are manipulated or he may observe behavior in a natural everyday situation where only his *observations* of the behavior are structured and controlled. Many problems in human behavior are found in the area of social interrelationships and personality where neither structured laboratory experiments, nor paper and pencil tests, nor interviews can duplicate real-life situations.

Systematic observation, a basic technique of field studies, refers to taking a representative sample of behavior as it occurs naturally in everyday life. From such samples of behavior, the researcher estimates typical behavior in real-life situations. Some researchers feel that the best way to understand an individual's personality is to watch him react to the conditions that are most significant for him.

Situational observation places all individuals in the same, controlled situation which may be quite different from what is encountered in real life. For example, a situational test might be designed to arouse a certain type of feeling to provoke exhibitions of critical behavior. One instance is an aggression-provoking situation consisting of procedures designed to annoy the individual. Its principal advantage may be the time saved by not having to wait for the desired conditions to occur in a natural setting. Its disadvantages lie in the narrow sample of behavior that is observed out of context and that may not represent important behavior patterns in a particular individual's life style. Ratings of an individual based on longer acquaintance generally have greater predictive validity than those obtained in contrived situations.

Content of Observations

In planning a structured observational study, an operational definition must be provided of the behavior unit being observed or measured. (Refer to Chapter 3 for a more detailed discussion of operational definitions.) If observations are to be made of independent behavior in kindergarten children, what actions are to be labeled "independent behavior" (e.g., the child playing by himself, initiating projects with other children, etc.)?

In a complex situation, no one can expect to observe everything that takes place. Observations must be selective and specific. The most relevant aspects should be chosen and defined in advance. Specific activities or behavior should be identified with the qualities to be observed. Most observational studies involve social interactions or personality development. Selltiz listed significant elements of every social situation. Only the most relevant items from the following list should be selected for study (Selltiz et al., 1959, pp. 209-210):

1. The participants — including who they are, how they are related to one another, and how many there are.

2. The setting — its appearance; the kinds of behavior it encourages, permits, discourages, or prevents; the kinds of behavior likely to be perceived as expected or unexpected, approved or disapproved, conforming or deviant.

3. The purpose — the official purpose and reactions to it, other goals that seem to be pursued and whether these goals are compatible or antagonistic.

4. The social behavior — what the participants do, how, and with whom; what was the stimulus for behavior, toward whom or what is the behavior directed, what form does the behavior take, what are its qualities (intensity, appropriateness, duration), what are its effects?

5. Frequency and duration — when did the situation occur, how long did it last, does it recur?

The *critical-incident* technique is a means of determining what is essential in order to accomplish a specific task. As the name implies, this technique refers to a study of significant aspects of some observable human activity. For example, it could be used to determine factors that lead to unusual success or failure on a job, such as teaching. A teacher could apply the same principles in identifying and reporting facts about behavior in any classroom situation of limited complexity. This method is designed to distinguish between behaviors that are critical and those that are not critical, but it does not discriminate between behaviors with regard to degrees of criticalness. Once the significant behaviors are determined, they can be used as the basis for forming categories in an evaluation instrument. Among its applications are the following (Flanagan, 1954, pp. 327-358):

1. Measures of typical performance (criteria)
2. Measures of proficiency (standard samples)
3. Training
4. Selection and classification
5. Job design and purification
6. Operating procedures
7. Equipment design
8. Motivation and leadership (attitudes)
9. Counseling and psychotherapy

Sampling of Behavior

Observation must be systematic. Careful planning and control should be exercised over such factors as the number of observations, replications to see whether the same results will be obtained on other occasions, length of the observation periods, and the interval between them.

A decision must be made as to whether all the designated behaviors in a given time period will be observed or whether samples of specified behaviors will be sampled randomly or systematically. Through *event sampling*, events or behaviors of a given class are selected for observation (i.e., temper tantrums, conversation with other people, etc.). Since some behaviors or events do not occur frequently, the researcher must wait until the event occurs for observing it. Such infrequent events may be missed in *time sampling*, where different points in time are selected during which to observe events or behavior. Time samples provide representative samples of behavior but lack continuity, and behavior may be observed out of context. This is particularly true when small units of time are selected. Short, well-distributed samples may be more typical, however, than an equal amount of time spent in longer observation periods. Reduced errors of memory are likely since records can be made immediately after a short time sample. Many observations are desirable to get a representative expression of the variable being measured as a means of determining how a person will behave "on the average." This determination represents the reliability of the observations.

Recording Instruments

Observations should be recorded objectively, indicating what actually happened rather than what the observer thought the behavior represented. Immediate recording in precise, concrete, and quantitative terms helps to increase accuracy. Shorthand records, still or motion pictures, and sound records are helpful in obtaining complete records which can be studied and analyzed thoroughly following the observation period.

There are two principal types of recording instruments for observations — categories and rating scales:

Category observation system. Under the category system, the observer assigns observed behaviors to specific categories. For example, the Bales System (Bales, 1950) provides 12 categories into which all verbal behavior in a small face-to-face group can be coded. These categories are reprinted in Figure 18.

Merrill (1946) used the category observation system to measure mother-child interaction. Each mother and child pair in the study was observed in an experimental room equipped with toys and a one-way screen. The mothers were told the research dealt with the child's play behavior. Therefore, they were unaware that they were being observed. Each mother's behavior was recorded on a category basis every five seconds. The categories embraced all possible behavior incidents that could occur during a play session: i.e., mother structurizes (s) or stimulates or influences the child, teaches (t), interferes (i) with in an attempt to stop the child's activity. Definitions and examples are provided for each category.

Rating scales. Simple rating scales are also used frequently to record observations in a social setting. Lippitt and Zander, in a field experiment on Scoutmaster training, used a five-point rating scale to rate the physical symptoms of group tension shown by a group of boys during meetings led by the trainees. The scale was marked whenever the group atmosphere or program activity changed during the meeting. Following is a description of the scale with instructions (Heyns and Zander, in Festinger and Katz, 1953, pp. 394-395):

0 position — *Can't rate*

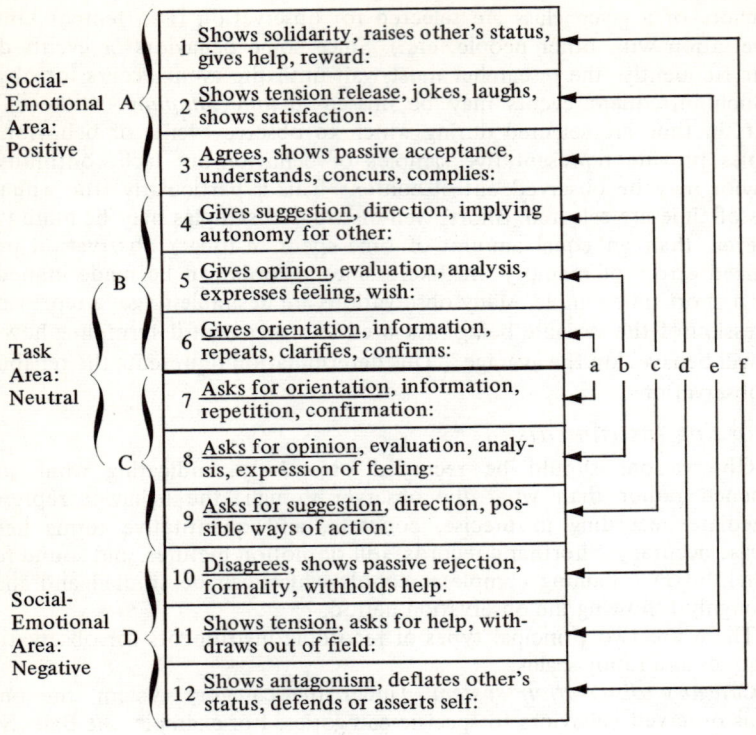

KEY:

a   Problems of Communication
b   Problems of Evaluation
c   Problems of Control
d   Problems of Decision
e   Problems of Tension Reduction
f   Problems of Reintegration

A   Positive Reactions
B   Attempted Answers
C   Questions
D   Negative Reactions

Figure 18. The System of Categories Used in Observation and Their Major Relations. Chart 1, p. 9, from *Interaction Process Analysis: A Method for the Study of Small Groups,* by R.F. Bales, 1950, reprinted with permission from Addison-Wesley Press, Cambridge, Massachusetts.

1 position — *Very relaxed:* The group is physically and psychologically "taking it easy." This does not mean that they are carrying on the kinds of activity which occur at a Scout meeting without any apparent air of tension. This may be a sprawled conversation group or it may be a relaxed game. The boys seem comfortable; they act and look the way people do after they rise from a good meal.

2 position — *Relaxed:* Mark this category if the group is relaxed but not as greatly relaxed as in the category above.

3 position — *Middleground:* This category is marked if the boys are acting as most people do most of the time. The goal has a more positive valence than might be true in positions 1 and 2. There is a small amount of tension, but it is not great enough to be expressed in physical signs of tension. They may be physically active or sitting still. Facial expression shows no apparent signs of strain.

4 position — *Restless:* This point is marked to describe group behaviors which indicate psychological tension. Boys may be "trying hard" in a signaling contest or a written examination. Sometimes tension may be apparent in the purposeless movements by the boy (purposeless in the sense that they seem to have no relation to the group goal at the time). These are such movements as hand-wringing, foot-twisting, tongue-chewing, drumming, and other nervous mannerisms.

5 position — *Keyed up:* Here tension is very obvious. Its physical signs are clenched fists, or hunched bodies, or extreme signs of restlessness, or a tense, anxious expression. A football crowd watching the kick for a point after touchdown would be "keyed up." The keyed-up behavior may be shown by boys who are in any posture or state of movement. During a fast basketball game, for example, the signs by which it is recognized might depend on the pitch and frequency of shouts, the facial gestures, etc. Boys who are required to sit through a tongue lashing may be keyed up but their tension might be shown in facial gestures and inhibited movements.

"One of the most ambitious attempts to measure parent behavior in natural settings is the research of Baldwin, Kalhorn, and Breese." (Kerlinger, 1964, p. 520) These researchers visited homes and rated the behavior of parents on a 30-item observation rating scale. (Baldwin, Kalhorn, and Breese, 1945, 1949) The scale was comprised of bipolar adjective pairs such as rejecting-devoted, disapproving-approving, dictatorial-democratic, etc. Specific directions were provided observers with respect to what to observe and rate. The researchers found that the 30 items grouped themselves into a smaller number of factors including warmth, democracy, and indulgence.

Anecdotal records. Anecdotal records are brief, specific, exact, and objective descriptions of significant behavior that is observed. A shorthand code can be used to record conversations and actions to facilitate the later writing of more detailed observational records. The observer is free to note any behavior rather than to focus on the same traits for all individuals. This technique requires less observer interpretation of behavior at the time of recording than would be necessary to categorize or rate the behavior. However, the data must be interpreted at the time of their analysis.

The Observer

The observer's presence is not considered to have a significant effect on the behaviors being observed. However, when the observer must interpret behavior unduly, validity and reliability may suffer. For increased accuracy, the observations of two or more observers should be compared. In moving from a sensory level of observation to levels involving abstraction, the agreement between different observers decreases.

A simple formula for finding the per cent of agreement between two observers is:

$$\frac{2 \times \text{number of agreements}}{\text{total of observer A} + \text{total of observer B}}$$

For example, if two observers agreed on 10 ratings, and each observer had made 25 independent ratings, the per cent of agreement would be:

$$\frac{2 \times 10}{25 + 25} = 40 \text{ per cent}$$

In a case where more than two observers were used (N represents the number of observers), the general formula would be:

$$\frac{N \times \text{number of agreements}}{\text{total A} + \text{total B} + \text{total C} \ldots \text{total N}}$$

LIMITATIONS

As is true of any research technique, observation has certain limitations. Since observers tend to see only what they are trained to look for, careful advanced planning, including a description of the characteristics to be observed, is necessary in order to obtain meaningful data. On the other hand, a person may become so obsessed with his hypothesis that he is looking for facts to support it and he ignores facts that are in disagreement. In some instances, people may be willing to give self-reports on events or behavior of a highly personal nature that could not be observed by an outsider. The presence of an observer may cause individuals or groups to change their usual behavior and try to create a good impression. The cost of observation is likely to be high, including the salaries of highly trained observers who may be required to devote several hours to each observation, and the expenses of recording, analyzing, and interpreting the data. Still another limitation is the difficulty in knowing exactly when a desired event might occur spontaneously so as to have an observer present on such occasions. Usually observations are focused on small aspects of behavior and the observer may fail to see this behavior in its true context.

Although it is easier to observe overt acts, an observer needs to be aware of important qualitative aspects that can help him know how to interpret the behavior which is observed.

RESEARCH EXAMPLES AND ANALYSES
*OBSERVATIONAL METHOD OF DATA COLLECTION

METHODOLOGY FOR THE STUDY OF PHYSICAL SPACE AND LIVING-PATTERN RELATIONSHIPS

RUTH H. SMITH, MILDRED T. LYNCH, AND DONNA BETH DOWNER

The choice of an appropriate methodological technique for data collection is a major hazard for the social scientist. Accurate and sufficient data, unsullied by intervening variables, is a difficult goal to attain when the research subjects are human beings.

The objectives of a study, in the final analysis, dictate the technique to be used for data collection. The methodology described here was developed for the purpose of studying possible relationships between a family's dwelling space and its living patterns. A composite technique, incorporating merits of both the controlled laboratory setting and observation, was developed. A descriptive study yielding intensive information on a limited number of representative cases resulted. By use of a computer, the observational data were transformed to quantities of time periods useful for comparisons and adaptable to statistical analysis.

The Controlled Laboratory

A realistic comparison of the influence of dwelling space on family living patterns necessitated adequate control over the dwelling environment. A complete dwelling, designed for the project and erected in a large laboratory in one of the campus buildings, offered assurance that all participant families would have the same amount of space in which to perform the individual and family activities which comprised their living patterns (1). Conversely, the research dwelling eliminated the possibility that differences in living space might account for differences in activity patterns.

Previous research had established minimum space requirements for separate household activities (2, 3). By combining minimum dimensional requirements for interrelated activities, multiple-use areas were developed which were adapted to specific house dimensions. The completed dwelling, containing a total of 1400 square feet, consisted of a living-dining room, kitchen with an adjoining eating area, three bedrooms, 1½ baths, and a laundry area.

Observational Technique

There are difficulties in obtaining objective data describing overt behavior. Methods dependent on the subjects' observations and recall are apt to be inaccurate and incomplete. The classic experiment of asking subjects to reconstruct a sequence of events has shown the wide range of recollections which come from eyewitnesses. Subjects also may make arbitrary decisions as to what

Reprinted with permission from *Journal of Home Economics,* Vol. 61, pp. 429-432, June, 1969. Copyright by the American Home Economics Association, Washington, D.C.

to report and what to omit, leaving the researcher with an incomplete record of occurrences or responses. Training the subjects to be otherwise destroys the spontaneity and normality of the reactions being investigated.

Observation is the most direct means of studying human behavior. Critics of the technique have pointed out that data obtained through a third person (the observer) are subject to that person's perception and bias. It remains that observation can provide insights into human behavior unattainable by other means. Henry, citing the new theories made possible by the revelations of the microscope and telescope, suggests:

> Direct observation of families functioning in their native habitats should be the microscope that reveals new phenomena of family existence and so provides the possibilities of new theory. (4, p. 31)

Valid observations depend upon factual, objective, and accurate annotations of responses by an observer.

The success of the observational procedure depends upon the investigator's answering several questions prior to initiating the research: What is to be observed? How should observations be recorded? What is the relationship to be between observer and observed?

Family living patterns were established as the subject or the "what" of the observation. Living patterns were defined as the arrangement of activities, locations, and performers into a design for action which keeps the family functioning in a satisfactory manner. A sequence of activities performed by certain family members may constitute a pattern for one family but be only a circumstantial occurrence for another. The problem of knowing when such events were going to occur was crucial; they may or may not occur at stated intervals. By the same token, the pattern may form from the totality of the day's happenings, rather than from single incidents.

To ensure a complete record, the observation period, for a total of seven days, was set to begin when the first family member arose in the morning and to end when the family was anticipating retirement at night.[1]

In alternate five-minute periods, the location and activity being performed were recorded for each family member. An alphabetical code was devised for recording both locations and activities. Sixteen locations were identified in the house, and abbreviated letter designations were assigned to each .... Fifty-seven activities, grouped in generalized categories, were also assigned letter designations for ease in recording.

Forms were designed for recording the observed behavior (see diagram 1). A space for comments was included; observers were encouraged to briefly describe any activity about whose letter designation they were uncertain. As the data were prepared for transferal to IBM cards, the editor could use those comments in maintaining continuity among observers.

---

[1] Similar records, kept by the homemaker in the family's own dwelling for one week prior to the "live-in" period, provided data on activity performance and use of space relative to their own home.

The observers, trained in the use of the code, were present and visible in the house at all times. It was imperative to the success of the study that the families be relaxed and comfortable in the experimental situation. Consideration was given to such observational devices as one-way screens and television cameras, but it was decided that their use would discourage the desired rapport between project personnel and project participants and might inhibit normal family activities.[2]

The influence of the observer's presence on the activities of the family was considered to be minimal. As Kerlinger points out:

> Individuals and groups seem to adapt rather quickly to an observer's presence and to act as they would usually act. This does not mean that the observer cannot have an effect. It means that if the observer takes care to be unobtrusive and not to give the people observed the feeling that judgments are being made, then the observer as an influential stimulus is mostly nullified. (5, p. 506)

Quantifying the Data

The five-minute time period became the unit for analysis. Any change in activity or location by any performer meant a new data card. All persons were accounted for at all times.

Analyzing the data by computer made it possible to examine the volume of observations in comprehensive detail. Original programs were written since neither the data nor the desired analysis lent itself to library programs. Three major tabulations were accomplished:

1. Location use — on the basis of 100 percent, the proportion of observed time periods that each of the 16 locations was used, by whom, and for what activities

• Multiple use of locations — the proportion of observed time periods that each location was shared by two or more family members, the combinations of people, and the simultaneous activities involved

2. Activity occurrence — on the basis of 100 percent, the proportion of observed time periods each of the 57 activities occurred, who performed them, and in what locations

• Episode sharing — the percentage of observed time periods in which two or more family members were engaged in the same activity in the same location, the combinations of family members involved, and the specific locations

3. Performers — on the basis of 100 per cent, the proportion of observed time periods that each family member used a location and, also on the basis of 100 per cent, the percentage of observed time periods that each individual performed specific activities

Significant differences between the scores of the family types were deter-

---

[2] Comments of the participants sustained the validity of this decision — they did not want to be *spied upon*.

Time Period	Comments	W		C_1		C_2		C_3		H	
		Loc	Act	Loc	Act	Loc	Act	Loc	Act	Loc	Act
7:30-7:35		KI	FP	BA	PW	KE	FE	KE	FE	BD	PD
		KI	FP	KE	FE	KE	FE	KE	FE	BD	PD
		KE	FM	KE	FE	KE	FE	KE	FE	KE	FE
		KE	FE	KE	FE	KE	FE	KE	FE	KE	FE
7:40-7:45		KE	FE	KE	FE	KE	FE	KE	FE	KE	FE
7:50-7:55		KE	FE	KE	FE	KE	FE	KE	FE	BA	PW
		FH	IC	KE	FE	KE	FE	KE	FE	FH	PD
		FH	IC	FH	IC	FH	IC	FH	IC	FH	IC
8:00-8:05		KI	FC	KI	FC	LR	XP	LR	XP	OF	OO

DIAGRAM 1. An example of recorded observations utilizing the code developed for the 57 activities. Line one would be interpreted as follows: Between 7:30 and 7:35 a.m., the wife is in the kitchen (KI), preparing food (FP); Child 1 is in the bathroom (BA), washing (PW); Child 2 is in the kitchen eating area (KE), eating (FE); Child 3 also is in the kitchen eating area (KE), eating (FE); and the husband is in the bedroom (BD), dressing (PD).

mined by analysis of variance. Percentages were converted into the corresponding arc angles to test significance.

Application of the Technique

The Sample. Twenty families, five in each of the four stages of the family life cycle, lived in the experimental house. The families were selected from the residents of the surrounding community, and their participation in the study was completely voluntary. Original contacts were made through an explanatory letter sent to social, church, and school organizations explaining the project. Anyone interested was asked to contact project personnel for more information. Names of subsequent prospective families were obtained through personal contact. (Previous participant families were the best "recruiters" for new families.)

Four stages of the family life cycle were selected for study as representative of those periods when differences in activity patterns are apt to create differences in house use. Families with preschool children, aged six months to six years, were one stage; families with children in school, including one teenager, were a second. All-adult families, stratified into those with husbands still actively employed and those with retired husbands, comprised the last two stages. Five-member families were specified.

A two-week period of residency for each family was established as both a minimum and a maximum. It was the minimal time span in which the members of a family could assume their normal living habits in the controlled space and still allow time for data collection; conversely, it was a maximal time allotment for families to live in the house without adapting their living patterns to the dwelling.

Obviously not everyone would be willing to serve as subjects in a study of this nature. The adult members of the families who did participate were given the Personal Orientation Inventory, a standardized test which provides a measure of the values and behavior important in the development of self-actualization (6). The Inventory provides a score on one's personal orientation – whether one is self-oriented or other-oriented (subject to influence from peer groups or other external forces). The scores achieved by the participant families were above the norms established as indicative of high self-actualization.

The data, collected and analyzed by the methods just described, provide graphic evidence of the patterns of family behavior. From the mathematical quantities it has been possible to describe living patterns, to identify activities contributing to familial traits such as role perception, to ascertain the priorities granted privacy and interaction – in short, to visualize the meaning individuals seek to derive from their dwelling.

Quantification of the data provides a basis for comparing families, groups of families, and individuals within the families. Statistical analysis has indicated that certain aspects of living patterns vary with the stage of the family life cycle, and others are unique to individual families. Concomitant with variations in living patterns are varying needs for space in which to perform the behavior patterns.

In this study, the constriction of living patterns by the limitations of space could only be ascertained through the family's evaluations of the residency experience. Dissatisfaction with lack of space for specific activities provides evidence that inadequate housing space does cause adjustment in living patterns. Studying families in diminished house space might give more specific answers. The report of data analysis and findings will be published at a later date.

Conclusions

As social scientists continue to seek explanations for human behavior, the significance of answers or solutions will be greatly dependent upon the method of asking the questions. The methodology developed for this study was successful in negating some of the limitations of both the laboratory setting and observational techniques. By moving the entire family to the laboratory, the setting became the real dwelling. The behavioral responses in and to the available space were normal and, hence, accurate. The code for recording behavior was quick, easily remembered by the observers, and allowed a minimum of observer bias to be injected. Data tabulation as percentages of observed time periods provided objective quantities which could be compared statistically among and between families.

By maximizing accuracy and minimizing bias, the technique would appear to be a useful tool in other areas of social and behavioral research.

REFERENCES

1. Smith R.H. Dwelling Environment: Multiple-Use Areas. Pennsylvania State Univ., Coll. of Home Econ. Research Publ. No. 241, June 1966.

2. McCullough, H., Philson, K., Smith, R.H., Wood, A.L., and Woolrich, A. Space Standards for Household Activities. Univ. of Illinois Agr. Expt. Sta. Bull. No. 686, Apr. 1962.

3. Smith, R.H., Beyer, G.H., Klinck, M.S., and Grady, E. Farmhouse Planning Guides: Household Activity Data and Space Needs Related to Design. Northeast Regional Publ., Cornell Univ. Agr. Expt. Sta., Dec. 1959.

4. Henry, J. My Life with the Families of Psychotic Children. In *The Psychosocial Interior of the Family*, G. Handel (Editor). Chicago: Aldine Publishing Company, 1967.

5. Kerlinger, F.N. *Foundations of Behavioral Research.* New York: Holt, Rinehart and Winston, Inc., 1965.

6. Shostrom, E.L. *Manual for the Personal Orientation Inventory.* San Diego, California: Educational and Industrial Testing Service, 1966.

ANALYSIS OF OBSERVATIONAL METHOD EXAMPLE

Methodology for the Study of Physical Space and Living-Pattern Relationships

Participants. Twenty families, five in each of the four stages of the family life cycle, lived in an experimental house for a two-week period.

Setting. Researchers observed the behavior of families in the experimental house in natural every day situations.

Content of Observations. Family living patterns were established as the content of the observations. Living patterns were defined as the arrangement of activities, locations, and performers into a design for action which keeps the family functioning in a satisfactory manner.

Sampling of Behavior. The observation period of seven days began when the first family member arose in the morning and ended when the family was anticipating retirement at night. Time sampling was used for recording activities taking place by different family members in different locations. In alternate five-minute periods, the location and activity being performed were recorded for each family member.

Recording Instruments. The category observation system of recording was used. The observer therefore assigned observed behaviors to specific categories. Fifty-seven activities, grouped in generalized categories, were assigned letter designations for ease in recording. Sixteen locations were identified in the house and abbreviated letter designations assigned to each. Forms were designed for recording the behavior within the categories. A space for comments was included.

A STUDY OF SOUND LEVELS IN HOUSES[1]

JESSIE J. MIZE, FERN TUTEN, AND JOSEPH W. SIMONS

Sound levels in houses are of growing concern to many families today. Increases in sound levels are due primarily to increases within houses of motor-driven appliances and sound-producing equipment, such as radios, televisions, and record players, and the extensive use of sound-reflecting surfaces, such as hard coverings on floors and glass over large areas.

The rise in sound levels presents various problems. According to medical researchers in the United States, sound can damage hearing and have an adverse effect on general health (1). Some attempts have been made to determine the psychological effects of sound upon people; however, there are no published data concerning the effects upon people of usual sound in houses. Sound is also of economic concern, for it has been estimated that 60 million dollars is invested yearly in sound-deadening materials for residential, commercial, and industrial buildings. (2)

Household fabrics are considered functional in reducing sound levels in houses. This is known from general observation and from the results of a few controlled laboratory studies of the effects of various fabrics, such as carpeting, upon sound control (3, 4, 5). A comprehensive investigation of the effects of both window fabrics and carpeting upon the sound levels in houses is currently being conducted; the study reported here is the first phase of this work and is concerned with the sound levels usual in family residences. These data were needed in order to plan controlled laboratory studies on the effects of household fabrics on noise levels.

Procedures[2]

A study of sound levels and frequencies of sound was conducted in 20 houses. In each, one or more persons were present during the two test periods: one of 24 hours' duration and the other a one-hour interval at the noisiest time of the day.

Records were made of the activity patterns of the family and the use of household equipment, such as washing machines, dishwashers, vacuum cleaners, and air conditioners. In addition, the houses were classified according to (1) location, age, and size; (2) type of house plan; (3) structural details; and (4) interior finishes.

Reprinted with permission from *Journal of Home Economics*, Vol. 58, pp. 41-45, January, 1966. Copyright by the American Home Economics Association, Washington, D.C.

[1] Journal Paper No. 440 of the College Experiment Station, University of Georgia. This project contributes to the Southern Regional Housing Research Project S-54 entitled "Environmental, Economic, and Structural Factors Related to Improved Rural Family Housing in the South."

[2] Appreciation is expressed to B.C. Haynes, Jr., of the agricultural engineering research division, Agricultural Research Service, USDA, for assembling and setting up equipment and for help in developing the procedures used in collecting the data.

Sound-pressure levels were measured in terms of decibel units.[3] A record was made of sound levels in each of the 20 houses during a 24-hour period. The equipment used included a sound-level meter which employed a system of four microphones, a decade amplifier, and a graphic-level recorder. The decade amplifier was used to boost the microphone signal through the microphone cable before the signal was measured in decibel units by the sound-level meter and subsequently recorded in decibels by the graphic-level recorder. The use of a selected chart-drive speed on the graphic-level recorder provided a record of time in which the data were recorded.

Because maximum-sound levels were of special interest in this phase of the study, the sound-level equipment and microphones were installed in the room where motor-driven equipment and family activities were concentrated. These rooms included kitchens, combination kitchen-family rooms, and combination kitchen-laundry rooms.

The proximity of the microphones to the sources of sound determined the intensity of the sound-pressure levels recorded. Careful consideration was given to the placement of the four microphones in each area. An effort was made to place the microphones in approximately the same positions in relation to electrical and mechanical equipment in each of the houses. In addition, the microphones were numbered in order that the same microphone could be placed near the same type of equipment. None of the microphones was installed higher than 65 inches above the floor level nor farther than 18 inches from the equipment to which it was related.

From the data collected during the 24-hour period, the noisiest hour of the day in each house was determined and the frequencies during this hour were identified. Two considerations were used as a basis for determining the noisiest hour of the day:

1.   The background sounds had to be continuous throughout the hour.

2.   A relatively high number of peaks in the decibel readings had to occur during the hour.

This hour was not necessarily the hour with the highest decibel level. In each of the 20 houses a one-hour tape recording of the sound produced during the noisiest hour was obtained.

When the tape recording was made during the noisiest hour of the day, the microphones were located in positions identical to those used during the original 24-hour period. Before each tape recording was made, a signal of 100 decibels at 1,000 cycles per second was impressed on the first 25 feet of the magnetic tape in order to identify the decibel level of the recorded sounds.

During the tape recording, families were asked to recreate as nearly as possible the activities which had occurred at the same hour during the 24-hour test; notations were made of the equipment in operation, the activities of the family, and the family members present.

---

[3] Sound-pressure level in decibels equals $20 \log_{10} \frac{P}{0.0002}$, in which P is the sound pressure in dynes per cm^2 and 0.0002 is the reference pressure equivalent to the weakest sound that can be heard by a person with good hearing in a very quiet place.

The tape recordings were analyzed in the laboratory to determine the range of frequencies at which the recorded sounds occurred. The sounds were channeled through a sound-level meter and a sound-and-vibration analyzer and recorded by a graphic-level recorder. The sound-and-vibration analyzer was set at the mid-point of each of 31 one-third-octave band settings ranging from 12.5 to 12,500 cycles per second. This range of frequencies was selected for study because sounds occurring within this range can be distinguished by a person with normal hearing ability.

Results

From the data recorded during the 24-hour period in each of the 20 houses, average decibel levels in four-minute intervals were read and over-all average decibel levels were determined for each hour of the day.

The highest average decibel level within a one-hour period occurred between 7:00 and 8:00 a.m. and from 9:00 a.m. to 12:00 noon in 10 of the houses, and from both 12:00 noon to 2:00 p.m. and 5:00 to 9:00 p.m. in 10 of the houses. Among the 20 houses, the highest average decibel levels ranged from 71.79 decibels in house number 15 to 83.77 decibels in house number 11 (table 1).

The lowest average decibel level occurred from 12:00 to 4:00 a.m. and 5:00 to 7:00 a.m. in 15 houses and from both 2:00 to 5:00 p.m. and 10:00 to 11:00

TABLE 1. HIGHEST DECIBEL LEVELS WITHIN
ONE-HOUR PERIODS IN 20 HOUSES

HOUR OF OCCURRENCE	HOUSE NUMBER	HIGHEST AVERAGE DECIBEL LEVEL
7:00- 8:00 a.m.	1	73.60
7:00- 8:00 a.m.	18	75.20
9:00-10:00 a.m.	3	80.75
9:00-10:00 a.m.	8	77.25
10:00-11:00 a.m.	5	81.20
10:00-11:00 a.m.	6	78.77
10:00-11:00 a.m.	20	77.84
11:00-12 00 noon	10	79.67
11:00-12:00 noon	12	76.74
11:00-12:00 noon	15	71.79
12:00 noon-1:00 p.m.	9	77.06
1:00- 2:00 p.m.	4	72.67
1:00- 2:00 p.m.	11	83.77*
5:00- 6:00 p.m.	13	78.22
5:00- 6:00 p.m.	17	72.58
6:00- 7:00 p.m.	19	74.22
7:00- 8:00 p.m.	2	74.93
8:00- 9:00 p.m.	7	74.15
8:00- 9:00 p.m.	14	74.17
8:00- 9:00 p.m.	16	72.64

*Over-all highest noise level

TABLE 2. LOWEST DECIBEL LEVELS WITHIN
ONE-HOUR PERIODS IN 20 HOUSES

HOUR OF OCCURRENCE	HOUSE NUMBER	HIGHEST AVERAGE DECIBEL LEVEL
12:00- 1:00 a.m.	10	59.46*
12 00- 1:00 a.m.	11	65.80
1:00- 2.00 a.m.	16	62.86
2:00- 3:00 a.m.	18	65.78
2:00- 3:00 a.m.	6	71.42
2:00- 3:00 a.m.	15	61.58
2:00- 3 00 a.m.	20	64.56
3:00- 4:00 a.m.	2	62.54
3:00- 4:00 a.m.	7	67.87
3:00- 4:00 a.m.	8	69.97
3.00- 4:00 a.m.	9	69.72
3:00- 4:00 a.m.	12	63.06
3:00- 4.00 a.m.	19	62.76
5:00- 6:00 a.m.	4	64.12
6:00- 7:00 a.m.	17	61.19
2:00- 3:00 p.m.	14	67.39
4:00- 5:00 p.m.	1	64.92
4:00- 5:00 p.m.	3	76.38
10:00-11:00 p.m.	5	72.23
10:00-11:00 p.m.	13	67.54

*Over-all lowest noise level

p.m. in 5 of the houses. Among the 20 houses the lowest average decibel levels ranged from 59.46 decibels in house number 10 to 76.38 decibels in house number 3 (table 2).

When tape recordings were made during the predetermined noisiest hour of the day in the houses, television sets and washing machines were being operated most frequently (table 3). It should be noted that some items of equipment were not in operation during the entire hour of recording. The number of persons present in the houses during the tape recordings ranged from one to nine. Preparing meals and dishwashing by hand were the most frequent activities of these persons.

From the analysis of the tape recordings, seven frequencies ranging from 125 to 8,000 cycles per second were selected for study in controlled laboratory tests of the acoustical properties of household fabrics (table 4). Decibel levels in the 20 houses ranged from 36.0 decibels at 8,000 cycles per second to 90.0 decibels at 125 cycles per second. Results from this study will be comparable with a similar study conducted at the National Bureau of Standards, where frequencies in one-octave bands ranging from 125 to 4,000 cycles per second were used. (3)

In addition to the immediate purpose of obtaining sound conditions in houses which could be simulated in a laboratory study, the investigation has served the following purposes:

TABLE 3. ACTIVITIES AND EQUIPMENT IN OPERATION
DURING THE NOISIEST HOUR OF A TYPICAL DAY IN 20 HOUSES

HOUR OF TAPE RECORDINGS	HOUSE NUMBER	PERSONS PRESENT		EQUIPMENT IN OPERATION
		Number	Activities	
9:15-10:15 a.m.	3	2	Washing dishes by hand Preparing meals	Washing machine Radio Range Vacuum cleaner
9:30-10:30 a.m.	19	6	Washing dishes by hand Loading washing machine Cleaning kitchen	Washing machine Television
10:00-11:00 a.m.	1	4	Preparing meals Children playing	Electric mixer Radio
10:00-11:00 a.m.	6	3	Storing groceries	Electric fan Washer-dryer combina Dishwasher Vacuum cleaner
10:00-11:00 a.m.	20	9	Loading washing machine	Washing machine
11:00-12:00 noon	7	1	Washing dishes by hand Preparing meals Unloading dishwasher	Dishwasher Electric mixer
11:00-12:00 noon	9	1	Washing dishes by hand	Washing machine Clothes dryer
11:00-12:00 noon	10	4	Children playing Washing dishes by hand	Washing machine Dishwasher
11:00-12:00 noon	12	1	Unloading dishwasher Cleaning kitchen	Television
11:05-12:05 p.m.	8	5	Loading dishwasher Children playing	Washing machine Clothes dryer Television
11:05-12:05 p.m.	15	2	Preparing meals	Garbage disposal
12:45- 1:45 p.m.	14	1	Storing groceries Loading dishwasher	Washing machine
1:00- 2:00 p.m.	4	4	Preparing meals Dining	Television Range
1:00- 2:00 p.m.	13	3	Dining Washing dishes by hand	Garbage disposal Dishwasher

TABLE 3 (cont.)

HOUR OF TAPE RECORDINGS	HOUSE NUMBER	PERSONS PRESENT		EQUIPMENT IN OPERATION
		Number	Activities	
3:00- 4:00 p.m.	11	1		Sewing machine Television
4:40- 5:40 p.m.	16	2		Washing machine Electric fan
5:00- 6:00 p.m.	5	4	Children playing Dining	Television
5:05- 6:05 p.m.	18	4	Preparing meals Children playing Dining Washing dishes by hand	Television Range
5:30- 6:30 p.m.	17	1	Preparing meals	Vent fan Electric fan Range Television
7:30- 8:30 p.m.	2	3	Loading dishwasher	Dishwasher Television Piano

TABLE 4. DECIBEL LEVELS OCCURRING DURING THE NOISIEST HOUR OF A TYPICAL DAY IN 20 HOUSES

FREQUENCY PER SECOND	RANGE	
	Lowest Decibel Level	Highest Decibel Level
125	55.00	90.00
250	58.00	85.00
500	58.00	80.00
1,000	51.00	83.00
2,000	49.00	67.00
4,000	45.00	60.00
8,000	36.00	63.50

1. The procedure developed for measuring and analyzing sound levels in housing and the findings from the study may be valuable in the design of other studies concerned with noise in homes.

2. The findings which indicate when the highest sound levels occurred in the houses and which items of equipment were being operated during these time intervals may be useful to families in planning rest periods and leisure and work activities.

Summary

Sound levels were measured in 20 houses to determine the maximum sound levels that exist in houses today. Sound-level equipment was installed in each of the houses for a 24-hour period to make a continuous record of the sound-pressure levels in terms of decibel units. From these records, the noisiest hour of the day in each of the houses was determined. Tape recordings made during the noisiest hour were analyzed in the laboratoy to determine the range of frequencies of the recorded sound levels.

Average decibel levels among the 20 houses during the 24-hour tests ranged from 59.46 decibels to 83.77. Decibel levels from the tape recordings ranged from 36.0 decibels at 8,000 cycles per second to 90.0 at 125.

REFERENCES

1. Noise, something more to worry about. *U.S. News and World Report* 55, No. 13 (Sept. 23, 1963), pp. 64-66.

2. Harris, C.M. *Handbook of Noise Control.* New York: McGraw-Hill Company, Inc., 1957.

3. Harris, C.M. Acoustical properties of carpet. *J. Acoustical Soc. of Am.* 27, No. 6 (Nov. 1955), pp. 1077-1082.

4. Sound Conditioning with Carpet, Carpet Institute, Inc., New York City, 10 pp.

5. Kunz, C.J., and Rodman, H.E. Acoustical Tests of Carpeting in a High School, *Noise Control.* Troy, New York: Rensselaer Polytechnic Institute, Jan./ Feb., 1961, pp. 11-20.

ANALYSIS OF OBSERVATIONAL METHOD EXAMPLE

A Study of Sound Levels in Houses

Participants and Setting. Twenty houses were analyzed for sound levels and frequencies. Activity patterns of families within the houses were also studied.

Content of Observations. Sound pressure levels and frequencies constituted the content of observations. Records were also made of the activity patterns of the family and the use of household equipment. In addition, the houses were classified according to location, age, and size; type of house plan; structural details; and interior finishes.

Sampling of Observation Unit. There were two test periods: one of 24 hours' duration and the other a one-hour interval at the noisiest time of the day. Thus, time sampling was used.

Recording Instruments. As indicated previously, observations may be made by the researcher with or without the assistance of scientific instruments. In this study, sound-level equipment was installed in each of the houses to make a continuous record of the sound-pressure levels in terms of decibel units. Equipment included a sound-level meter which employed a system of four microphones, a decade amplifier, and a graphic-level recorder.

From the data collected the noisiest hour of the day in each house was determined. A one-hour tape recording was then made of the sound produced during the noisiest hour. For this recording, families were asked to recreate as nearly as possible the activities that had occurred at the same hour during the 24-hour test. Notations were made of the equipment in operation, the activities of the family, and the family members present.

INDIVIDUAL DIFFERENCES IN HUMAN NEONATES' RESPONSES TO STIMULATION

BEVERLY BIRNS

This investigation of individual differences in the behavior of neonates helps fill a gap in existing longitudinal research. Several recent investigators have demonstrated behavioral differences that are stable during childhood (Chess, Thomas, & Birch, 1959; Escalona & Heider, 1959; Schaefer & Bayley, 1963). However, these investigators, having acknowledged the importance of measuring traits at birth, began their observations at a later stage in the infancy period when complex environmental variables may already have exerted an influence.

The study here reported focused on responsiveness to stimulation as one aspect of individual differences in neonatal functioning. This behavior was selected as a possible precursor of temperamental and personality differences.

Individual temperamental differences are acknowledged to be important by

Reprinted from *Child Development*, Vol. 36, pp. 249-256, 1965, with permission from The Society for Research in Child Development, Inc.

A version of this paper was read at the biennial meeting of the Society for Research in Child Development, Pennsylvania State College, March, 1961. This research was submitted in partial fulfilment of the Ph.D. degree at Columbia University, 1963. This study was supported, in part, by National Institutes of Mental Health Grant No. MF-10, 992.

The author wishes to thank Sibylle Escalona, Wagner H. Bridger, Marion Blank, Lore Rubin, and Eve Lazar, who served as raters and co-investigators. Gratitude is also expressed to Arthur T. Jersild, who supervised the research, and to Rosedith Sitgreaves, for statistical consultations. Author's address: Department of Psychiatry, Albert Einstein College of Medicine of Yeshiva University, Bronx, N.Y. 10461.

theorists who have various frames of reference. Systems as divergent as those of Freud and Pavlov consider biological factors to play an important role in behavior. When Freudians speak of differences in instinctual drives and in the "stimulus barrier" (Freud, 1950), they are referring to constitutional differences. Pavlovians (Pavlov, 1955; Teplov, 1961) consider that individual organisms differ in nervous-system processes such as strength, mobility, and equilibrium. Other workers, while avoiding the psychoanalytic concept of instinct and without postulating the specific physiological mechanisms of behavior, still emphasize the view that behavior is determined by internal factors in the organisms as well as by external circumstances. Thus, Chess, Thomas, Birch, and Hertzig (1960) maintain that infants manifest primary reaction patterns that cannot be explained solely on an experiential basis. Despite differences on many points, writers as diverse as Pavlov, Freud, and Chess et al. agree that the way in which both internal and external stimuli are experienced is an important aspect of the organism's equipment.

This study is an attempt to determine whether there are individual differences in neonates' intensity of response to various sensory stimuli. Day-to-day constancy of response to different stimuli was tested to determine whether such differences were stable during the first few days of life. The relationship between responses in different modalities was also investigated to see whether those babies who gave the most intense response to one stimulus also gave the most intense responses to other stimuli.

Method

Subjects. The subjects were 30 healthy full-term babies born at Bronx Municipal Hospital Center. Recently circumcised boys were excluded because they seemed too irritable. The sample thus consisted of 24 girls and 6 boys.[1]

Procedure. Babies were tested and observed during four sessions. The first session always occurred on the second day of life and the last session on the fourth or fifth day. Babies were always observed from 30 to 90 min. postprandially and most frequently after the 10:00 a.m. feeding.

The stimuli were a soft tone, a loud tone, a cold disk applied to the baby's thigh, and a pacifier inserted in the baby's mouth. The tones and the disk were excitatory stimuli, whereas the pacifier was considered to result in inhibition. The pure tones were produced by an audio-frequency oscillator. The frequency (pitch) used was 250 cps. The soft tone was measured as 65 db. and the loud tone as 90 db. at the baby's bassinette. The metal disk measured 2½ in. by 1½ in. and was curved. It was immersed in ice water (temperature, 8°C.) for three min. between applications. Immediately after removal from the ice water, it was applied to the thigh. The pacifier was dipped in dextrose prior to insertion in the baby's mouth. All stimuli were applied by the experimenter. The first three stimuli were applied for 5 sec. each and the pacifier for 20 sec. The interval between stimulus applications was at least 60 sec.

---

[1] Both Graham (1956) and Brownfield (1956) reported no sex differences in their studies, and this study confirmed that finding.

Each stimulus, with a few unavoidable exceptions, was applied three times at each session for a total of 12 trials per stimulus for the four sessions (a complete set of trials would have numbered 1,440; the number actually completed was 1,425). The procedure was for the stimuli to be applied in the following sequence: soft tone, loud tone, cold disk, pacifier. An attempt was made to have the baby quiescent prior to stimulation, but this was not always possible. As a result, occasional changes in the sequence of stimuli were made (e.g., when a baby was irritable, the pacifier trial was used since this quieted the baby; similarly, if a baby became too aroused, the cold disk was omitted). Deviation from the prescribed stimulus sequence, although perhaps lessening the rigorousness of the procedure, occurred only when it was essential if the experiment was to be continued.

Ratings. Since human observation was the instrument used to record the data, considerable effort was devoted to establishing rating scales that were explicit. The major variable was a measure of the intensity of the subject's response to each experimental stimulation. Intensity of response to the excitatory stimuli consisted primarily of changes in body movement (Table 1).

Intensity of response to the pacifier was rated differently from responses to arousing stimuli. Although sucking on a pacifier frequently altered activity level, the most significant feature of the response was sucking, and thus intensity of sucking was measured and changes in bodily movement were excluded from this rating. The rating scale for sucking is presented as Table 2.

Observers made numerical ratings and descriptive statements on mimeographed forms. For each trial, intensity of response was rated. A total of six psychologists and psychiatrists served as observers. The group worked together for several months observing babies and elaborating the rating scales and test procedures. Once the data collection was begun, two or three observers were present at each session. To minimize a halo effect (the influence of a first impression on subsequent ratings), the observers were rotated so that no one, except the author, was present at consecutive sessions.

TABLE 1. DESCRIPTION AND NUMERICAL DESIGNATION OF RESPONSES TO AROUSING STIMULI

Description	Numerical Designation*
Inhibition or diminution of activity	↓
No response	0
Small eye, toe, or finger flicker; movement of only one body part	1
More intense flutter or flicker of more than one part; a small movement of one extremity	2
Partial or incomplete startle; large movement of extremities; any major flexion or extension	3
Startle; any movement with crying; over-all activation	4
Hard crying and any activity; major intense over-all activation	5

*Intensity scale, ↓ (inhibitions); 0; 1; 2; 3; 4; 5.

TABLE 2. DESCRIPTION AND NUMERICAL DESIGNATION OF
RESPONSES TO PACIFIER

Description	Numerical Designation*
No response	0
Occasionally sucks on the pacifier	1
Mild and not continuous sucking	2
Discontinuous sucking of moderate intensity; constant sucking of mild intensity	3
Strong, but not continuous sucking	4
Vigorous and continuous sucking	5

*Intensity scale, ↓ (inhibitions); 0; 1; 2; 3; 4; 5.

Rater Reliability. In a pilot study rater reliability was established at 0.95; that is, at least two of the three raters agreed precisely in 95 per cent of the trials. In less than 1 per cent of the trials were there disagreements of more than one point (on a seven-point scale). Rater reliability was computed for ten randomly selected babies, throughout the experimental period. This procedure was selected to assure that rater reliability be maintained. Rater reliability was computed for all trials without considering the nature of the stimulus.

Results

The major finding was that babies could be differentiated within the first 5 days of life in terms of the consistency of their reactivity to external stimuli. Some neonates consistently responded vigorously to all stimuli, whereas others responded moderately, and others were characterized by mild-intensity responses. In general, babies who responded vigorously to one stimulus responded vigorously to all stimuli and stability from day 2 to day 5 was established.

These differences among babies were determined as follows. Initially, the data from each baby for the four sessions were combined for each stimulus condition. Then a median intensity of response per stimulus for each baby was derived. This median was based on the 12 trials from all sessions combined. Table 3 presents these data.

A Kendall coefficient of concordance (W) was then computed (based on the rankings of the medians), and it was found that neonates significantly maintained their ranks relative to other neonates in response to each of the different stimuli ($W = .477, df = 29, \chi^2 = 55.68, p < .01$).

The babies tended to maintain their relative rankings in response to all four stimuli, and the differences among babies were significant. This finding implies that a baby who gave low-intensity responses to one stimulus tended to give low-intensity responses to all stimuli. Therefore, babies could be differentiated on the criterion of intensity of response.

This analysis was based on pooled data; that is, no differentiation was made

TABLE 3. MEDIANS OF INTENSITY OF RESPONSE TO THE 12 TRIALS UNDER EACH STIMULUS CONDITION

SUBJECTS	STIMULUS CONDITIONS*			
	Soft Tone	Loud Tone	Cold Disk	Pacifier
1.	0.3	2.5	3.0	2.5
2.	0.5	1.5	2.7	0.3
3.	0.8	1.9	1.5	1.2
4.	0.5	2.5	3.0	2.7
5.	1.0	2.5	3.3	3.5
6.	2.	2.8	2.9	2.8
7.	0.3	1.0	3.3	3.5
8.	0.7	1.8	2.9	1.5
9.	1.8	3.1	3.7	2.8
10.	1.7	2.5	2.8	2.5
11.	0.7	2.8	3.6	0.3
12.	0.4	1.2	3.3	1.5
13.	1.2	3.5	3.5	2.5
14.	2.	2.9	2.7	0.0
15.	1.	2.4	2.8	3.0
16.	1.5	1.8	3.5	3.5
17.	0.8	2.5	2.9	1.5
18.	1.9	2.7	2.3	0.3
19.	−0.5	1.5	2.6	0.1
20.	1.8	3.0	4.1	3.0
21.	1.0	2.6	3.2	0.4
22.	0.5	2.5	2.9	0.3
23.	0.9	1.5	3.3	0.1
24.	1.5	2.7	3.9	2.8
25.	0.3	0.5	2.3	0.2
26.	2.8	3.5	3.1	2.7
27.	0.9	1.8	2.4	3.6
28.	1.3	2.0	2.8	4.8
29.	2.1	1.8	3.5	2.8
30.	2.7	3.0	3.2	2.3

*Intensity scale, 0; 1; 2; 3; 4; 5.

among the trials from the four different sessions. Implicit in the finding of individual differences (based on data obtained at several sessions) is the assumption of day-to-day constancy. For if there were marked variability, measures of central tendency would converge. However, a separate test was made to obtain an independent evaluation of constancy of response. The question asked was whether a baby who responds vigorously on the second day of life also responds vigorously on the third, fourth, and fifth days. All trials on all stimuli for each day were combined so that there would be 12 trials per day. Table 4 presents the ranks of the babies according to their median scores for each of the four sessions across all stimuli. A coefficient of concordance (W) was computed ($W = .406, df = 29, \chi^2 = 47.10, p < .02$). This result demonstrates that babies who responded

TABLE 4. BABIES RANKED ON EACH OF FOUR SESSIONS
ACCORDING TO MEDIAN INTENSITY OF RESPONSE
(COMBINES ALL STIMULI)

Subject	Session 1	Session 2	Session 3	Session 4
1.......	23.5	9.0	19.5	6.0
2.......	26.5	1.0	11.0	7.5
3.......	2.5	14.5	22.0	2.0
4.......	21.5	23.0	19.5	4.5
5.......	17.0	19.0	27.5	17.0
6.......	10.5	25.0	17.0	20.0
7.......	17.0	5.0	27.5	27.5
8.......	5.0	25.0	7.0	4.5
9.......	29.0	28.0	11.0	25.0
10.......	21.5	9.0	4.5	20.0
11.......	5.0	14.5	25.5	10.0
12.......	7.0	9.0	4.5	7.5
13.......	26.5	28.0	19.5	10.0
14.......	17.0	22.0	11.0	12.0
15.......	8.0	12.0	25.5	27.5
16.......	17.0	14.5	19.5	15.0
17.......	26.5	19.0	7.0	13.0
18.......	13.0	9.0	15.5	3.0
19.......	2.5	9.0	3.0	10.0
20.......	23.5	28.0	29.0	29.0
21.......	20.0	19.0	13.5	17.0
22.......	17.0	6.0	1.0	17.0
23.......	5.0	3.0	2.0	25.0
24.......	26.5	19.0	15.5	27.5
25.......	1.0	4.0	9.0	1.0
26.......	30.0	25.0	13.5	20.0
27.......	14.0	19.0	7.0	14.0
28.......	10.5	2.0	30.0	25.0
29.......	10.5	14.5	23.5	30.0
30.......	10.5	30.0	23.5	27.5

at a certain intensity at the first session responded at a similar intensity at
subsequent sessions.

Discussion

Consistent individual differences in response intensity during the first few
days of life were the major finding in this study. Babies seen on successive days
tended to respond in characteristic ways.

This method of studying neonates provides an index of neonatal respon-
sivity which may profitably be used in longitudinal studies of children that
attempt to relate early-appearing patterns of response to later behavior.

Another significant finding was the fact that rankings of babies' responses to
different stimuli tended to be the same. This result suggests that most babies
could be characterized as being either slightly, moderately, or intensely respon-

sive to stimuli, regardless of the modality or the nature of the stimulus. Perhaps this general quality refers to babies whose development will follow a normal course. Perhaps, too, as suggested by clinical research (Kanner, 1944; Bergman and Escalona, 1949), those babies who show unusual responsiveness in one modality may be more prone to atypical development. This question could only be resolved through longitudinal studies.

This study does not reveal the determinants of the individual differences that were obtained. The genic background of both parents and the mother's state during pregnancy and labor may, to varying degrees, determine what a child's characteristics are at birth. The effects of some of these influences (such as anesthesia and difficult labor) are likely to lose their significance soon after birth. However, some prenatal or perinatal influences may leave a more lasting mark.

It seems likely that similar maternal behavior will have a different effect on different babies. Perhaps the behavior of the neonate will in part determine the behavior of the mother. The baby who responds vigorously to all sensory stimuli will evoke different responses than a baby who is unperturbed by most occurrences in his environment.

Several interesting questions derive from this research concerning the fate of the babies among whom differences have been found. Does the trait of vigorousness of response remain constant through development? Is vigorousness of response related to later, more complex development of personality, cognitive style, interpersonal relationships, defense mechanisms, and adaptation? Can vulnerability to stress be predicted? Will the baby who is generally unresponsive to stimuli or the one who seems most responsive require greater protection from the environment? How will babies at the extremes of the continuum develop in interaction with mothers who provide different degrees of stimulation? What will become of an unresponsive baby of a somewhat withdrawn mother, or an easily aroused baby who has a tense, intrusive mother? Is "intensity of response to external stimuli" in neonates related to later-developing psychological functions, such as attention, concentration, and "capacity to delay"?

Current psychological theories regard development as a function of the continuous interaction between intrinsic and experiential factors. This research provides a method for evaluating normal neonates prior to their participation in an increasingly complex environment which will both influence and respond to characteristics observable in the first few days of life.

REFERENCES

Bergman, P., and Escalona, Sibylle K. Unusual sensitivities in very young children. *Psychoanal. Stud. Child.*, 1949, **3-4**, 332-352.

Brownfield, Edith D. An investigation of the activity and sensory responses of healthy newborn infants. Unpublished doctoral dissertation, Cornell Univer., 1956.

Chess, Stella, Thomas, A., and Birch, H. Characteristics of the individual child's behavioral response to the environment. *Amer. J. Orthopsychiat.*, 1959, **29**, 791-802.

Chess, Stella, Thomas A., Birch, H.G., and Hertzig, Margaret. Implications of a longitudinal study of child development for child psychiatry, Paper read at Amer. Psychiat. Ass., Atlantic City, May, 1960.

Escalona, Sibylle, and Heider, Grace M. *Prediction and outcome.* New York: Basic Books, 1959.

Freud, S. *Beyond the pleasure principle.* New York: Liveright, 1950.

Graham, Frances, K. Behavioral differences between normal and traumatized newborns. I. Test Procedures. *Psychol. Monogr.,* 1956, **70**, No. 20 (Whole No. 427).

Kanner, L. Early infantile autism. *J. Ped.,* 1944, **25**, 211-217.

Pavlov, I.P. *Selected works.* Moscow: Foreign Languages, 1955, 313-342.

Schaefer, E.S., and Bayley, Nancy. Maternal behavior, child behavior, and their intercorrelations from infancy through adolescence. *Monogr. Soc. Res. Child Develpm.,* 1963, **87**, No. 3.

Teplov, B.M. Typological properties of nervous system and their psychological manifestations. In N. O'Connor (Ed.), *Recent Soviet psychology.* New York: Liveright, 1961.

ANALYSIS OF OBSERVATIONAL METHOD EXAMPLE

Individual Differences in Human Neonates' Responses to Stimulation

Participants and Setting. The subjects were 30 healthy full-term babies at Bronx Municipal Hospital Center.

Content of Observations. The major variable was a measure of the intensity of the subject's response to experimental stimulation. Intensity of response to the excitatory stimuli consisted primarily of changes in body movement.

Sampling of Behavior. Babies were observed during four sessions. The first session occurred on the second day of life and the last session on the fourth or fifth day. Time sampling was used, with observations made from 30 to 90 minutes after feeding, most frequently after the 10:00 a.m. feeding.

Recording Instruments. A rating scale system was used in making observations. The scale consisted of numerical ratings and descriptive statements. (See **Tables 1 and 2 of Birns's article for two intensity scales.**)

CHAPTER 12

Questionnaire and Interview Techniques

As indicated in Chapter 11, the observational method makes it possible to record behavior as it occurs, ruling out the disadvantage of depending upon someone else's memory and interpretation of an event. However, there are studies which are concerned with securing information about past behavior and with individuals' perceptions, feelings, attitudes, and goals. The observational method cannot be used in such instances.

Questionnaire and interview techniques have been devised to collect data directly from the subjects in the form of their verbal or written self-reports. The validity of these reports is open to question. People may not only be reluctant to express their personal feelings, attitudes, etc., but they may not have sufficient understanding of themselves to give an accurate appraisal. In spite of these limitations, the self-report provides information that may not be available through other techniques or may be more expensive and time-consuming to obtain by other means. In instances where the information needed is straight-forward and not threatening to the subject, valid information may be obtained providing, of course, the questionnaires are constructed properly and interviews are handled by well-trained interviewers.

INTERVIEWS VERSUS SELF-ADMINISTERED QUESTIONNAIRES

As is true of any research instrument, both questionnaires and interviews have advantages and limitations. Familiarity with these possibilities can enable one to select the technique having optimum value for a certain type of study. In some studies, interviewing a small sample of respondents provides worthwhile supplementary information to a questionnaire study. Another way of combining interviews and questionnaires is for the interviewer to intersperse short questionnaires dealing with complex parts of the interview so the respondent can reread these items if he wishes.

Questionnaires

The questionnaire includes any kind of instrument that has items or questions to which individuals respond directly. It is usually associated with self-administered instruments composed of items of a closed or fixed alternative type. The information obtained is limited to written responses of subjects to prearranged questions. Self-administered questionnaires are either handed to the subjects or simply mailed to them. In either case, a minimum of explanation is given. The respondent can take as much time as he wishes to think about his answers without feeling under pressure to respond. It is an impersonal instrument with standardized instructions and wording. Unusual or personal kinds of activities may be discussed more freely than in an interview. There may be less desire on the part of the respondent to try to impress the investigator. The questionnaire is less expensive and requires less skill to administer than the interview. Also, it can provide anonymity of the respondents and can be administered to a large group simultaneously.

Galfo and Miller stated two "philosophic objections" to the use of questionnaires: "(1) the fallacious belief that what is should be; and (2) the notion that the truth of a fact is directly proportional to the number of people who accept its accuracy." (Galfo and Miller, 1965, p. 26)

Among the limitations of questionnaires are the diversity of meaning attributed to a question by various respondents, the amount of education that may be required of a person in order to understand the questions and procedures, the difficulty of securing valid personal or confidential information, and the uncertainty of receiving an adequate number of responses to represent the population.

A number of factors influence the percentage of mailed questionnaires returned. Greater return is likely when the questionnaire is short, the questions are easy to answer, it is sponsored by a group with prestige, and is sent to correspondents who are literate and not so mobile that they are not likely to receive it. Of course, a self-addressed, postage-paid envelope should be provided.

Interviews

The interview is a face-to-face method of verbal communication in which one person, the interviewer, asks another person, the respondent, questions designed to elicit information or opinions pertinent to the purposes of the research study.

Among the major advantages of an interview is the possibility of obtaining information that very likely could not, or would not, be obtained by any other method. For example, a person might be willing to talk about certain family problems on which he would not wish to comment in writing. A person may be willing to spend more time giving information when he has direct personal contact than when he is asked to take time to complete a questionnaire. In some instances, the personal contact encourages cooperation from persons who might neglect to respond to a questionnaire. Gorden stated that the "motivation factor becomes more decisive as the amount of needed information increases, as the degree of answer-structuring decreases, and as the extrinsic rewards for supplying the information decrease." (Gorden, 1969, p. 53)

An interview provides more flexibility in obtaining information than the self-administered questionnaire provides. It may yield more accurate information and greater depth of response than could be obtained through a questionnaire. This is true particularly when respondents are poorly educated or when they are from a low socioeconomic area. These people might have difficulty reading or understanding the questions, or they may not be able to express themselves clearly. An interview can be adapted to the level of understanding of the interviewee. The interviewer may clarify by repeating or rephrasing questions, following up leads in the responses, or probing more deeply to obtain a clear picture of the interviewee's ideas. In so doing, he must be careful not to influence the respondent's answer.

The interview permits greater control regarding the sequence of questions. Since questions are hidden from the respondent, later questions cannot affect earlier replies. The respondent is prevented from consulting someone else about how to answer a question.

The interviewer has an opportunity for personal growth through contacts with many types of home or community situations different from those with which he is most familiar. Through observation of the environment and personal characteristics of the interviewees, an interviewer can gain deeper insight into factors related to the research problem.

Possible limitations of interview data arise from three sources: the interview situation, the respondent, or the interviewer.

The *interview situation* may be a very expensive one, especially if a random sample is selected from a wide geographic area in which transportation costs are high. In a comparative study of the cost of mailed questionnaires and interviews, Jackson and Rothney reported that, for every dollar spent on questionnaires, interview procedures cost $60. (Jackson and Rothney, 1961, pp. 569-571)

The process of interviewing is time-consuming. In addition to the time actually spent in personal contact with the interviewees, time must be allowed for transportation and for arranging in advance for an appointment or for returning to homes where the person to be visited was not available when first contacted. Evening or weekend hours often must be used in reaching persons who are employed full time.

The *respondent* may be a limiting factor because of his inability to understand the questions or to express himself clearly, lack of information or unwillingness to reveal what he does have, unreliable memory of events, suppression of facts or memories, rationalization or deliberate distortion in order to make a good impression, or the poor quality of his judgment concerning relationships between causes and effects.

An *interviewer* may be a source of bias, directly or indirectly. Errors introduced by him may be of several types: omitting a question, rewording a question, giving insufficient time for a respondent to express his ideas, failing to probe when necessary or to probe adequately, not listening carefully, giving his own interpretation of what the respondent says, using inadequate or inappropriate motivation, and actually cheating in recording answers to questions he did not ask.

PREPARATION OF QUESTIONNAIRE AND INTERVIEW SCHEDULES

Both self-administered questionnaires and interviews have too often been used simply for gathering facts. They can and should also be used to test hypotheses and to study relations between variables. In this respect, they become measuring instruments, subject to the same criteria of reliability and validity as other measuring instruments.

Construction of the Instrument

In preparing questions, either for self-administered questionnaires or for an interview schedule, great care must be taken. Questions must be pretested and revised to eliminate misunderstanding and ambiguities through improper wording of questions. The following criteria should be kept in mind when constructing the instrument or developing techniques for interviewing that will elicit the desired information:

1. Each question should relate to the research problem being studied. Except for certain factual information about the respondent or subject, only those questions should be included which have a specific function in relation to the research study. In other words, each question should have as its purpose the eliciting of some information to be used to test the hypotheses of the study.

2. The type of question used should be appropriate to the research being conducted. An appropriate form for questions is determined by the method of administration, the subject matter, the sample of people to be studied, and the kind of analysis to be made. Questions may be asked in two forms: closed or open.

Open-end or free response questions permit an individual to respond in his own words. His responses may give insight into his feelings, background, hidden motivations, interests, or decisions. Free-response questions can stimulate a person to think about his feelings or motives and to express what he considers to be most important. In this manner, some of the disadvantages of a checklist type of questionnaire are overcome, for where unequivocal replies are sometimes demanded a respondent's thinking may be conditioned by the suggestions or limited by an incomplete list.

The open-end question is suggested when the researcher cannot anticipate ahead of time the type of answer a question may bring and when he wants the respondent to volunteer his responses rather than to be prompted by the questionnaire.

A major problem for the researcher in open-end questionnaires is that he has to classify the responses when analyzing the data and he may receive fifty different responses to a particular question. Moreover, had the respondents made the classification, they may have classified themselves differently.

Following are examples of open-end questions used in an interview schedule: (Sears, Maccoby and Levin, 1957, pp. 495, 496, 500)

"Some people feel it is very important for a child to learn not to fight with other children, and other people feel there are times when a child has to learn to fight. How do you feel about this?"

"How does X react generally when you go out of the house and leave him with someone else?"

"Do you think X behaves better with you or with his father? How do you account for that?"

In the *closed-type* or structured questions, possible answers are suggested. The respondent checks those with which he agrees, or he responds to each item indicating whether or not he agrees with it. When answers are of the "yes-no" type, provision should be made for a person to say that he is uncertain or that he has no opinion about an item. A checklist should include most of the answers that a person might wish to give, and provision should be made for writing some additional response if he so desires. Ease of response and tabulation are major advantages of closed questions or checklists.

The following questions illustrate those that elicit merely "yes-no" responses as well as those that enable the respondent to choose one or several fixed alternatives:

"Do you prefer Product X to Product Y?" Yes _____ No _____

"Did you vote for John Smith?" Yes _____ No _____

"Do you think our new product is: (1) Excellent _____ (2) Very good _____ (3) Good _____ (4) Fair _____ (5) Poor _____ ?"

"Which factor is of most importance to you in purchasing a dress? (1) Price _____ (2) Color _____ (3) Current fashion _____ (4) General appearance on me _____ ."

Closed questions are easy to administer because they are precoded and each alternative answer is classified in advance. Of course, this system forces the respondent to answer a question in terms of the researcher's criteria.

3. *A new topic should be introduced skillfully and developed by using an appropriate sequence of questions.* Gorden suggested several tactics that allow the respondent maximum freedom to develop his own sequence for discussion:

Lead-in questions are not directly related to the objectives of the study but they introduce a relevant subject area by preparing the respondent to give more accurate and valid information.

Example: "In a study of the differences in the amount of interaction between the child, his family and the school in high and low delinquency areas of a large city, the opening question was, 'Do you think this neighborhood is a good or a bad place to raise kids?' " (Gorden, 1969, p. 258)

Pivot or filter questions attempt to determine whether the line of questioning would be appropriate in light of the individual's experiences.

> Example: In a study of the effects of a disaster on the community, an interviewer might start by asking: "Where were you when the storm struck Judsonia?" "Were you injured in any way?" (Gorden, 1969, p. 260)

Transition questions provide a bridge from one topic to another so the respondent will not carry over an inappropriate context from a previous question or be confused about the purpose of the interview.

> Example: "In a study of the effects of foreign travel, we included the following five topics in the order indicated:
> 1) The respondent's specific experiences abroad within the past two years.
> 2) The effects of these experiences in *changing* his views of the foreign country.
> 3) The effects of these experiences in *changing* his views of his own country.
> 4) Courses taken in college that influenced the meaningfulness of the foreign experience.
> 5) Certain personality traits that might affect the respondent's adjustment to the foreign culture." (Gorden, 1969, p. 261)

In a *funnel* sequence, the most general question is asked first and then the more restricted questions. This approach helps the respondent to recall details so the interviewer is less likely to have to interrupt with specific questions. Also, the respondent speaks from his own perspective before a frame of reference is imposed on him. Funneling the questions helps a researcher to discover unanticipated responses.

> Example: "If we were interested in discovering how people's views of social problems are related to the magazines they read ... the sequence given below would be a funnel sequence:
> 1) What do you think are some of the most important social problems in the world today, and why?
> 2) Of all the problems you have just mentioned, which one do you think is the most important one to solve?
> 3) Where have you gotten most of your information about problem X?
> 4) Do you read *U.S. News and World Report*?" (Gorden, 1969, p. 266)

4. Leading questions should be avoided so that there is no suggestion to the respondent of the most appropriate answer. For example, if you wished to elicit attitudes toward mobile housing, an open-end question in this respect could take several forms: "How do you feel about mobile housing?" or "You wouldn't say that you were in favor of mobile housing, would you?" The latter question is obviously biased and tends to make it easier for the respondent to answer "no." Such an answer seems to agree with the researcher rather than to contradict him. Another way in which a question may suggest a positive or negative answer is by the use of emotionally loaded words. For example, different responses were received to a question referring to Nazi Germany as compared to Germany.

5. *The language used in a questionnaire should be similar to the language used and understood by the subjects.* Questions must also be worded so that they are in keeping with the respondent's present level of information and education.

6. *The questions should not be loaded with "social desirability."* (Kerlinger, 1964, p. 475) People tend to give answers which they know to be socially desirable. Therefore, questions dealing with such concepts as motherhood, love, and peace, must be handled carefully, for these terms are desirable ones that everyone is supposed to favor. No matter what a person's true attitude, he is aware that any form of prejudice is disapproved socially and so he may give an invalid response when asked for his reactions to minority groups. The following is an open-end question in which the researcher puts the respondent at ease about the desirability of one answer in preference to another:

> "All babies cry, of course. Some mothers feel that if you pick up a baby every time it cries, you will spoil it. Others think you should never let a baby cry for very long. How do you feel about this? What do you do about this with X? How about in the middle of the night?" (Sears, Maccoby, and Levin, 1957, pp. 491-492)

Pretesting the Instrument

It is important to try out the questions and procedures on a small scale to determine whether or not the purpose of the research will be fulfilled. This preliminary or exploratory study is called a *pilot* study. The pretesting of instruments should be with a sample of individuals from a population similar to that to be drawn for the major part of the research. Space should be provided on the questionnaire for the respondents' reactions in terms of the need for additional responses not included in the questionnaire, ambiguous questions, etc.

A large sample is not necessary for pretesting. For a well-defined professional group such as home economics teachers, about twenty cases may be sufficient. For a more heterogeneous group such as housewives, a larger pretest sample group would be advisable.

The results of the pretest should be evaluated with a view toward revising and improving the instruments and the procedures for gathering and analyzing data. Responses to each question should be checked separately, noting items that are frequently left blank or are answered in an unexpected manner. Such items may have been misinterpreted.

A brief analysis of the data should be made to determine whether the plan for classifying and quantifying the data to test the hypotheses will be satisfactory.

GATHERING QUESTIONNAIRE OR INTERVIEW DATA

Generally when questionnaires or interviews are to be used, preliminary contacts are made with potential respondents to explain the purpose and scope of the study. Building rapport in the initial phases is important in obtaining cooperation and usable responses.

Letter of Transmittal

Obtaining a sufficient percentage of responses to a mailed questionnaire is a major problem. The letter of transmittal is an important factor in eliciting a high degree of response and enabling the researcher to draw general conclusions from a representative sample.

The letter of transmittal that is sent originally with the questionnaire should state clearly the purposes of the study so the subject will be motivated to respond. What groups or individuals are being asked to cooperate and the value of the information they can supply should also be stressed. An offer to share the results of the completed study is often effective. If the study can be associated with a professional organization or institution respected by the respondents, the importance of the study may be strengthened. It may also be desirable to point out the anonymity of the respondents and the confidentiality with which the data will be handled.

The following is a sample letter of transmittal:

Dr. A. B. Smith, Head
Department of Housing and Environmental Design
Middle State University
Middletown, Ohio

Dear Dr. Smith:

The attached questionnaire, concerned with research related to human ecology being conducted in U.S. colleges and universities, is part of a national study being carried on cooperatively by the Environmental Quality Association and Central State University. The specific purpose of the project is to determine the present status of research dealing with the interrelationships of man and his environment, particularly with respect to environmental problems being studied, research methodology and instruments used, and departments and schools in which the researchers are located. The results of this study will help to provide information regarding the types of problems for which solutions are being sought through research. They should be of value to other researchers as well as to environmental planners.

We are particularly interested in obtaining your responses because your experience with an important aspect of man's environment will contribute significantly toward identifying methods used in attempting to solve environmental problems. The average time required for completing the questionnaire in a preliminary trial was 30 minutes.

Please complete the questionnaire by March 15 and return it in the enclosed stamped, self-addressed envelope. We will be pleased to send you a summary of the results of the study if you desire.

Thank you for your assistance.

Sincerely,

R.E. Jones
Director of Research

In general, the higher the per cent of response, the more likely the responses are to represent the total group to whom the questionnaires were given. Respondents and nonrespondents might be compared on certain objective characteristics for which information is available. If the two groups are not significantly different on these factors, the group may be considered representative of the larger population.

In many studies, an attempt is made to follow up the persons from whom no reply has been received. Various procedures are used. A common one is to send a card or letter within a few weeks after sending the questionnaire. The follow-up card or letter should state in a direct, straightforward manner the significance of the study, the need for obtaining a reply from each person who received the questionnaire, and willingness to send a duplicate questionnaire in case the other copy is no longer available.

Even in studies where the replies are anonymous and confidential, an identifying number is necessary on each questionnaire or return envelope if a follow-up notice is to be sent only to the nonrespondents. As each reply is received, the respondent's name is checked off. Follow-up cards or letters are sent to the persons from whom no reply has been received by the suggested deadline, or within a week following the deadline. Just in case a person has sent his reply while the follow-up letters are being mailed, the letter might say: "If you have not already returned your completed questionnaire. . . ."

Interview Techniques

Valid data can be collected in an interview only if the questions have been well designed and assembled so as to meet the objectives and test the hypotheses of the research. Interviewing is an art which consists largely of creating a situation in which the respondents will be cooperative and honest. The first requirement for successful interviewing, therefore, is to create a situation in which the respondents will answer in a reliable and valid manner. When this requirement has been met, the interviewer's task is to ask the questions properly to obtain accurate responses and to record those responses accurately and in detail.

Gorden (1969, pp. 1-2) summarized the difficulties of obtaining valid, reliable, and meaningful data:

> Accompanying this increasing consciousness of the need for greater validity and reliability in methodology is an increase in the methodological difficulty intrinsic to the types of problems being posed. For example, social anthropology has seen a shift from the description of external

environment, artifacts and behavioral patterns to analysis of the subjective meaning of these for the members of the culture. Thus there has been increasing emphasis on values, world-view, beliefs, expectations, and socialization of the child.

In social psychology there has been a gradual shift in empirical studies from observation of external forms of behavior, where high reliability is relatively easy to obtain, to more theoretically meaningful categories of human phenomena that tend to have greater predictive value but which present more difficult problems of data gathering.

In sociology there has been an increasing shift of emphasis from the use of easily observable facts such as sex, race, and residential location to more meaningful but less obvious categories such as social distance, expectations, cognitive dissonance, attitude, definition of the situation, latent and operative values, channels of influence and decision making. There has also been a historical shift in emphasis from static descriptions of public opinion or social class, for example, to the more dynamic problems of the formation and function of public opinion and social stratification systems. There has also been a historical shift away from reliance on the use of data already collected for some official or practical purpose toward the collection of information more directly relevant to the theoretical or practical requirements of the specific problem at hand. These general trends in the basic behavioral sciences of social anthropology, social psychology and sociology are reflected in trends which follow in applied areas such as industrial relations, race relations, family relations, mental health, and education.

Obtaining data by the personal interview method is a very complicated task requiring a considerable amount of training.

Contemporary social science does not provide the interviewer with adequate methods for dealing with all the variables at work in the interview. To some extent this might be thought of as a symptom of the youthful inadequacy of social science in general and social psychology in particular. To a considerable extent, however, it is also a function of the unusual complexity of the subject matter on which the interviewer, as a scientific technician, is exercising his techniques. Much of the available literature consists of rules of thumb, presented as lists of "do's" and "don'ts" for the interviewer and for the questionnaire framer. These do's and don'ts are essentially nonsystematic compilations of interviewing experience derived from a variety of situations over a considerable period of time. (Cannel and Kahn in Festinger and Katz, 1953, p. 333)

The following is a set of well-tested procedures which the research interviewer uses:

Introduction to the Interview. In the initial contact the respondent or subject must be motivated to permit the interview to be conducted. Ordinarily the following sequence of procedures is followed by the interviewer: (1) Explanation of purpose of the research; (2) Description of the method of selecting the sample and the respondent as one member of the sample; (3) Identification of the group conducting the research; and (4) Indicating the confidential nature of the interview.

Questioning the Respondent. Using the questionnaire as part of the interview may be compared to the scientific experimenter's role of using a measuring instrument in the standard manner. It is important in interviewing respondents to ask the question of each respondent in the same manner. The only instance in which the procedure should vary is when a respondent is unable to understand the question as worded and it must be repeated to him, or, if necessary, interpreted for him. If it is desired to quantify data, then it is important to treat the questionnaire and the interview in a scientific way by administering it as a standard stimulus to a population of respondents. In such instances, the questions must be identical and the situation or manner in which the questions are asked must be identical.

In exploratory research or where subjective analysis is planned, the interviewer may be permitted to use more flexibility in the use of the questionnaire and may tailor his questions to his respondents. It may sometimes be necessary for the interviewer to probe for additional information or to clarify or make more specific, information which the respondent has already given. This must be accomplished without biasing the data.

When there is a discrepancy between the information given by the respondent and that needed for the research study, a skilled interviewer draws upon a variety of probing techniques as outlined by Gorden (1969, pp. 272-291):

1. A *silent probe* is the most permissive and often very productive way of allowing the respondent to proceed in any direction that he finds interesting or meaningful. This is one way of being sure the interviewer does not interrupt too quickly. Too much silence, however, may be embarrassing to a respondent who has said all he wants to say, doesn't know what the interviewer is seeking, or needs support or direction.

2. *Neutral probes* encourage the respondent to elaborate without specifying any direction. They indicate the interviewer has understood and accepted what was said and wants to hear more. Encouragement probes might be "uh huh," "I see," etc. Elaboration probes include: ". . . and then?" "What happened next?" "Tell me more about that."

3. *Clarification probes* specify the kind of additional information that is desired. For example:

> R: In general, I got along fine with both of my parents. We lived out in the country and I went to high school on the bus, so none of the kids came to my house. Of course, we had a little skirmish now and then, but basically I liked my parents and they liked me, even when I was a wild teenager.
>
> I: I see. Tell me a little about some of the skirmishes you had now and then. What were they about? (Gorden, 1969, p. 282)

4. A *reflective probe* repeats the respondent's implicit or explicit state-

ment in one of three ways: (a) an *echo* probe simply repeats words from the previous response; (b) an *interpretive* probe reflects the meaning or feeling behind the words without actually repeating the words; and (c) a *summary* probe combines several elements from previous responses. An example of an echo probe is:

> R: The main reason I came to Antioch College was because of the combination of high academic standards and the work program. It appealed to me a lot.
>
> I: It appealed to you a lot? (Gorden, 1969, p. 286)

Recording the Responses in an Interview. It is important for the interviewer to get an accurate report of the responses given. Errors in recording might result from recording something that the interviewee did not say or failing to record something he did say. Responses should be recorded accurately, either at the time they are being given or immediately following the interview. It takes a highly skilled interviewer to be able to write intelligible notes while he is carrying on the interview. Oldfield pointed out that note-taking possesses certain incidental advantages. It enables the interviewer to take his eyes occasionally off the respondent, who may find constant regard to be disconcerting. If the interviewer perceives what the interviewee considers to be important, and makes notes accordingly, the respondent's confidence in the interviewer is built up. (Oldfield, 1951, pp. 58-60)

Verbatim and rather complete replies may be recorded in several ways, such as using abbreviations, taking shorthand, or writing key words at the time and completing the details later. Asking for examples or using minor questions are ways in which the interviewer can have time for recording the full responses to major questions without long pauses. Using a tape recorder permits a complete and unbiased transcription of the responses later.

It is beyond the scope of this book to give a detailed analysis of interviewer training. Suggested references in the bibliography should be consulted for this purpose.

Sociometric Techniques

Sociometric studies involve social interactions among any group of people. Such studies commonly use questionnaires or interviews and involve simply asking each member of a group to specify which other members of that group he would like to have as a companion in some activity (e.g., study with) and which ones he would not like to have as a companion. The subject is sometimes allowed to name as many people as he wishes but more frequently is limited to naming a specific number.

Sociometry yields very simple scores — basically ones and zeros. Yet it can involve analysis of a high level of sophistication mathematically. These mathematical methods will not be discussed here. However, the type of analysis shown in Figure 19 in the form of a sociogram is frequently used, especially for practical purposes. The data plotted in this sociogram may be manipulated to describe several properties of group structure or to define an individual member's social

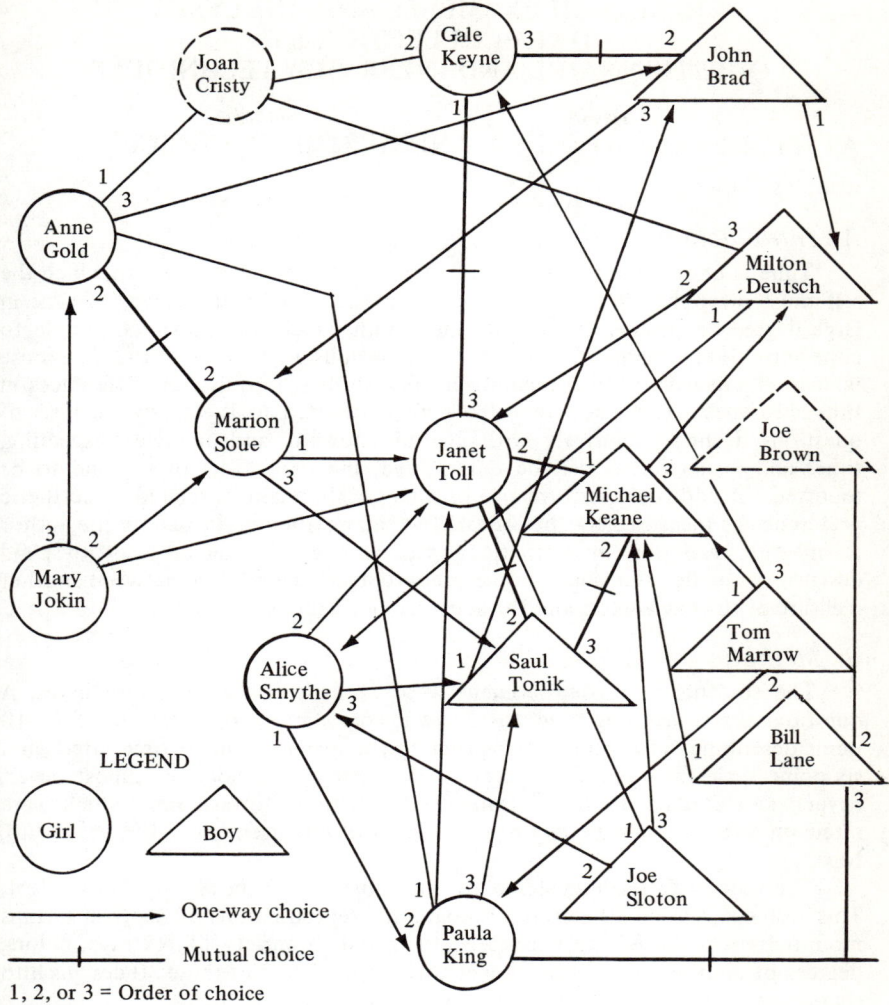

Figure 19. Sociogram. Fig. 3, p. 22, from *Sociometry in Group Relations: A Work Guide for Teachers,* by H.H. Jennings, 1948, reprinted with permission from American Council on Education, Washington, D.C.

relationships with other members of the group. Whenever a conceptual arrow from one person to another person can be drawn, with the arrow indicating interacts with, dominates, leads, likes, is friendly with, is like me, and so forth, sociometric methods have potential usefulness for observation and measurement of variables.

RESEARCH EXAMPLES AND ANALYSES
DATA COLLECTION BY
QUESTIONNAIRE AND INTERVIEW TECHNIQUES

ATTITUDES TOWARD TIME AND AESTHETIC CHOICE[1]

ROBERT H. KNAPP

A. Introduction

Time is one of the two basic parameters of the physical world to which the self must inevitably relate itself, and the mastery and management of time in large degree determines the effectiveness with which the individual is able to cope with his environment. Yet despite the obvious importance of the time sense in man, there have been comparatively few studies of individual differences in time awareness. The study reported here is devoted to the factor analysis of questions dealing exclusively with attitudes toward, and practices respecting, time, and is, so far as can be determined, the first effort of its kind to be reported. In addition, performance on this questionnaire is related to aesthetic preference as measured by the Tartan Test, an instrument devised by the author to measure variation in aesthetic appeal among 30 selected Scottish plaid designs. An earlier study has, in fact, reported a closer relation between another measure of time awareness and this measure of aesthetic choice (4).

B. Method

The subjects in this experiment were 77 male college undergraduates. A questionnaire concerning time was devised, consisting of two sections: first, 10 items describing actual practices respecting the management of time rated on a six-point scale (always, almost always, frequently, occasionally, almost never, never); and second, 13 items dealing with attitudes toward time which were rated on a five-point scale expressing degrees of endorsement (YES, yes, ?, no, NO).

The second test administered to our subjects was the Knapp Tartan Test. This test consists of 30 selected lithographic reproductions of Scottish tartans mounted on 5″ x 8″ cards selected to include a variety of textures, colors, degrees of contrast, etc. Each subject was required to sort these 30 designs into six groups of five each, according to their aesthetic appeal.

C. Results

All 23 items of the time questionnaire were correlated to yield a 23 x 23 matrix. It was evident immediately that some of the items yielded very low

Reprinted with permission from *The Journal of Social Psychology*, Vol. 56, 1962, pp. 79-87.

[1] This research has been partially supported by funds made available through a grant from the Ford Foundation to David C. McClelland for the study of motivation and economic behavior and partially by U.S. Public Health Grant #M-2178.

correlations with all others, and in the interests of economy these were eliminated from further consideration. The resulting matrix was thus reduced to 17 items, seven taken from the Practices Scale and 10 from the Attitudes Scale. They are given below in Table 1 with their original numbers, prefaced by an initial to indicate the scale from which they were derived.

The correlation matrix relating these 17 items was then subjected to a centroid factor analysis and two factors extracted, after which the residuals were so small that further factoring did not seem warranted. Table 2 gives the rotated factor loadings of each of these items on both factors.

A consideration of the rotated factor loadings for the several items given above will reveal two fairly sharply defined clusters which include all but four of the 17 items. The first of these clusters yields high loadings on the first factor and negligible loadings on the second. Table 3 presents these items. It is evident from a superficial consideration of the positively loaded items that they all express a feeling of harassment with the passage of time together with an effort to manage and control it. Conversely, the negatively loaded items suggest an Olympian unconcern with time. It would appear appropriate to characterize this factor as a "time servant-master" dimension. Items expressive of a time-serving have, of course, positive loadings on this first factor; those representing a superior masterful sense, negative loadings.

The second factor comprises the five items as shown in Table 4. The impression one gathers from this cluster of items is that it defines a polarity of attitude running from "time efficiency" to "time obliviousness." The presence of clear affective feeling toward time is not so manifest here as in the case of the first cluster. It is also probably important to note that all but one of the items deal with simple practices in the management of time. In contrast, the first factor is

TABLE 1. SELECTED ITEMS FROM PRACTICES AND ATTITUDES SCALES

P	1.	Do you wear a watch?
P	2.	Do you keep your clock or watch set ahead?
P	3.	Do you use an alarm clock?
P	4.	Do you arise at the same time each morning whether necessary or not?
P	5.	Are you often early for appointments?
P	7.	Do you ever make out written time schedules?
P	10.	Do you have trouble remembering what day or date it is?
A	11.	Do you feel particularly guilty when late for appointments?
A.	12.	Does it annoy you to find your watch has stopped or does not run properly?
A	13.	Do you feel anxious when you are not certain of the time?
A	14.	Do you feel guilty if you sleep late in the morning?
A	16.	Do you feel you waste time or spend it uselessly?
A	17.	Do you find you have lots of leisure time?
A	20.	Do you feel that you are a slave to time?
A	21.	Do you ever wish you lived in a world without time?
A	22.	Do you like the idea of changing our clocks ahead to Daylight Saving Time?
A	23.	Does a close time schedule make you feel anxious?

TABLE 2. ROTATED FACTOR LOADINGS ON ITEMS FROM
PRACTICES AND ATTITUDES SCALES

			Factor I	Factor II
P	1	(wear watch)	+.12	+.37
P	2	(clock set ahead)	−.06	−.46
P	3	(use alarm clock)	+.15	−.27
P	4	(arise same time)	+.10	+.43
P	5	(early for appointments)	−.30	+.02
P	7	(written time schedules)	+.40	−.12
P	10	(trouble remembering day or date)	00	−.52
A	11	(guilty when late for appointments)	+.30	−.13
A	12	(annoyed with stopped watch)	+.53	+.07
A	13	(anxious if uncertain of time)	+.42	−.03
A	14	(guilty if sleep late)	+.48	+.07
A	16	(feel may waste time)	+.45	−.16
A	17	(lots of leisure time)	−.31	−.03
A	20	(slave to time)	+.45	−.46
A	21	(world without time)	+.07	−.51
A	22	(Daylight Saving Time)	+.37	+.35
A	23	(anxious about close time schedule)	+.34	−.49

heavily determined by attitudinal items expressing emotional involvement with time.

Four items remain unaccounted for. Of these, two, namely A 20 (considers self a slave to time) and A 23 (close schedules make anxious), yield high positive loadings on the first factor and negative loadings on the second. They occupy the center of a quadrant lying between time obliviousness and time harassment, which is logical, considering their nature. A third item, A 22 (favors Daylight Saving Time), gives substantial loadings on both the first and second factors and occupies the quadrant lying between time efficiency and time harassment. The final item, P3 (use of alarm clock), does not yield any significant loading on either factor.

Next, factor scores were computed for each of the two factors described by summing the ratings assigned each of the significant items reported above and subtracting those with positive from those with negative loadings. These factor scores were then correlated with the preference ranking assigned each of the 30 tartans of the Knapp Tartan Test. Since results on the second factor were somewhat inconclusive, they will not be reported here. However, the correlations of each tartan with the factor score of the first cluster, that embodying what we have called the "master-servant" attitude, revealed an interesting pattern. Table 5 shows the correlations of these tartans with this factorial score, as well as the rank order of the correlation. It will be seen that the correlations range from +.40 through −.38 without any corrections for coarseness of grouping or for the imperfect reliability of the measures. Given our N of 77, a correlation would have to attain .23 to be significant at the five per cent level of confidence, .29 to be significant at the one per cent level. In all, therefore, five exceed the one per

TABLE 3. SIGNIFICANT FACTOR LOADINGS ON ITEMS COMPRISING FACTOR I

			Factor I	Factor II
A	12	(annoyed by bad watch)	+.53	+.07
A	14	(guilty if sleep late)	+.48	+.07
A	16	(feels may waste time)	+.45	−.16
A	13	(anxious if uncertain of time)	+.42	−.03
P	7	(makes times schedules)	+.40	−.12
A	11	(feels guilty when late)	+.30	−.13
A	18	(has lots of leisure time)	−.31	−.03
P	5	(frequently early for appointment)	−.30	+.02

TABLE 4. FIVE ITEMS YIELDING SIGNIFICANT LOADINGS ON FACTOR II

			Factor I	Factor II
P	4	(arise at same time)	+.10	+.43
P	1	(wear watch)	+.12	+.37
P	2	(set watch ahead)	−.06	−.46
A	21	(wish world without time)	+.07	−.51
P	10	(trouble remembering date)	00	−.52

cent level and eight the five per cent level of confidence. We shall assume that the null hypothesis would require that there be a random relation between the stimulus qualities of the tartans and their rank position in the correlation series. If it transpires that this ordinal ranking is not randomly related to the stimulus properties of the tartans, then we feel justified in declaring a positive relation between the time attitude cluster considered and aesthetic preference.

On inspection, it appears that the tartans, far from being randomly mingled in the ordinal series, show a striking pattern such that those occupying the lower ranks are consistently somber, and frequently of blue and green coloring. Those in the higher ranks, on the other hand, tend to be predominantly red and yellow. A Chi-square table classifying the 10 correlating most positively with Factor I and the 10 correlating most negatively divided according to the predominance of blue-green or red-yellow is shown in Table 6. It may be seen that there is not a random relationship between the first and last 10 in the ordinal series, rather that those yielding positive correlations with our first cluster tend overwhelmingly to the somber blue-green while this quality is totally absent from the last 10. As a matter of fact, only one of the first 10 is a bright red, i.e., the Drummond. The second tartan in doubt among this group is the Macdonald of Clanranald, which is distinctly somber though with some deep rust-colored striations.

Of the 10 tartans yielding the most negative correlations with our time

TABLE 5. CORRELATIONS OF TARTAN TEST WITH FACTOR I

No.	Tartan	r with Factor I	Rank Order of r
2	MacLeod of Lewis	−.38	30
3	Balmoral	−.31	28
5	Brodie	−.13	24
6	Anderson	−.10	19
7	MacPherson, Hunting	−.34	29
8	Leslie	+.13	9
9	Innes	−.13	23
10	Logan	+.20	4
11	MacLachlan	−.12	22
13	Sinclair	−.16	25
15	Cumming	+.06	13
16	Drummond	+.19	5
17	Barclay	−.26	26
18	Cameron of Erracht	−.03	16
19	Ramsay	−.41	27
20	Oliphant	+.28	2
21	Stewart of Appin	−.10	20
22	MacDonell of Glengarry	+.08	11
24	Ogilvie	00	14
26	Campbell of Breadalbane	+.16	8
28	MacDonald of Clanranald	+.26	3
31	Macrae	−.06	18
33	MacDonald of Staffa	−.03	17
37	Clergy	+.12	10
41	Sutherland Ancient	+.17	7
43	Stewart, Prince Charles Edward	−.02	15
44	Douglas	+.18	6
46	Colquhoun	+.05	12
47	Hay	−.12	21
48	Elliot	+.40	1

Five per cent level of confidence = .23
One per cent level of confidence = .29

factor, the division is as follows. Six are dominated by vigorous red, two striking yellow and black contrasts. The two remaining are grey, one of which, Balmoral, is distinctly on the light side. None are, by any stretch of the imagination, dominated by blue-green coloration; only three have blue or green even as a very minor feature of their design.

Finally, it may be of some interest to observe how this ordering of tartans compares with orderings based upon correlations with other measured psychological variables as determined in other studies. We shall select three of these. The first (2) is the ordering established with respect to need for achievement measured with the Thematic Apperception Test according to the method described by McClelland (5). The second is an ordering derived from the correlations of the tartans with the Strong Vocational Inventory factor for interest in physical sciences (1). The third is an ordering established in research relating

TABLE 6. CHI-SQUARE TABLE SHOWING COLOR
PREDOMINANCE IN ORDINAL SERIES

	Rank 1-10	Rank 21-30
Blue, green	8	0
Red, yellow, grey	2	10

Chi-square with Yates correlation = 10.26

TABLE 7. CORRELATIONS OF TARTAN TEST WITH
OTHER MEASURED PSYCHOLOGICAL VARIABLES

Questionnaire Factor No. I with n Achievement	+.34
Questionnaire Factor No. I with "science interest"	+.40
Questionnaire Factor No. I with underestimation of time	+.55

tartan preference to the tendency to underestimate or overestimate time required for a moving target to reach a specified target (4). Table 7 shows these correlations.

Thus, it appears that there is a roughly similar pattern of aesthetic preference associated with four measured psychological variables in which the principle is preference for somber blue-green designs over bright red and yellow designs. These four independent variables are (1) the tendency to be harassed by time and to seek to control it, (2) high achievement motivation, (3) interest in science and technology, and (4) the tendency to underestimate time intervals in calculating the progress of a moving target.

D. Discussion

The purpose of the foregoing has been primarily to present a factorial structure of attitudes and practices respecting time. We have been able to identify two primary factors in this area: first, a time-servant vs. time-master dimension; second, a time efficient vs. time oblivious dimension. We have further shown that correlated with the first of these is a pattern of aesthetic preference showing preference for somber blue-green designs to be positively associated with concern and worry about time, scheduling, etc. Finally, we have shown that the pattern of aesthetic preferences related to worry about time and scheduling is similar to patterns established in other reported experiments. Specifically we have shown this pattern of aesthetic preference to be similar to that established for *n* Achievement, interest in physical science, and tendency to underestimate time intervals, which we shall call henceforth time parsimony. A proper understanding of the thinking which has prompted this and other researches cannot be obtained without a short excursion into the theory and speculations which prompted them. To this purpose the following is devoted.

In the history of Western civilization, the rise of North European Protestantism marks a significant development in the psychological evolution of Western man, as Weber (7), Tawney (6), and others have noted. One of the foremost aspects of the rise of Protestantism, apart from the promulgation of religious doctrines themselves, has been the emergence of certain secular psychological attitudes and interests. Among these have been an interest in the nature and measurement of time culminating in the Newtonian theory of time and the rise of the technology of time measurement. This sense of time, which we tentatively identify historically with the Protestant, and more especially the Calvinistic, character structure, has made possible some of the unique attainments of European culture, notably the rise of science and technology, the development of industrialism, the organization of capitalistic enterprise, etc. Further aspects of this Protestant character structure as it has historically evolved include, we believe, *emphasis upon achievement motivation, asceticism in matters of taste and decor, interest in science and technology*, and probably the preferred *employment of repression* as a means of coping with instincts and affect. Seeking to divorce this character syndrome from purely religious terminology, we have called it the "Puritan Pragmatic" constellation. It is to the investigation of this hypothesized structure that this and other reported studies have been devoted.

In the present study we have shown that acute time awareness and a need to control and use time effectively is associated with asceticism of aesthetic taste. Elsewhere we have shown that achievement motivation is associated with preference for images of time involving haste and direction (3), that underestimation of time intervals is associated with aesthetic asceticism, i.e., preference for blue-green tartan designs (4), and that achievement motivation is associated again with preference for somber ascetic tartan designs (2). Thus, a sort of triad has been demonstrated relating asceticism of aesthetic taste, as we define it, acute time awareness, and high achievement motivation. We have further been able to show that aesthetic asceticism is related to interests in the physical sciences, but we have not been able to demonstrate a significant positive correlation between scientific interest and achievement motivation as measured by McClelland's method (5). Neither have we yet shown that scientific interests correlate with attitudes toward time, though this possibility has not at this writing been explored. Finally, the preferred use of repression as a defense mechanism, which we believe to be part of this general character constellation, has been subject to no experimental inquiry at this point. Its participation with the others in a character syndrome remains, therefore, purely a theoretical speculation.

One concluding comment should probably be made regarding our theoretical hypothesis. As we have described it, it is a psychological hypothesis drawn from a historical analysis of North European Protestantism, a hypothesis related to the rise of capitalism, democracy, industrialism, and science. We have, we believe, partly succeeded in showing that psychological qualities ascribed to this tradition may be found correlated in contemporary populations of American students. Now two explanations of this reality are possible. First, it may be argued that these intercorrelations exist among our subjects only as a survival of a character heritage. The linkage of these several qualities becomes in this view merely one of historical accident. An alternative hypothesis, to which we subscribe, is that the association of these qualities in a common complex was not a matter of simple historical combination which survives in our time. Rather, we would contend that there are coherent and persuasive psychodynamic reasons for the intercorrelation of the several qualities which we have identified with the "Puritan pragmatic character."

E. Summary

A questionnaire has been constructed containing items dealing with the management of time and with attitudes toward time. A factor analysis of the responses of 77 male undergraduates on this instrument reveals two significant factors, the first identified as a "time servant-master" factor in which attitudes of emotional concern and harassment over time are bipolar to attitudes and practices suggesting masterful management of time and scheduling. The second factor is marked at one pole by attitudes of time obliviousness and at the other by attitudes of efficient time management. The first of these factors is shown to bear a significant relation to aesthetic preference for Scottish tartan designs such that "time-driven" persons prefer somber blue and green designs, while brighter designs of predominantly red and yellow are preferred by individuals with reported ease in the management of time. The results of this research are in general consonance with those reported earlier in which the tendency to underestimate time intervals required for a moving target to reach a mark were similarly correlated with preference for somber tartan designs (4). The results of these and other studies are related to a hypothesized "Puritan Pragmatic" character syndrome in which achievement motivation, acute time awareness, asceticism, interest in science and technology, and the preferred use of repression as a defense are positively related (3).

REFERENCES

1. Hofmann, E.G., and Knapp, R.H. Aesthetic preference and vocational preference. Unpublished study, Wesleyan University.

2. Knapp, R.H. *n* Achievement and aesthetic preference. *In* J.W. Atkinson (*Ed.*), *Motives in Fantasy, Action and Society*. Princeton, N.J.: Van Nostrand, 1958.

3. Knapp, R.H., and Garbutt, J.T. Time imagery and the achievement motive. *J. Personal.*, 1958, **26**, 426-434.

4. Knapp, R.H., and Green, H.B. Time judgment, aesthetic preference and need for achievement. *J. Abn. Soc. Psychol.*, 1959, **58**, 140-142.

5. McClelland, D.C., Atkinson, J.W., et al. *The Achievement Motive.* New York: Appleton-Century-Crofts, 1953.

6. Tawney, R.H. *Religion and the Rise of Capitalism.* New York: Penguin, 1922.

7. Weber, M. *The Protestant Ethic.* New York: Scribner, 1952.

ANALYSIS OF EXAMPLE OF QUESTIONNAIRE AND INTERVIEW TECHNIQUES

Attitudes Toward Time and Aesthetic Choice

In this study measurement of one variable — attitudes toward time — was made through the use of a questionnaire. Subjects responded to questions relating to their actual *practices* in time management, rating 10 items on a six-point scale (always, almost always, frequently, occasionally, almost never, never). Another 13 items dealing with *attitudes* toward time were rated on a five-point scale expressing degrees of endorsement (YES, yes, ?, no, NO). This questionnaire would be classified as a "closed" in contrast to an "open" one.

Responses to this time questionnaire were subjected to a statistical technique called "factor analysis." All 23 items were first correlated. Six items yielding low correlations (or relationship) with all others were eliminated. The 17 items remaining were subjected to factor analysis and two factors were extracted. In other words, most of the 17 items (all except 4) fit into two fairly sharply defined clusters.

All of the items in one cluster (positively loaded in Table 3) express a feeling of harassment with the passage of time plus an effort to manage and control it. The negatively loaded items suggest an unconcern for time. The factor was therefore labeled a "time servant-master" dimension (Factor I).

All of the items in the second cluster of items (Table 4) relate to "time efficiency" or "time obliviousness" (Factor II).

This study illustrates how responses to a questionnaire can be organized and analyzed in terms of meaning and quantified.

POTENTIAL CANDIDATES FOR THE DESIGNERS' PARADISE, A SOCIAL ANALYSIS FROM A NATIONWIDE SURVEY*

WILLIAM MICHELSON

Several themes stand out among the contemporary plans of many prominent urban designers. Faced with enormous population growth in a limited number of metropolitan areas, their plans typically aim to house people in

---

Reprinted with permission from *Social Forces*, Vol. 46, December, 1967, pp. 190-196, a publication of the University of North Carolina Press.

*I am grateful for the kindness of Professor John B. Lansing of the Survey Research Center, Institute for Social Research, University of Michigan in making available the results of his 1965 survey of families in metropolitan areas of the United States, without which this analysis would have been impossible. He also offered helpful suggestions on an earlier draft of this paper as did Charles Tilly and Mrs. Eva Samary. I wish to thank also Miss Janet Lytle, who assisted with the analysis. This paper was presented at the annual meeting of the American Sociological Association, San Francisco, California, August 1967.

high-rise apartments or town houses near the centers of cities so as to conserve land and promote efficient development, the antithesis of suburban sprawl.[1]

In making these plans, the designers assume the existence of a sufficient number of people with particular desires. These people would wish to give up single family housing for multiple dwellings, and they would prefer less private open space than they have now. Although they may now live in relatively uncrowded areas, what they really want is geographic centrality and easy access to community facilities. Finally, they would ideally eschew the private automobile in favor of mass transit facilities.

This paper will explore the extent to which people with such desires represent an identifiable subgroup of the population. I shall analyze whether people with each of these desires, as expressed in a nationwide survey, differ from the rest of the population in ways that are significant to past hypotheses and to practical planning for the future of cities.

Hypotheses

The literature on the social bases of housing choice has isolated a few factors thought to explain a person's choice of residential environment. They are: (1) stage in the life cycle, (2) life style, and (3) socioeconomic status, when considered apart from life style. Let us examine each of these briefly.

Stage in the life cycle refers to where a person stands in the sequence of childhood, marriage, childbearing, and later life. It is closely related, of course, to one's age, but in complex societies, it often represents a finer indicator of age-based behavior than does age alone. With respect to the residential environment, it has often been hypothesized that home occupancy and low density living are most desirable for those with growing children.[2] Younger adults and older people whose children have left the family nest or whose spouses may be deceased are assumed to prefer the efficiency and convenience of multiple dwellings and central locations.[3]

Life style is a general variable that includes several factors such as interactive behavior and use of time. It is often mentioned as class specific, but yet can vary within broad class groups and hence be considered apart from socioeconomic status. In one use of the concept, for example, Bell posits "suburbanism" as a function of "familism" — an emphasis on activities and pastimes reflecting the immediate interests of the nuclear family rather than on consumption or occupational achievement.[4] Others point to styles of life which emphasize the extended

---

[1] This is particularly true among the architecturally-oriented designers.

[2] A most suggestive discussion of this is found in Anthony F. C. Wallace, *Housing and Social Structure: A Preliminary Survey with Particular Reference to Multi-Storey, Low Rent Public Housing Projects* (Philadelphia: Philadelphia Housing Authority, 1952), mimeo. See also Margaret Willis, *Environment and the Home* (London: London County Council, Architect's Department, October 1954).

[3] See, for example, William H. Whyte, Jr., "Are Cities Un-American?" in *Fortune, The Exploding Metropolis* (New York: Doubleday Anchor Books, 1957), pp. 1-31.

[4] Wendell Bell, "Social Choice, Life Styles, and Suburban Residence," in William M. Dobriner (ed.), *The Suburban Community* (New York: G.P. Putnam's Sons, 1958), pp. 225-247.

family in either "peer group" or matriarchal arrangements as being most compatible with high density areas.[5] Still others point to an emphasis on cultural activities as a motivation for residence in a central location in cities.[6]

Socioeconomic status, whether considered in terms of income, occupation, or education, has been related to environmental choice. White-collar workers, for example, are likely to expend a greater part of their income on a high quality of housing than are blue-collar workers,[7] and education is felt to be a strong determinant in this context.[8] Those in the upper levels of the status hierarchy have been hypothesized particularly to desire homogeneous, suburban, single family home living as an influence in the proper choice of a mate by their children.[9]

In addition to the above variables, for which hypothesized relations to particular variations in the urban environment spring easily from past literature, several other variables may be analyzed in this context. The environment in which a person spent his formative years may well influence his preferences for current residential environment. It is not inconceivable that a rural upbringing would lead to desires for larger sized lots, for example. A person's sex may also have an influence; research indicates that women are more greatly affected by their residential surrounding than are their husbands, who typically spend the greater part of their day elsewhere.[10] Finally, it has been asserted that whether or not people own automobiles influences their conceptions of ideal environment; those without them prefer public transit and central locations.[11]

Method of Study

Survey Research Center of the University of Michigan conducted interviews with a sample representative of families in all metropolitan areas of the United

[5] Herbert Gans, *The Urban Villagers* (New York: The Free Press of Glencoe, 1962), and Michael Young and Peter Willmott, *Family and Kinship in East London* (London: Routledge & Kegan Paul, 1957). The same phenomenon is reported in Lagos, Nigeria by Peter Marris in *Family and Social Change in an African City* (Evanston, Illinois: Northwestern University Press, 1962).

[6] Raymond Vernon, *The Myth and Reality of Our Urban Problems* (Cambridge: Joint Center for Urban Studies of M.I.T. and Harvard University, 1962), and Janet Abu-Lughod, "A Survey of Center-City Residents," in Nelson Foote, Janet Abu-Lughod, Mary Mix Foley, and Louis Winnick, *Housing Choices and Constraints* (New York: McGraw-Hill Book Co., 1960), pp. 387-447.

[7] A prominent statement of this is by Otis Dudley Duncan and Beverly Duncan, "Residential Distribution and Occupational Stratification," in Paul K. Hatt and Albert J. Reiss, Jr. (eds.), *Cities and Society* (rev. ed.; New York: The Free Press of Glencoe, 1963), pp. 283-296.

[8] Charles Tilly, "Occupational Rank and Grade of Residence in a Metropolis," *American Journal of Sociology*, 67 (November 1961), pp. 323-330, and Arnold S. Feldman and Charles Tilly, "The Interaction of Social and Physical Space," *American Sociological Review*, 25 (December 1960), pp. 877-884.

[9] See, for example, James Beshers, *Urban Social Structure* (New York: The Free Press of Glencoe, 1962).

[10] Herbert J. Gans, "Effects of the Move from City to Suburb," in Leonard Duhl (ed.), *The Urban Condition* (New York: Basic Books, 1963), pp. 184-198.

[11] This was suggested strongly in a personal communication by Miss Constance Perin.

States except New York, which was considered atypical. Seven hundred and forty-eight people were interviewed in the early fall of 1965 on a variety of aspects of their environment and on their uses and opinions of transportation. A thorough analysis of the basic results may be found elsewhere,[12] and this effort represents a secondary analysis of the original data to assess the extent that people meeting designers' criteria exist and have definitive characteristics apart from the rest of the population.

Questions from the interviews made it possible to identify people, assumed to exist in great numbers by designers, who fit each of the following categories:

1. Those who now live in a single family home but who desire to move to some type of multiple dwelling.

2. Those whose lot is larger than the median sized urban lot but who feel it is too large for them.

3. Those who feel that their present dwelling area is uncrowded but who would like to live closer to the center of the city.

4. Those who could travel to work by either public transit or private automobile and who, if cost and time were the same, would choose public transit.

No person fits all the categories! In fact, only two people fit all the first three categories, and none of these categories represented the position of more than six per cent of the population. The people thus fitting into each of the first three categories, one by one, were contrasted with those who didn't with respect to a series of variables representing the factors outlined in the hypotheses. For the fourth category, the contrast was only with those who had a choice of travel mode and chose the private automobile.

The series of social variables was relatively straightforward. Stage in the life cycle was expressed in two ways. The division was made between single person households, households without children currently resident and those with children.[13] Age was used as the second way of operationalizing this factor in order to contrast its utility in this context. Style of life could be viewed only incompletely from the questions asked. However, some idea of it could be gleaned from a series of questions asking which spare-time activities respondents enjoyed the most. Data was thus available on whether or not a person mentioned each of the following pastimes:

A. going for a drive in the car
B. gardening or working in the yard
C. cooking out in the yard at home
D. going on picnics away from home
E. fishing
F. hunting
G. golf

---

[12] John B. Lansing, *Residential Location and Urban Mobility: The Second Wave of Interviews* (Ann Arbor: The University of Michigan, Survey Research Center, Institute for Social Research, 1966).

[13] Prior investigation showed no difference in the results from forming separate categories for families whose children were in different age groups.

H. going to plays and concerts
I. workshop activities
J. watching television

While these pastimes are not inclusive of all alternatives, the individual activities have intrinsic meaning. Finally, clearcut data enabled the following variables to be part of the series: residence during childhood, education, occupation, sex, race, and number of cars available.

Contingency tables were computed to assess whether those people fitting designers' requirements differed significantly from all appropriate others on any or all of these social variables. I shall discuss below those ways in which the size of the difference between the two groups could have been expected on the basis of chance alone no more than five times in a hundred.

Results

1. Home to Multiple Dwelling. People living in single family homes who desire to move to multiple dwellings differ from others first in their stage in the life cycle. As Table 1 shows, the overwhelming majority of those wishing to change to an apartment do not have children living at home, a direct contrast to the rest of the population, the majority of whom are living with children in their households. Thus, although relatively few people desire to make such a move, those who do are predominantly those who either have not yet had children or whose children have grown up and left home.

Second, with respect to the activities in which people participate, Table 2 shows that those who desire to give up their homes enjoy the active pastimes of hunting, fishing, and going away from home to picnics much *less frequently* than the rest of the respondents. In fact, they mention enjoying a pastime more frequently than the residual group only in the case of going to plays or concerts, and even in this situation the difference is minuscule (*33%-32%*). Thus, as a group, those wanting to go from a home to a multiple dwelling seem to have fewer recreational interests than does the rest of the population, and this is particularly true for active pastimes.

TABLE 1. HOUSING PREFERENCES BY STAGE IN THE
LIFE CYCLE (in percent)

	Home to Apartment	Others
Single	33.3	21.9
Married, no children resident	40.0	25.8
Married with resident children	26.7	52.2
Total of percentages	100.0	99.9
N	30	662

Others and N.A. = 56
$\chi^2 = 7.56$ $\chi^2{}_2$ (.05) = 5.99

TABLE 2. HOUSING PREFERENCES BY WHETHER ENJOY SELECTED PASTIMES (in percent)

	Home to Apartment (N = 34)	Others (N = 711)	x^2
Mention enjoying picnics away from home	29.4	50.1	4.75*
Mention enjoying fishing	23.5	43.6	4.54*
Mention enjoying hunting	5.9	24.3	5.68*

*.05>x^2>.01

Some additional light is shed on the social basis of the desire to move away from single family housing by contrasting all those who had moved from multiple dwellings to single homes and later thought it was a good idea with those who made the same move and thought it was a poor idea. Although the categories formed in the relevant tables have too few cases for strict statistical analysis, it is clear that the major area of difference between the groups lies in the realm of activities. As Table 3 demonstrates, people who think the move a poor idea enjoy far less frequently the activities so often associated with ownership of a single family home in America — gardening, cooking out in the yard at home, and workshop activities. In addition, they are also less likely to go away for picnics or fishing, activities mentioned above as uncharacteristic of those wishing to give up their homes for apartments. It thus appears from fragmentary data that dissatisfaction with a single home is associated with a failure to adopt aspects of a style of life commonly practiced by those living in homes.

2. Large to Smaller Lot. Those homeowners who wish to exchange a relatively large lot (all lots 1/5 acre or larger are above the median in this sample) for less private open space form a subgroup among the respondents in this study

TABLE 3. SATISFACTION WITH MOVE TO SINGLE FAMILY HOME BY WHETHER ENJOY SELECTED PASTIMES (in percent)

	Satisfaction Poor (N = 9)	Satisfaction Good (N = 156)
Mention enjoying gardening or yard activities	33.3	59.6
Mention enjoying cooking out in yard at home	44.4	59
Mention enjoying workshop activities	11.1	31.4

with respect to their stage in the life cycle. As Table 4 points out, married couples without children in their home are greatly overrepresented in this group. This is not surprising inasmuch as larger lots require more maintenance, and it is common among childless couples for both husband and wife to work, while age becomes a limiting factor among couples whose children have grown up and moved out.

3. Centralizers. The third group studied was those who now live in what they consider uncrowded areas who still would prefer to live closer to the city center. They differ from the rest of the sample with respect to their activity preferences.

Table 5 shows that the centralizers are *more* likely than others to prefer attending plays and concerts than are the others. On the other hand, as Table 5 also points out, they are *less* likely to enjoy hunting. This contrast between enjoyment of cultural versus active outdoor activities supports well the past assertions that many who wish to move closer to city centers are motivated by the cultural attractions found there. But it is equally clear that the desire for such a move, as with the other moves, is held by only a minority, even of those who like culture.

4. Mass Transit. Those who would prefer to make their regular daily trips by

TABLE 4. LOT SIZE PREFERENCES BY STAGE IN THE LIFE CYCLE (in percent)

	Large to Small	Others
Single	6.9	23.1
Married, no children resident	48.3	25.4
Married with resident children	44.8	51.4
Percent	100.0	99.9
N	29	663

Others and N.A. = 56.
$\chi^2 = 11.89 \; \chi^2{}_2 \; (.01) = 9.21.$

TABLE 5. LOCATION PREFERENCES BY WHETHER ENJOY SELECTED ACTIVITIES (in percent)

	Centralizers (N = 42)	Others (N = 702)	χ^2
Mention enjoying plays and concerts	47.6	31.1	4.32*
Mention enjoying hunting	9.5	24.3	4.00*

*.05 > χ^2 > .01

mass transit rather than by automobile if time and expense were the same differ from their opposites by stage in the life cycle. As Table 6 demonstrates, single people are far overrepresented among the mass transit devotees, while people with children are far underrepresented in this group. The reverse is true among those preferring to drive. This may well reflect a type of "halo" effect; if people need automobiles for the many stops often needed to supply a growing family, they may find it handier and more comfortable to have the same car with them on their daily trip to and from work, during which time they can run those errands without appreciable added costs or time spent. Nonetheless, exactly half of those who would like taking mass transit to work say they enjoy pleasure driving as a recreational activity; however, this percentage is far lower than it is among those who would also drive to work.

Discussion

The data of this study were organized to assess whether people holding environmental preferences assumed by many physical designers to exist in the current population possess some of the social attributes previous work had hypothesized as related to the physical environment. As summarized in Table 7, these data bring out the importance of stage in the life cycle in three of the four subgroups isolated, of style of life in two of them, and of none of the other variables in any of the subgroups.

However, the influence of the different stages in the life cycle works differently with respect to specific aspects of the environment. With respect to desiring to give up a single house for a multiple dwelling, it is the presence or absence of children that makes all the difference. When it comes to lot size, it is the "married but without children at home" group that most wants the smaller area. And with respect to transportation preferences, the great contrast is between the single and those with children at home. Clearly then, even though

TABLE 6. TRANSPORTATION CHOICE BY STAGE IN
THE LIFE CYCLE (in percent)

	Private Automobile	Mass Transit
Single	15.0	34.8
Married no children resident	24.9	26.1
Married with resident children	60.1	39.1
Percent	100.0	100.0
N	193	23

Others and N.A. = 56.

χ^2 = 4.48 χ^2_1 (.05) = 3.84. The test of significance was taken after lumping the married groups together in order to maintain adequate sized numbers in the "expected" table. This is not out of order given the nature of the results.

TABLE 7. SUMMARY OF STATISTICAL ANALYSES

	Now Live in Single Home but Want Multiple Dwelling	Moved from Apartment to Single Home but Think it a Poor Idea Now	Have Large Lot but Prefer Smaller	Live in Uncrowded Area but Would Prefer to Centralize	Prefer Mass Transit to Private Automobile
Stage in the life cycle	X		X		X
Age					
Activities (life style)					
Driving					
Gardening		(X)			
Cooking out at home		(X)			
Picnics away	X	(X)			
Fishing	X	(X)			
Hunting	X			X	
Golf					
Theater and concerts				X	
Workshop activities		(X)			
Television					
Education					
Occupation					
Childhood environment					
Race					
Sex					
Cars available					

Key: X = Relation significant at .05 level or better.
(X) = Strong relationship indicated by data but statistical yardsticks inapplicable because of small number in category.

stage in the life cycle appears from this data as closely related to environmental preferences as hypothesized, one must still observe the dimensions of environment independently of one another to achieve the benefit of this knowledge.

Furthermore, age per se does not contribute significantly to the identity of the subgroups, indicating the utility in this context of stage in the life cycle as opposed to simple age as a variable.

Although measures of style of life are extremely crude and incomplete in this analysis due to its secondary character, some of the ways in which respondents spend their time are significantly related to their environmental preferences — in a logical manner consistent with previous work. This suggests strongly the value of future studies in which the quantitative as well as qualitative uses of time found in substantially different physical environments could be ascertained.[14] One could profitably isolate such modal patterns as exist and discover, as suggested in this study, what strains may result from adhering to a style of life which deviates from modalities.

One must note with care that *none* of the subunits of the population meeting designers' requirements could be characterized by either education or occupation, key elements of socioeconomic status. People's housing and its distribution in the city may now be largely a result of economic ability or its lack, but even though some kind of economic differentiation and segregation in housing may be inevitable (and in some respects desirable), the qualitative nature of desired environment does not vary by status, but rather by other factors. Other variables with none of the hypothesized relevance in this context are childhood environment, sex, and number of cars available.

Finally, it should be clear that in no case do many people want what the designers require. Their numbers may be just large enough to prevent economic hardship from entrepreneurs who follow these dictates, particularly during periods when the housing market is less than flexible, but they are hardly the kind to serve as evidence for a reorientation of housing policy. Given a choice, most people don't want centrality living in multiple dwellings and a dependence on mass transit. However, among those who do, the variables discussed above seem relevant.

ANALYSIS OF EXAMPLE OF QUESTIONNAIRE AND INTERVIEW TECHNIQUES

Potential Candidates for the Designer's Paradise

A Social Analysis from a Nationwide Survey

In this study data collected by the interview technique in a large survey were organized and subjected to a secondary analysis to assess whether people holding environmental preferences assumed by many physical designers to exist in the current population possess some of the social attributes previous researchers had hypothesized as related to a person's choice of residential environment. These attributes included (1) stage in the life cycle, (2) life style, and (3) socioeconomic status.

Statistical contingency tables (chi-square) were computed to assess whether

---

[14] Recent interest in time and activity budgets leads to my optimism about their future utility. One fruitful implementation of it, but in a different application from what I suggest, is by F. Stuart Chapin, Jr. and Henry C. Hightower, *Household Activity Systems* (Chapel Hill: The University of North Carolina, Center for Urban and Regional Studies, Institute for Research in Social Science, 1966). An exemplary use of this instrument is by Charles Tilly in his current "Boston Housing Study."

people fitting designers' requirements differed significantly from those not meeting their requirements (others) on any or all of these social variables. For example, Table 1 shows the results of testing of the hypothesis that the desire to move from a single dwelling to an apartment is related to stage in the life cycle. In this case, a relationship is shown between the two variables. The overwhelming majority of those wishing to change to an apartment do not have children living at home, in contrast to the rest of the population (others) who do not want to move to an apartment, the majority of whom are living with children in their households.

CHAPTER 13

Objective Tests and Scales

As measuring instruments, tests and scales are similarly defined. The individual tested is presented with a set of constructive stimuli to which he responds and his responses enable the tester to assign him a numeral or numerals to indicate his possession of the attributes the test is supposed to measure. Likewise, a scale indicates the individual's possession of whatever the scale is supposed to measure. However, scales do not usually imply competition and success or failure as tests do.

Objective tests and scales can be divided into several classes such as intelligence and aptitude tests, achievement tests, personality scales, interest scales, attitude scales, and value scales. They are used in a variety of ways ranging from the rating of an object to the evaluating of personal traits. Some can be answered quickly and without much thought, while others are complex and the rater is forced to make fine discriminations between degrees of behavior or preference.

Many such instruments are available in published form. The researcher can choose one of these tests or can devise a test himself. However, the construction of tests is a formidable job, the details of which are beyond the scope of this book. If a good measure for a particular variable is available, there is little advantage in constructing a new one. The question that must be asked is: "Does a good measure exist?" The answer to this question will require much searching and studying. First, the individual must know what kind of variable he is trying to measure. Second, once he knows whether his variable is an aptitude, personality, attitude, or some other kind of variable, his next step is to consult books which discuss tests and measures. The periodical research journals should also be searched, for many worthwhile instruments have never been published commercially. The measures can be checked through *Psychological Abstracts, Review of Educational Research, Encyclopedia of Educational Research,* and the *Mental Measurements Yearbook*. The latter book presents reviews of various research instruments. If no measure for the variable exists and the researcher finds it necessary to construct his own test or scale, it would be advisable to take a course in psychometrics and test construction, to consult good references on the subject, and, if possible, to consult a psychometrics expert for assistance. The construction of an instrument is a research project in its own right.

PERSONALITY SCALES

The most complex area of psychological measurement is that of personality testing (or scaling). The major problem with such testing or measurement is validity. Items do not always measure what they are supposed to measure. For example, a scale that is assumed to measure social responsibility might actually be measuring a tendency to agree with socially desirable statements. Such a scale might be validated by locating a group of individuals known to be high in social responsibility and another group known to be low in social responsibility to see if the scale is successful in differentiating between the two groups.

Personality instruments generally measure traits that are relatively stable characteristics of individuals so as to indicate the way people tend to respond in all situations.

Many problems arise when you try to obtain ratings on the extent to which a person possesses certain traits. Thorndike and Hagen (1961, pp. 355-361) discussed the following problems:

Factors affecting the rater's willingness to rate conscientiously
    Unwillingness to take the necessary pains
    Identification with the persons being rated
Factors affecting the rater's ability to rate accurately
    Opportunity to observe the person rated
    Covertness of trait being rated
    Ambiguity of meaning of dimension to be rated
    Uniform standard of reference
    Specific rater idiosyncrasies

Among the errors that enter into ratings are: a tendency to rate everyone too high, neglecting to use the "below average" side of the scale; rating everyone too low (because of the judge's personal bias); rating everyone in the middle position (especially on a three-point scale); using similar ratings for several attributes possessed by one individual (allowing one's general impression of the person to influence ratings of his specific traits); and misinterpreting the meaning of various statements.

ATTITUDE SCALES

An attitude is a tendency to think, feel, and behave toward an object beyond one's self. Attitudes are really an integral part of personality, although they are often treated separately in terms of measuring instruments.

There are three major types of attitude scales; equal-appearing interval scales, summated or Likert-type scales, and cumulative or Guttman scales. (Kerlinger, 1964, p. 484)

Equal-Appearing Interval Scales

Thurstone originated a technique for measuring attitudes that is called "equal-appearing" intervals. This method involves writing a large number of items expressing widely different attitudes toward a particular subject. The statements are presented to judges who work independently in classifying the items. Each item is placed in one of 11 piles, ranging from the most favorable to the least favorable attitudes. The median of the judges' ratings becomes the scale value of an item. Items differ in scale value and the intervals between the items are equal. An item is discarded as ambiguous if the judges' ratings vary beyond an acceptable semi-interquartile range (Q).

The following items have been selected from the Thurstone and Chave scale (1929) for measuring attitudes toward the church. The lower the scale value, the more positive the attitudes toward the church. This example shows the lowest and highest items of this scale as well as one from the middle range:

Scale value
0.2 I believe the church is the greatest institution in America today.
5.4 I believe in religion, but I seldom go to church.
9.6 I think the church is a hindrance to religion for it still depends upon magic, superstition, and myths.

The scale should include approximately an equal number of items from the various points along the continuum. The number of items may be reduced to as few as 20 if the scale is a reliable measure of a single attitude.

An individual responds to this type of scale by checking only the items with which he agrees, and his score is the average of the scale values for these items. Normally, his responses will represent items of similar scale values if his beliefs are consistent and the scale is valid. An individual whose responses are scattered over several scale positions probably does not have well-crystallized attitudes on that subject, or the attitude scale is not functioning well in measuring his attitudes.

Selltiz et al. (1959, pp. 362-363) discussed the following objections to the Thurstone-type of scale:

First, many have objected to the amount of work involved in constructing it.... A second criticism has been that, since an individual's score is the mean or median of the scale values of the several items he checks, essentially different attitudinal patterns may be expressed in the same score.... A still more serious question has to do with the extent to which the scale values assigned to the items are influenced by the attitudes of the judges themselves.

Likert-type Rating Scales

The Likert technique overcomes some of the objections to the Thurstone methods, particularly in eliminating the judges. In responding to each item, a person indicates how strongly he approves or disapproves, likes or dislikes, agrees or disagrees. Responses that are the most favorable are given the highest ratings (or lowest, as long as the same plan is followed throughout the scale). An individual's score is the sum of his ratings on each item. The statements are selected on the basis of the scale's internal consistency — that is, each item discriminates well between people who obtain high scores and those who receive low scores on the scale.

The advantages and disadvantages of the Likert-type scale were summarized by Selltiz et al. (1959, p. 368) as follows:

> First, it permits the use of items that are not manifestly related to the attitude being studied. . . . Second, a Likert-type scale is generally considered simpler to construct. Third, it is likely to be more reliable than a Thurstone scale of the same number of items. . . . Fourth, the range of responses permitted to an item given in a Likert-type scale provides, in effect, more precise information about the individual's opinion on the issue referred to by the given item.

Pace and Wallace included six items on the Household in their survey of the opinions of Syracuse University graduates. Respondents indicated the degree to which they agreed with each statement, according to the following scale: SA — strongly agree; A — agree; ? — no opinion at all; D — disagree; SD — strongly disagree. The first item of the scale was:

SA	A	?	D	SD	
1	2	3	4	5	Keeping a family or personal budget is more trouble than it is worth. (Pace and Wallace, 1948)

The common practice is to give a *verbal* description to every point on a numerical rating scale as in the following example from a Scale for Aesthetic Appeal: (9) Extremely appealing; (8) Very appealing; (7) Moderately appealing; (6) Slightly appealing; (5) Neither appealing nor unappealing; (4) Slightly unappealing; (3) Moderately unappealing; (2) Very unappealing; (1) Extremely unappealing.

Such scales can be *graphic* in form, whereby judges are asked to indicate on a physical continuum, or straight line segment, the location which they feel represents the place of the item being rated on some attitude or other psychological continuum or dimension. The line is a continuous one so the rater may locate his mark at any point along it. The numerical scoring is done later.

Very High	Moderate	Very Low
Aesthetic	Aesthetic	Aesthetic
Appeal	Appeal	Appeal

The graphic rating scale is suitable to use with young students or with adults who have not been privileged to complete high school or college. Behaviors to be rated can be stated very concisely, response categories can be very simple, and the respondent merely places a check at any point along a continuum. A neutral or average position usually is at the center of the scale.

Cumulative or Guttman Scales

The cumulative or Guttman scale is a unidimensional scale, measuring one variable only. It gets its name from the cumulative relation between the individual's response to each item and his total score. Ideally, an individual who checks a given response would also have checked the responses below that level.

The following is an example of the Bogardus Social Distance Scale (Bogardus, 1933), which was one of the earliest scales of this type used in the measurement of attitudes (from Selltiz et al., 1959, p. 371):

Directions: For each race or nationality listed below, circle each of the classifications to which you would be willing to admit the average member of that race or nationality (not the best members you have known, nor the worst). Answer in terms of your first feeling reactions.

	To close kinship by marriage	To my club as personal chums	To my street as neighbors	To employment in my occupation	To citizenship in my country	As visitors only to my country	Would exclude from my country
English	1	2	3	4	5	6	7
Negro	1	2	3	4	5	6	7
French	1	2	3	4	5	6	7
Chinese	1	2	3	4	5	6	7
Russian	1	2	3	4	5	6	7
etc.							

On the whole, the assumption that these items in the Bogardus Scale form a cumulative scale has been borne out. For example, it is likely that if an individual circles 2 in relation to the Chinese (accepting him to his club as a personal chum), he would also circle 3 (to my street as neighbors) and 4 (to employment in my occupation) and 5 (to citizenship in my country). It is likely that he would not circle 6 and 7, since these items are essentially statements of exclusion, absence of the circle constituting the favorable response to these two items.

VALUE SCALES

Value scales are closely related to attitude scales. A value is a culturally weighted preference for a thing or things, for people, for institutions, or for some kind of behavior. (Kluckhohn, in Parson and Shils, 1962) Values have also been defined in terms of very inclusive general attitudes. Values express the good and bad of human behavior, putting things on an approval-disapproval continuum. Unfortunately, the topic of values has not been subjected to much scientific investigation.

A well-known, commercially available value scale is the Allport-Vernon-Lindzey Study of Values which uses six categories: theoretical, economic, aesthetic, social, political, and religious values. (Allport, Vernon, and Lindzey, 1951)

Dyer and Paolucci developed a forced choice values test using descriptive stories about homemakers. The respondent was to select the story that *best* described his idea of what a homemaker ought to be or do, the next best, etc., and on to the *least* desirable. The nine stories emphasized the following values: family-centeredness, health, economy, freedom, aesthetic interests, prestige, friendship, religion, and education. For example:

> 2. Mrs. H. believes that a healthy family is the key to a happy family. She protects her family members so as to avoid situations that might lead to physical fatigue, ill health, or accidents. She arranges activities in which the family can get lots of fresh air and sunshine. She doesn't approve of children devoting lots of time to television viewing because they become less physically active. Mrs. H. plans on the children getting adequate rest, and avoids activities that interfere with their nap time. She arranges nutritious meals because good diets are essential to good health. (Dyer and Paolucci, 1963)

INTEREST SCALES

Interest scales or inventories are self-reporting instruments in which the individual indicates activities that he likes or dislikes. These scales are often related to occupations. For example, the Strong Vocational Interest Blank (1959) measures interests interpreted in terms of various occupations. Each interest blank (one for men and one for women) contains 400 items listing occupations, school subjects, hobbies, kinds of people, etc., to which those taking the instrument respond in terms of "like," "dislike," or "indifferent." The individual's responses are compared in scoring with the known responses of persons who have been successful in the occupations included.

An interest inventory for home economics was developed by Johnson (1955). This inventory was designed "to differentiate, on the basis of interests, women employed in each of a number of occupations for which home economics training is desirable preparation from home economists in other occupations." (Johnson, 1955, p. 11)

MISCELLANEOUS OBJECTIVE SCALES AND ITEMS

Several other methods of testing and scaling which are used in research are presented in the remainder of this chapter: ranking, paired comparisons, Q sort, and semantic differential.

Method of Ranking

One of the simplest types of scales involves the placing of individuals or items in order, according to their excellence. If the rater is competent and he is judging a specific characteristic, the results can be highly reliable. Usually ranking is done by picking out the highest and the next highest, then the poorest and the next poorest, and finally fitting the middle ones into position. The resulting scale is an ordinal scale, giving merely the rank order of stimuli on a given characteristic but no information on the size of difference that separates the ranks.

Ranking is particularly useful in the judging of stimuli that may be moved around physically. However, the method is not confined to such situations. Ranks can be assigned to famous authors or makes of automobiles, but ranking is not as convenient as rating when many items must be judged. Stimuli all have to be available at once for comparison. No problem arises as to the sequence of presentation. However, to assure that the arrangement made by one subject does not influence the ranking or arrangement made by the next subject, items should be randomly mixed between presentation to judges. An example of ranking could be a group of paintings which subjects are asked to rank in their order of preference. A frequency distribution showing how many times each picture was ranked in each position can be made to study the popularity of the paintings.

Thorndike and Hagen (1961, p. 371) summarized the advantages of ranking as follows:

> It forces the persons doing the evaluation to make discriminations among those being evaluated. The ranker cannot place all or most of the persons being judged in a single category, as may happen with other reporting systems. Secondly, it washes out individual differences among raters in generosity or leniency. No matter how kindly the ranker may feel, he must put somebody last, and no matter how hard-boiled he is, someone must come first. Individual differences in standards of judgment are eliminated from the final score.

Paired Comparisons

With this method, stimuli are paired and compared with each other instead of with any numerical rating scale or set of ranks. Two items (one pair) are responded to at a time. Judges or subjects merely say which member of each pair is preferred or possesses more of the quality being judged. Each stimulus should be presented as often on the right as on the left to keep a space error from distorting the data. Judges must be told to take each pair as a new problem and they must make a forced choice in each case.

Paired comparisons can be used for scaling values, attitudes, or products. This approach is useful only with a small number of items. When 10 items are used, 45 pairs must be compared. Fifteen items would necessitate 105 comparisons. The number of pairs necessary can be determined by:

$$n(n-1)/2$$

In analyzing the data, the relative frequency with which a stimulus is preferred is compared with every other stimulus. The proportion of times each is chosen provides data from which scale values may be derived. The article on the Compton Fabric Preference Test, at the end of this chapter, is an example of a paired comparison instrument.

In some ways, the paired comparison technique is the most satisfying of psychometric methods for it is simple and economical and a good deal of information can be obtained with a limited amount of material. Most important, paired comparison items force the subject to choose. (Kerlinger, 1964, pp. 497-498)

The Q Sort

Although a large part of research is based upon the testing of groups, Stephenson thought it should be possible to make a scientific study and reach valid conclusions based upon the measurement of one individual. The technique which he developed is called the "Q sort." Basically it is a type of correlation.

The first step is to prepare a list of statements (or other stimuli) toward which the individual is to react. Validity of the set of statements is a prime factor in determining the usefulness of the responses. About 60-90 statements are usually included in the set. However, as few as 50 or as many as 150 might be included. Each statement is written on a separate card and numbered at random. The cards are given to an individual with the instructions that he is to sort them into piles, placing a specified number of statements in each pile. The following example shows typical numbers of cards that might be used in a 100-item series and in a 50-item series, to force a normal distribution as a respondent sorts items into 11 groups.

	Prefer least									Prefer most	
Pile	1	2	3	4	5	6	7	8	9	10	11
Number of cards											
(100 items)	2	4	8	12	14	20	14	12	8	4	2
(50 items)	1	2	4	7	7	8	7	7	4	2	1

When 50-80 items are used, the number of piles might be reduced to nine. When more than 100 items are included, the number of piles might be increased to 13. Although the number of piles and the number of statements to be placed in each pile might vary, the distribution is approximately a bell-shaped or normal curve. The advantage of a forced choice is that the distribution is the same for all raters. The disadvantage is that an individual cannot be scored. His responses are compared with those of other individuals or with his own responses (self-sort) on other occasions.

The respondent is instructed to pick out the items for the four best-liked categories first (or those that are most descriptive of him). Then he chooses the four least-liked categories and, finally, he fills in the middle categories. This procedure is used because it is usually easier to declare what one likes or dislikes intensely than what he feels neutral about. Moreover, the extreme positions are more important than the middle ones in determining the size of correlations and so it is important that they be as reliable as possible.

The purpose of sorting is to get a picture of the subject's view of or attitude toward the object or concept being considered. The Q sort is most frequently employed in the study of personality. Sorting instructions vary according to the objectives of the research. If the study deals with attitudes, attitudinal statements may be sorted on a continuum of agree to disagree. Personality traits may be sorted on a "like me" and "not like me" continuum or an individual may be described by judges on a similar continuum. Objects such as paintings, food, photographs, or art objects can be sorted according to one's strength of preference for them.

Semantic Differential

How an individual reacts to a situation is determined by what the situation means to him rather than by the intrinsic properties of the event. Osgood developed a way of measuring "meaning," of determining how an object, person, or idea affects an individual. (Osgood et al., 1957) The semantic differential is the result of an attempt to subject meaning to systematic quantitative measurement.

The semantic differential measures connotative rather than denotative meaning. Underlying the semantic differential is the hypothesis that the connotative, or affective, components of meaning can be measured by rating objects or ideas with respect to bipolar adjectives. It is assumed that pairs of bipolar adjectives (such as strong versus weak) are continua along which connotative meanings are expressed. Each pair of adjectives is called a scale. An individual is asked to respond to a number of these scales and he may be asked to rate one or more objects or ideas on the scales. Seven-step scales are used and the individual makes one check mark on each scale to indicate how closely he associates the concepts with the end points of that scale. If the bipolar adjectives seem to him to be unrelated to the concept, he would presumably place a mark toward the middle of the scale. Any concept can be rated — a person, painting, food, etc.

Factor analysis has shown that it is not necessary to think in terms of many small dimensions. Three "super" dimensions are sufficient to treat most of the meaning in the concepts. The individual scales are not really independent — things that are rated as good are generally rated as valuable, beautiful, sweet, nice, honest, pleasant, wise, positive, and reputable. Therefore, only a few scales need be used to sample the important super dimensions or factors: Evaluation, Potency, and Activity. *Evaluation* is the most important factor and this is illustrated by such scales as good-bad, pleasant-unpleasant, valuable-worthless. *Potency* is indicated by scales such as strong-weak, rugged-delicate, hard-soft, heavy-light. *Activity* and motion are illustrated by active-passive, fast-slow, dull-sharp. In other words, one can rate a concept or object in terms of (1) his evaluation of it (corresponding to the favorable-unfavorable dimension of the traditional attitude scale), (2) his perception of the potency of power of the concept of object, and (3) his perception of its activity or action. Osgood gives a list of fifty scales which have been tested empirically and are available for use. (See Table 4)

The first step in constructing a semantic differential for research is to choose the concepts (or objects) one is going to rate with the polar adjectives. A number of concepts must be chosen that are relevant to the research problem. The next step is to construct the instrument by selecting appropriate scales or adjective pairs. Of course, these adjective pairs must be relevant to the concepts used. For example, if one of the concepts being judged is teacher, adjective pairs

TABLE 4. OSGOOD SCALES
ROTATED FACTOR LOADINGS – ANALYSIS I

1. good-bad
2. large-small
3. beautiful-ugly
4. yellow-blue
5. hard-soft
6. sweet-sour
7. strong-weak
8. clean-dirty
9. high-low
10. calm-agitated
11. tasty-distasteful
12. valuable-worthless
13. red-green
14. young-old
15. kind-cruel
16. loud-soft
17. deep-shallow
18. pleasant-unpleasant
19. black-white
20. bitter-sweet
21. happy-sad
22. sharp-dull
23. empty-full
24. ferocious-peaceful
25. heavy-light
26. wet-dry
27. sacred-profane
28. relaxed-tense
29. brave-cowardly
30. long-short
31. rich-poor
32. clear-hazy
33. hot-cold
34. thick-thin
35. nice-awful
36. bright-dark
37. bass-treble
38. angular-rounded
39. fragrant-foul
40. honest-dishonest
41. active-passive
42. rough-smooth
43. fresh-stale
44. fast-slow
45. fair-unfair
46. rugged-delicate
47. near-far
48. pungent-bland
49. healthy-sick
50. wide-narrow

like good-bad, young-old, loud-soft, etc. are suitable since any of these pairs can be used to modify teacher. Usually three or four scales are used to measure each of the three super dimensions and the score for the concept on each factor is determined by averaging the scores for the scales used to measure that factor.

The meaning of the scales of bipolar adjectives and their relation to other scales vary with the concept being judged. Therefore, their meaning should be determined through a statistical analysis of the related factors or dimensions which tend to cluster together when rating a particular concept. This technique is called factor analysis.

Under the direction of one of the authors, Torreta (1968) used a semantic differential scale to determine the meaning attached by college students to the texture of fabrics. These students had previously rated several fabrics on a scale from "very pleasant" to "very unpleasant." The fabric which received the most pleasant rating and that which received the most unpleasant rating were selected for further rating with the semantic differential on the 32 pair words in Table 5. Pair words not relating to texture impression were included in the scale as buffers.

The data for the semantic differential were subjected to factor analysis. In summary, two principal factors or components were found — an *affective factor* and a *physical factor*. Variables contributing heavily to the affective factor included pleasant-unpleasant, harsh-soft, demanding-relaxing, pleasurable-painful, beautiful-ugly, lively-dead. These words seemed to indicate affective (feeling) qualities and, therefore, the researcher named the factor "affective." The physical factor was so named because it was loaded heavily with weight and density characteristics such as dense-sheer, bulky-sleazy, light-heavy.

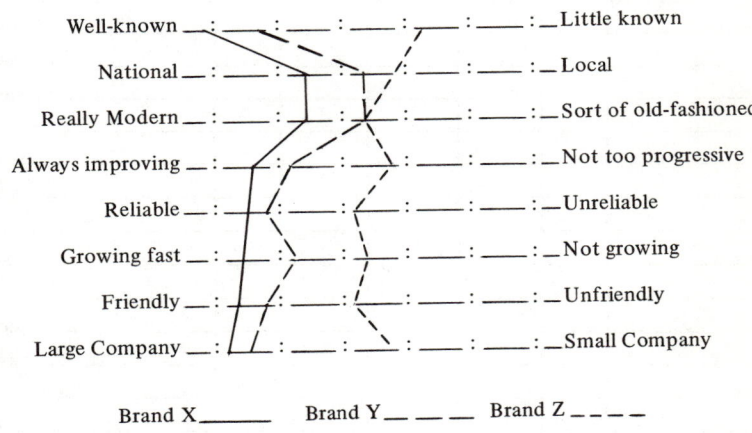

Figure 20. Specific Product Image. Modified from "Fitting the Semantic Differential to the Marketing Problem," by W. Mindak, reprinted from *Journal of Marketing,* April, 1961, Vol. 25, pp. 25, 28, published by the American Marketing Association.

TABLE 5. BIPOLAR WORD SCALE

Record No. _____

	Extremely	Quite	Slightly	Equally or Neither	Slightly	Quite	Extremely
cold							warm
quick							slow
high							low
sticky							slippery
limp							stiff
good							bad
dense							sheer
comfortable							uncomfortable
beautiful							ugly
supple							crisp
quiet							loud
loft							thin
pleasurable							painful
smooth							rough
lively							dead
scratchy							smooth
soft							firm
rich							poor
light							heavy
pleasant							unpleasant
dirty							clean
restraint							free
conceal							expose
full							lean
demanding							relaxing
harsh							soft
bulky							sleazy
active							passive
appropriate							inappropriate
sharp							dull
secure							insecure
shallow							deep

Source: Toretta, 1968, p. 123.

With respect to the texture of fabrics, then, the rating of pleasant and unpleasant fabrics in terms of bipolar adjectives seemed to result in the clustering together of characteristics dealing with the subjects' feeling about the texture (affective component) and the physical characteristics of the fabric itself.

Figure 20 presents in graphic form a modified semantic differential from another study. This graph is a compilation of the image of three companies producing brands of a product as measured in terms of eight semantic-differential scales. Brand X appears to rate higher than Brands Y and Z on all dimensions measured.

RESEARCH EXAMPLES AND ANALYSES
DATA COLLECTION BY
OBJECTIVE TESTS AND SCALES

DEVELOPMENT OF A FABRIC PREFERENCE TEST [1]

NORMA H. COMPTON

The Compton Fabric Preference Test (CFPT) was constructed for the purpose of conducting research dealing with relationships among individuals' color, design and texture preferences in clothing fabrics and their physical and personality characteristics. Preliminary research with the test indicates that the self is expressed in one's selection of clothing fabrics (Compton, 1962a, 1962b, 1963, 1964).

Development of the CFPT began in 1961 (Compton, 1962a) and has since been expanded in terms of variables measured. It has also been converted from its original fabric swatch form to reproducible 35-mm. colored slides. It is being released, not as a finished product, but as a useful tool for teaching and research and is still subject to modification. It is designed primarily for use with girls enrolled in junior high, high school, and college and women participating in Extension Service programs.

Description of Test

Fabric swatches (5 x 7 in.) cut from apparel fabrics purchased on the retail market were used in constructing the original preference testing instrument. These swatches were mounted in pairs, labeled "A" and "B" on numbered 8½-in. x 11-in. cards, cut from heavy white illustration board.

Variables Measured. Five series of slides have been prepared, three for color, one for design size, and one for texture, as follows.

The color series includes chroma (saturation) and value: (a) saturated hue, (b) tint, and (c) shade. This group of slides involves selection of plain weave cotton fabrics of the six hues of red, yellow, orange, blue, green, and purple with respect to a tint, shade, or highly saturated hue. For a given hue, each of the three fabrics is presented for comparison with each of the other two fabrics, so that a total of 18 paired comparisons is made. Color notations from the *Munsell Book of Color* (Munsell Color Co., 1929) were used in determining value and chroma differences for classifying fabrics as saturated, tint, or shade (Compton, 1962a).

The figure-ground value contrasts were (a) strong and (b) weak. In this series of slides were 15 patterned fabric pairs of strong versus weak contrasts in the value of color between the design or pattern and the background of the fabric.

Reprinted with permission of publisher from *Perceptual and Motor Skills*, Vol. 22, 1966, pp. 287-294.

[1] Development of the Compton Fabric Preference Test in slide form was supported by Utah State University Division of Research Grant NSF U-256.

Value notations from the *Munsell Book of Color* were used in calculating differences in figure-ground contrasts between fabric pairs (Compton, 1962a).

The series of slides for the warm-cool dimension of color made use of 15 fabric pairs for (a) warm color and (b) cool color.

Design size (15 patterned fabric pairs) was large and small and the 15 fabric pairs for texture included rough and smooth textures.

Each of the five series of fabrics was developed from as diverse a selection as was available in the retail market. In measuring each variable on the test, all other variables are controlled as rigidly as possible within the limitation of market availability. For example, with respect to design size, both fabrics within a pair are of the same design, color, and fabric construction, differing only with respect to the size of the design.

Each fabric of a pair within a series and slides for all series are randomized within the test. *S*s thus are not aware of the specific variables being assessed.

Administration and Scoring. Detailed instructions for administering and scoring the CFPT appear in the *Compton Fabric Preference Test Manual* (Compton, 1965). In brief, those taking the test are asked to choose the fabric on each slide which they would prefer for their own clothing. They are given one point for each choice. A total score for each variable is determined by summing the number of choices for each one. A high of 12 points can be scored for any one of the color variables of saturation, tint, and shade. The binomial expansion method of probability determination was used to determine the score which would constitute a strong preference. The likelihood of scoring 10 or more points by chance was only .019 for each variable (total probability = .057). Therefore, a score of 10 to 12 points for any of these color variables may be considered an expression of a strong preference for that aspect of color. Fifteen points may be scored for any one of the other color, design size, and texture variables measured by the test. The probability of scoring 3 or less, or 12 or more for either of the variables within a pair was .036. Therefore, a score of 12 to 15 points for any of these variables may be considered a strong preference.

Test Validity

The American Psychological Association (1954) suggests that four factors determine content validity of a test: (1) item selection, (2) item description, (3) range and balance of items, and (4) manner of item presentation. These factors have been discussed with reference to the CFPT in the description of the test given above.

A concurrent validity study was conducted with the CFPT to determine whether *S*s would respond to fabric and slide forms of the test in the same manner. Approximately 1 mo. elapsed between the two test administrations. Correlation coefficients of scores on the two forms of the test are presented in Table 1. *S*s ($N = 60$) included college students, young wives of college students, and homemakers.

Half of the *S*s were shown the slides first and half the fabrics. By assigning a number to each *S* as she arrived to take the CFPT, it was possible to show slides first to those having odd numbers, and fabrics to those with even numbers. Two

TABLE 1. PEARSON CORRELATIONS OF SCORES ON
FABRIC SWATCH AND SLIDE FORMS OF THE CFPT (N = 60)

CFPT Variable	r^*
Saturated Color	.58
Tints	.52
Shades	.71
Warm-cool colors	.68
Strong-weak contrasts	.70
Large-small designs	.75
Rough-smooth texture	.67

*Critical region $a.01$ = .354.

testers and two rooms were used. At the retest after 1 mo. the order of materials was reversed.

All correlations reported in this paper were computed at the Utah State University Computer Center, using the Pearson product-moment technique.

Correlations between preferences on the fabric and slide forms of the test were significant for all color, texture and design variables ($p < .01$). It was therefore concluded that Ss respond to the slide presentation of the test in much the same way as they respond to presentation of actual fabric swatches.

An important measure of practical validity is that which reveals the degree to which a test relates to performance in a real-life situation. The CFPT was designed to determine or predict consumer choices in the retail market, but it also isolates and controls variables for experimental measurement in a laboratory situation. Because this may stimulate doubts about the practical validity of results, wardrobes of about 60% (N = 45) of all Ss participating in research with the slide form of the test were analyzed. Before the wardrobes were selected for analysis, each S was asked to fill out a questionnaire to determine whether she usually selected her own clothing. This permitted the researchers to eliminate all Ss who did not choose their own clothes. Wardrobes of 45 Ss who usually chose their own clothing were then randomly selected for analysis.

Wardrobes were rated with respect to each variable measured on the CFPT. However, since fabrics in the wardrobe are not controlled as they are on the CFPT, special rating scales had to be devised. In classifying wardrobes into the saturated-tint-shade categories, the *Munsell Book of Color* was used as a guide. A color was classified as *saturated* if it appeared in its maximum chroma or strength; as a *tint*, if it were in its lightest form; as a *shade*, if it were highly darkened. Each time a color appeared in one of these three forms in an item of apparel, it was given a score of 2 in that category. But few apparel colors are so clearly defined. Most colors are somewhere in between two of the above three categories. Therefore, they were rated *saturated-tint, shade-saturated,* or *shade-tint*, depending upon their position in relation to the saturated color. If the color of a clothing item fell in any of the above three classifications, it was given one point under each appropriate category.

The *Munsell Book of Color* was also used in determining the amount of contrast within a garment. Only those garments containing two colors could be used in this rating. First, one color from the garment was matched with its mate on the color chart and accorded the value number Munsell assigned it. Then the process was repeated with the other color. The difference between the two Munsell value numbers was the contrast score for the garment.

All items in the wardrobe which were yellow, yellow-orange, orange-yellow, etc., through purple were rated warm. All items which were yellow-green, green-yellow, green, etc., through blue-purple were rated cool. Items which contained both warm and cool colors were not rated. The number of items in each category was compared with the number of times warm and cool colors were preferred on the CFPT.

Before analyzing wardrobes, fabric swatches representing varied textures were selected of cotton, silk, wool, and synthetic fibers. Ten judges, who were clothing and textile instructors, other professional home economists, and graduate students, placed the fabrics into five categories for each of the fiber groups. These categories were smooth, medium-smooth, medium, medium-rough, and rough. The two swatches most often appearing in each category were used as a guide fabric when rating wardrobes. These swatches were mounted on a card for easy reference when analyzing wardrobes. Each item in a wardrobe was rated on a continuum of 1 to 5 (from smooth to rough) on the basis of which category it was most like.

Varied printed fabrics were rated for size in the same manner as were the textures, by the same judges. The five design-size categories were small, medium-small, medium, medium-large, and large. It was found that "small" included all prints under ½ in. in diameter, "medium small," all those about 3½ in. in diameter, and "large," all over 5 in. in diameter. A problem arose here in determining the predominant motif in some prints. All-over prints could not be rated. Each item in the wardrobe was again assigned 1 to 5 points depending on which category its main motif fitted best. Plaids were also rated on the basis of the size of the main squares.

Two research assistants individually scored 10 wardrobes of Ss not included

TABLE 2. PEARSON CORRELATIONS OF WARDROBE ANALYSES OF TWO RESEARCH WORKERS ($N = 10$)

Rated Fabric Categories	r^*
Saturated Color	.933
Tints	.905
Shades	.974
Warm-cool colors	.985
Strong-weak contrasts	.998
Large-small designs	.990
Rough-smooth textures	.989

*Critical region $a.01 = .735$

in the main study. The score each judge gave the wardrobes was analyzed by the Pearson product-moment correlation technique, with the results reported in Table 2. As these correlations were all significant ($p < .01$), it was assumed that the scoring of the wardrobes would be reliable, even if the validity of the measures used was questioned.

The wardrobes of the 45 selected women randomly selected from the group of 60 mentioned above were analyzed as items appeared in their closets by the two research assistants for whom the reliability coefficients are reported. The correlation coefficients for these Ss' choices on the CFPT and the ratings of their wardrobes are presented in Table 3. It will be noted that there were significant correlations between Ss' choices on the CFPT and their wardrobe selections for deep shades of color ($p < .01$) and for highly saturated colors ($p < .05$).

Test Reliability

Test-retest reliability coefficients for the scale were calculated for a group of 27 students enrolled in the College of Family Life at Utah State University. There was a lapse of one month between testings. These correlations are reported in Table 4. The correlations for the color and texture variables were

TABLE 3. PEARSON CORRELATION OF CFPT CHOICES AND WARDROBE RATINGS ($N = 45$)

Related Fabric Categories	r^*
Saturated Colors	.290†
Tints	.171
Shades	.474‡
Warm-cool colors	.138
Strong-weak contrasts	.156
Large-small designs	.144
Rough-smooth textures	.161

*Critical region $a.05 = .288$.
†$p < .05$ ‡$p < .01$.

TABLE 4. TEST-RETEST RELIABILITY COEFFICIENTS FOR THE COMPTON FABRIC PREFERENCE TEST ($N = 27$)

CFPT Variables	r	p
Saturated Color	.702	0.01
Tints	.740	0.01
Shades	.819	0.01
Warm-cool colors	.847	0.01
Strong-weak contrasts	.857	0.01
Large-small designs	.460	0.05
Rough-smooth textures	.681	0.01

significant at the .01 level of confidence. Correlations for preferences for large or small designs were significant at the .05 level. Therefore, we may conclude that the CFPT is reliable in these respects.

Intercorrelation of CFPT Variables

Table 5 reports the simple correlations of scores for all variables on the CFPT for the 60 Ss participating in the concurrent validity study described previously. That there were significant negative correlations among variables of saturation, tint, and shade which indicate inverse relationships of these measures, is consistent with the design of the test. Preferences for tints are also negatively correlated with rough-textured choices. Ss preferring tints therefore tend to choose smooth fabrics. It may also be noted that Ss choosing rough-textured fabrics also tend to choose fabrics with larger designs than Ss choosing smooth fabrics.

The author is planning to use the CFPT to provide additional insight regarding the perceptual dynamics involved in color, design, and texture preferences in clothing fabrics.

TABLE 5. INTERCORRELATIONS OF FABRIC PREFERENCE
TEST VARIABLES ($N = 60$)

	Tint	Shade	Strong	Warm	Large	Rough
Saturated	−.48‡	−.39‡	−.06	.22	.04	.14
Tint		−.62‡	.14	.04	−.11	−.25 ‡
Shade			−.10	−.25†	.08	.12
Strong				−.05	−.02	−.11
Warm					−.01	.12
Large						.34‡
Rough						

†$p < .05$. ‡$p < .01$.

REFERENCES

American Psychological Association. *Technical recommendations for psychological tests and diagnostic techniques.* Washington, D.C.: Author, 1954.

Compton, N.H. Clothing fabric preferences in relation to selected physical and personality characteristics. Unpublished Ph.D. dissertation, Univer. of Maryland, 1962. (a)

Compton, N.H. Personal attributes of color and design preferences in clothing fabrics. *J. Psychol.*, 1962, 54, 191-195. (b)

Compton, N.H. Clothing fabric preferences in relation to selected physical and cultural background factors of a group of Maryland homemakers. *Home Demonstration News,* Cooperative Extension Service, Univer. of Maryland, June 1963.

Compton, N.H. Body-image boundaries in relation to clothing fabric and design preferences of a group of hospitalized psychotic women. *J. Home Econ.*, 1964, 56(1), 40-45.

Compton, N.H. *Compton Fabric Preference Test Manual.* Logan: Utah State Univer. Agricultural Experiment Station, August, 1965. (Special Rep. 19)

Munsell Color Company, *Munsell book of color.* Baltimore: Munsell Color Company, Inc., 1929.

ANALYSIS OF EXAMPLE OF OBJECTIVE TESTS AND SCALES

Development of a Fabric Preference Test

The method of paired comparisons was used by Compton in developing this instrument. As indicated previously, with this method stimuli are paired and compared with each other instead of with any numerical rating scale or set of ranks. Subjects merely say which member of the pair is preferred or possesses more of the quality being judged. Each pair is considered a new problem and subjects must make a forced choice in each case. The relative frequency with which a stimulus is preferred is calculated in analyzing the data. For example, a subject chooses between warm and cool colors on fabrics on 15 sets of paired fabrics on the CFPT. The frequency or number of times he chooses warm colors is calculated and provides his score for warm colored preference. Likewise, he receives a score for the number of times he chooses a cool colored fabric. Other color, texture, and design variables are studied through this test in the same manner.

In Chapter 10 the importance of the reliability and validity of measuring instruments was emphasized. Results of reliability and validation studies on the CFPT are presented in this article on development of the instrument.

DIMENSIONS AND CORRELATES OF TEXTURE PREFERENCES[1]

C.M. CHRISTENSEN

That personality characteristics are related to preferences for textures and forms is suggested by theory and supported by research. In the realm of esthetic theory, the relationship between form and feeling has received considerable

---

[1] This research was supported by grant from the Alberta Advisory Committee on Educational Research.

attention. Pratt (1961, p. 80) refers to "the expressiveness of art as a property closely bound up with the perceptual structure" as a "prominent theme in present day aesthetic theory."

Several investigations have dealt with the dimensions and correlates of preferences for esthetic objects. For example, Eysenck's (1947, 1953) analysis of preferences for visual stimuli yielded a bipolar factor representing simple, obvious stimuli versus complex, subtle stimuli. Barron (1952, 1953a, 1953b) and Welsh (1959) also identified a complexity-simplicity dimension in a series of studies involving preferences for black and white drawings. They have reported significant correlations between preference for complex figures and a wide variety of personality characteristics.

Rorschach theory deals extensively with form, shading, and texture responses (Beck, 1951; Bohm, 1960). Form responses are regarded as indicative of intellectual control whereas shading and texture responses reflect general feeling or affect, particularly anxiety. Factorial analyses of Rorschach scores have yielded separate factors on which form and shading responses load. Consalvi and Canter (1957) found that form dominant shading scores had high loadings on an "intelligence" factor and the shading and texture scores loaded on a "low form" factor. Geertsma (1962) obtained separate shading and vista factors. Singer, Wilensky, and McCraven (1956) obtained high shading response loadings on an "emotional surgency" factor. The factor on which shading and texture scores loaded were generally interpreted as an emotional or affective experience dimension. A somewhat different interpretation was given by Williams and Lawrence (1954) in their factor analysis of the Rorschach and MMPI. Shading scores, MMPI K and Es, and verbal IQ had positive loadings on a factor labeled "ego strength." MMPI Pt, Sc, and F scores had negative loadings on this factor.

To help clarify the nature and meaning of texture preferences, research was done on the dimensions of texture preferences and some correlates of these dimensions. A Texture Preference Inventory, Minnesota Multiphasic Personality Inventory, and Kuder preference record were administered to samples of college students and intercorrelations computed. Previous research and theory indicated that preferences for textures are related to personality, including interest, variables.

Method

Texture Preference Inventory. Description and development of preference inventory. The Texture Preference Inventory is based on a correlational analysis of preferences for photographs of texturous materials (Christensen, 1961). A variety of materials such as brick, bark, cloth, leather, and metal was photographed. The photographs were randomly paired and presented to a sample of subjects with instructions to indicate which texture of each pair they preferred. All items or pairs were intercorrelated and a cluster analysis was carried out to sort the items into homogeneous groups. A professional artist then inspected the cluster of items and recommended some rearrangement of items to increase the homogeneity. Twelve clusters of items resulted.

The Texture Preference Inventory was made up by printing in a booklet 144 pairs of photographs representing the 12 clusters. Photographs from each cluster are paired twice with photographs from all the other clusters, i.e., permutation of 12 different things taken two at a time. Thus each kind of texture is presented 22 times. Twelve pairs are repeated. Subjects are instructed to briefly look at each pair of textures and decide which texture they like better and then indicate their preference on a separate answer sheet. Twelve scores are obtained by counting the number of textures within each cluster that is preferred by the subject.

Intercorrelation and description of clusters. Although cluster analysis of item intercorrelations maximizes the correlations within clusters and minimizes correlations between clusters, it does not insure independence of clusters. Information regarding relationship between clusters was obtained by administering the Texture Preference Inventory to a sample of 52 female undergraduate education students and a sample of 76 male undergraduate education students. Product-moment correlations coefficients between the 12 clusters were computed separately for male and female students, and the results are given in Table 1. First note the similarity for the intercorrelations for female and male students.

Consider now the classes or groups of textures suggested by the intercorrelations and some characteristics of the textures included in each of the classes. The first class includes clusters numbered 1, 2, 5, 8, and 11 with an average intercorrelation of approximately .52. An inspection of the textures included in this class suggest the following description: complex, ambiguous, unstructured, rhythmic lines and forms, varied pattern of lights and dark, and three dimensional. These textures will be referred to as complex unstructured.

In contrast to the complex unstructured textures are the simple structured textures found in clusters numbered 3, 4, and 9. These textures can be described as simple, structured, rigid, repetitive forms, and linear. The average intercorrelation of these three clusters is approximately .55.

Clusters numbered 7, 10, and 12 represent textures differing somewhat from the complex unstructured and simple structured and have been labeled simple unstructured. Textures included in this class can be described as follows: slight variation of form, indefinite form, and two-dimensional. Intercorrelation of the clusters is approximately .30.

Cluster Number 6 does not relate clearly to the other three classes. All the correlations between the complex unstructured textures (Clusters 1, 2, 5, 8, and 11), and the simple structured textures (Clusters 3, 4, and 9) are consistently negative with a mean of approximately −.44. Similarly, the correlations between the complex unstructured textures and the simple unstructured textures (Clusters 7, 10, 12) are consistently negative with a mean of approximately −.48. However, the correlations between the simple structured textures and the simple unstructured textures are generally small, include both positive and negative values, and yield a mean of .11. The textures appear to vary along two dimensions, one dimension representing complexity or intricacy and the other dimensions representing structuredness or definiteness of form.

TABLE 1. INTERCORRELATION AND RELIABILITY
COEFFICIENTS OF TEXTURE PREFERENCE CLUSTERS

Clusters	1	2	5	8	11	6	3	4	9	7	10	12
1.	83[a]	45	−04	17	12	07	−42	−31	−53	−27	−16	03
	80	53	−26	16	00	39	−60	−40	−60	11	−21	11
2.		91	34	56	66	07	−44	−50	−66	−55	−57	−33
		80	20	63	53	29	−53	−61	−69	−17	−65	−48
5.			78	49	54	33	−32	−32	−51	−24	−54	−43
			73	47	64	10	−16	−12	−26	−34	−39	−62
8.				86	56	33	−38	−44	−59	−13	−55	−62
				78	64	41	−38	−59	−62	−09	−76	−61
11.					92	01	−20	−30	−61	−50	−78	−42
					75	17	−22	−41	−50	−28	−69	−69
6.						88	−46	−43	−38	33	−21	−13
						76	−61	−60	−60	37	−36	−08
3.							72	43	65	−09	08	−09
							84	63	67	−31	20	01
4.								65	38	11	18	10
								76	58	−31	41	23
9.									89	22	57	10
									80	−17	58	22
7.										75	35	12
										69	21	28
10.											88	38
											77	47
12.												82
												82

First value in each cell based on 52 female students.
Second value in each cell based on 76 male students.

Reliability. Test-retest reliability coefficients, with one week elapsing between administration of the inventory, were obtained for a sample of male and a sample of female students. The coefficients, given in Table 1, ranged from .65 to .92.

Results

Product-moment correlations between the Texture Preference Inventory (TPI) and the Minnesota Multiphasic Personality Inventory (MMPI) and the Kuder Preference Record, Vocational (Kuder) are reported in Tables 2 and 3.

TABLE 2. CORRELATIONS BETWEEN TEXTURE PREFERENCE INVENTORY AND MINNESOTA MULTIPHASIC PERSONALITY INVENTORY

Texture preference cluster	Minnesota Multiphasic Personality Inventory												
	L	F	K	Hs	D	Hy	Pd	Mf	Pa	Pt	Sc	Ma	Si
1.	-15	00	-01	-12	-01	-15	14	-29*	-09	-07	-07	-01	-01
	01	-08	01	-10	-36**	-31**	-11	-21	-23*	-19	-21	00	-01
2.	-03	06	24	-38**	-11	-07	00	-41**	-15	-20	-18	05	-21
	07	-04	01	-03	-18	-08	-06	-09	-19	-12	-12	-08	-07
5.	-06	05	10	04	01	34*	-09	-18	-21	-07	-01	10	-21
	-03	01	09	06	16	06	11	04	17	05	00	-09	10
8.	00	-19	18	-17	-10	07	-19	-14	-34*	-23	-21	-12	-21
	06	-07	04	01	-07	-02	-02	01	-05	02	-03	-10	00
11.	02	12	19	-15	-20	06	07	-40**	-09	-19	-03	28*	-32*
	00	02	07	05	00	07	06	15	-04	01	00	00	-04
6.	-17	-01	-28*	23	00	09	-11	11	-12	27*	17	-01	15
	-02	-03	-03	-07	-14	-21	09	-06	-03	-10	-14	02	01
3.	03	05	00	04	13	-15	00	33*	15	08	15	-03	27*
	-11	00	-04	07	24*	20	00	16	18	31**	30**	01	11
4.	-03	-07	00	07	-06	-03	03	32*	34*	06	06	13	00
	-03	05	-06	17	21	29**	10	17	18	26*	27*	07	11
9.	04	-11	-02	-02	09	-16	-08	42**	23	-01	01	-18	17
	-09	-02	05	02	20	25*	04	-03	12	10	10	00	-06
7.	-01	-05	-31*	26	-04	05	-03	30*	-11	25	19	-04	09
	13	03	-13	-10	-05	-27*	-02	-12	08	-04	-01	08	11
10.	08	-04	-07	03	18	01	01	25	12	05	-07	-18	14
	00	03	-03	-07	-02	-08	04	-05	05	-10	-02	04	-03
12.	18	13	-12	30*	08	07	23	-18	11	20	08	07	11
	03	05	00	-05	-07	-10	-18	-01	-13	-17	-11	07	-07

*Significant at .05 level.
**Significant at .01 level.

Correlations between the TPI and MMPI were computed separately for males and females and the first value in each cell of Table 2 is the correlation for females. Correlations with the Kuder were computed for a sample of 63 male and female students. Raw scores were employed throughout and the MMPI

TABLE 3. CORRELATIONS BETWEEN TEXTURE PREFERENCE INVENTORY AND KUDER PREFERENCE RECORD, VOCATIONAL

Texture preference cluster	Kuder Preference Record, Vocational									
	Out-door	Me-chani-cal	Com-puta-tional	Scien-tific	Per-sua-sive	Art	Liter-ary	Musi-cal	Social Ser-vice	Cleri-cal
1.	02	22	−03	02	−03	05	−18	18	−08	−26*
2.	−08	−04	−09	−01	14	11	−13	13	00	−07
5.	−04	−25*	−33**	−22	10	42**	−01	15	−08	−12
8.	03	−10	−09	04	06	11	−03	−10	03	−04
11.	−08	−27*	−16	−02	10	18	−02	07	09	−06
6.	−01	12	18	23	−21	06	−23	−10	−20	03
3.	−08	−25*	−04	−18	01	−08	28*	−04	17	16
4.	−05	−11	−02	−18	−11	06	26*	−02	13	02
9.	−02	−01	02	−09	−01	−13	17	−10	12	14
7.	33**	36**	38**	44**	−31*	−33*	−25*	−31*	−18	13
10.	06	25*	16	08	−03	−17	18	−16	−16	03
12.	−02	15	03	−01	12	−21	−12	15	02	04

*Significant at .05 level.
**Significant at .01 level.

scores were uncorrected for K. It should be noted that the MMPI Mf raw score for females is the reverse of the T score typically reported, i.e., a high raw score indicates femininity.

Consider first the correlates of preferences for complex unstructured textures (Clusters 1, 2, 5, 8, and 11). Female preferences for complex unstructured textures correlated positively with Hy (Hysteria) and Ma (Hypomania) and negatively with Si (Social Introversion), Hs (Hypochondriasis), Mf (Masculinity-Femininity) and Pa (Paranoid). Male preferences correlated negatively with D (Depression), Hy (Hysteria), and Pa (Paranoid). Kuder Artistic interest correlated positively; and Mechanical, Computational, and Clerical interest correlated negatively with preferences for complex unstructured textures.

Relying primarily on the work of Drake and Oetting (1959) with MMPI profiles for college students, a general description of subjects preferring complex unstructured texture is attempted. Women are characterized as socially outgoing, free from social problems, "marriage oriented," and having vague goals. The vague goals may reflect a nonconformist attitude where the typical feminine goals are rejected. Similarly, men are characterized as socially secure and free from worries. The results suggest that preference for complex unstructured textures is indicative of responsiveness, good morale, tolerance of anxiety, and a preference for intuitive, creative activities rather than concrete, routine activities.

Correlates of preferences for simple structured textures (Clusters 3, 4, and 9) can be contrasted with those of complex unstructured. Mf, Pa, and Si correlate positively with female preferences. *D, Hy, Pt* (Psychasthenia), and *Sc* (Schizophrenia) correlated positively with male preferences. Again using Drake and Oetting's (1959) descriptions, women preferring simple structured textures are characterized by shyness, social insecurity, and feelings of physical inferiority. Males are characterized by self-consciousness, social insecurity, tenseness, nonresponsiveness, indecisiveness, worry, conflict, unhappiness, and confusion. Literary interest correlated positively and mechanical interest correlated negatively.

Preferences for simple unstructured textures (Clusters 7, 10, and 12) did not correlate as clearly with the MMPI. For women, *Mf* and *Hs* correlated positively and *K* negatively. This could be indicative of reliance on physical symptoms and a nonpsychological orientation. Only *Hy* correlated negatively with male preferences. Correlations with the Kuder are clearer. Persuasive, Artistic, Literary, and Musical interest correlated negatively with Outdoor, Mechanical Computational, and Scientific interest correlated positively with preferences for simple unstructured textures. This appears to reflect an interest in things versus an interest in people. It may also indicate either an avoidance or unawareness of feeling, a blandness.

Discussion

The results can be conceptualized in terms of the relationship between four variables: ambiguity and complexity of stimuli, arousal level, and reaction to arousal. Complexity refers to the intricacy, variety, and number of dimensions involved in the stimuli, and ambiguity to the vagueness of structure. For example, a blank piece of paper would be considered very simple and highly ambiguous or unstructured. Similarly, an intricate geometric design would be considered complex and unambiguous or structured. Arousal level has reference to a general level of activation as conceptualized by Lindsley (1957) and anxiety would represent the upper end of the arousal continuum. Reaction to arousal is concerned with an individual's desire to seek or avoid arousal and his methods for coping or dealing with the arousal.

Considerable research has shown that complexity and ambiguity are positively associated with the arousal value of stimuli. Barron (1953a) and Welsh (1959) obtained positive relationships between anxiety and preference for complex figures. Dibner (1958) obtained a positive relationship between ambiguity of interview and four out of five measures of anxiety. Hamilton (1957) found that Conversion Hysterics and Obsessionals avoided ambiguity more than Anxiety states. Cox and Sarason (1954) reported that high anxiety subjects gave fewer texture responses to the Rorschach than low anxiety subjects. However, Waller (1960) reported more shading responses by psychiatric subjects than normal subjects when an inquiry procedure was used that made it easy for the subject to report determinants of the responses. Waller concluded that anxiety is related to shading but a subject under stress may have difficulty in reporting it. Berlyne (1960) concluded:

. . . ambiguity and complexity are, in some way, associated with, or equivalent to, anxiety ... fear, complexity, uncertainty, and conflict all contribute to a common fund of arousal (p. 215).

Although others have not made a clear distinction between ambiguity and complexity, it is theoretically helpful to do so and this is consistent with the results of the present study. It is assumed here that only the complexity of the stimuli is positively associated with arousal level and individuals differ not only in their sensitivity to be aroused but also in their ability to cope with a high level of arousal. Of the individuals who are sensitive to and aroused by complex stimuli, some will be able to cope effectively with the arousal and prefer ambiguous stimuli while others who cannot cope effectively with a high level of arousal will be "intolerant of ambiguity" and prefer structured stimuli.

Frenkel-Brunswik (1949, 1951) has described the individual who is intolerant of ambiguity as a rigid, prejudiced person adhering to conventional values and who responds in a stereotyped and "all-or-none" fashion. Development of these traits is attributed to strong ambivalent feelings toward parents with repression of the negative feelings and confusion lurking behind the facade that is maintained. One gains the impression that this difficulty is not lack of feeling or sensitivity to stimuli, but rather an inability to cope with feelings aroused. Ambiguity is avoided because the individual is unable to structure and deal with it effectively. Therefore he must rely on structures provided by others. Jensen (1957) arrives at a similar conclusion based on correlations between the MMPI and authoritarianism. His survey of nine studies plus his own research revealed a fairly consistent relationship between MMPI scales and various measures of authoritarianism. D, Pt, Sc correlated positively and K, Hy correlated negatively with authoritarianism. Jensen (1957) concludes that:

> The impression is that prejudiced, authoritarian persons have less well-developed ego defenses and are thus more exposed and vulnerable to psychological stress, in the face of which they develop tendencies toward pessimism, cynicism, low moral (D), and psychological isolation (Sc), along with the more primitive defenses of a compulsive, ritualistic, and schizoid nature (the triad D, Pt, Sc) (p. 310).

Other research also supports the assumption that intolerance of ambiguity is a function of capacity to cope effectively with a high level of arousal. Many researchers, employing a variety of stimuli, have reported a positive relationship between authoritarian attitudes and intolerance of ambiguity. Barron (1953a) and Rosenberg and Zimet (1958), for example, obtained such a relationship with figure drawings and designs as stimuli. Similar results were obtained by Block and Block (1951) and Taft (1956) with the autokinetic phenomenon, and O'Connor (1952) with an attitude scale as a measure of intolerance of ambiguity. Hamilton (1957), using a variety of test situations, found that neurotic subjects avoid ambiguity more than normals. It has also been demonstrated that experimentally induced stress and frustration (Brim & Hoff, 1957; Smock, 1955a, 1955b) result in an increased intolerance of ambiguity and desire for certainty.

Research by Barron and Welsh (Barron, 1952, 1953a, 1953b; Barron & Welsh, 1952; Welsh, 1959) indicate that individuals who prefer complex-ambiguous stimuli are responsive to stimuli and equipped to cope with arousal producing situations. Such individuals were more independent of group opinion and social conventions, aggressive, impulsive, expansive, original, fluent, and they were more highly aroused (anxious) without being repressive.

Returning now to the results of the present study, a brief description is given of individuals preferring the three different types of textures.

Individuals who are able and eager to cope with their environment prefer complex unstructured textures. These individuals are sensitive and responsive to stimuli, comfortable with the feelings evoked, seek stimulation, and obtain satisfaction from structuring an ambiguous situation. Results reported earlier are supportive. Preferences for the complex unstructured stimuli correlated positively with *Ma* and Artistic interest and negatively with *Mf, Hs, Pa, Si, D,* Clerical interest, Mechanical interest, and Computational interest.

Individuals who are sensitive and responsive to stimuli but unable to cope effectively with their environment prefer structured textures. Ambiguity is intolerable because the individual is unable to create his own structures. When faced with an ambiguous situation such an individual is likely to become anxious and obsessive and he will likely deal with the situation by either seeking premature closure or repressing. Note positive correlations with *Mf, Pa, Si, D, Hy, Pt, Sc,* Literary interest and negative correlations with Mechanical interest.

Individuals who prefer simple unstructured textures are not sensitive and responsive to stimuli. Generally strong feelings are not aroused and consequently the problem of coping with feelings does not exist. If strong feelings should be evoked as in a stressful situation, these individuals would be more likely to develop a physical symptom than worry about it or become depressed. That is, these individuals are not psychologically minded, nor are they introspective or repressive, but rather they are extroverts in the Jungian sense. The MMPI results are not as clear in this instance, but the positive correlation with *Hs* and negative correlation with *Hy* are not inconsistent with the description given. Correlations with the Kuder are more persuasive. Positive correlations were obtained with Outdoor, Mechanical, Computational, and Scientific interests. Negative correlations were obtained with Persuasive, Artistic, Literary, and Musical interests. These individuals prefer activities that are not primarily concerned with human feelings and values.

Summary

A Texture Preference Inventory measuring preference for 12 clusters of photographs of texturous material, the Minnesota Multiphasic Personality Inventory, and the Kuder Preference Record were administered to samples of college students. Intercorrelation of the texture clusters and correlation of texture preference with the MMPI and Kuder were determined.

Intercorrelation of texture clusters suggested a threefold classification: complex unstructured, simple structured, and simple unstructured textures. Two dimensions, complexity and structuredness or ambiguity, appeared relevant.

Preferences for complex unstructured textures correlated positively with *Ma* and Artistic interest and negatively with *Mf, Hs, Pa, Si, D,* Clerical, Mechanical, and Computational interests. Individuals preferring these textures were described as sensitive and responsive to stimuli, seekers of stimulation, and capable of dealing effectively with unstructured situations. Preferences for simple structured textures correlated positively with *Mf, Pa, Si, D, Hy, Pt, Sc,* and Literary interest and negatively with Mechanical interest. Individuals preferring these textures were also described as sensitive and responsive to stimuli but lacking in ability to cope with an ambiguous situation. Preferences for simple unstructured textures correlated positively with Outdoor, Mechanical, Computational, and Scientific interests and negatively with Persuasive, Artistic, Literary, and Musical interests. A positive correlation with *Hs* and a negative correlation with *Hy* were also obtained. Individuals preferring these textures were described as insensitive and unresponsive to stimuli, preferring activities devoid of human feelings and values.

Complexity, ambiguity, arousal value of stimuli, and the individual's reactions to arousal were notions used to interpret the findings.

REFERENCES

Barron, F. Personality style and perceptual choice. *J. Pers.*, 1952, **20**, 385-401.

Barron, F. Complexity-simplicity as a personality dimension. *J. abnorm. soc. Psychol.*, 1953, **48**, 163-172.(a)

Barron, F. Some personality correlates of independence of judgment. *J. Pers.*, 1953, **21**, 287-297. (b)

Barron, F., & Welsh, G.S. Artistic perception as a factor in personality style: Its measurement by a figure-preference test. *J. Psychol.*, 1952, **33**, 199-203.

Beck, S.J. The Rorschach test: A multi-dimensional test of personality. In H.H. Anderson & Gladys L. Anderson (Eds.), *An introduction to projective techniques.* New York: Prentice-Hall, 1951. Pp. 101-122.

Berlyne, D.E. *Conflict, arousal and curiosity.* New York: McGraw-Hill, 1960.

Block, J., & Block, Jeanne. An investigation of the relationship between intolerance of ambiguity and ethnocentrism. *J. Pers.*, 1951, **19**, 303-311.

Bohm, E. The Binder chiaroscuro system and its theoretical basis. In Maria A. Rickers-Ovsiankina (Ed.), *Rorschach psychology.* New York: Wiley, 1960. Pp. 202-222.

Brim, O.G., & Hoff, D.B. Individual and situational differences in desire for certainty. *J. abnorm. soc. Psychol.*, 1957, **54**, 225-233.

Christensen, C.M. Use of design, texture, and color preferences in assessment of personality characteristics. *Percept. mot. Skills*, 1961, **12**, 143-150.

Consalvi, C., & Canter, A. Rorschach scores as a function of four factors. *J. consult. Psychol.*, 1957, **21**, 47-51.

Cox, F.N., & Sarason, S.B. Test anxiety and Rorschach performance. *J. abnorm. soc. Psychol.*, 1954, **49**, 371-377.

Dibner, A.S. Ambiguity and anxiety. *J. abnorm. soc. Psychol.*, 1958, **56**, 165-174.

Drake, L.E., & Oetting, E.R. *An MMPI codebook for counselors*. Minneapolis: Univer. Minnesota Press, 1959.

Eysenck, H.J. *Dimensions of personality*. London: Kegan Paul, 1947.

Eysenck, H.J. *The structure of human personality*. New York: Wiley, 1953.

Frenkel-Brunswick, Else. Intolerance of ambiguity as an emotional and perceptual personality variable. *J. Pers.*, 1949, **18**, 108-143.

Frenkel-Brunswik, Else. Personality theory and perception. In R.R. Blake & G.V. Ramsey (Eds.), *Perception: An approach to personality*. New York: Ronald, 1951. Pp. 356-419.

Geertsma, R.H. Factor analysis of Rorschach scoring categories for a population of normal subjects. *J. consult. Psychol.*, 1962, **26**, 20-25.

Hamilton, V. Perceptual and personality dynamics in reactions to ambiguity. *Brit. J. Psychol.*, 1957, **48**, 200-215.

Jensen, A.R. Authoritarian attitudes and personality maladjustment. *J. abnorm. soc. Psychol.*, 1957, **54**, 303-311.

Lindsley, D.B. Psychophysiology and motivation. In M.R. Jones (Ed.), *Nebraska symposium on motivation: 1957*. Lincoln: Univer. Nebraska Press, 1957. Pp. 44-105.

O'Connor, P. Ethnocentrism, "intolerance of ambiguity," and abstract reasoning ability. *J. abnorm. soc. Psychol.*, 1952, **47**, 526-530.

Pratt, C.C. Aesthetics. *Ann. Rev. Psychol.*, 1961. **12**, 71-92.

Rosenberg, B.G., & Zimet, C.M. Authoritarianism and aesthetic choice. *J. soc. Psychol.*, 1958, **46**, 293-297.

Singer, J.L., Wilensky, H., & McCraven, V.G. Delaying capacity, fantasy, and planning ability: A factorial study of some basic ego functions. *J. consult. Psychol.*, 1956, **20**, 375-383.

Smock, C.D. The influence of psychological stress on the "intolerance of ambiguity." *J. abnorm. soc. Psychol.*, 1955, **50**, 177-182. (a)

Smock, C.D. The influence of stress on the perception of incongruity. *J. abnorm. soc. Psychol.*, 1955, **50**, 354-356. (b)

Taft, R. Intolerance of ambiguity and ethnocentrism. *J. consult. Psychol.*, 1956, **20**, 153-154.

Waller, Patricia, F. A comparison of shading responses obtained with two Rorschach methodologies from psychiatric and nonpsychiatric subjects. *J. consult. Psychol.*, 1960, **24**, 43-45.

Welsh, G.S. *Preliminary manual, Welsh Figure Preference Test*. Palo Alto, Calif.: Consulting Psychologists Press, 1959.

Williams, H.L., & Lawrence, J.F. Comparison of the Rorschach and MMPI by means of factor analysis. *J. consult. Psychol.*, 1954, **18**, 193-197.

ANALYSIS OF EXAMPLE OF OBJECTIVE TESTS AND SCALES

Dimensions and Correlates of Texture Preferences

Christensen used several types of objective tests and scales in this study. He developed a Texture Preference Inventory measuring preference for 12 clusters of photographs of texturous material. Intercorrelations of texture clusters suggested three classifications: complex unstructured, simple structured, and simple unstructured textures. Two dimensions or factors were therefore identified: complexity and structuredness (or ambiguity).

To help clarify the meaning of texture preferences, a personality scale and a vocational interest scale were also administered. The MMPI (Minnesota Multiphasic Personality Inventory) measures thirteen personality traits. The Kuder Preference Record, Vocational measures preferences for the following interests: outdoor, mechanical, computational, scientific, persuasive, art, literary, musical, social service, and clerical.

CHAPTER 14

Projective and Other Indirect Research Methods

Projective tests probe into the unconscious depths of behavior and give a more complete picture of personality than is usually possible with most instruments. They do this by using relatively unstructured stimuli for which there are no obvious or socially acceptable responses.

A projective technique is one that provides a relatively ambiguous, unstructured stimulus which the individual is assumed to structure in terms of his own personality and functioning. When an individual is presented with objective items to test his knowledge of subject matter, he is given little opportunity to project himself. He has few choices and little opportunity for interpretation. On the other hand, a stimulus of low structure has no meaning in itself and so the individual is forced to "project" something of himself into his response. The individual has a wide variety of choices. He chooses his own interpretation or reaction from within himself, thereby expressing the way he perceives himself and his individual world. The principle of projection may be used by getting subjects' responses to stimuli of many forms — describing inkblots, using finger paints, describing pictures, playing with dolls, reacting to colors and sounds, etc.

Projective techniques were developed for use in clinical psychology, but today applications are being made in many research fields, including the measurement of consumer behavior in marketing research. The techniques are largely independent of the subject's self-insight and of his willingness to reveal himself. He is generally unaware of what is being measured. In a projective test, the individual's responses are not taken at face value, with the meaning the subject would expect them to have, but are interpreted in terms of preestablished conceptualizations with respect to what his responses to the test stimuli mean. Such conceptualization provides the framework for interpreting the responses. Usually a total record of numerous replies must be studied before deriving a response tendency for an individual.

Since projective devices lack objectivity, it is difficult to establish reliability and validity. With objective tests, it is easy for observers to agree on the scoring of responses. When projective tests are used, it is much more difficult for different observers to come to the same conclusions about an individual's responses. Nevertheless, if they are to be used in research, projective methods must satisfy the same scientific standards as all methods of observation and measurement. They must be subjected to the same type of reliability testing and empirical validation as any other research procedure, even though this may be difficult. Competent judges must compare their scoring and interpretation of data that are yielded by any observation method. Judges' ratings with projective techniques can be compared by correlating the ratings or judgments made by the researchers. To the extent that the ratings correlate highly, objectivity has been achieved.

It is advisable not to use a projective technique if a more objective instrument is available that adequately measures the same variable. Many projective techniques require highly specialized training and a great deal of questionable interpretation. However, the following examples show attempts to objectify projective techniques and to use them in restrictive ways for research projects.

Lindzey (1959) has proposed a five-way classification for projective measures, based on types of response: association, construction, completion, choice or ordering, and expressive.

ASSOCIATION TECHNIQUES

In association techniques, the subject is presented with the stimulus and is asked to respond with the first word, image, or percept that comes to his mind. The two most commonly used forms of association are word association and inkblots.

Word Association

The word association technique is one of the oldest procedures used in personality study. It may well be considered the forerunner of projective techniques. With this method, clues to personality of the subject are obtained in three typical ways: (1) by analyzing stimulus words on which the subject "blocks"; (2) by analyzing associations or actual responses to stimulus words on which the subject shows some emotional disturbance, blocking, etc.; and (3) by analyzing usualness or unusualness of the subject's responses as compared to the norm for his culture or group. In the word association method, emotionally charged words are ordinarily included with neutral words and subjects are asked to respond with the first word that comes to mind. The words they express presumably indicate their feelings and attitudes, especially toward other persons.

Ortega (1962) used the association method in "A Study of Word Recognition and Concomitant Galvanic Skin Responses of a Group of Schizophrenic Patients and a Group of Graduate Students." The mental hospital subjects were 16 schizophrenic patients (eight men and eight women). The graduate students were approaching course examinations, comprehensive examinations, or both, and were working on or planning graduate research projects.

The following three sets of familiar and socially acceptable words were used in the experiment. One set was most meaningful to the schizophrenic patients, a second set most meaningful to the graduate students, and the third was neutral for both groups.

*Lock	**Report	***Stove
*Visit	**Grade	***House
*Ward	**Degree	***Earth
*Aide	**Major	***Salt
*Drug	**Thesis	***Bread
*Group	**Oral	***Table

*Meaningful to patients.
**Meaningful to graduate students.
***Neutral to both patients and graduate students.

Instead of having the subjects respond verbally with the associations each word had for them, psychophysical measurement was used.* Thresholds of recognition were first determined by presenting each word initially for 10 milliseconds and then at durations increased successively by 10-millisecond intervals until correct report was obtained. A psychogalvanometer was used to take GSR (galvanic skin response) measures for each presentation until the recognition threshold was obtained. The galvanic skin response is measured in ohms of reduction in skin resistance to an electric current. Some research evidence supports the idea that positive-rated stimuli elicit larger GSR responses than neutral-rated stimuli and that negative-rated stimuli elicit larger GSR's than positive-rated ones.

Rorschach Inkblots

Another example of an association technique is the Rorschach. With this instrument, the individual is asked by highly trained persons to respond to ten inkblots of varying shapes and colors. The subject is shown each card in a series, one at a time, and is asked to tell what he sees in it or what it may be. After he has responded to each of the ten cards, a period of inquiry follows in which the psychologist administering the test probes for information to clarify what the subject saw and what aspect of the blot determined his perception. Every response to the inkblots is determined both by the qualities of the blot and the individual response of the subject. Perceptual responses play an important part.

Scoring systems provide for the analysis of both structure and content of responses. The researcher is concerned with the way the subject uses movement, color, shading, and form in determining his responses. These are called the *determinants* of the responses. Once the responses are scored and tabulated, they are interpreted according to Rorschach's hypothesis concerning the meaning of

---

*Psychophysical measurement is oriented toward scaling and quantification. A scale is established for measuring the individuals' responses to physical stimuli. The identification of zero points and the determination of the smallest discriminable sensory differences (thresholds) are important parts of such scaling of sensations.

movement and color. These hypotheses have been well validated clinically and students of Rorschach's method find from their actual study of patients that they hold up in practice. The tendency to project movement into the blots reflects intra-psychic activity and fantasy-thinking. The tendency to utilize color in determining responses reflects responsiveness to emotionally toned stimulus material. The need to take interrelationships of various factors into account makes Rorschach's interpretation very complex.

Several attempts have been made to objectify the inkblot technique: e.g., the SORT (Structured Objective Rorschach Test), the Holtzman Ink Blot Test, and Fisher and Cleveland's method of scoring for the body boundary or barrier measure. (See example of the latter scoring technique as well as application of the traditional Rorschach technique in Compton's clothing fabric study reproduced at the end of this chapter, Compton, 1964).

CONSTRUCTION TECHNIQUES

Construction projective techniques emphasize the product created or constructed by the subject. In this technique the subject is required to produce something like a picture or a story. This technique is relatively demanding of the subject, although the stimulus may be simple. Usually a standardized stimulus is used.

Thematic Apperception Test

The TAT (Thematic Apperception Test), or parts or variants of it, has been used to a great extent in research studies. TAT is comprised of a set of vague pictures of relatively low structure to which the subject responds by telling a story about what is happening in each picture, what led up to this scene, and what the outcome will be. In so doing, the individual expresses a variety of feelings and needs.

Although the TAT is probably not used often in its original form, the idea behind it has been used considerably. One of the adaptations uses pictures representative of situations with which adolescents are concerned (Symonds Picture Story Test). Several vague pictures have been shown to children with instructions to write or tell brief stories. Then the responses made by the individuals may be scored on specific variables defined by the researcher, such as originality, expression of aggression, etc.

Blacky Pictures

The Blacky Pictures (Blum, 1950) is a modified TAT. It consists of 12 cartoons showing various scenes in the life of a dog named Blacky. Dogs, rather than humans, are used to facilitate personal expression in situations that might provoke inhibitory resistance. Each card is presented with a brief identification and the subject is requested to tell a story in TAT style. Analysis is in terms of psychoanalytic variables of sexual development.

Drawing and Painting

The Draw-a-Man Test (Goodenough, 1926) emphasized drawing as an indication of cognitive as well as personality development in children. Both drawing and painting have since been used as projective devices. One of the best known is Machover's Draw-a-Person Test (Machover, 1948). Through her method, the subject is asked to draw a person and then to draw a person of the opposite sex. The article by Badri and Dennis (Human-Figure Drawings in Relation to Modernization in Sudan), reproduced at the end of this chapter, illustrates this technique in a research project.

COMPLETION TECHNIQUES

The sentence completion method is the best known completion technique, but other measures such as story completion and argument completion are available also. The projective aspect of these completion techniques is that the subject is supplied with an incomplete stimulus which he is required to complete as he wishes.

Sentence Completion

One of the simplest methods is that in which the beginning of a sentence is provided and the individual writes an ending. Responses can be analyzed for content, moods, motives, feelings, expectations, attitudes, etc. Since the nature of the response is apparent, an individual may easily control his responses and not reveal his inner feelings.

Figure 21 gives an example of the sentence completion technique as used in the field of consumer marketing research.

I like Product X when . . . .

Other People like Product X because . . . .

The best thing about Product X is . . . .

The best time to serve Product X is . . . .

The one thing children don't like about Product X is . . . . .

The word that would best describe Product X is . . . .

My family would like Product X better if . . . .

Figure 21. Sentence completion test like this is a projective technique. Instructions to people filling in the blanks above are: "This is a little game . . . All you have to do is complete some sentences with the first thought that comes into your mind. Just tell me the very first thing you think of . . . a word, a phrase or a whole sentence." Fig. 1, p. 49, from *Consumer Behavior and the Behavioral Sciences,* edited by Stewart H. Britt, 1966. Copyright © 1966 by John Wiley and Sons, Inc.

Balloon Test

Another approach is to ask a respondent to fill in the blank balloon, or write a reply to what one person in a cartoon has said. An example in consumer marketing research is shown in Figure 22.

Rosenzweig Picture-Frustration Study

The Rosenzweig Picture-Frustration Study consists of two anonymous figures in cartoon form reacting to mildly frustrating situations. The respondent is asked to write in the blank caption box what the frustrated person would say. The assumption is that the respondent identifies with the frustrated character and projects his own reaction tendencies in his replies.

Forms are available for adults and children. The Children's Form is intended for use with children from ages 4-13. Instructions are as follows:

> We are going to play a game. Here are some pictures of people doing and saying different things. Look at the pictures carefully one at a time. One person is always shown talking. Read what the person is saying. Write in the empty space what you think the boy or girl would answer. The

Clerk   **Woman Customer**

Figure 22. Balloon test like this is a pictorial variation of projective technique. Instructions to people filling in blank balloon are: "This is another little game that I would like to have you play. In the picture one person is shown saying something to another person. . . . Write in the reply made by the second person . .."" Fig. 2, p. 49, from *Consumer Behavior and the Behavioral Sciences,* edited by Stewart H. Britt, 1966. Copyright © 1966 by John Wiley and Sons, Inc.

answer you give should be the first thing you think of. Do not make jokes. Work as fast as you can.

Following are two of the 24 situations included in the instrument:

A woman is telling a boy that she does not know how to fix his trucks.

A girl on a swing is telling another girl that she is planning to keep the swing all afternoon. (Rosenzweig, et al., 1948, pp. 141-191)

CHOICE OR ORDERING

Choice or ordering techniques provide multiple choice responses to projective stimuli and, in this sense, are modified projective techniques. A multiple choice Rorschach Test is available.

EXPRESSIVE TECHNIQUES

An expressive technique is similar to a constructive technique except that the emphasis in the former is on the manner in which the subject forms a product out of raw material. The end product is not so important. The methods commonly used in expressive techniques are drawing, painting, role playing, and doll play.

Play Techniques

Doll play seems well suited to research in which young children are subjects because it is easy and natural for children to project themselves into the dolls. Such doll play is a promising method for research with children in the nursery school, kindergarten, and early primary grades. The child reveals attitudes toward family members as well as his fears, aggressions, and conflicts. The examiner observes what the child chooses to play with, what he says and does, and his emotional expressions.

Finger Painting

Finger painting was used by Alper, Blane, and Adams (1955) as they sought to answer the question: "Are there social class differences in the approach to, and the use of, finger painting?" Lower and middle class children were given finger paints with the instructions: (1) to paint anything you want, and (2) to paint a picture of your family. (A controlled experiment in which crayons were used was also run. The assumption was that crayons do not have the expressive power of finger paints.)

Sixteen aspects of finger painting were measured in this study. Among them were the time to begin painting, use of whole hand versus fingertip approach, use of both hands, use of whole versus partial use of sheet, and washing up behavior. Significant differences were found in the behavior in most of the tasks. For example, middle class children more often tried to avoid the finger painting task and less often used both hands and the whole sheet.

Role Playing

Although role playing has not been used extensively as a measurement tool for behavioral research, it holds great promise as an experimental method and as an observational measurement tool. "Role playing is the acting out of an assigned personal or social situation for a brief period of time by two or more individuals who have been assigned specific roles." (Kerlinger, 1964, p. 533) With the role playing technique, the researcher usually uses an observation system to measure his variables. Role playing can be used also in experimental manipulation. Group processes and interpersonal interaction can be studied conveniently through the role playing method. This method tends to project motives, needs, and attitudes of the subjects that may be below the surface and may not be expressed directly. The researcher may be a participant in the role playing process, playing one of the roles and therefore be able to control in structure the role playing situation. This may be advisable in research studies.

Among the limitations in the use of role playing as a research tool is its lack of standardization in administration, recording, and interpretation. Another question concerns its validity, since an individual's behavior on stage may not correlate with his behavior in normal life situations.

RESEARCH EXAMPLES AND ANALYSES
PROJECTIVE AND OTHER INDIRECT METHODS
OF DATA COLLECTION

BODY-IMAGE BOUNDARIES IN RELATION TO CLOTHING FABRIC AND DESIGN PREFERENCES OF A GROUP OF HOSPITALIZED PSYCHOTIC WOMEN[1]

NORMA H. COMPTON

Although the body-image concept may be defined with respect to different levels of physiological and psycho-physiological integration, the higher levels of these integrations show a similarity to the mechanisms of the psychic sphere. In the course of the socialization process, the individual experiences his body in manifold situations and is influenced by the varied responses of others to him. His image of his own body evolves gradually from these experiences, and its earliest crystallizations represent the nucleus upon which the ego structure is built. The body image becomes the individual's organized model of himself against which he measures many of his perceptions which influence his behavior and total adjustment.

It has been hypothesized that the body image reflects the self and that its boundaries play an important role in maintaining homeostasis in the course of the individual's transactions with the world. People have shown wide differences in the degree to which they experience their body boundaries as definite and firm or indefinite and weak. Individuals differ considerably with respect to where they set their body-image boundaries. While the body wall may be a primary reference point for many persons, the boundary may, by others, be perceived as encompassing clothing and aspects of the environment which might appear to be far distant from the individual. It is widely recognized that airplane pilots and automobile drivers may, in varying degrees, experience the machines as extensions of themselves. Schilder (1) and Garma (2) have called attention to the intimate relationships between clothes and other body decorations and psychological variables of a body-image order. As an extension of the body scheme, clothing may have the same symbolic significance as parts of the body. Clothing may be considered an extension of the self and can serve as a means of reinforcing body walls or of transforming the body image entirely. It appears probable to the investigator that women with concepts of their body boundaries as weak and indefinite rather than firm and definite may attempt to define these

Reprinted with permission from *Journal of Home Economics*, Vol. 56, January, 1964, pp. 40-45. Copyright by the American Home Economics Association, Washington, D.C.

[1] The author wishes to thank Dr. Seymour Fisher of the Medical Center, State University of New York, for reviewing the scoring of all Rorschach records used and Dr. Margaret Mercer and her staff of the Clinical Psychology Program of the Behavioral Studies Branch of Saint Elizabeths Hospital for their cooperation and assistance. The views expressed herein are solely those of the author and do not necessarily reflect those of Saint Elizabeths Hospital.

boundaries through clothing choices emphasizing such aspects as large fabric designs, strong figure-ground contrasts, bright colors, rough textures, and maximum body coverage.

Fisher and Cleveland (3) have developed two Rorschach scoring categories defining aspects of the body image: Barrier (container, covering, or boundary-like response); Penetration (description of the surface, channels between exterior and interior, or permeable or fragile qualities of surfaces). The Barrier score is defined as an index of the degree to which the individual regards his body exterior as a defensive barrier.

As a result of a series of studies, Fisher and Cleveland concluded that those who emphasize the barrier qualities of their body boundaries differ from those who do not in a greater interest in muscular expression, higher aspiration, a greater frequency of physical complaints involving the exterior layers of the body, and a tendency to perceive others as concealing their true intentions behind a deceptive facade. The individual who conceives of his exterior as armored seems to stress his own selfhood and its expression. (4)

Fisher and Cleveland have defined the Penetration of Boundary score as an index of the degree to which the individual regards his boundaries as readily penetrated. Studies have demonstrated that it has meaningful application to certain special groups but lacks the scope of the Barrier score. Theoretically, one would expect the two scores to be negatively correlated, but such is not the case. When one corrects for length of record the scores have been found to be independent. (In the present study rho = .15.) Because the Penetration score is measuring something independent of the Barrier concept, it has been studied here to see if there are relationships to clothing fabric preferences which may aid in defining its theoretical significance.

The question arises as to the relation of the Barrier concept to the actual physical appearance or structural characteristics of the body. Fisher and Cleveland regarded it as having little to do with them.

> ... the Barrier score manifests little relationship to indices which describe the actual structure or condition of the body. There is no correlation between the Barrier score and Sheldon's body-type classification. Also, persons who have experienced extreme body disablement from poliomyelitis do not differ in their Barrier scores from persons with mild or no polio involvement. Further, persons who have lived with colostomies for many years do not show greater boundary indefiniteness than comparable individuals who have not had colostomies. The implication of these findings is that within broad limits the manner in which an individual experiences his body-image boundaries is determined more by forces from inside than by the actual characteristics of his body. (3)

Secord and Jourard, however, found that the actual measured size of the body was a correlate of the degree of satisfaction (body cathexis) which women express for various body parts. (5)

Consideration of the possible relationships between the Barrier and Penetration concepts, clothing fabric and design preferences, and physical appearance led to the formulation of the following null hypotheses:

1. There are no significant relationships between percentage of Barrier and percentage of Penetration of Boundary responses of a group of psychotic women patients and their preferences for:
   a. Tints, bright (saturated) colors, or shades of fabrics
   b. Warm versus cool colors
   c. Strong versus weak color-value contrasts between the design and background of fabrics
   d. Large versus small fabric designs
   e. Rough versus smooth-textured fabrics
   f. Maximum versus minimum body coverage with respect to neckline-sleeve design
2. There is no significant relationship between percentage of Barrier and percentage of Penetration of Boundary responses of a group of psychotic women patients and their weight/height ratios.

Because Fisher and Cleveland have reported the relationship of various Rorschach factor scores to the Barrier and Penetration scores these relationships also will be examined in this study.

Method and Procedure

Subjects. The subjects of this study are 30 women patients at Saint Elizabeths Hospital in Washington, D.C., all living in the same ward of a continued treatment service. In comparison with many such wards, there is better prognosis and more general activity. An active rehabilitation program is in process, and most of these women have jobs on the hospital grounds. The group is heterogeneous with respect to diagnoses, period of hospitalization, and age. The ages range from 23 to 66 (median 44). Length of time since first admission ranges from 9 months to 26 years (median 7 years). In many cases hospital residence has been interrupted by home visits of varying length and frequency. Diagnoses cut across diagnostic categories. Twenty-three patients were in the various classifications of schizophrenia, three were manic depressive, and four chronic brain syndrome.

Participation in the study was voluntary. All subjects accepted the test situation readily and gave full cooperation.

Tests Used.

1. The Rorschach was administered individually and scored according to Klopfer's method (6). The individual responses were then evaluated according to Fisher and Cleveland's method of content analysis previously described. These records were checked independently by the investigator and a senior member of the psychology staff at Saint Elizabeths Hospital. Few differences resulted in the Boundary and Penetration scores obtained by the two scorers. All records were submitted to Dr. Seymour Fisher who checked the scores and provided the additional definitions necessary to resolve the few difficulties which had arisen in scoring. In the studies reported by Fisher and Cleveland various methods were used to control for the influence of the length of the record on Barrier and Penetration scores (3). In the present study, the scores were converted to percentages of the total number of responses. This procedure resulted in independence of the Barrier and Penetration ratings (rho = .15).

2. The Clothing Fabric and Design Preference Test, developed by the investigator, was administered individually to each subject. This instrument consists of 93 cards, 8½" x 11" in size, each mounted with two 5" x 7" fabric swatches or dress designs. Each subject was asked to choose the fabric or design on each card that she would prefer for clothing for herself. One group of choices involved selection of plain weave cotton fabrics of the six hues of red, yellow, orange, blue, green, and purple with respect to a tint, shade, or saturated hue. For a given hue, each of the three fabrics was presented for comparison with each of the other two fabrics so that a total of 18 paired comparisons was made.

Five other series of fabrics each consisted of 15 choices between fabrics or dress designs varying on the following dimensions:

1. Strong compared to weak contrasts in the value of color between the
    · background and the fabric pattern (figure-ground relationship)
2. Warm compared to cool colors
3. Large compared to small fabric designs
4. Rough compared to smooth-textured fabrics
5. Minimum compared to maximum body coverage with respect to neckline-sleeve design

Each fabric of a pair within a series and cards for all series were randomized before presentation to subjects for choices.

SPEARMAN RANK CORRELATIONS OF BODY-IMAGE BARRIER AND PENETRATION OF BOUNDARY SCORES WITH WEIGHT/HEIGHT RATIOS AND CLOTHING FABRIC AND DESIGN PREFERENCES

ITEM	PERCENTAGE OF BARRIER SCORES* (N = 30)	PERCENTAGE OF PENETRATION SCORES* (N = 30)
Weight/height	.32†	.08
Color preferences:		
Saturated	−.31†	.15
Tint	.10	−.12
Shade	.13	.07
Warm	−.08	.32†
Strong figure-ground contrasts	−.49‡	.14
Large patterns	−.20	.40†
Rough texture	.16	−.23
Maximum dress coverage	−.04	−.22

*Scores were translated to percentages to correct for variations in record length.

†Significant at the 5 per cent level, Old's Table of Critical Values for the Spearman Rank Correlation Coefficient (7).

‡Significant at the 1 per cent level or better, Old's Table of Critical Values for the Spearman Rank Correlation Coefficient (7).

Preference scores for each subject were calculated by summing the number of choices for each variable. Spearman rank order correlations were computed between the percentages of Barrier and Penetration responses and the scores on the Clothing Fabric and Design Preference Test, the weight/height ratios of the subjects, and certain Rorschach factors.

Results

The table shows the Spearman rank correlations of Barrier and Penetration of Boundary scores with weight/height ratios and clothing fabric and design preferences.

Weight/height ratios are significantly related to Barrier scores but not to Penetration scores. Preferences for saturated colors and strong figure-ground contrasts are negatively related to Barrier scores. Preferences for warm colors and large patterns are positively related to Penetration scores.

Spearman rank correlations also were calculated for Barrier and Penetration of Boundary scores and the usually measured attributes of Rorschach protocols which have been reported on in other studies (whole responses, popular responses to form or shape, color responses, and human movement responses). An insufficient number of shading responses was given by these subjects for analysis. The only significant correlation found was between Barrier scores and percentage of human movement responses (rho = .61). This correlation was significant beyond the .01 level.

Discussion

Clothing Fabric and Design Preference Test. The results of the Clothing Fabric and Design Preference Test indicate that women with low Barrier percentages preferred brighter, more highly saturated colors and stronger figure-ground contrasts in selecting clothing fabrics than women with high percentage of Barrier scores. These results are consistent with the report of Fisher and Cleveland, who say that some of their data suggest that, in the absence of a body-image capable of supplying a minimum constancy in new situations, the individual finds it necessary to create exterior conditions which will artificially provide a substitute boundary.

Two factors in the Clothing Fabric and Design Preference Test — preference for large designs and preference for warm colors — show a significant relationship to Penetration of Boundary scores. In order to learn more about the meaning of the Penetration score it is desirable to see what qualities other investigations have shown to be associated with these color and design preferences.

Only one study, made by the present investigator with college women, has been reported on preferences for large and small designs. In that study, women preferring large fabric designs scored significantly lower than women preferring small designs on the good impression personality dimension as measured on the California Psychological Inventory (8). High scorers in "good impression" are described as wishing to present themselves to others in the best possible light by representing themselves as unaffected, natural, and modest (9). Apparently college women choosing large designs were less concerned with impressing others favorably in this respect than were women choosing small designs. If we may extend the findings of this study and assume that women who are unconcerned with impressing others favorably choose large designs, we could interpret the patients' preferences for large designs as reflecting lack of concern with presenting themselves as unaffected, natural, and modest.

Warm color preference in this study is associated with a high Penetration score. However, these qualities which other investigators relate to preferences for warm colors are those that Fisher associates with a high Barrier score.

Several investigators have studied warm and cool color preferences of mentally ill patients. The conclusions of these studies indicate that emotionally elated and physically active patients prefer the warm and brighter colors (red, yellow, orange) and that emotionally depressed and physically inactive patients prefer cooler colors (green, blue, purple) (10, 11, 12, 13, 14, 15, 16, 17). Bullough reported in the *British Journal of Psychology* (18) that color preferences are determined in the last analysis by the individual's desire to be stimulated (preference for warmth) or to be soothed (preference for coolness). In a study with college students, Bjerstedt found that preferences for warm colors represented activity, directness, and need gratification. Subjects preferring warm colors expressed an attitude of life enjoyment rather than of moral or intellectual selection. (19)

Structural Body Characteristics. Results of the present study do not confirm Fisher and Cleveland's impression previously mentioned that Barrier scores have little relationship to indices describing the actual structure of the body. For this group of women hospital patients there is a significant positive relationship between the weight/height ratio and the percentage of Boundary scores ($p < .05$). This, of course, does not contradict their opinion that the concept is primarily internally determined.

Judging from the results of the Secord and Jourard studies (5) and those of Fisher and Cleveland (3), it would appear that women small in size should have positive, secure feelings with respect to their bodies which should be reflected in higher Barrier scores than women large in size. In the present study, the reverse relationship resulted. Women with high weight/height ratios tended to score significantly higher in Barrier concepts than women with low ratios. Therefore, if these results are to be explained in psychological security terms, it would appear that women with large weight/height ratios feel more secure than women with small ratios.

To the college girl, security in relation to her body is associated with her conformity to an internalized cultural ideal of attractive physical dimensions. In contrast, the women patients not only are older but feelings of security for them may be the result of defensive operations rather than social conformity to standards of attractive appearance.

Rorschach factors. Fisher and Cleveland studied the relationship between six often measured attributes of Rorschach protocols and Barrier and Penetration scores of college students. They found a significant relationship only between Barrier scores and number of W (whole) responses and F+% (popular form response). These relationships were also examined in the present study of psychotic patients. These subjects did not give enough shading responses to permit analysis. Of the remaining Rorschach factors analyzed, the only significant correlation found was between percentage of Barrier scores and percentage of human movement responses. This correlation was significant beyond the .01 level. This finding would appear to be consistent with several theoretical formulations appearing in the literature. Schilder emphasizes that a connection exists between one's own body and the bodies of others and that an interest in particular parts of one's own body provokes interest in the corresponding parts of the bodies of others. Fisher and Cleveland report a high level of physical activity (i.e., participation in athletics) and high levels of aspiration and need achievement manifested by individuals with high Barrier scores (3). A factor isolated in a study of responses to the Holtzman ink blots also indicated a relationship between Barrier and movement (20). This factor was defined:

Factor I — Movement, Integration, Human, Barrier, and Popular. Indicative of well-organized, ideational activity, good imaginative capacity, well-differentiated ego boundaries, and awareness of conventional concepts.

Summary and Conclusions

The present study was designed to investigate the relationship between the Body-Image Boundary (Barrier) and Penetration of Boundary aspects of the body-image concept, as defined by Fisher and Cleveland (3), and clothing fabric and design preferences of a group of thirty psychotic women hospital patients.

The Rorschach was administered individually and scored according to Klopfer's method. The individual responses were then evaluated for Barrier and Penetration according to Fisher and Cleveland's method of content analysis. Clothing fabric and design preferences were determined by administering the paired-choice Clothing Fabric and Design Preference Test developed by the investigator.

Because Fisher and Cleveland reported the relationship of various Rorschach factor scores to Barrier and Penetration scores, these relationships were also examined in this study. A significant positive correlation ($p<.01$) resulted between percentage of Barrier scores and percentage of human movement responses. For college students Fisher and Cleveland found a significant relationship between Barrier scores and number of W responses and F+%.

It was hypothesized that there would be no significant relationship between percentage of Barrier and percentage of Penetration of Boundary responses and each of the color and design preferences described above. These null hypotheses were rejected for the Barrier concept by significant negative correlations between percentage of Barrier scores and preferences for highly saturated colors ($p < .05$) and for strong figure-ground contrasts in clothing fabrics ($p < .01$). These relationships suggest that subjects with weak body boundaries tend to define or reinforce them through their clothing fabric choices. Such clothing may artificially provide them with a defense, supplying them a minimum constancy in new situations.

The null hypotheses concerning the Penetration concept were rejected as a result of significant positive correlations between percentage of Penetration scores and preferences for warm colors and for large fabric designs ($p<.05$).

A secondary hypothesis was derived from Fisher and Cleveland's interpretation that Barrier scores are primarily internally determined and have little relationship to indices describing the actual structure of the body. In the present study we find the weight/height ratio is significantly related to percentage of Barrier responses ($p < .05$). Women with high Barrier scores had significantly larger weight/height ratios than women with low Barrier scores. This significant positive correlation suggests that large body size has already provided a defense in body-image terms for these psychotic patients. The psychological meanings evolving from body size appear to differ with respect to college women. For them small body size, apparently representing an internalized cultural ideal, is associated with secure body feelings which are reflected in the high Barrier scores. (3), (5)

The results of this study suggest that clothing fabrics may function to strengthen weak body-image boundaries for women patients of mental hospitals. This finding may be a possible explanation for the recently acknowledged positive effects of "fashion therapy" in mental hospitals. Since the confusion of psychotic patients may involve the limits of their own bodies, it would appear that efforts directed at attempting to redefine and reidentify these limits through clothing should be valuable. It would be desirable to have further information concerning the relation of the Barrier score to clothing selection and structural characteristics of the body for women of different ages and different degrees of personality adjustment.

REFERENCES

1.   Schilder, P. *The Image and Appearance of the Human Body*. London: Kegan Paul, French, Trubner and Co., 1935.

2.   Garma, A. The origin of clothes. *Psychoanalytical Quart.* 18 (1949), pp. 178-190.

3.   Fisher, S., and Cleveland, S. *Body Image and Personality*. New York: D. Van Nostrand Co., Inc., 1958.

4.   Fisher, S., and Cleveland, S. Body-image boundaries and style of life. *J. Abnorm. Soc. Psychol.* 52 (1956), pp. 373-379.

5.   Secord, P., and Jourard, S. Body size and body-cathexis. *J. Consulting Psychol.* 18 (1954), p. 184.

6.   Klopfer, B., *et al. Developments in the Rorschach Technique*. New York: Harcourt, Brace and World, Inc., 1954.

7.   Olds, E.G. The 5% significance levels for sums of squares of rank differences and a correction. *Ann. Mathematical Statistics* 20 (1949), pp. 117-118.

8.   Compton, N. Personal attributes of color and design preferences in clothing fabrics. *J. Psychol.* 54 (1962), pp. 191-195.

9.   Gough, H.G. *C.P.I. Manual*. Palo Alto, California: Consulting Psychologists Press, 1956.

10.   Bullough, E. On the apparent heaviness of colors. *British J. Psychol.* 2 (1907), pp. 111-152.

11.   Stefanescu-Goanga, F. Experimentelle Untersuchungen zur Gefuehlobetonung der Farben. *Philosophische Studien* 7 (1911), pp. 284-335.

12. Allesch, G. von. Die Aesthetische Erscheinungwerse der Farbe. *Psychologische Forschung* **6** (1924), pp. 1-91, 215-281.

13. Pfister, O. Farbe und Bewegung in der Zeichnung Geisteskranker. *Schweizer Archiv für Neurologie und Psychiatrie* **34** (1934), pp. 325-365.

14. Birren, F. *Color Psychology and Color Therapy: A Factual Study of the Influence of Color on Human Life.* New York: McGraw-Hill Book Co., Inc., 1950.

15. Goldstein, E. Some experimental observations concerning the influence of color on the function of the organism. *Occupational Therapy & Rehabilitation* **21** (1942), pp. 147-151.

16. Bricks, M. Mental hygiene value of children's art work. *Am. J. Orthopsychiatry* **14** (1944), pp. 136-146.

17. Goldberg, G. The Choice of Color in Projective Techniques. Unpublished master's thesis, George Washington University, Feb. 1961.

18. Bullough, E. The perceptive problem in the aesthetic appreciation of single colors. *British J. Psychol.* **3** (1908), pp. 406-463.

19. Bjerstedt, A. Fargarrangemang ach Fargassociationer. *Nordisk Psykologi* **11** (1959), pp. 96-106.

20. Holtzman, W., *et al. Inkblot Perception and Personality.* Austin, Texas: Hogg Foundation for Mental Health by University of Texas Press, 1961.

ANALYSIS OF EXAMPLE OF PROJECTIVE TECHNIQUE

Body-Image Boundaries in Relation to Clothing Fabric and Design Preferences of a Group of Hospitalized Psychotic Women

The projective technique used in this study was the Rorschach. As indicated previously, with this instrument the subject is asked to respond to ten inkblots of varying shapes and colors. He is asked to tell what he sees in it or what it may be. Following his responses to each of the ten cards, a period of inquiry follows in which the psychologist administering the test probes for information on which the subject based his responses. The determinants of the subject's responses are recorded — the way he uses movement, color, shading, and form in determing his responses. The interpretation of these responses depends upon Rorschach's hypothesis concerning the meaning of movement and color. Such interpretation is complex and requires special training in Rorschach technique.

These determinants were scored and analyzed by Compton in this study in relation to preferences on her CFPT. However, the primary purpose of the study was to score the Rorschach responses according to Fisher and Cleveland's method of content analysis to measure body-image boundary or barrier. The details of this scoring technique appear in their book *Body Image and Personality.* Essentially, container, covering or boundary-like responses to the inkblots are scored for barrier. Barrier therefore is defined as an index of the degree to which the individual regards his body exterior as a defensive barrier. In effect, he *projects* such a feeling about himself onto the inkblots.

HUMAN-FIGURE DRAWINGS IN RELATION TO MODERNIZATION IN SUDAN[1]

MALIK B. BADRI AND WAYNE DENNIS

A. Introduction

From a consideration of drawings of a man made by children in a heterogenous assortment of groups, it appears probable that children in nearly all groups draw the kinds of men of which they approve. While a brief report has appeared (1), most of the data supporting this position are as yet unpublished. If this principle is upheld, human-figure drawings, and drawings of other subjects, may provide easily obtained and indirect indices of social attitudes and of changes in attitudes.

One of the topics that may be elucidated by this method is the nature of some of the psychological changes that occur in the course of the modernization of a nation or of a smaller social unit.

The term "modernization" refers to a complex of changes that take place as a group progresses from a more primitive, traditional way of life to one based largely on modern industry and technology. The visible signs of modernization include products such as locomotives, automobiles, airplanes, paved streets and highways, refrigerators, plumbing, telephones, cinemas, and television. Accompanying the introduction of these artifacts are many other changes, such as an increase in literacy and education, increases in health facilities, new forms of recreation and of employment, changes in child-rearing practices, etc. Many of these social changes take place concurrently, so that a community which is advanced in one respect is likely also to be advanced in other aspects of modern life.

It may be assumed that the changes which constitute modernization do not take place voluntarily unless positive attitudes toward modernization are present in the population which is undergoing change. It is in the measurement of these attitudes that we are interested.

In this context, drawings of the human figure provide a useful research tool. In a traditional society, the approved-of-man often has an appearance that distinguishes him from the men of other groups. The distinctive items of appearance may involve hairstyle and headgear, the treatment of facial hair, scarification, and, of course, clothing. Social change usually results in the disappearance or diminution of local styles and the adoption of the more widespread "modern" dress.

It is the authors' hypothesis that children who, when asked to draw a man, draw chiefly men in modern dress show thereby a preference for modern dress and for the complex of social changes of which it is a part. On the other hand,

Reprinted with permission from *The Journal of Psychology*, Vol. 58, 1964, pp. 421-425. Copyright by The Journal Press.

[1] Expenses in this study were defrayed by a grant from the Rockefeller Brothers Fund to the American University of Beirut.

children who for the most part draw men having the traditional appearance of men of their group are either (a) unacquainted with modern dress or (b) hold negative attitudes toward it.

Unpublished data obtained by Dennis suggest that changes in human-figure drawings occur early in the process of modernization. This is what one would expect if, as has been suggested, psychological acceptance must precede the modernization that is sponsored by the changing group itself.

For example, unpublished data from Lebanon show that few men in traditional dress are drawn by children in villages in which traditional dress is still worn by the older men. The same results have been obtained from Indian groups in Mexico. These results suggest that drawings obtained from countries which have been less exposed to modern influences than have been Lebanon and Mexico would be of interest.

The present paper, as the title indicates, is concerned with drawings obtained in Sudan, a country many parts of which meet the requirement proposed above. The data were gathered by one of the authors (Badri) who is Sudanese and who is familiar with the schools and the communities in which drawings were obtained. The assistance of several Sudanese students at the American University of Beirut and at the Ahfad College of Omdurman, Sudan, is gratefully acknowledged.

B. Procedure in Obtaining Drawings

All drawings were obtained by Dr. Badri or by a trained assistant. They were made in the children's usual classrooms. They were drawn with pencil on plain white 9″ x 12″ paper. The children were asked to draw a man, any kind of man they wished, but to draw a whole man — not just a head or torso. There was no time limit.

The test was given in Grade 4, in which the pupils were primarily 10 and 11 years of age. This grade was chosen because children draw a man less well before ages 10 and 11 and because a considerable degree of elimination from school occurs beyond these ages.

C. The Groups Tested

Data are presented only for boys. Drawings were obtained from four boys' schools in Omdurman and Khartoum, the two major cities in Sudan. In addition, a boys' school in each of two villages was tested.

In terms of modernization of the families of the students, Dr. Badri and several Sudanese university students ranked these schools as follows (prior to classification of the drawings): Rated as most modern were the families of students in an American school for boys which has been operated in Omdurman for some time. While all of its teachers and students are Sudanese and instruction is in Arabic, by tradition it is "modern" and parents who wish their sons to have this sort of outlook send them to this school. This school was rated "A" in respect to modernization.

The other Omdurman and Khartoum schools which were tested were rated "B." They have been combined for the purposes of this paper. It was unanimously agreed by the raters that both villages rank below the urban groups and that village "D" is below village "C." Village C has a large center for religious training and for native psychotherapy. This village has electricity in the religious center and is situated on a main traffic highway. Because village C is nearer to Khartoum, its people have more opportunity to visit the capital. Village D is farther away from the capital and is much smaller. It has no electricity, its houses are poorer, its people are poorer. It has poor communication with the capital.

D. The Classification of the Drawings

In the case of each drawing it was determined by inspection whether it represented (a) a man of traditional appearance, (b) a man in modern dress, or (c) a man of uncertain or ambiguous appearance. The decisions depended primarily upon clothing, but other items sometimes played a part.

The most distinguishing aspect of the appearance of a traditional Sudanese man, as depicted in the drawings, is his chief article of apparel: the galabia. This is a long loose garment extending from the shoulders to the ankles. To a person accustomed to modern dress, it is likely to suggest a nightgown. It is made of cotton and ordinarily is white. Because of its simplicity, it is easily drawn and is not difficult to distinguish from drawings of modern dress.

Under the galabia are worn thin cotton trousers resembling pajamas. Children in their drawings frequently draw these trousers although they are, in fact, not visible. Shoes without laces may be worn with the galabia, but the poorer Sudanese wear a native type of slipper.

The traditional Sudanese dress includes several forms of headgear, which need not be described here, but traditional Sudanese headgear is easily distinguished from modern hats and caps. Formerly many Sudanese had their cheeks scarified, but scarification of the face is seldom represented in the drawings. Apparently the abandonment of facial scarification is one of the first steps toward modernization.

In Sudanese drawings, modern dress can be distinguished from traditional dress by the presence of one or more of the following items: a hat or cap, collar, necktie, shirt, coat, belt, and trousers not accompanied by a galabia.

In "good" drawings the distinction between traditional and modern appearance is easily made. However, many of the drawings are not good. In poor drawings, if the drawing contained a mixture of modern and traditional, such as a galabia combined with a wristwatch, it was classified according to the aspect of appearance that seemed to predominate: in this case, the galabia. Some drawings, however, were not classifiable, either because they represented unclothed figures or were so poorly executed that they could not be interpreted or because they appeared to represent a man neither in current traditional dress nor in current modern dress. As was noted earlier, we have therefore three classes of drawings: (a) traditional, (b) modern, and (c) neither traditional nor modern.

After the non-Sudanese author (Dennis) had been familiarized with the drawings and with the costumes which they represented, the two authors independently scored 100 papers chosen from the four ranks. The agreement with respect to placement in the three categories was 98 per cent. The data included in Table 1 were classified by Badri and by Sudanese assistants whose independent scoring also agreed highly with that of Dr. Badri.

E. Results

The results to be considered are shown in Table 1. In this table the successive columns show for each group (a) the number of drawings, (b) the number which were classified as traditional, (c) the number classified as modern, and (d) the per cent of the combined traditional and modern drawings which were modern.

The results require little comment. The per cents of modern drawings parallel the group rankings for modernization. The per cents of modern drawings vary from 82.9 in the most modernized group to 4.9 in the least modernized. If each group is compared with all other groups, in all such comparisons the group designated as more advanced in modernization has the higher per cent of modern drawings. In all such comparisons, the differences are significant at the .001 level of confidence.

The fact that modern dress is seldom drawn in the two villages is not due to lack of acquaintance with it. The teachers of these boys are men in modern dress. The drawing test was administered by a psychologist in modern dress. Other men in modern dress, such as policemen, agricultural officers, and health officers, either live in the village in question or frequently visit it. However, the prominent local citizens usually wear traditional dress. The data, therefore, are consonant with the interpretation that most of the village boys and some of the urban boys have not yet developed a preference for modern clothing, although it is familiar to them. It is predicted by the authors that before these villages in Sudan adopt the technological changes associated with modernization, the content of drawings will begin to show a preference for modern dress.

TABLE 1. NUMBER AND PER CENT OF TRADITIONAL AND
MODERN DRAWINGS BY SUDANESE CHILDREN

Group	Number of cases	Drawings Traditional	Modern	Per cent modern
A	41	6	29	82.9
B	178	86	64	42.6
C	28	19	5	20.8
D	46	39	2	4.9

F. Summary

It is proposed that the relative frequencies of traditional appearance and modern appearance in children's drawings of a man made by children who are familiar with both kinds of dress reflect the extent to which the child favors one form of dress over the other. It is further proposed that in Sudan, where some groups are much more "modernized" than others, the degree of adoption of the modern style of life would be reflected by the relative frequency of modern dress in the drawings of various groups. Drawings were obtained from Sudanese groups appropriate for the study. The findings are consonant with the interpretation proposed.

REFERENCES

1. Dennis, W. Values Expressed in Children's Drawings. In W. Dennis (Ed.), *Readings in Child Psychology* (2nd ed.), Englewood Cliffs, N.J.: Prentice-Hall, 1963. Pp. 265-271.

ANALYSIS OF EXAMPLE OF PROJECTIVE TECHNIQUE

Human-Figure Drawings in Relation to Modernization in Sudan

As indicated previously, drawings and paintings are used as projective devices. Badri and Dennis stated that "from a consideration of drawings of a man made by children in a heterogenous assortment of groups, it appears probable that children in nearly all groups draw the kinds of men of which they approve."

Badri and Dennis used human figure drawings in Sudan to test the following hypotheses:

1. Children who when asked to draw a man, draw chiefly men in modern dress show thereby a preference for modern dress and for the complex of social changes of which it is a part.

2. Children who for the most part draw men having the traditional appearance of men of their group are either unacquainted with modern dress or hold negative attitudes toward it.

Drawings were classified by inspection according to whether they represented (a) a man of traditional appearance, (b) a man in modern dress, or (c) a man of uncertain or ambiguous appearance. The decisions depended primarily upon clothing.

Drawings were obtained from boys in four schools — two in major cities and two in villages in Sudan. Schools were ranked in terms of modernization of the families of the students, prior to classification of the drawings. To test the hypotheses, the per cents of modern drawings were compared with group rankings for modernization.

SEX-ROLE CONCEPTS AND SEX TYPING IN CHILDHOOD AS A FUNCTION OF SCHOOL AND HOME ENVIRONMENTS

PATRICIA MINUCHIN

This century has seen a broadening in the range of prevailing attitudes toward social sex roles for men and women and sex-appropriate behavior for boys and girls. Increasingly flexible attitudes have grown up and now coexist with more conventional and sex-typed conceptions. Though there has been little specific attention paid to the change as it affects American schools, social scientists have described and discussed this change in the American culture and family (Bronfenbrenner, 1958; 1961; Miller and Swanson, 1958; Parsons, 1942; Riesman, 1958; Sanford, 1958; Sears, Maccoby, & Levin, 1957). They have described an increasing similarity in parents' relations with boys and girls. They have also noted a lessening of dichotomous, sex-typed expectations on the part of parents concerning the interests, abilities, and personality characteristics of their sons and daughters.

These trends are stronger in some sections of the culture than in others. They are more characteristic of the middle than the lower class and more prevalent among the well educated (Bronfenbrenner, 1961; Parsons, 1942; Rabban, 1950; Sanford, 1958). They also vary, obviously, within the educated middle class; some families and schools have been more responsive to these trends, intellectually and psychologically, than others. Where changing attitudes toward sex roles and sex typing have taken root — usually as part of a generalized move away from the traditional — children have been growing up in subcultures different from those with equivalent class characteristics but more traditional orientations. Children who belong to these families or attend schools of similar orientation experience sex-role standards that are less specific, dichotomous, and imperative than those described as traditionally typical of American culture.

It is a primary research task, at this point, to examine the nature of the effects on children — to determine whether children of otherwise comparable backgrounds are developing different sex-role concepts and sex typing in behavior as a function of differences in attitudes and models offered by their schools and homes. This paper presents data bearing on this question.

The material to be presented is drawn from a study that had multiple purposes and a broad scope. It was designed to assess the effects of different educational and home environments on the psychological development of children (Biber, Zimiles, Minuchin, & Shapiro, 1962; Minuchin, Shapiro, Dinner-

Reprinted from *Child Development*, Vol. 36, 1965, pp. 1033-1048, with permission from The Society for Research in Child Development, Inc.

Based on a paper presented at the 41st annual meeting of the American Orthopsychiatric Association, Chicago, March, 1964. The study described in this paper was undertaken by Bank Street College of Education and supported by the National Institute of Mental Health (Grant M-1075) and the U.S. Office of Education (Cooperative Research Project 1401). The author wishes to thank Barbara Biber, Edna Shapiro, Herbert Zimiles, and also Virginia Stern and Doris Wallace, as well as other members of the research staff who worked on the study and on the material presented in this paper.

stein, & Biber, 1961). The different environments were defined in terms of their relatively traditional or modern philosophies and practices. Psychological development was broadly defined and included cognitive functioning, interpersonal attitudes, and aspects of self-image. Material relevant to sex-role concepts and sex-typical reactions constituted a part of the data obtained on the children's development.

The research design involved the study of four urban elementary schools as social institutions, the observation of children in fourth-grade classrooms of these schools, six individual sessions with 105 children from these classrooms, and interviews with mothers of the children selected for study. Since this paper will concentrate on comparing sex-role concepts and sex-typical reactions of children from traditional and modern backgrounds, the description of procedures and methods will be limited to facts essential to an understanding of the findings to be presented.

Background and Procedures

Selection of Schools. Four schools from a large metropolitan area were selected as the study settings, after consultation with local school officials, visits to the schools, and interviews with their principals. They were selected for their variability on a modern-traditional continuum of values, goals, and methods, combined with their equivalence on other basic dimensions: socioeconomic background of the parent population, stability of administration and viewpoint, reputation as good schools, and willingness to cooperate in the research. The differences in modern or traditional viewpoints of the schools constituted the major independent variable of the study.

The "traditional" viewpoint (in school or home) is defined in this study as stressing the socialization of the child, through known and standardized methods, toward established and generalized standards. The schools selected as relatively traditional, therefore, were those that stressed the teaching and mastery of a definite and established body of facts, the competitive and comparative evaluation of achievement, and the maintenance of a distant and inflexible authority role on the part of adults. Relatively fixed conceptions of sex-appropriate roles and behavior were considered part of this constellation.

The "modern" viewpoint is defined in this study as fostering the individual development of the child, through more varied methods and toward more complex and individually relevant standards. By definition, the modern environment incorporates more of the accumulating knowledge of personality formation, child development, motivation, and learning into its methods and goals. The schools selected as modern were those that stressed intellectual exploration and involvement, the shaping of curriculum to basic developmental trends, the individualized evaluation of mastery, and flexible, close relationships between teachers and children. Relatively open conceptions of sex-appropriate roles and behavior were considered part of this constellation.

Two schools (Adams and Browning) were selected as traditional, two (Conrad and Dickens) as modern. Subsequent detailed study of the four schools confirmed the original categorization. Three schools are part of the public school system, but Conrad, the most modern, is an independent school.

Subjects. The sample consists of 105 children, 57 boys and 48 girls, drawn from fourth-grade classrooms in the four schools. Children whose families did not meet the socioeconomic criteria were eliminated from the research. The study children were white, middle-class, urban nine-year-olds, who had been attending their schools since the earliest grades. Fifty-two subjects attended traditional schools and 53 attended modern schools.

Children in all schools except the modern private school came from homes that varied in modern-traditional orientation. For these schools the home and school viewpoints were not correlated. Children in the modern private school, however, tended to come from homes that varied less and were predominantly modern in orientation.

Categorization of Families. A Socio-Economic-Cultural Index (SEC), comprised of family income, parents' education, and the social status of parents' occupations, was applied to all families whose children were considered for inclusion in the study. The SEC Index served as a means for eliminating families with too low a status to match the private-school families and as a means for comparing families that met the selection criteria. Though there is a range among the selected families, the entire sample can be categorized as middle middle class or upper middle class. Income and occupational status tend to be high. Most parents are college graduates.

The basic distinctions between modern and traditional families are the same, ideologically, as those for the schools, but, in keeping with the different functions and relationships within the family, the definition is different in detail.

Traditional families are defined as those that stress the social acceptability of the child's behavior and his adaptation to the expectations and standards of his society. In these families adults exercise authority as a fixed prerogative of the adult role. Modern families are defined as those that stress the individual child's needs and rate of growth. They attempt to balance demands for socialization with provision for impulse gratification and individual expression, and they exercise authority in a relatively functional and flexible way.

Ratings of the Modern-Traditional Orientation (MTO) of the families were based on questionnaires and interviews conducted with the mothers of the study children. The questionnaire was concerned with the mother's values and attitudes on child-rearing and education. The interview centered on the mother's attitudes, her actual enactment of her parental role, and her views about education. The composite MTO rating was based on scores considered relevant to the modern-traditional dimension. These were questionnaire and interview scores of modern-traditional ideology and interview ratings on the following measures: enactment of authority role, emphasis on standards of behavior and achievement, encouragement of child's individual interests. The composite MTO rating is along a 7-point scale from most traditional to most modern.

In view of the fact that sex-role attitudes are known to vary with education and socioeconomic status, it is of some importance to describe the relationship, in this sample, between socioeconomic variables and the modern-traditional orientations of the families. There is no correlation between the educational level of the parents and the MTO rating ($r = .09$), probably because the educational level is generally high and the range relatively small. There is no correlation between the SEC Index and the MTO rating for the total sample ($r = .15$) or for the parents of boys ($r = -.09$). There is a significant correlation, however, for the families of girls between higher socioeconomic status and modern orientation ($r = .39$; $p < .01$). While not highly correlated, these factors are not totally independent for parents of girls, even in this sample of relatively restricted range.

In the presentation of findings, correlations with the SEC Index will be included wherever they are at significant levels.

Testing Procedures. The techniques were administered to the children in six individual sessions. They included interviews, intelligence tests, problem-solving tasks, projective techniques, and several miscellaneous tasks. Material for this paper has been drawn from the interviews, the Stick Figure Scale (a self-scaling technique), a play session, and the Children's Picture Story Test. Description and scoring of the tests will be indicated in the subsections below.

Protocols were masked for name, school and sex before scoring. Data were analyzed for school and sex differences through analysis of variance.

Results

The material will be presented in two sections, representing two categories of data: social sex-role attitudes, and sex typing in play and fantasy. It was predicted that the traditionally educated and reared children would hold more conventional sex-role attitudes and demonstrate more conventional sex typing than children from more modern backgrounds.

Social Sex-Role Attitudes. The children were asked about their sex-role preferences and opinions through two techniques, each calling for consciously held opinions expressed directly to the interviewing adult.

Interview. — In a direct interview question, the child was asked whether it was "best to be a boy or girl."

Stick Figure Scale. — In this technique, based on the work of Mary Engel (Engel and Raine, 1963), the child was presented with ten items, for each of which two stick figures were drawn at opposite sides of the page. The interviewer described the figures in terms of contrasting qualities along some dimension of self-description. The child was then asked which one was more like himself and requested to draw himself in. Of the ten items two are relevant to this paper:

Item A

Here's a boy [girl for girl Ss] who thinks boys have the most fun and the best life.

Here's a boy [girl for girl Ss] who thinks girls have the most fun and the best life.

Responses were coded along a 3-point scale: opposite sex, middle choice, own sex. "Middle" choices were those responses where the child drew himself in the middle, usually with some comment that both have fun, each has advantages, he cannot choose because he has never been a girl, etc. These were considered more open, less committed responses than the "own-sex" choice.

Item B

For boys:

Here's a boy who likes the kind of girl who's a good athlete, strong, likes to play games.

Here's a boy who likes the kind of girl who's sort of sweet, shy, and likes to dress up.

For girls:

Here's a girl who likes the kind of boy who's a good athlete, strong, likes to play games.

Here's a girl who likes the kind of boy who is smart, likes to make things and reads a lot.

It was considered that general cultural stereotypes favor the strong athletic boy and the sweet, reticent, clothes-conscious girl. Responses were coded along a 3-point scale, from less to more stereotyped.

Findings. The interview question yielded a strong group trend and little range of response: 85 per cent of the children chose their own sex as best. Of the remaining children, five — all girls — chose the opposite sex, and these girls came from varied school and home backgrounds.

Item A of the Stick Figure Scale (SFS), though it also showed a clear group trend toward own-sex choices, drew a greater range of response. Sixty-one per cent unequivocally chose their own sex, with boys tending to this choice more than girls ($F = 5.24$; $p < .05$). Of the remaining children, 28 made middle choices and 12, 9 of whom were girls, chose the opposite sex. Children who chose the opposite sex were scattered through the schools and through the range of modern and traditional homes. It seems likely that individual factors were stronger than consistent styles of modern or traditional influence in bringing out this kind of articulate and direct protest.

A comparison of own-sex choices with middle choices, however, yielded a

TABLE 1. CHOICE OF "BEST SEX" BY MODERN AND TRADITIONAL SCHOOL CHILDREN[a] (STICK FIGURE SCALE)

Item A	No. Traditional School Children (Browning + Adams)	No. Modern School Children (Dickens + Conrad)	Total
Own-sex choice.	34	28	62
Boys	19	19	
Girls	15	9	
Middle choice	8	20	28
Boys	5	9	
Girls	3	11	
Total	42	48	90

[a]χ^2 (traditional vs. modern) = 4.34; $p < .05$.

significant connection between the response and the modern or traditional orientations of both schools and homes (see Tables 1 and 2).

Table 1 indicates that traditional school children more consistently chose their own sex as having "the most fun and the best life." Modern school children were more likely to make a middle choice, the difference being carried primarily by the girls. As Table 2 indicates, the relation between the responses and home orientation is in the same direction. The correlations are of a low order, but in the case of the total group, significant. A low order but significant correlation also obtained for girls between own-sex choices and a lower family SEC Index ($r = -.24$; $p < .05$), though not for boys or for the total group.

In relation to both home and school, an unequivocal commitment to the advantages of their own sex tended to be characteristic of children from traditional backgrounds. More open responses were more characteristic of children from modern backgrounds. Overt commitment to the advantages of the opposite sex, however, was not characteristic of either group.

In Item B of the SFS, there was a significant association between modern-traditional school background and the extent to which responses reflected cultural stereotypes. Table 3 presents the means of boys and girls from the modern and traditional schools and indicates a significant difference in the expected direction.

The relation between responses to Item B and home background is more complex, as indicated in Table 2, at least for the girls. While the preference among girls for strong, athletic young males is associated with more traditional school backgrounds, it is apparently associated with less traditional home backgrounds, as suggested by a low but significant correlation. To illuminate this

TABLE 2. CORRELATIONS BETWEEN MODERN-TRADITIONAL
ORIENTATION OF HOME AND CHILDREN'S RESPONSES CONCERNING
"BEST SEX" AND PREFERRED QUALITIES IN
OPPOSITE SEX (STICK FIGURE SCALE)

Stick Figure Scale	Boys	Girls	Total
Item A:			
Own-sex choice	+ .18[a]	+ .21	+ .20**
N	(52)	(38)	(90)
Item B:			
Preference sex-typed			
qualities opposite sex	+ .21*	- .26	+ .05
N	(53)[b]	(48)	(101)

[a]Product-moment correlations. Positive correlations signify relationship between described choice and more traditional home orientation.

[b]Discrepancies in N's, on tables, reflect instances where children did not receive tests, respond to certain items, etc.

*Significant at $p < .10$.
**Significant at $p < .05$.

TABLE 3. PREFERENCE FOR CULTURALLY SEX-TYPED QUALITIES
IN THE OPPOSITE SEX: MEANS OF MODERN AND
TRADITIONAL SCHOOL CHILDREN (STICK FIGURE SCALE, ITEM B)

	Traditional School Children						Modern School Children					
	Browning		Adams		B. + A.		Dickens		Conrad		D. + C.	
	N	Means	N	Means	N	Means	N	Means	N	Means	N	Means
Boys	9	1.89	17	2.12	26	2.04	11	1.55	16	1.19	27	1.33
Girls	8	2.50	16	2.38	24	2.42	12	1.92	12	2.25	24	2.08
Total . . .	17	2.18	33	2.24	50	2.22[a]	23	1.74	28	1.64	51	1.69[a]

[a] $t = 3.46; p < .01$.

finding, it might be necessary to explore the particular qualities of these girls' fathers. It should be noted that no relation obtains between girls' responses to this item and the SEC Index of the family ($r = .06$).

Among the boys, the findings from both school and home comparisons are consistent. The boys from traditional backgrounds showed some interest in the sweet and nicely presented girl, while boys from modern schools and homes tended to choose "pals" and reject the decorative girl. No boy from Conrad, the modern private school, reversed this pattern.

Interview discussion about reasons for best-sex choices tended to corroborate the implications drawn from the findings. Only traditionally schooled boys talked of female lives as dull and uninteresting, only traditionally schooled girls projected female advantages in terms of attractiveness, clothes, and the protection and deference accorded adult women. It might be noted, however, that when girls from the most modern background defended their preference for being girls, they tended to describe the disadvantages of the opposite sex rather than offering positive reasons for preferring their own sex role. It seems possible that these girls had neither incorporated cultural stereotypes of their own role nor, at this age at least, developed alternative images that were clear and specific.

The data tapping conscious, directly expressed attitudes about sex-role advantages and social sex images can be summarized as follows:

1. There is a group trend toward stated preference for one's own sex and toward conventional role imagery, but this trend is more consistently characteristic of children from traditional backgrounds. More open attitudes are associated, as predicted, with more modern backgrounds.

2. An open stance toward sex-role preferences is more characteristic of the girls than the boys. It is particularly characteristic of the girls from schools and homes with modern orientations and from families of higher socioeconomic status.

3. A clearly stated preference for opposite sex roles is rare in this sample and not systematically related to either modern or traditional backgrounds.

4. Both school and home orientation appear to influence these attitudes.

Sex Typing in Play and Fantasy. The idea that certain interests, fantasies, and personality reactions are typical of a particular sex tends to be well documented and accepted. It is generally expected, for instance, that aggression will be typical of boys, dependency and family orientation typical of girls (Kagan, 1964). These differences are considered a partial function of intrinsic factors, but they are generally attributed in large measure to cultural expectations and reinforcements. The modern homes and schools of this study were less bound by conventional cultural expectations than the traditional. They considered a wider range of expression and exploratory behavior acceptable and normal for both boys and girls. It might thus be expected that the play and fantasy concerns of children from modern subcultures would be less consistently sex typed. Projective data were therefore examined for the relation between modern-traditional environments and sex typing in play and fantasy, with particular attention to themes of aggression, dependency, and family orientation.

Techniques. Relevant data were drawn from two projective techniques:

Children's Picture Story Test. — The CPST is a story-telling test, similar to the TAT, consisting of 12 pictures selected for relevance to the age level.

Play session. — A session of approximately 1½ hours in which the child selected from a wide array of miniature toys (people, animals, vehicles, etc.) to play out and verbalize dramatic stories.

Protocols were rated on the following variables:

1. Sex-typed (play): a rating of the extent to which the child's play was exclusively concerned with content considered typical for sex (rating 1-2).

2. Aggressive-destructive thema (play): a rating of the incidence of aggressive-destructive themes (war scenes, battles with animals, fire, etc.) in the play session (rating 0-3).

3. Primacy of family life (play): a rating of the extent to which play was centered on family figures and themes (rating 1-3).

4. Incidence of parent figures (CPST): a count of the presence of parent figures in the stories (range 1-10).

5. Projection of benevolent adult behavior (CPST): a rating of the projected emphasis on socializing, disapproving aspects of adult behavior with children as opposed to nurturing, affectionate aspects (rating 1-4; high rating indicates greater projected benevolence).

Findings. There was a general tendency in the group to play out themes easily identified as "typical" for the sex. Boys played out stories of combat, of adventure and action, of boys as central characters. Girls played out stories of family life and interaction, of girls as central characters. There was much play that was not clearly typical for the child's sex, however. Children played out themes considered characteristic of the opposite sex, or developed play involving life sagas, farms and animals, trips, circus performances, city scenes, varying characters, etc., in ways that might characterize their own sex, the opposite sex, or neither.

The incidence of sex-typed play was significantly higher among boys than girls (see Table 4). Two-thirds of the boys played out exclusively sex-typed themes, while most of the girls included themes in their play that were not clearly typical for their sex. This quality of play was most evident among the

TABLE 4. SEX-TYPED PLAY, AGGRESSIVE-DESTRUCTIVE THEMA, AND ORIENTATION TOWARD FAMILY AND FAMILY FIGURES IN PROJECTIVE MATERIAL: MEANS OF MODERN AND TRADITIONAL SCHOOL BOYS AND GIRLS[a]

Projective Variables	Traditional School Children			Modern School Children			Statistical Comparisons
	Browning	Adams	B. + A.	Dickens	Conrad	D. + C.	
Play							
Sex-typed play:							
Boys	1.70	1.67	1.68	1.67	1.82	1.76	B > G: $F = 9.12$***
Girls	1.63	1.38	1.46	1.58	1.25	1.42	Conrad: B > G: $t = 3.52$***
Total	1.67	1.53	1.58	1.62	1.59	1.61	
Aggressive-destructive thema:							
Boys	2.20	1.89	2.00	1.67	1.50	1.57	B > G: $F = 46.44$***
Girls	0.25	0.56	0.46	0.42	0.58	0.50	B.+A. boys > D.+C. boys: $t = 1.10$ N.S.
Total	1.33	1.26	1.29	1.04	1.11	1.08	Browning: B > G: $t = 4.53$***
							Adams: B > G: $t = 4.16$***
							Dickens: B > G: $t = 2.98$***
							Conrad: B > G: $t = 2.36$*
Primacy of family life:							
Boys	0.80	0.72	0.75	0.42	0.63	0.54	G > B: $F = 46.16$***
Girls	2.50	1.75	2.00	2.33	1.17	1.75	Browning: G > B: $t = 4.15$***
Total	1.56	1.21	1.33	1.38	0.86	1.10	Adams: G > B: $t = 3.03$***
							Dickens: G > B: $t = 5.97$***
							Conrad: N.S.
Children's Picture Story Test							
Incidence of parent figures:							
Boys	5.00	5.18	5.11	4.17	4.35	4.28	Dickens: G > B: $t = 2.24$*
Girls	5.75	4.33	4.83	5.58	4.58	5.08	
Total	5.33	4.78	4.98	4.88	4.45	4.64	
Projection of benevolent adults:							
Boys	1.30	1.18	1.22	1.58	1.38	1.46	G > B: $F = 23.96$***
Girls	2.38	1.93	2.09	2.75	1.55	2.17	Browning: G > B: $t = 3.21$***
Total	1.78	1.52	1.61	2.17	1.44	1.78	Adams: G > B: $t = 2.68$**
							Dickens: G > B: $t = 3.44$***
							Conrad: N.S.

[a]Total sample of 105, with occasional missing cases. See Table 3 for approximate N's.
*Significant at $p < .05$.   **Significant at $p < .02$.   ***Significant at $p < .01$.

girls from Conrad, the most modern school. There were no general differences, however, between modern and traditional school groups on the measure of sex-typed play.

As seen in Table 5, there is a significant correlation, for girls, between family orientation and sex-typed play. Wider ranging play is associated with more modern families. No correlation obtains between sex-typed play and the SEC Index. In a separate analysis of 47 children who came from the most clearly traditional or modern families (rated 1, 2, 6, or 7 on the MTO Scale), the general trend was further sharpened (Minuchin and Shipiro, 1964). Girls from clearly modern families were significantly less sex typed in their play than either girls from clearly traditional families or boys from either group (all at $p < .01$).

On the measure of aggressive-destructive thema, there were strong sex differences. Boys tended to play out aggressive themes more than girls (see Table 4). There was considerable variability among the boys, however, and this variability was related to background factors. More aggressive play appeared among the boys of the traditional schools, less among boys of the modern schools, though differences were not statistically significant. Boys and girls of all schools were significantly different from each other in the extent of aggressive play, but the distinction was least evident in Conrad, the most modern school.

For the total group, but especially among boys, there was a low but significant correlation between aggressive-destructive thema and traditional family orientation. The study of the 47 children from clearly modern or traditional families strengthened this trend. Boys from clearly traditional families were significantly more aggressive in their play than boys from modern families (at p

TABLE 5. CORRELATIONS BETWEEN MODERN-TRADITIONAL
HOME BACKGROUNDS AND CHILDREN'S SCORES ON
SEX-TYPED PLAY, AGGRESSIVE-DESTRUCTIVE THEMA,
AND ORIENTATION TOWARD FAMILY AND FAMILY FIGURES

Projective Variables	Boys	Girls	Total
Play:			
Sex-typed play	+ .05[a]	+ .32**	+ .15
Aggressive-			
destructive thema	+ .22*	+ .10	+ .19**
Primacy of family life	− .05	+ .26*	+ .03
CPST:			
Incidence of parent			
figures.	+ .11	+ .33***	+ .21**
Projection of			
benevolent adults	− .06	+ .29**	+ .09

[a]Product-moment correlations. Positive correlations signify relationship between high score and more traditional home background.
*Significant at $p < .05$.
**Significant at $p < .02$.
***Significant at $p < .01$.

< .05) and much more aggressive than girls from clearly traditional families (at p < .01). Boys and girls from modern families were not significantly different from each other.

In general, the direction of association on the measure of aggressive-destructive thema is consistent. It suggests that boys from modern backgrounds are less aggressive in their expressed fantasies than boys from traditional backgrounds. It suggests also that the discrepancy between boy and girl aggressive reactions is less extreme among children of the modern subcultures than among those of the traditional.

On the three remaining measures, there were consistent general sex differences. The girls of the sample tended far more than the boys to play out family drama, to make up stories involving parents, and to project adults who were benevolent and nurturing in their attitudes toward children (Table 4). Variations among the girls were great but did not follow lines of modern-traditional difference in school experience. The girls from Conrad, as might be expected, were least oriented toward such themes and were most like the boys, but the strongest orientation toward such themes appeared among the girls of one traditional and one modern school (Browning and Dickens).

There were significant correlations for girls, however, between all three measures and home orientation (see Table 5). Primacy of family life in play themes correlated both with traditional family orientation ($r = .26; p < .05$) and a lower SEC Index ($r = .25; p < .05$). The other two measures did not correlate with the SEC Index but did correlate with family orientation. Traditional family orientation was associated with a high incidence of parent figures in CPST stories and greater projection of benevolent adults. The tendency to project benevolent adult figures in the CPST stories was in contrast to the group trend, which emphasized adult-child conflicts. It seems likely that these girls used the fantasy situation to project their dependent need of protective adults. The study of the 47 children from clearly modern and traditional families bore out the particular family oriented position of girls from traditional homes, as contrasted with the boys and with girls from modern homes.

The data on sex typing in play and fantasy can be summarized as follows:

1. There is a substantial group trend toward sex-typical reactions and concerns, but this trend is more characteristic of children from traditional backgrounds. Less sex-typical reactions are associated, as predicted, with more modern backgrounds. The direction of association is consistent on all measures, though the order of magnitude is not generally high.

2. Girls from modern backgrounds are particularly apt to depart from sex-typed expectations.

3. In areas where sex-typed expectations are particularly strong for one sex (aggression in boys, family orientation and dependence in girls), variability of reaction within that sex is relatively great. Higher aggression in boys and stronger family orientation and dependence in girls are associated with more traditional backgrounds.

4. The influence of family orientation is more evident, in these projective data, than that of the school.

Discussion

The data reported here suggest a consistent connection between modern-traditional background factors and the social sex-role attitudes or sex-typed behavior of children. Previous research in this area has established a connection between children's attitudes and other variables, such as sex membership and socioeconomic family status. Open role commitment and lesser sex typing have been found to be more characteristic of girls than boys and more characteristic of upper middle- than lower middle-class children (Brown, 1956; Emmerich, 1959; Rabban, 1950). The present study corroborates the finding that girls are less sex typed and more flexible in role commitment than boys. It also offers partial support for the relevance of socioeconomic factors, albeit tenuously in this relatively homogeneous sample. Primarily, however, this study suggests that psychological dimensions — differing philosophies of child-rearing and education — are influential in the formation of sex-role attitudes and reactions.

Seen in terms of group patterns, the reactions of the children in this study would be considered typical for boys and girls of this age. They stated a preference for their own sex membership and role and tended to play along sex-typed lines. Boys expressed more aggressive fantasies than girls; girls showed a stronger home and family orientation than boys. As predicted, however, it was mostly children from modern subcultures who departed from conventional expectations and group patterns. These children came from families and schools where socialization toward generalized cultural standards was not the touchstone of child-rearing and education and where expectations for boys and girls were not so dichotomous as in traditional environments.

That this relation was clearer for girls is of particular interest, and not unexpected. Roles for both men and women have been changing, but the most obvious and dramatic changes, certainly, have involved women. The contrast between traditionally accepted standards for female behavior and the modern vision of individual expression and development makes for sharp differences in the experience of girls from different backgrounds. This is particularly true if female adults holding "modern" viewpoints are themselves models for exploratory and complex role integrations. The girls from modern backgrounds, exposed perhaps to both modern attitudes and complex models, exhibited the more open attitudes toward social sex roles. They showed a greater and less sex-typed range of reactions than would conventionally be expected and were relatively free of predetermined stereotypes. At the same time, they were somewhat unclear about the specifics of their own role. Hartley (1964) has noted that we know more about how upper middle-class girls do *not* define their sex roles than about the details of how they *do* define them. The problem may lie not only in a research lag, as she suggests. It may lie also in the complexity of the image that girls from middle-class, modern-oriented backgrounds are attempting to form and integrate.

The relative influence of families and schools is difficult to assess in this study, partly for methodological reasons and partly because they are actually interwoven in the child's experience. There is nonetheless some psychological plausibility to the suggested pattern of findings. The families seem more systematically influential at a level of inner fantasy and personality organization. The schools seem influential at attitudinal levels, where children may be affected not only by direct attitudes toward social sex-role development but by attitudes toward the formation of thought and opinion and the value of exploratory reactions rather than rapid, conventional responses.

In addition to further exploration of the relative roles of home and school, two lines of research seem indicated. One involves elaboration of the background variables contributing to different sex-role attitudes and reactions. It is self-evident that child development in complex areas must be affected not only by specific teachings but by a constellation of general factors, such as authority structure, methods of socialization, attitudes toward individual growth. Such constellations are difficult to describe and measure, and their influence is seldom demonstrated. The establishment of a relation between general modern-traditional attitudes, as defined in this study, and sex-role reactions of children is interesting and important at its own level. To account in greater part for the children's reactions, however, it would clearly be necessary to integrate these findings with research on other factors: the influence of peer-group attitudes, the influence of parents and teachers as identification figures, of sibling structure in the family, of parental sex-role preferences, etc.

The second line of research involves the relation between sex-typed reactions and the process of maturation toward a resolved sex identity. It does not seem valid to assume, though psychological research has sometimes done so, that all departures from sex-typical behavior indicate faulty identification and a poor prognosis for normal, integrated development. Modern homes and schools have, in fact, followed different reasoning. They have assumed that the loosening of stereotypes in social roles and the provision of opportunity to develop in keeping with individual propensities would result in more integrated development and more resolved identity. Research would need to evaluate the course of development for children from modern and traditional backgrounds, assessing sex-role resolution as these children move into stages of adolescence and maturity.

REFERENCES

Biber, Barbara, Zimiles, H., Minuchin, Patricia, & Shapiro, Edna. A study of the psychological impact of school experience: a series of papers on selected findings. Papers read at New England Psychol. Ass., Boston, November, 1962.

Bronfenbrenner, U. Socialization and social class through time and space. In Eleanor E. Maccoby, T.E. Newcomb, & E.L. Hartley (Eds.), *Readings in social psychology*. New York: Holt, Rinehart & Winston, 1958. Pp. 400-425.

Bronfenbrenner, U. The changing American child — a speculative analysis. *J. soc. Issues*, 1961, **17**, 1.

Brown, D.G. Sex-role preference in young children. *Psychol. Monogr.*, 1956, **70**, No. 14.

Emmerich, W. Parental identification in young children. *Genet. Psychol. Monogr.*, 1959, **60**, 257-308.

Engel, Mary, & Raine, W.J. A method for the measurement of the self-concept of children in the third grade. *J. genet. Psychol.*, 1963, **102**, 125-137.

Hartley, Ruth E. A developmental view of female sex-role definition and identification. *Merrill-Palmer Quart.*, 1964, **10**, 3-16.

Kagan, J. Acquisition and significance of sex typing and sex role identity. In M.L. Hoffman & Lois W. Hoffman (Eds.), *Review of child development research.* New York: Russell Sage Foundation, 1964. Pp. 137-167.

Miller, D.R., and Swanson, G.E. *The changing American parent.* New York: Wiley, 1958.

Minuchin, Patricia, Shapiro, Edna, Dinnerstein, Dorothy, & Biber, Barbara. The psychological impact of school experience: methodological report of a study in progress. Unpublished manuscript. New York: Bank Street College of Education Library, 1961.

Minuchin, Patricia, & Shapiro, Edna. *Patterns of Mastery and Conflict Resolution at the Elementary School Level.* New York: Bank Street College of Education, 1964. (U.S. Office of Educ. Coop. Res. Proj. No. 1401)

Parsons, T. Age and sex in the social structure of the United States. *Amer. sociol. Rev.*, 1942, **7**, 604-616.

Rabban, M. Sex-role identification in young children in two diverse social groups. *Genet. Psychol. Monogr.*, 1950, **42**, 81-158.

Riesman, D. Permissiveness and sex roles. *Human Developm. Bull.*, 1958, 47-57.

Sanford, N. Changing sex roles, socialization and education. *Human Developm. Bull.*, 1958, 58-75.

Sears, R.R., Maccoby, Eleanor E., & Levin, H. *Patterns of child rearing.* Row, Peterson, 1957.

ANALYSIS OF EXAMPLE
OF PROJECTIVE TECHNIQUE

Sex-Role Concepts and Sex Typing in Childhood as a Function of School and Home Environments

Three projective techniques were included among the measuring techniques used in this study — Stick Figure Scale, a play session and the Children's Picture Story Test.

Stick Figure Scale. The child was presented with ten items, for each of which two stick figures were drawn at opposite sides of the page. The interviewer described the figures in terms of contrasting qualities along some dimension of self-description. The child was asked which one was more like himself and requested to draw himself in. Minuchin includes the following illustration in her article:

Here's a boy [girl for girl Ss]   Here's a boy [girl for girl Ss]
who thinks boys have the most fun   who thinks girls have the most fun
and the best life.   and the best life.

Responses were coded along a 3-point scale: opposite sex, middle choice, own sex. "Middle" choices were those responses where the child drew himself in the middle, usually with some comment that both have fun, each has advantages, he cannot choose because he has never been a girl, etc. These were considered more open, less committed responses than the "own-sex" choice.

Play Session. For approximately 1½ hours the child selected small toys (people, animals, vehicles, etc.) to play out and verbalize dramatic stories. As indicated previously, this method of role playing tends to project motives, needs and attitudes of subjects that may be below the surface and not expressed directly. In Minuchin's study girls tended to play out stories of family life and interaction, with girls as central characters. Boys tended to play out stories of combat, adventure and action, with boys as central characters.

Children's Picture Story Test. This test is similar to the TAT. It consists of 12 pictures selected for relevance to young children. A count was made of the incidence of parent figures in the stories and of the projection of benevolent adult behavior. With respect to the latter, ratings were made of the projected emphasis on socializing, disapproving aspects of adult behavior in relation to children as opposed to nurturing, affectionate aspects.

PART V

Analysis and Interpretation

After the data have been collected, they need to be summarized in order to answer the questions posed by the research problem. However, this analysis must be planned at the time the research is designed, before the collection of any data. The design of the study and the hypotheses formed will guide the researcher with respect to the proper breakdown and analysis of the data, but each of these processes affects the others and they should be planned together. If the researcher lays out analysis models as he states each hypothesis, only the mechanical manipulations of the data will be necessary after their collection.

Interpretation involves examining the data for their meaning and implications. Each statistical result carries a meaning which must be understood by the researcher and applied to his data. For a broader interpretation, the researcher should also compare his results and conclusions with those of other researchers conducting similar studies. Finally, he should compare them with the theories on which research is based to determine whether or not they confirm theoretical expectations or predictions.

CHAPTER 15

Statistical Significance of Data

Before gathering data, the researcher should plan methods of analysis that will enable him to interpret his results and generalize from his study. During the planning stage he should consult with a statistician and computer programmer. Such consultation is important in planning a good research design. There are numerous packaged computer programs in existence to which the researcher can be steered. However, he should be sufficiently knowledgeable about statistics and the computer to be able to read the computer printout and to interpret the analyses which have been computed for him. It is his responsibility to recognize gross errors. He does not need to master the computer formula by memory but he should be sufficiently knowledgeable in statistics and in the theories upon which his research is based to predict the general range within which his data should fall: Are the means, standard deviations, the correlation coefficients, etc. within the bounds of reasonable expectancy? If not, an error can be assumed in some process in the computer analysis.

In a few instances the researcher may need to write his own program in the language of the computer available to him (e.g., FORTRAN, COBOL, PL/I, BASIC). The effort and time involved in learning this language should be determined in consultation with the computer programmer.

The researcher should also consider the fact that some types of data are not appropriate for computer analysis and may be more easily analyzed with a calculator (i.e., nonparametric statistics such as rank order correlations, Mann Whitney U test, coefficient of congruence, etc.). On the other hand, multivariate procedures are hopeless without the computer.

Many questionnaires require extensive intellectual work to quantify them. In some instances answers can be tallied and chi-squares calculated easily by hand. Before printing a questionnaire, the researcher should consult with someone familiar with data processing. Then quantification can be done ahead of time and notations made for the key punch operator if a computer is to be used.

The researcher must guard against limiting his thinking to those elements that can be computerized. For many studies, nonverbal clues and personal meanings can be very valuable even though they may not lend themselves to computer processing.

DESCRIPTIVE STATISTICS

Categorizing the data and making a frequency distribution are preliminary steps to the analysis and interpretation of data. Descriptive statistics present a picture of a group in terms of such characteristics as the central tendency and variability of the data.

Categorizing the Data

To organize data, measurements or responses must be summarized in a meaningful way. The first step in organizing is to categorize. Categorizing is a useful technique for reducing the number of items to be studied and for revealing similarities among items.

A method of classification must be selected in accord with the research questions to be answered or hypotheses to be tested. If the study is concerned with the relationship between family income and school achievement, presumably these concepts would be operationally defined and measured in the study. To analyze the data, the school children studied would have to be classified into categories based upon family income and high and low school achievement. Each category must be mutually exclusive, i.e., each school child can be assigned to only one family income category and one school achievement category.

Before classifying data, the researcher needs to determine what relationships between factors are to be studied and whether it is necessary to retain a picture of individual cases or merely of the group as a whole. Categories should be small enough to insure the homogeneity of all cases falling within a single category, yet large enough to permit an observer to differentiate cases in various categories.

Frequency Distribution

A *statistic* is a number which represents some aspect of a group of data; it summarizes measures meaningfully. The simplest way to present data statistically is in the form of a frequency distribution. Such a distribution, as the name implies, is the number of cases falling into different categories. A frequency distribution of scores is made by placing the score values in numerical order, from largest to smallest, and indicating the frequency with which each value occurs. Table 6 shows a frequency distribution of achievement scores attained by 40 female college students.

Measures of Central Tendency

Large numbers of measures are difficult for the eye and mind to group and

TABLE 6. FREQUENCY DISTRIBUTION OF ACHIEVEMENT SCORES ATTAINED BY 40 FEMALE COLLEGE STUDENTS

Score	Frequency
80-89	8
70-79	12
60-69	10
50-59	6
40-49	4

understand. Therefore, an entire distribution of measures is described by taking typical (or average) scores. These "typical" scores are called measures of central tendency, representing central points in the frequency distribution around which scores tend to cluster.

Arithmetic Mean. The mean is the most reliable index of central tendency, varying least as different samples of data are studied. The mean is the arithmetical "average," computed by adding all the scores in a series and dividing by the number of scores $(M = \frac{\Sigma X}{N})$.* Computing the mean is one of the initial steps in applying many of the more advanced statistical tools.

The means of two or more subgroups may be combined, making possible further statistical manipulation of the data. Since each value affects the size of the mean, an extremely high or low score may exert undue influence on the mean. The mean is appropriate for most sets of data in which consistency from sample to sample is desired and where the distribution is symmetrical.

Median. The median is a point on a measurement scale, above and below which half of the scores in the frequency distribution lie. When an odd number of scores is involved, this point is identical with the value of the middle score. If an even number of scores is used, the median is midway between the two middle scores. The median is useful when reporting percentile scores, since the median is the same as the 50th percentile. It is more appropriate than the mean when there are a few extremely high or low scores that cause a marked skewness in a distribution. It is well to calculate the median as well as the mean when the set of data contains extreme values, either very high or very low, when they are not balanced by values at the opposite end.

The median is appropriate when answering such questions as:

1. What is the average age of women at the time of their marriage?

2. What is the median scale value assigned by a group of judges to an item on a Thurstone-type attitude scale?

3. Is Mary Jones's score in the upper or lower half of the scores made by entering freshmen at a given college on the *Cooperative Reading Test?*

Mode. The mode is the score value or item in a frequency distribution that occurs most often. When scores are arranged in order of their size, as in a

---

*M = mean; Σ = sum of; X = individual scores; N = total number of scores

frequency table, the mode can be determined readily by inspection. The mode is easy to determine and to understand. It is not necessary to know the values of the highest and lowest scores in the series since these extreme scores do not affect the mode. This value does not describe the entire distribution of scores. The mode fluctuates widely from one sample to another and is not as reliable as the median or mean, especially in small samples.

When interested primarily in a quick, rough estimate of the most typical item, trait, or score in a group, the mode is useful. For example:

1. What is the most typical major curriculum of high school students who are enrolled in child development courses?

2. How many minutes in length is the typical class period for a seventh grade home economics class?

3. What brand of laundry product is used by the average homemaker in Spring Valley?

Measures of Variability

A measure of the central tendency of a group gives a picture of what is the typical or average case, but it does not indicate whether the cases tend to cluster near the average or how much they spread out. The extent and manner of variation are the distinctive properties of a frequency distribution. Three measures of variability are common — the range, quartile deviation, and standard deviation.

Range. The crudest measure of variability may be obtained simply by noting the difference between the lowest and the highest scores in a series. Since only two scores are used in determining the range, it is not as reliable as other measures of variability. The range is easily determined and understood. It is a useful estimate of population variability when the sample is drawn from a normal population. Usually it is more meaningful when combined with other measures. When comparing two distributions, the range should be used only when the units of measurement are the same and the sizes of the two groups are similar.

Quartile Deviation. A quartile deviation is most likely to be used in situations where the median and percentiles are applicable, since it is obtained by locating the 75th percentile (Q_3) and the 25th percentile (Q_1). The distance between Q_3 and Q_1 is divided in half to obtain the value of Q (called the semi-interquartile range). In a symmetrical distribution, the quartile deviation is useful in showing the range of the middle 50 per cent of the cases. It is independent of the effects of extreme cases.

Standard Deviation. Just as the quartile deviation is linked with the median, the standard deviation is a measure of the spread of a distribution from the arithmetic mean. Since it is affected by the deviation of each score, it should not be used when there are a few extreme values in a series. The standard deviation is the most commonly used measure of variability because of its reliability and its usefulness in further statistical analyses. It is the square root of the variance. Further discussion of the standard deviation is in the following section on the normal distribution.

The Normal Distribution

Many frequency distributions consisting of a large number of measures tend to follow a certain pattern when plotted, called a normal distribution. The shape of the curve drawn tends to be bell-shaped. (See Figure 23.) The majority of measures cluster close to the mean (central tendency). In moving further and further from the mean, there are fewer and fewer cases.

The score values in Figure 23 can represent any measure — body weight, calories consumed, academic test scores, personality scale scores, etc. The frequencies on the vertical axis would be the number of cases for each score value. The mean, median, and mode are identical in a normal distribution.

It is possible for actual data to be distributed into any shape; scores may be "skewed" to the right or left. The normal distribution, or symmetrical bell-shaped curve, is derived from a mathematical equation. It is an ideal and, theoretically with large numbers of cases, data are expected to fall in such a pattern. Therefore, many statistical tests assume a normal distribution of the sample.

The standard deviation is an important characteristic of the normal distribution. It is generally considered to be the most useful and stable measure of variability. Like the mean, it is a necessary step to applying many of the more advanced statistical tools. The standard deviation can best be understood in relation to the ways in which data tend to distribute themselves theoretically in the "normal distribution." It divides the normal curve into a number of equal units and takes into account the distance between every individual score and the mean. Figure 24 shows the point of inflection of the curve, the point where it moves horizontally more than vertically. A perpendicular line has been drawn from this point to the base line on both sides of the symmetrical curve. The distance along the base line between the mean and the dotted line is the standard deviation of the distribution. The point to the right of the mean is one standard deviation or 1 S.D. The point to the left of the mean is −1 S.D.

All the scores in the distribution are represented in the total area under the curve, which can be divided into parts representing percentages of the whole. The area to the right of the mean contains 50 per cent of the scores. Also, it has

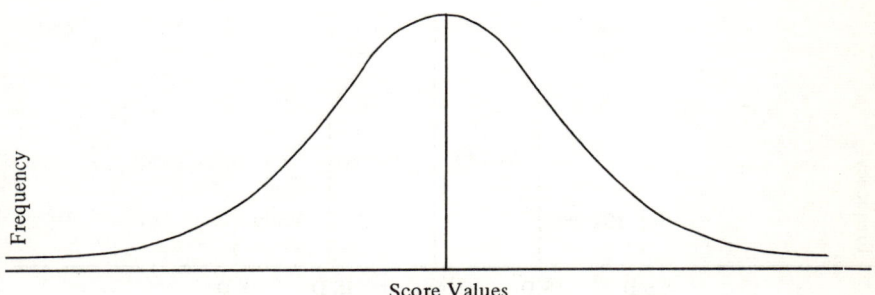

Figure 23. The Normal Distribution

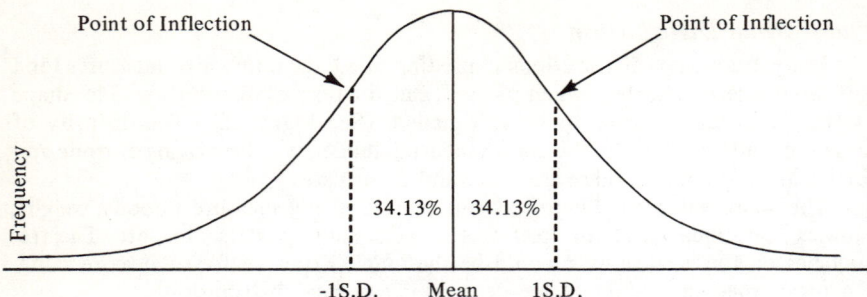

Figure 24. The Normal Distribution (± 1 S.D.)

been determined that 34.13 per cent of the area under the curve lies between the mean and the vertical dotted line in Figure 24. This is 1 S.D. from the mean. The range of scores between the mean and 1 S.D. encompasses 34.13 per cent of the scores. This is applicable to both sides of the mean.

The second standard deviation (2 S.D.) is located the same distance from 1 S.D. as 1 S.D. is from the mean. Therefore, 2 S.D. and −2 S.D. are shown in this relationship in Figure 25.

To determine 3 S.D., a base line is located which is three times as far from the mean as 1 S.D. (See Figure 26.) As shown in Figure 26, a very small percentage of scores or measurements lies between 2 S.D. and 3 S.D.

Once the mean and the standard deviation have been computed for a distribution of measurements, the percentage of measurements lying above and below any given measurement or score value can be determined. The distribution presented in Figure 27 shows the mean I.Q. score is 100 and the S.D. of the scores is 15 points. At 1 S.D. from the mean, therefore, the I.Q. score is 115 and at −1 S.D. the score is 85. Using the percentages associated with the various S.D. units, any person's position can be determined relative to the total group by com-

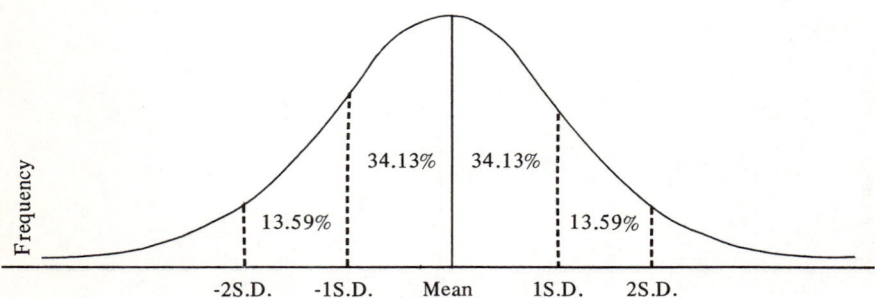

Figure 25. The Normal Distribution (± 2 S.D.)

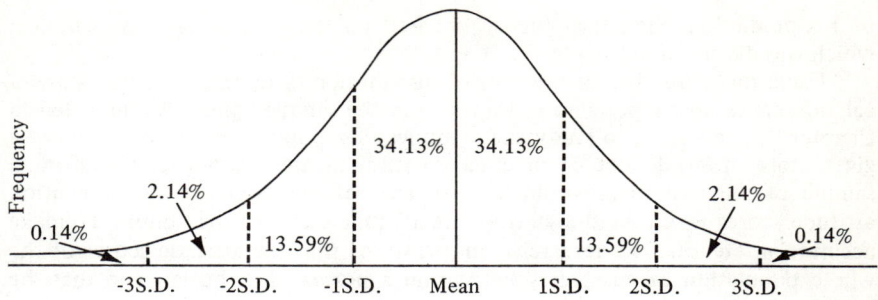

Figure 26. The Normal Distribution (± 3 S.D.)

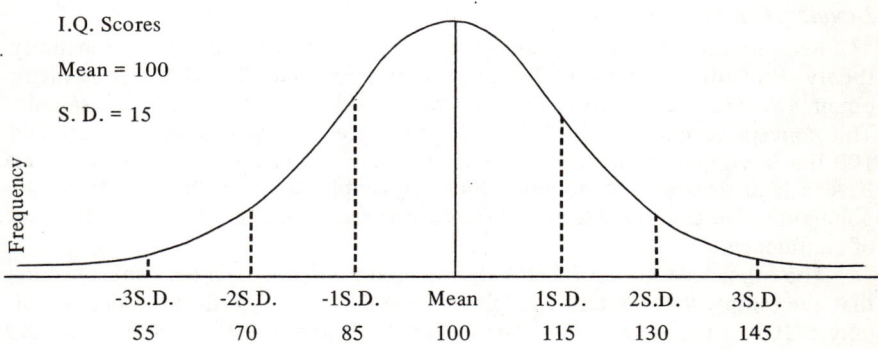

Figure 27. Normal Distribution of I.Q. Scores

puting how far, in standard deviation units, his score deviates from the mean score of the group. Using Figures 26 and 27, for a person with an I.Q. of 115, 84.13 per cent of the total group have scores below his and 15.87 per cent above his. Statistical tables are available for the percentages of scores associated with S.D. values in the normal distribution.

STATISTICAL INFERENCE AND TESTS OF ASSOCIATION

A complete treatment of statistical inference is beyond the scope of this book. Everyone conducting research should register for a course or courses in statistics. However, many authors of statistics books and statistics instructors are so absorbed with the manipulation of symbols and equations that students gain little understanding of the logic behind them. At the risk of oversimplification, a logical, nonmathematical treatment of the subject will be attempted here.

One of the most remarkable things about using statistics is that the information obtained from a rather small group can be used as the basis for estimating what a larger group would be like. The researcher can even estimate the accuracy of his prediction. Statistical theory is based on the idea of random sampling which was discussed in Chapter 9.

Using the properties of the normal distribution, a researcher makes statistical inferences about population values from the sample values. As indicated in Chapter 9, if planning to study the attitudes of a population of customers of a given store, it would not be practical to study all the customers. Therefore, a sample of the customers would be used and inferences about the population attitude scores would be drawn from the attitude scores of the sample. To make accurate inferences, the researcher must assume that the attitude scores of the whole population of customers fall within a normal distribution and that the sample is representative of the whole population. The aspect of statistics dealing with the conditions under which such inference is valid is called *statistical inference*.

Levels of Significance

Because inference is not absolutely certain, it is based upon probability theory. Probability refers to the number of times out of 100 that one might obtain a value as deviant from the expectancy as the one obtained in this sample. This concept is tied in with "levels of confidence." If the chances are only 1 in 100 that a sample mean would deviate this much from the true mean, one can have a high degree of confidence that his sample mean is different from the population. He can say that this difference is established at the 1 per cent level of confidence.

The other level of confidence that is used frequently is 5 per cent, meaning that the sample value is rare enough to come from the hypothesized population only 5/100 of the time or less. The probability fraction that the researcher uses is called the level of significance.

There are four possible results when testing a hypothesis about a population:

1. A true hypothesis will be accepted.
2. A false hypothesis will be rejected.
3. A true hypothesis will be rejected.
4. A false hypothesis will be accepted.

When applying a statistical test, a researcher hopes to achieve one of the first two results. "Type I error" is a term that refers to the possibility of rejecting a true hypothesis and "Type II error" refers to accepting a false hypothesis. The problem is complicated because if a person takes steps to reduce the risk of making a Type I error he is increasing the risk of making a Type II error. For example, he can reduce the risk of rejecting a true hypothesis by choosing the 1 per cent level of significance (meaning that he would reject not more than one true hypothesis in 100). At the same time he must keep in mind that a hypothesis which is not rejected is considered to be acceptable and so he is actually increasing the risk of accepting a false hypothesis. If an experimenter were studying a new method of teaching which would require drastic changes in class size and expensive equipment, he would want to be quite confident that the new method would be better than the old method. On the other hand, if the new method would be no more expensive and as practicable as the old, he could accept weaker evidence in rejecting the null hypothesis that the new method is no better than the old method. Generally, a low probability or small region of rejection would be selected when there are serious consequences of rejecting a true hypothesis.

Walker and Lev have outlined the steps in formulating and testing a statistical hypothesis:

1. Select the measures on which the investigation will be based.

2. Specify the general nature of the population and parameter or parameters needed for the investigation.

3. Formulate a hypothesis about the population and decide on the alternatives.

4. Determine a statistic by which the hypothesis is to be tested.

5. Ascertain the distribution of the statistic.

6. Choose a level of significance.

7. Determine the region of rejection on the basis of the level of significance and the alternatives to the hypothesis.

8. Draw a random sample of size N from the population.

9. Compare for this sample the value of the previously specified statistic.

10. Determine whether the computed value of the statistic is in the region of rejection.

11. Reject the hypothesis if the value of the statistic is in the region of rejection; otherwise accept it. (Walker and Lev, 1958, p. 232)

In an effort to achieve control and obtain significant results, remember Greenwood's caution: "We must not confuse the exactness of the findings with their significance." (Greenwood, 1945, p. 92)

As an example of how levels of significance work, a null hypothesis follows. The null hypothesis form states that there is no significant difference or relationship between groups. The procedure is to reject the null hypothesis if a statistical test yields a value whose probability of occurrence by chance is equal to or less than the small probability level chosen. If the probability of its occurrence by chance is small, then, provided the research study is properly designed, it may be assumed that the results of the study are beyond chance and are due to the experimental (independent) variable being studied.

The researcher's attitude should be that of the null hypothesis. His mind should be set to expect that his results will be null so that he can avoid the bias of seeing significant differences where there are none. The null hypothesis is the evidence that he has in fact set his mind to expect nothing.

Null Hypothesis. There is no significant difference in weight between students receiving a diet supplement (Group I – Experimental Group) and students not receiving the supplement (Group II – Control Group). The level of significance (or critical region for rejection) is selected at .05 ($P<.05$). This means that the probability of being wrong or of the results being due to chance or sampling error is to be .05 or less.

To test the hypothesis of no significant difference between weights of the two groups, the mean weights of the two groups are computed and a *t test* is performed for difference between means. This determines the likelihood of the two means being drawn from the same population. In this hypothetical study, the mean weight of Group I (receiving diet supplement) was 99.2. The mean weight of Group II was 102.3. Through a mathematical process, a t value of -1.31 is calculated for the data. A statistical table indicates that the critical region for rejection at the .05 level is 2.05. In other words, the hypothesis of no difference between means can be rejected only if the t value is less than -2.05 or greater than 2.05. Since the t value obtained was -1.31, which is not less than -2.05, the researcher fails to reject the hypothesis. His conclusion must be that there is no significant difference in weight between the two groups.

If a t value had been obtained within the critical region of rejection (less than -2.05 or greater than 2.05), the hypothesis could have been rejected. Then, the researcher could have assumed that the difference in weight between the groups was significant and that the probability of the difference being due to chance was less than .05. In other words, such a difference would likely occur by chance less than 5 times in 100 (or 5 per cent of the time). If he selected the .01 level of significance, a larger difference between the sample means would have been needed to reject the hypothesis. The .01 level is more rigid than the .05 level, involving less risk that one could be wrong in rejecting the hypothesis (one time in 100).

Differences Between Groups

Several statistical techniques are applicable in determining whether the differences between groups are significant: i.e., the t test, analysis of variance, and chi square.

t Test. The t test is used to test the significance of the difference between means of two sample groups. Its use was illustrated in the previous section where a null hypothesis was tested.

Analysis of Variance. The analysis of variance (or F test) has wider application than the t test, permitting a study of the action of two or more independent variables simultaneously on an affected or dependent variable. Like the t test, mean scores are used. The analysis of variance determines whether there is a significant difference between mean scores of two *or more* groups. The t test is limited to two groups. The analysis of variance permits computing the equivalent of several t tests at once. It indicates whether there is more variability between the groups than within the groups.

In addition, interactions cannot be determined with separate t tests. Such interactions occur when the two or more variables being investigated work together with the measurement involved to reveal differences that are not visible in comparing means in pairs. For example, in a study to determine children's emotional reactions to aggressive acts on television, such reactions could be analyzed in relation to the type of aggressive model used (human or cartoon) and to the sex of the children, as follows:

		Type of Aggressive Model	
		Human	Cartoon
Sex	Male		
	Female		

Three statistical hypotheses could be tested simultaneously: the significance of the differences in emotional reactions between human and cartoon models, between male and female children, and the significance of the *interaction* between these two variables. The researcher may be interested in the effects of human and cartoon models but he may be more interested in whether human and cartoon models work differently with boys and girls.

A more complicated technique is the *analysis of covariance*, in which differences between groups are compared, with differences due to the covariant being removed. In studies where it is impossible to match groups before applying an experimental variable, the analysis of covariance technique makes it possible to eliminate the effects of some important factor such as intelligence.

Chi Square. The chi square (χ^2) statistical technique is used for summarizing differences in distribution found between two or more sample groups in a counting experiment. This approach deals with frequencies rather than mean scores. It can thus be determined whether there is a difference in the number or frequency of people responding in certain ways. For instance, a group of people may be asked if they prefer Brand A or Brand B cereal. The number (or frequency) of people preferring Brand A and the number preferring Brand B may be counted and the differences compared. With the chi square technique, one can determine the probability that the frequencies observed in his study differ from an expected theoretical frequency. In the cereal survey, for example, from a sample of 50 people, it should be expected that 25 people would prefer Brand A and that 25 would prefer Brand B. In the chi square test, these are called the *expected* frequencies that would be expected to occur by chance. If 20 people in the survey actually preferred Brand A and 30 people preferred Brand B, these preferences are termed the *observed* frequencies. The question to be asked is: "Do the observed frequencies differ sufficiently from the expected frequencies to justify rejection of the null hypothesis?" If they do, the null hypothesis of no significant difference is rejected with the conclusion that there is a preference for Brand B over Brand A.

The chi square can also be used to test the departure of two observed distributions from one another. In this instance the difference in distribution between the two groups is tested. Frequencies are entered in cells as shown in Table 7. The computation of chi square in this instance is based upon the mathematical distribution of row and column frequencies uniformly over the table. The distribution of column totals up the column are expected to be in the same proportion as the distribution of row totals across the rows. This distribution constitutes the expected value.

As with the t test, statistical tables provide the value of chi square needed to reach significance at $P = .05$ and $P = .01$. For the data in Table 7 (preferences of cereal brands by males and females), the critical region or level of significance (as determined by consulting a statistical table) was $\chi^2 > 5.99$. The chi square which was computed was 10.67. Therefore, males and females differed in their preferences for cereal brands more than could be expected by chance so the null hypothesis of no significant difference is rejected. Another way of stating this hypothesis to be tested by chi square is that preference for cereal brands is independent of the sex of the subject. The hypothesis was rejected, indicating that preference for cereal brands is not independent of sex in the study represented by these data.

TABLE 7. CHI SQUARE

Cereal Brands	Sex		Total
	Male	Female	
Brand A	32	12	44
Brand B	14	22	36
Brand C	6	9	15
Total	52	43	95

Correlation

The relationship between the changes in two variables is expressed mathematically as a correlation coefficient and graphically as a scatter diagram. (See Figures 28-30.) In the figures a point represents a person as the intersection of his two measurements. Correlations lie between the limits of +1.0 and -1.0, which represent a perfect direct (positive) relationship or inverse (negative) relationship respectively. A positive relationship means that as the measures for one of the variables increase the measures for the other variable also increase. Likewise, as one decreases the other decreases. A negative (or inverse) relationship means that as the measures for one variable increase the measures for the other variable decrease. The correlation technique is used when there are scores or measures on two variables for each individual in a group and the researcher wishes to determine whether there is a relationship between these variables.

The following hypothetical scores for eight children are based on a psychology and a child development test, from which to determine the degree of correlation between the scores on the two tests:

Student	Psychology Score	Child Development Score
A	60	60
B	40	40
C	30	30
D	20	20
E	80	80
F	50	50
G	10	10
H	70	70

A quick examination of these data reveals that the scores for each individual on the two measures are identical and therefore a perfect correlation exists. To show this relationship graphically, the data are plotted on a scatter diagram in Figure 28.

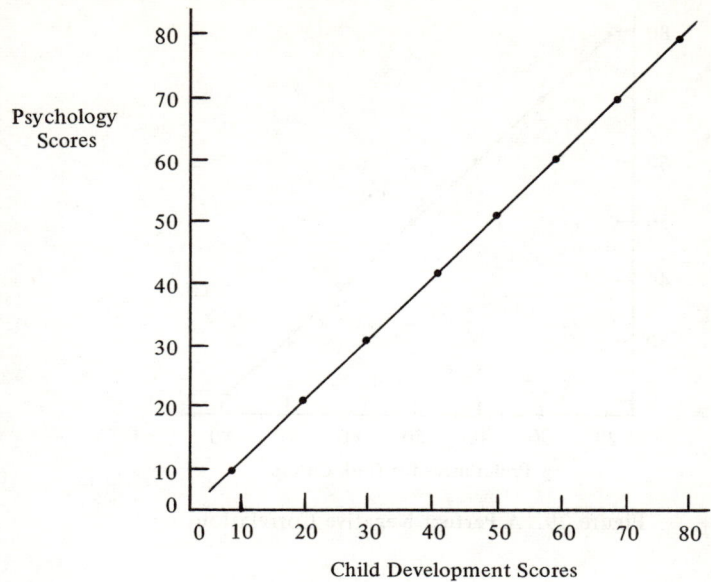

Figure 28. A Perfect Positive Correlation

A scatter diagram showing a perfect negative correlation is given in Figure 29.

In the diagram depicting a hypothetical perfect negative correlation, it is evident that preferences for dark colors are inversely related to preferences for light colors. It is perfect because if a straight line is drawn through the dots, the dots fall exactly on the line and the amount of increase in one variable is in proportion to the amount of decrease on the other variable.

An imperfect relationship between variables is illustrated in Figure 30. The dots tend to lie in a positive direction, indicating a positive correlation.

By using a statistical formula, such as the Pearson product-moment correlation, one can compute the correlation coefficient from the two sets of scores. The coefficient is an estimation of the closeness of the points to the line, which is the same thing as the estimation of the closeness of the relationship of the measurements to a perfect relationship. Through statistical tables one can determine whether the correlation is sufficiently significant to reject the hypothesis of no significant relationship between the two sets of scores. The Pearson product-moment correlation involves the use of a scatter diagram unless a calculator or a computer program is used. The computation requires just one step in addition to those necessary for finding the means and standard deviations of two sets of data. The additional step, which can be taken simultaneously with the other steps, can be found in the computational procedures set forth in Garrett (1966).

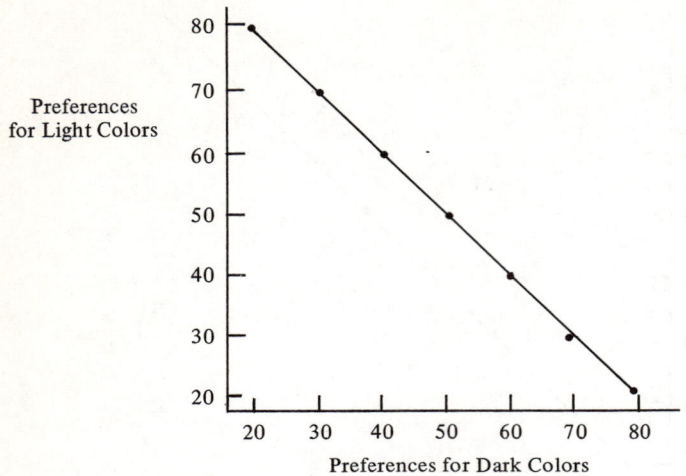

Figure 29. A Perfect Negative Correlation

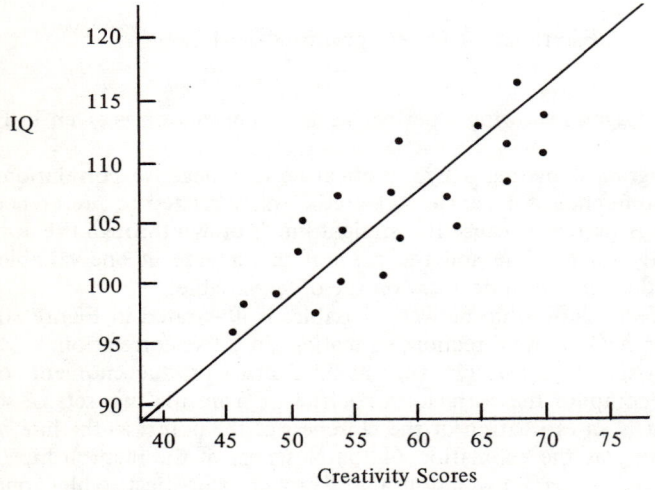

Figure 30. Scatter Diagram of I.Q. and Creativity Scores

The Spearman rank order correlation is adaptable particularly to small groups, in which the number of paired scores is 30 or less. Since it depends upon placing scores in their order, from highest to lowest, it may be used when exact scores are not available and only the rankings are available. Rank order correlation assumes that the measures are independent of each other.

There are several other statistical techniques for examining the relationships between two sets of measurements. Some of these are the tetrachoric r, the biserial r, and the phi coefficient. These techniques are used when the data have special characteristics such as non-continuity or low orders of measurement.

It is not easy to determine how significant a correlation is, since its meaning can be interpreted only in relation to the situation in which it was obtained. Arny (1953, pp. 301-302) cautioned against three common errors in the interpretation of correlation coefficients:

1. Assuming that if two variables are highly correlated, one causes the other. Both may be influenced by another factor or factors.

2. Generalizing from the sample for which the computation was made to groups of which it was not representative.

3. Assuming that a correlation coefficient of a given size always has equal significance. We can place more faith in a correlation coefficient which was computed for a large number of cases than when only a few were involved; when the distributions were "normally" distributed than when they were not; and when each group was relatively homogeneous than when it was very heterogeneous.

SUMMARY

It has been recognized by researchers for a long time that statistical analysis is a way of establishing significance in a study when no significance is obvious. Every researcher dreams of the research study whose results are so evidently significant that no statistical analysis is necessary. However, since that dream is seldom realized, statistical investigation of the characteristics of a set of data remains a valuable and sometimes fascinating auxiliary to the main activity of research, which is always the conception, design, and execution of a study based on sound theory. Beware of the temptation to salvage a poor study by extensive analysis!

CHAPTER 16

Presentation and Interpretation of Data

Interpretation of the research findings to others is an important part of any study. Tables or graphs evolved from the data can highlight significant findings.

GENERAL GUIDES FOR PRESENTING DATA

Style manuals differ in specific recommendations about presenting data. After selecting a style, the researcher should follow it and be consistent in handling comparable kinds of data. Illustrations of various styles for tables and graphic materials may be found in the research examples included in Chapters 5-8 and 11-14. Reference books and assistance from experienced researchers will also help the beginner to present data clearly and succinctly.*

A table containing only four or five items or a graph presenting limited data is usually included in the body of the text immediately following the paragraph in which it is first mentioned (or on the next page, if necessary, to present it in full). A table or graph is referred to in the text by its number.

Titles of tables or graphs must be concise, clearly indicating the content,

---

*Among the widely used reference books are these:

Stephen V. Ballou, *A Model for Theses and Research Papers.* Boston: Houghton Mifflin Company, 1970.

William G. Campbell, *Form and Style in Thesis Writing.* 3rd ed. Boston: Houghton Mifflin Company, 1969.

Kathleen Dugdale, *A Manual of Form for Theses and Term Reports.* Rev. ed. Bloomington, Ind.: The Indiana University Bookstore, 1962.

A Manual of Style. 12th ed. Chicago: The University of Chicago Press, 1969.

Rudolf Modley and Dyno Lowenstein, *Pictographs and Graphs.* New York: Harper and Row, Inc., 1952.

participants or population, and other information essential to understanding the data.

Tables

When specific numbers are necessary for clarity and the series of numbers is of manageable size, a table may be effective. If long series of raw data must be included, the tables may be placed in the appendix.

The goals of a table are accuracy, neat appearance, and ease of interpretation. These goals are more likely to be achieved when a table is simple, presenting only one kind of information and only a few aspects related to it. A table should stand alone, not being dependent upon the text for meaning or clarity.

Long box headings may be placed vertically (broadside), reading up from the bottom of the table. Tables that are too wide to fit broadside may be typed on a wider page that can be folded inconspicuously and neatly into place. A photostatic copy may be used to reduce the size sufficiently so the table is readable and yet is of normal size.

Cut-in headings may be used to combine materials which would otherwise have to be placed in two or more small tables.

Abbreviations are sometimes used in the box headings or body of a table. Whenever possible, these should be standard forms. Footnotes are used to explain abbreviations, to point out significant differences between parts of the data, or to explain how a difficult table should be read.

Graphs and Illustrations

Visual presentation is widely used and is often more effective than tabular or verbal description. Its benefits have been summarized by Modley and Lowenstein (1952, pp. 3-4):

> Visualized information is faster, more direct, more dramatic and easier to remember. For the large part, also, visual communication conveys a personal feeling which arouses the interest of the average reader.

Because of these advantages, Campbell found it necessary to caution that: "As a general rule, Figures are not both easily and inexpensively reproduced." (Campbell, 1954, p. 50) Be selective, then, and use them where they are most effective. Graphs can be used to clarify numerical data, present relationships among variables, reveal trends or changes over a period of time, or to show how a total is made up of its component parts.

Criteria for Effective Graphic Presentation. To be effective, visual materials must be planned carefully, executed with high standards, and interpreted with caution. Graphic materials should fulfill the following criteria:

1.   Accuracy. All of the data must be correct to start with. The points must be plotted accurately. Intervals should be appropriate in size to show the data clearly and without distortion. Numerical figures shown as part of a graph must be checked for accuracy. They should be placed in a position where they will not distort the data. Numerical values placed outside bars or segments of a pie chart may change the apparent proportions being represented.

2. Clarity. Graphic data may be clarified by including numerical data as part of the graph. Independent variables (such as dates) are placed on the horizontal axis with the low values at the left and high values at the right. The dependent variable, or measured trait, is on the vertical axis with low values at the bottom and high values at the top. A key or legend should be given when necessary. The title should be clear and complete, yet concise. When curve lines are used, they must be distinguished sharply from each other and from the background rulings.

3. Simplicity. Relatively large intervals and as few words as possible contribute to the ease of interpreting a graph. Only the coordinate lines that are necessary to guide the reader's eye to the proper position should be shown. As Spear stated, "The purpose of a chart is to display facts — not to disguise them." (Spear, 1952, p. 37)

4. Ease of reading. A careful selection of the best method for showing data is important for readability. All numbers and lettering should be large enough to read easily. Whenever possible, they should be placed in the proper direction for easy reading. Different colors or various types of lines are efficient ways of differentiating between parts of a line graph.

5. Orderliness and neatness of arrangement. The quality of workmanship is an important factor in the effectiveness of visual material. All pencil lines should be erased. Black India ink or clear dark colors may be used for drawing graphs. Gummed tape (such as Zip-a-tone or Contak sheets) is available in an assortment of lines. When two or more designs are needed on one chart, they should be distinctive in pattern and shading. The gummed sheets can be cut easily to any desired size or shape. If an error is made, the tape can be removed and relocated easily without leaving a trace. Since this tape has a tendency to loosen in time, its use is recommended for photostatic work rather than for original copies to be placed in a thesis.

Types of Illustrative Material. Each of the following types of illustrative material might have a place in human ecology research:

1. Bar graphs. A bar graph normally is composed of horizontal bars showing relationships of two variables for which information is given for one or more groups (usually not more than three groups). Bar graphs are widely used, quick to prepare, and easy to understand. Bars may extend horizontally with the zero position at the left, vertically with the base line at the bottom, or in both directions from a position in the middle of a base line (as in a profile chart).

All of the bars within a single chart should be of the same width. When two or more groups are being compared, the bars for any one item touch each other and a space separates those bars from the ones pertaining to the items on either side of it. The number of cases may be indicated on each bar.

When all of the bars are of equal length, representing 100 per cent for each group, they are referred to as *100 per cent bars*. Shaded areas within each bar, showing the size of its components, should be indicated in the same order on each bar.

2. Line graphs. Line or curve charts are used to show the relationship between two variables such as time, age, or test scores. Several series of data may be compared over a period of time. Not more than four or five lines can be

shown clearly in one figure. To differentiate between groups, a variety of lines should be used (such as solid, hollow, dash, dotted, and a combination of line and dot).

Color is satisfactory when each copy of a report is to contain an original copy. However, color cannot be reproduced in microfilm, which is used commonly to make doctoral dissertations available for interlibrary use. The expense of color reproduction in printing may make its use prohibitive, especially where more than one color is necessary.

Several types of simple line graphs are useful in presenting data:

Frequency chart — to show the distribution of a group
Percentile chart — to make comparisons between groups
Profile chart — to give the relative rank of an individual on a series of measures
Surface chart — to emphasize the movement or the magnitude of a trend.

3. Pictographs. A pictograph often starts with a bar graph. An appropriate symbol is selected to fill in the bar and add interest to the chart. To be effective, a symbol must be interesting and of good design. Whenever possible, a symbol should be small enough so that one whole symbol stands on the shortest bar. Each symbol represents 10, 100, or some other unit of children, food, or whatever is being shown. Increasing numbers are shown by adding more symbols of equal size rather than by increasing the size of the symbol (doubling the size of a figure actually increases its area four times).

4. Pie charts. — A pie chart (or area or volume chart) shows how an entire area or volume is divided. This is often used in the form of a three-dimensional silver dollar to show a family or national budget, or the way in which money has been spent. For materials having not more than five or six parts, a pie chart may make an attractive, simple presentation. The pie chart is of greater interest when its sections are of uneven size than when each one is equal.

The largest segment is usually the lightest and is often placed at the top. Other sections follow in a clockwise direction, according to their size, and each is progressively darker. A picture or symbol may be used in each segment along with the printed name of the category and the numerical size. If space within the circle is too small, the labels or pictures may be placed outside. Emphasis may be given to one portion by cutting it and withdrawing it slightly from its normal position in the circle. The areas for each segment must be of correct size. The proper number of degrees on the circumference of the circle should be measured with a protractor.

5. Flow charts. A flow chart (or organization chart) is a diagram showing the relationship of various parts of an organization. It is used to illustrate such matters as the relative positions of authority, the flow of work in an organization, or the number of persons being admitted to or dropping out at various stages of a process. Each name or office is centered in a rectangle with the highest position at the top. Lines connect each office to the others with which it is related.

6. Sociograms. A sociogram indicates the name of each person in a group

and shows how he interacts with the other members of the group. Connecting lines with an arrow in one direction reveal a preference of one individual for another. Arrows in both directions indicate mutual choices. (See Chapter 12.)

7. Maps. A circle or other symbol may be used to spot locations on a printed outline map. If larger areas are to be shown, gummed tape or coloring are helpful.

8. Photographs. Color photographs may be effective, but the precautions that were mentioned under line graphs must be kept in mind when photographs are to be used in a dissertation or in printed matter. Photographs should be mounted with dry mounting tissue or stationer's rubber cement. Excess rubber cement can be rubbed off, leaving no trace.

9. Photostats. Photostatic copies are useful in reducing tables or figures to normal page size. A new black typewriter ribbon is important to ensure clean, clear copy. Pale blue lines on graph paper are eliminated in the photostatic process.

DISCUSSION AND INTERPRETATION OF DATA

Whitney pointed out that there are two distinct steps in reporting research data — discussion and interpretation. He emphasized that *discussion* alone is not sufficient; a research worker must be able to present an "illuminating *interpretation* of his data." (Whitney, 1950, p. 410)

Discussion of Data

When analyzing data, it is helpful to keep each segment of the data on a separate page. A flexible system such as this enables one to arrange the data in logical sequence for discussion.

Just as tables and graphs should stand alone, the text in which findings are discussed should be complete and understandable by itself. The goal for discussion is to clarify the data and present significant aspects more forcefully. It is neither necessary nor desirable to refer to all parts of a table or graph, or to restate each item. One helpful procedure is to select the items to be discussed and then present them in the order of their appearance, working from left to right and from the top to the bottom.

The discussion of data might call attention to such facts as the following: outstanding or significant points, common elements in various parts of the data, prevailing tendencies or averages, trends in the data, inconsistencies within the data, differences between parts of the data, deviations from normal expectancy, and relationships of two or more items.

Interpretation of Data

The aim of interpretation is to bring out the true meaning of the data. Illuminating interpretation answers such questions as:

1. What are the basic principles applicable to the data and how do they apply?

2. How reliable is the information? When interpreting research data, be

honest in evaluating possible weaknesses that could have affected the results (e.g., extraneous factors such as ambiguity of questions or a nonrepresentative group of respondents). Could one expect these results to be duplicated on another occasion? Inconsistencies within the data should be explained on such bases as inadequate sampling or improper controls.

3. To what extent are the measures true and dependable? One way of indicating validity is by comparing results with related data already in existence.

4. What other information is necessary before one can be sure of his interpretation of the data? Statistical measures of significance are helpful, but one must be alert also to the social and educational significance of his findings.

5. What are the implications of the data? Although the researcher must refrain from making judgments as to cause-effect relationships, his interpretation might include an analysis of possible causes for the conditions described, a prediction of their probable effects, or a recommended course of action suggested by the data.

CHAPTER 17

Conclusions and Recommendations Based Upon Research

Perhaps the most frequently read portion of a research paper is the section that summarizes the study and highlights the author's conclusions. Busy people, who must plan efficient use of a limited amount of time, can read a wider variety of materials by concentrating on the most significant parts. The summary, then, must be very stimulating and sound if these readers are to be attracted sufficiently to read the entire report.

For suggestions regarding what to include and how to present the summary and conclusions, the reader should refer to the research examples which have been included in Chapters 5-8 and 11-14.

SUMMARY

An overview of the purposes and findings of a study not only gives the reader an effective, concise presentation, but it also paves the way for a clear understanding of the author's conclusions and recommendations. A summary is simply a miniature picture of the study. If a famous oil painting of museum size were photographed and reduced to the size of a small snapshot, the same general features would be recognizable even though specific details would no longer be evident. In the same manner, when a detailed research report is reduced to a summary, the essential framework must be retained. The summary should contain a statement of the problem, the method of attack, a review of the findings, and their meaning or application. A summary should not attempt to present details of the data or to introduce findings that have not been discussed elsewhere in the report.

The length and content of a summary are dependent upon the purposes for which it is intended. Several types of summaries are in general use:

Introductory Summary. A technique that is used in reporting research results to lay people is to begin the report with a striking conclusion or some of the most interesting findings. The interest of the reader may thus be captured so that he will want to read the rest of the paper. Some professional journals introduce each research article with a brief summary.

Final-Chapter Summary. The final chapter of a thesis usually contains an overview of the study along with conclusions and recommendations based upon the findings. This summary helps the reader to keep the general plan in mind and guides him in thinking about the meaning of the study.

Abstract. Many graduate schools require each candidate who submits a thesis to accompany it with an abstract. Sometimes an abstract is used as an introduction to a research bulletin.

Abstracts of doctoral dissertations and selected master's theses which have been produced on microfilm are available in research libraries (see Chapter 4).

CONCLUSIONS

Occasionally the writer of a research paper has a section called "conclusions" in which he presents a description of the method used, the purpose of the study, or a detailed repetition of the findings. In such instances, the writer has failed to fulfill the real function of conclusions. Worthwhile and sound conclusions may consist of general factual summaries, critical analyses of the shortcomings or limitations of the study, or advisory hints on the application of results, but their essential function must not be overlooked — they should be generalizations that are warranted by the evidence obtained in the study.

Conclusions are the building blocks which help the reader synthesize the knowledge he has gained from the research paper. Davis stressed that synthesis is basic to understanding and it requires the ability to see relationships:

> In unifying experiences, ideas and the like, the joining together is possible when the individual SEES where one experience may "hook into" another, where one concept may "hook into" another. This process is continued until a cluster is formed. . . . The old saying that there is nothing more useless than an unattached fact is balanced by, "There is nothing more dangerous than an unconnected idea." (Davis, 1961, p. 122)

Each conclusion should be analyzed critically since it is possible to reach a wrong conclusion. The principles involved in drawing conclusions are very much like those necessary for logical thinking:

Ability to See the Point. Mander said that the ability to recognize what is the point in question, and to stick to it until it has been dealt with, is the first essential to clear thinking. (Mander, 1947, p. 3) Merely restating the hypotheses in different words is not a satisfactory way of drawing conclusions; nevertheless, conclusions should have a definite relationship to the purposes of the study.

Ability to Restrict Generalizations. Conclusions should be kept within the boundaries established by the purposes and limitations of the study. Replication of the findings through the use of other samples is one basis for being able to generalize. A frequent criticism of research workers is that they try to make sweeping conclusions from limited data. This criticism can be avoided by introducing conclusions with a statement defining the limits within which the findings from the study might be generalized to a larger population.

Ability to Base Conclusions on Sound Facts. Conclusions should be based only on facts or findings that have been subjected to careful analysis. Evidence must be clear and give strong support to the conclusions drawn. Several steps might be taken to avoid conclusions that are inaccurate or unsound: (1) Take precautions throughout the study to prevent errors of observation, arithmetic, or personal bias; (2) Be sure to fulfill the assumptions required for whatever statistical procedures are used; and (3) Make a clear separation between facts and opinions throughout the report.

Ability to Analyze the Limitations of the Study. An investigation does not always yield the kind of data the research worker hopes to find. In his disappointment over not obtaining results that enable him to accept his hypothesis, he may overlook the benefits of negative findings. If the researcher can recognize and report the shortcomings of his own study, he may help another investigator to conduct a similar study with better controls. By eliminating false hypotheses, he is narrowing the field in which the answer must lie.

The amount of confidence that can be placed in a generalization depends upon several factors, such as the number of cases studied, how they were selected, the variety of circumstances under which they were observed, skill of the observer, reliability and validity of the instruments, and the appropriateness and accuracy of the statistical analyses. After stating a conclusion and establishing that it is dependable, the researcher may want to point out its connection with other facts. In doing so, however, he should exercise caution in claiming cause-and-effect relationships.

RECOMMENDATIONS

A single research study may seem to the investigator to be very small and insignificant. Its value may depend to some extent upon how much he can help to put the findings into action. Some research workers feel that their obligation ends when they have reported their findings, whereas others feel that their work is incomplete until they have done something about implementing the findings.

Experience gained through careful and devoted attention to a specific problem over an extended period of time places the researcher in a position where he has much to offer other people who are interested in related problems. An evaluation of the procedures and techniques which he used may help another person to plan a similar study in a different setting and thereby clarify some of the findings or verify certain conclusions.

Recommendations may be presented in several ways. Sometimes a finding is stated and then a recommendation that is based upon it. Another approach is to state a generalization followed by a series of specific recommendations, each with supporting evidence from the study.

Recommendations may be grouped according to the type of action needed to carry them out. For example, a study of the dietary practices of school students might contain recommendations on ways in which the school district could help to improve the students' food habits. It could also give suggestions regarding the sampling and design of other studies which could expand and follow up this study.

Recommendations probably should not be highly specific as to the exact means of carrying them out. Specific suggestions as to the frequency of repeating a study, details of selecting a sample, or procedures to be followed may discourage another person from beginning a study or taking necessary action to carry out the recommendations.

Davis presented a series of suggested aids to help one *change a belief* and some criteria for the acceptance of beliefs. These might well be given serious thought before making recommendations for changes in practices or policies as outgrowths of a research study:

> Some suggested *criteria to consider in accepting a belief* are: compatibility with other presently held beliefs; desirability; supportability (based on sound foundation); reliability; validity; attainability; understandability; feasibility; applicability. (Davis, 1961, pp. 129-137)

PART VI

Research Communication

The environment in which a graduate student or researcher is working can facilitate high quality research or can discourage a person from putting forth much effort. Communicating an attitude that seeks to solve problems and welcomes change can make research a significant part of graduate study and professional responsibilities.

Research results need to be communicated to others if they are to add to the theoretical knowledge of areas related to human ecology and if they are to be used by teachers in the classroom as well as by individuals in their daily living, where applicable. The results of research may be communicated in technical language to other scientists, in language applied to the classroom teacher, and in popular language to reach the public through such media as newspapers, magazine articles, and university extension bulletins.

CHAPTER *18*

Proposals For Research Studies

A research proposal, which should always be written *prior* to commencing a research project, serves as a blueprint to guide each step. For the student's thesis committee and for reviewing committees of institutions to whom the researcher may apply for financial grants, the research proposal provides a basis for evaluating the merit of a project.

GUIDE FOR RESEARCH PROPOSALS

Preparing a successful research proposal requires careful planning of the aims and procedures of the study. In addition, it requires ability to sell one's ideas to committees or agencies who are in a position to offer grants and to one's administration so that time and assistants may be available to carry out the study.

Content of the Proposal

The specific wording of headings suggested for a research proposal differs with various universities and granting agencies, but the following items are usually included in proposals. The procedures for each step have been discussed previously in this book and will not be repeated here:

1. Title of Project. The title should reveal the major objective of the study in concise form.

2. Statement of Problem and Justification. The statement of the general problem to be studied, along with its justification as a research problem, should convince the reviewers of the importance of the proposal.

3. Review of Literature and Present Outlook. A brief review of related research should be included in the proposal. (This review should appear in greater detail in the final research report.) This previous research should be summarized in relation to the present outlook with respect to the problem. Preferably, the proposed study should help to close the gaps in current knowledge.

4.   *Specific Objectives and Hypotheses.* Examples of the statement of hypotheses are given in Chapter 3.

5.   *Procedures.* In this section the researcher tells *how* he will solve the problem to be studied (i.e., *how* he will test the hypotheses).

The researcher must specify the population being studied and the method used to sample that population and gain access to the subjects. (See Chapter 9 for sampling techniques.) If a control group is to be used, the criteria for obtaining comparability between individuals in the experimental and control groups must be specified.

Procedures for conducting the study must be described (i.e., method for making and recording observations or other forms of data collection, instruments used, reproduction of verbal directions given to subjects, etc.).

6.   *Proposed Presentation of Findings and Analysis of Results.* The presentation of data and their actual analysis must await their collection. However, anticipation of the way the data will be organized and analyzed is related to the ease with which the project is carried to completion.

"Selling" a Proposal

To "sell" a research proposal to a university research committee or a granting agency requires convincing the reviewers that the proposal is worthwhile and the director is able to carry out the study. The previous section summarized points to consider regarding the content of the study. Just a few more suggestions might be appropriate to give the content importance:

1.   Take into account what is now taking place in the world; make the proposal timely.

2.   Build a new project on an outgoing project, taking advantage of the momentum and enthusiasm while it is at a peak.

3.   Point out the innovative aspects of the proposal and the new information that might result.

4.   Show the broad applications and usefulness this study could have in colleges or other organizations.

Since various granting agencies are looking for different things, it is important for the investigator to choose the best agency for the type of study he is proposing. One or two giant foundations may be the first ones that come to his mind, but he should not overlook other likely, but smaller, foundations and industrial organizations. To familiarize himself with the idiosyncrasies of a particular granting agency, he should obtain a current statement of the requirements and preferences of that agency. A personal contact within that organization might be helpful. Also, it might be advisable to talk with someone whose proposal has recently been accepted by that agency.

The researcher may save time by submitting a "concept paper" or preliminary letter of inquiry in which he presents briefly the nature of the problem to be studied and its unique features. If interested, the granting agency may request the individual to submit a proposal and may even participate in developing the final contract.

The proposed time elements for a research study can be very important. Be sure that sufficient time will be devoted to the project to fulfill its objectives. At the same time, be sure that the required work can be completed in the time period indicated.

The qualifications of the research investigator need to be made manifest in a proposal to a funding agency. His educational background and his success in directing and communicating previous research studies can help the reviewers predict the likelihood of his achieving worthwhile results.

Just as it is difficult for individuals to obtain research grants on their own, it is becoming difficult for a department or an institution to make it alone. Interdisciplinary cooperation is encouraged. Also, consortia of several institutions may be expected. Such cooperation might include various levels or kinds of educational organizations (e.g., community colleges, state colleges, state universities, private colleges). It might also involve the cooperation of community agencies and educational institutions (e.g., a university working cooperatively with human resources development, family planning, or child welfare agencies). The availability of consultants and their willingness to help with the study can be an important selling point. When possible, persons whose advice will be sought later in the study should be involved in the initial development of the proposal.

When requesting financial assistance, be sure to clarify what facilities are available (e.g., computer center) and what equipment will need to be purchased. Also, a budget should be planned in detail to show the salaries and benefits to be provided for research staff members, related travel expenses, and any indirect costs that might be covered by the grant.

Developing a research proposal takes time. It should be started well in advance of the deadline set by the granting agency. Very likely it will need to be approved by a department head and representative of the research planning division of the institution employing the investigator. Careful editing is essential and requires time.

RESEARCH PROPOSAL REJECTION

Table 8 presents a summary of shortcomings found in a review of research grant applications disapproved by the National Institutes of Health. At the time this review was conducted, Dr. Allen was Chief of the Division of Research Grants. (Allen, 1960)

Table 8 shows that 58 per cent of the sample of 605 research proposals reviewed had shortcomings related to the *problem* or the question the proposed research would seek to answer. The problem was considered to be of insufficient importance or unlikely to produce any new or useful information in 33.1 per cent of these proposals.

The largest percentage of shortcomings (73 per cent) dealt with the *approach* to be used (or the method and procedure). This result emphasizes the

TABLE 8. SHORTCOMINGS FOUND IN STUDY-SECTION REVIEW OF 605
DISAPPROVED RESEARCH GRANT APPLICATIONS, APRIL-MAY
1959. ALL PERCENTAGES ARE TO THE BASE NUMBER 605.

No.	Shortcoming	%
	Class I: Problem (58 per cent)	
1	The problem is of insufficient importance or is unlikely to produce any new or useful information.	33.1
2	The proposed research is based on a hypothesis that rests on insufficient evidence, is doubtful, or is unsound.	8.9
3	The problem is more complex than the investigator appears to realize.	8.1
4	The problem has only local significance, or is one of production or control, or otherwise fails to fall sufficiently clearly within the general field of health-related research.	4.8
5	The problem is scientifically premature and warrants, at most, only a pilot study.	3.1
6	The research as proposed is overly involved, with too many elements under simultaneous investigation.	3.0
7	The description of the nature of the research and of its significance leaves the proposal nebulous and diffuse and without clear research aim.	2.6
	Class II: Approach (73 per cent)	
8	The proposed tests, or methods, or scientific procedures are unsuited to the stated objective.	34.7
9	The description of the approach is too nebulous, diffuse, and lacking in clarity to permit adequate evaluation.	28.8
10	The over-all design of the study has not been carefully thought out.	14.7
11	The statistical aspects of the approach have not been given sufficient consideration.	8.1
12	The approach lacks scientific imagination.	7.4
13	Controls are either inadequately conceived or inadequately described.	6.8
14	The material the investigator proposes to use is unsuited to the objectives of the study or is difficult to obtain.	3.8
15	The number of observations is unsuitable.	2.5
16	The equipment contemplated is outmoded or otherwise unsuitable.	1.0
	Class III: Man (55 per cent)	
17	The investigator does not have adequate experience or training, or both, for *this* research.	32.6
18	The investigator appears to be unfamiliar with recent pertinent literature or methods, or both.	13.7
19	The investigator's previously published work in *this* field does not inspire confidence.	12.6
20	The investigator proposes to rely too heavily on insufficiently experienced associates.	5.0
21	The investigator is spreading himself too thin; he will be more productive if he concentrates on fewer projects.	3.8
22	The investigator needs more liaison with colleagues in this field or in collateral fields.	1.7
	Class IV: Other (16 per cent)	
23	The requirements for equipment or personnel, or both, are unrealistic.	10.1

TABLE 8 (cont.)

No.	Shortcoming	%
24	It appears that other responsibilities would prevent devotion of sufficient time and attention to this research.	3.0
25	The institutional setting is unfavorable.	2.3
26	Research grants to the investigator, now in force, are adequate in scope and amount to cover the proposed research.	1.5

Reprinted with permission from *Science*, Vol. 132, 25 November 1960, p. 1533.

importance of understanding scientific procedures and research methodology. Related to this is the competence of the *researcher* (man). In 55 per cent of these proposals, the researcher appeared to lack adequate experience or training, to be unfamiliar with pertinent literature or methods, etc.

CHAPTER 19

Preparation of a Written Research Report

Research, in itself, is a challenging experience for the investigator. However, its greatest value is lost unless the reseacher is willing to share his methods and results with others. To communicate effectively, he must have not only the ability to write and explain clearly what he meant but also to attract attention and stimulate interest.

To guide a student in writing a report, this chapter offers some criteria for evaluating a research paper. Then attention is directed to the organization of a research report, and finally, specific suggestions are included for writing clearly and concisely. While reading this chapter, remember what Good (1966, pp. 389-390) has said:

> In the technical report the soundness of the data and insight in interpretation are the important considerations rather than form and style as such, although commonly there is a relationship between careful organization of materials, sound interpretation of data, and effective style.

CHARACTERISTICS OF A RESEARCH PAPER

Effective research writing has the following characteristics:

Objectivity. The entire report is written in the third person, with no personal pronouns used. If the investigator wishes to refer to himself, he uses some appropriate term such as "the investigator," "the author," or "this writer."

Logical Organization. A suitable title for the paper is selected. Usually a research report is organized in sections; each division is essential to developing an understanding of the main ideas and each has its own appropriate subheading. A smooth transition is made between the various divisions by using an introductory paragraph to present the general plan of organization and to prevent one subheading from following immediately after another one.

Accuracy. When reviewing related literature, it is important to take adequate notes on the sources and content of each study. Any materials that are paraphrased or quoted directly must be documented. All statistical data must be gathered, reported, and interpreted with accuracy.

Conciseness. Woodrow Wilson realized the art of achieving brevity without sacrificing impact when he said that it would take him two weeks to prepare a 10-minute speech, one week for an hour's speech, and he was "ready right now" for a two-hour speech. Some people approach a subject as if they would surely hit an important point if they just write or speak long enough. The real art of writing is to be able to present clearly and concisely sufficient information for the reader's complete understanding of the problem.

Readability. The characteristics of a research paper that contribute to its readability are its content and focus, its organization, its format, and an effective choice of words. A report that is both readable and challenging takes into consideration what the reader already knows and at the same time stimulates his interest in learning more about areas that are unknown to him. Although a research paper is written in an objective manner, it can be personalized in such ways as relating it to the interests of the readers, giving illustrative cases, and pointing out unusual findings.

ORGANIZATION

The title of a research report should be stated as briefly as possible, yet it should contain the essential descriptive elements. Phrases that do not contribute to a better understanding of the title should be omitted (e.g., "A study of," "An investigation of," and "An analysis of"). The title should contain the essence of what was studied and include, when possible, the method used and the sample (e.g., "Food Practices of Families with Adolescent Children in Three Indiana Communities").

Major Divisions

Prior to gathering data for a study, it is helpful to plan the study thoroughly. Part of this planning includes developing a tentative outline or table of contents for the paper. Try to think of descriptive titles for the various chapters and subheadings. These can make the report interesting and readable.

Although the length of a paper influences how many divisions may be needed, a research report generally contains four sections:

Introduction. The introductory section or chapter should aim to capture the reader's attention with the first sentence and paragraph. The function of an introduction is to present the following types of information:

1. Nature of the study: the subject area, the specific problem that was studied, the purpose and scope of the study.

2. Background for the study: historical background to aid the reader in understanding the problem area, reasons for the investigation, the researcher's point of view in dealing with the subject, and the contributions the study can be expected to make to the area of home economics.

3. Plan to be followed: basic assumptions fundamental to the study, hypotheses, definitions, delimitation of the study, and its possible limitations.

4. Relation to previous studies: a review of related literature may be incorporated into the introductory chapter or it may constitute a separate chapter.

Methods of Procedure. The research paper should present enough details of the research design to enable the reader to evaluate the study and to repeat it under similar circumstances if he should desire to do so. Methods of selecting the sample, controlling extraneous variables, gathering and recording data, and analyzing and synthesizing data should be included. Materials or instruments that were used should be described and, whenever possible, illustrations or duplicate copies should be contained in the report.

Analysis and Interpretation of Data. The presentation of evidence is a bridge between the introduction and conclusions. The evidence should be stated clearly and consistently. Separate chapters may be devoted to the analysis of each part of the problem. Sometimes the presentation of findings is separated from the discussion or interpretation of their meaning in order to maintain an objective view of the results. In any event, a clear distinction must be made between fact and judgment. Any information the reader must have to evaluate the data should be included (e.g., the validity and reliability of the instruments).

Summary, Conclusions, and Recommendations. From his close contact with an investigation, the research worker is best qualified to select the essential parts of his study and to summarize them concisely. In stating his conclusions, he should be sure they are based on his hypotheses and are justified by the data. Recommendations for further research and for specific action to bring about changes in keeping with the research results are means of sharing with others and assisting them to see how these findings might have implications for strengthening programs related to home economics.

Subheadings

In addition to determining the major sections of a paper, a detailed outline should be planned to show the sequence and content of each subdivision. Various groups have different preferences for the style of subheadings. Select a style that is clear and easy to follow. Then be consistent in using it to show the rank and relationship of topics. Usually two or three ranks of headings are sufficient. Each heading and subheading should be brief.

STYLE OF WRITING

Research writing need not be heavy, monotonous, or dull. By choosing words carefully and by following basic principles of writing for understanding, an individualistic and interesting style can be developed.

Writing for Understanding

Richardson and Callahan proposed the "R/C recipe for effective Communications." Although the steps were suggested as a means of reaching homemakers through popular writing, they also have applications in research style. The "R/C recipe" (Richardson and Callahan, 1962, p. 8) contains five fundamental steps:

1.   Visualize your Audience. Research reports generally reach a more restricted and homogeneous group than would be visualized by a writer of a popular article. Nevertheless, defining the audience is still a basic step. The readers of an article in a professional journal are likely to include persons from related professional fields who have not had technical, specialized background. When bringing research findings to lay people through newspaper or magazine articles, the researcher must be highly selective in content and must present the results in an interesting manner.

2.   Analyze your Problems. In writing, as well as in speaking, one can verbalize extensively and never actually define the point. To prevent this, the writer needs to define his subject and purpose exactly and clearly. Then, very early in his report, his purpose and plan of organization should be explained to the reader.

3.   Organize your Thinking. Organization of a report has been discussed previously in this chapter. Logical organization can be achieved by dividing the content of a paper into a few main parts, each of which covers only one phase of the topic and includes only closely related and adequately developed ideas. Appropriate summaries can emphasize the major points. In brief: ". . . tell the reader where he is going, take him there, and then tell him where he has been." (Good, 1966, p. 398)

4.   Dramatize your Presentation. Dramatizing, or bringing life to a piece of copy, is highly important when writing for the general public. Research writing can be personalized by showing the reader how the findings tie in with his needs and problems or with those of his professional peers. This is hard to achieve while being objective. A possible danger that must be avoided is making one's writing so dramatic that the report of the actual research becomes superficial.

Choice of Words

Sentence structure and choice of words influence the effectiveness with which ideas are communicated. Although the following suggestions could lead to highly stilted writing if followed mechanically, their intelligent use should help to develop clarity and conciseness in writing research papers:

1. Use *one* exact word rather than a longer phrase. (Flesch, 1951, p. 26)

Unnecessary wordiness	More exact word
accordingly	so
for the purpose of	for
inasmuch as	since, or because
in order to	to
in the event that	if
in the neighborhood of	about
on the basis of	by
with reference to	about

2. Omit words that contribute nothing to the meaning of a sentence.

"The following table (serves to) show. . . ."
"It is known that. . . ."
"It is evident that. . . ."
"The investigator has (tried to) compare. . . ."

3. Avoid using words that are redundant (e.g., "refer back," "repeat again," "same identical").

4. Clarify the subject of a sentence. Avoid "it," "they," "experts," unless the reference is very clear.

5. Use connectives when necessary for clarity (e.g., "however," "furthermore," "likewise," "nevertheless").

6. Be reserved and avoid the use of intensives (e.g., "obviously," "certainly," "extremely," "much," "very").

7. Be cautious about using words that infer cause or relationship, such as: "due to," "prove," "cause," "effect," "determine," "influence."

8. Be familiar with the exact meaning and possible implications of abstract ideas or technical terms used.

9. Use intellectual and vitalized expressions rather than cliches, "big-sounding," or emotional words. The following examples show types of cliches that should be avoided: (Grace and Grace, 1952, p. 93)

(a)	figurative description	soft as silk, sweet as honey
(b)	descriptive of type	talented artist, brilliant thinker, distinguished colleague
(c)	dependent on professional phraseology	deep insight, remarkable technique, in the light of recent developments, after carefully weighing the evidence
(d)	proverbial expression substituted for precise thought	Virtue is its own reward.

10. Use strong, active verbs (e.g., "The table shows that. . . ." rather than "It is shown that. . . .").

11. Use concrete words rather than "slippery" or vague words (e.g., avoid "equal," "bright," "comparable," "fast").

12. Finish comparisons so the reader will not have to ask, "For what?" or "To whom?" Examples of unfinished terms are: "unfit," "desirable," "good," "progressive," "dangerous," "valuable."

13. Change the pace or emphasis to avoid monotony. Vary the length of words, clauses, sentences, and paragraphs. Develop a natural, individualized style of expression. Find a variety of ways to express similar ideas.

14. Simplify sentence structure, avoiding complicated qualifications.

15. Be consistent in point of view. The *past* tense is used in most parts of a research report, such as in stating facts reported by others and the findings and conclusions of the author's study. The *present* tense is used when stating a well-established principle (assumption) and when referring to data shown in a table, graph, or appendix.

The following examples have been selected from actual year-end reports of projects sponsored by federal funds. Notice how difficult it is to decipher the real meaning behind these words. These statements underline the importance of clarity, conciseness, and accuracy in a research paper:

Purpose of the project

Counsel the parents of the special problem child to avoid dropouts in their later high school years.

Activities carried on

Group counseling sessions with behavior problems were held with students.

Results of the project

All parents have been seen and collected data interpreted with a view to mutual goals.

Evaluation of project

From student, parent and faculty comments concerning this project have been of favorable and active acceptance.

When writing the first draft of a manuscript, strive for a logical organization of ideas. Most writing has to be rewritten and edited before it is really smooth and effective. When revising a paper, give attention to such aspects as the logic of its organization, accuracy of facts, choice of words, grammar, paragraphing, and spelling.

CHAPTER 20

Individual and Professional Responsibilities for Research

A publication on research in educational administration raised a challenging question: If all of the research that has been done in the last three years were to be wiped out, would our lives be materially changed? Lamke stated that we would really notice differences in those areas of our lives that are touched by advances in medicine, agriculture, physics, and chemistry. However, he felt that educators would continue about the same as usual, because few studies affect educational practice. He asked whether research shouldn't be of as much worth to educators as agricultural research has been to farmers. (Griffiths, 1959, p. 6)

What can individuals and members of professional associations do to make research more significant? The remainder of this book offers some suggestions and raises questions about the functions of research in strengthening areas related to human ecology.

DEVELOPING PERSONNEL FOR RESEARCH

If research is to be significant, professional preparation must emphasize how to conduct research as well as how to use research results. Actually, developing a research attitude can be started with very young children. The fun of discovery and an experimental approach to problem-solving can enrich family living and school programs at all levels.

College courses can encourage young people to become interested in careers where part or all of their duties will be related to research. For example, many courses require a term paper that can be a creative experience involving a simple research approach. In a seminar for seniors, some institutions acquaint their students with professional problems and require each student to carry out a small research project. The candidate upon whom a graduate degree is conferred should be capable of understanding and applying research results and of contributing to the solution of professional problems through the use of sound research methods.

In this period of rapid change, it is utterly impossible for a person to learn in high school or college all the knowledge he will need in adjusting to the world about him throughout his lifetime. Recent developments in research deserve considerable emphasis in programs of in-service education. A research investigator needs periodic refresher training on how to observe, record, assess or reassess, control, and make applications of knowledge. Hopefully this book will encourage the free, inquiring scholar to probe and discover in the best interests of mankind. After a period of probing, the creative and productive scholar may embark on a series of related studies within sharply restricted spheres of interest.

FACILITATING RESEARCH PROJECTS

Perhaps the best way to stimulate interest in research is through the enthusiasm of those already engaged in research. An attitude of trying to improve some phase of one's work through research communicates to his co-workers that research is worthwhile in helping to solve practical problems. Inertia is one of the biggest obstacles to research. It is easier to continue doing things as they have been done than to put forth the extra effort to bring about change.

Corey's summary of conditions favorable for action research by classroom teachers may be encouraging also to young researchers in other areas: (1) providing an atmosphere in which a person feels free to admit limitations of his work; (2) providing opportunities to develop creative ideas about new or promising practices or materials; (3) encouraging a person to try out promising ideas; (4) improving methods of group work; (5) striving to obtain better evidence than is presently available rather than seeking a *final* answer; and (6) providing time and other resources (such as instructional materials, mimeographing, and clerical assistance) for persons who are participating in research studies. (Corey, 1953, p. 86)

In addition to a receptive attitude toward research, individuals usually need specific help in developing plans for research studies. Such help is readily available in universities. Statisticians and computer center staff should be consulted during the planning of a project rather than used as rescue personnel after the gathering of data. From his wide experience as a teacher and consultant on action research, Shumsky (1958, p. 197) prepared a checklist for consultants. Some of these questions could be applied by the researcher in his relationships with the subjects cooperating in his study:

1. Do I overpower others by acting as an answer man and quiz master, or do I encourage a climate of cooperative work?

2. Do I rush forward prematurely with suggestions, or do I try to understand the other's perspective?

3. Do I know how to listen, or do I put on a front or go off on a tangent?

4. Am I involved in the other's problem from the standpoint of content and process?

5.   Do I make progress on my own and plan my next conference, or am I dependent on others?

6.   Is my research based primarily on repetition of ideas read in books or on my own experience and thinking?

7.   Am I open to experiences and ideas, or do I tend to overplan and manipulate?

8.   Am I accessible to others as a human being or only as a scholar?

9.   Do I only teach or do I also learn?

FINANCING RESEARCH PROJECTS

One significant way to encourage research is to provide time free from one's regular duties so an individual can serve on a research team. Paraprofessional and/or clerical assistants are real assets. In the past, much research was done in spite of inadequate time, facilities, and financial support. Only the future can reveal the accomplishments that are possible when proper recognition is given to the worth of research.

Among the major sources for financial support are the scholarships and fellowships offered by professional associations. An individual who is considering graduate study may obtain information about these opportunities and how to apply for them by writing to the national office of a professional association such as the American Home Economics Association. Very likely a research proposal will have to be submitted as a basis for receiving an award. (See Chapter 18.)

Many colleges and universities offer teaching or research assistantships for graduate students who wish to combine study toward an advanced degree with valuable part-time professional experiences. Information may be obtained directly from an institution offering a graduate program.

Several branches of the United States government and a number of foundations offer support for projects of major importance, with clearly formulated hypotheses and a competent principal investigator.

IMPROVING RESEARCH QUALITY

Informing the public of the purposes and results of a research study can be an excellent means of gaining confidence and trust. On the other hand, the purposes of such communication can be defeated if the research is poorly planned, with untried and perhaps unsound methods used.

Improving the quality of research projects cannot be separated from the other topics that have been discussed in this chapter. For example, one way of improving research is to work cooperatively with professional persons from other geographic areas or institutions to pool ideas and engage in larger, more worthwhile projects. Another approach is to cooperate with specialists from other disciplines in attacking problems of mutual concern. A third need is for individuals to become more sophisticated in planning research designs and using sound statistical procedures for analyzing and interpreting data. Also, more professional persons are needed who can devote a major part of their work to research planning and guidance. As it is, much research is carried on by graduate students or professional workers who must limit their studies to those that fit somewhat conveniently into their heavy schedules.

Common criticisms of research are that it is trivial, pedantic, and irrelevant. In truth many studies have been shoddy, redundant, and ill-conceived. The "research craze" has encouraged projects of dubious worth, even with large expenditures of government funds.

What kinds of research should be encouraged? The arts, humanities, and social sciences strive to achieve unique intellectual or aesthetic insights. In the arts and humanities, quality research creates new and significant symbols, or it re-creates and reinterprets knowledge and ideas. A worthy goal of the sciences is to amplify and extend comprehension of the external world in its physical, biological, and social aspects. Quality research in the sciences increases or deepens knowledge and ideas by the discovery of new facts, the formulation of new ideas, or the critical interpretation, organization, and evaluation of knowledge. Applied sciences, such as food technology and public health, use predictions of the natural and social sciences for the improvement of human welfare.

Research has enriched man's life by increasing his understanding of himself and nature, by opening new vistas of interest and activity, and by increasing man's control over his environment and himself.

This book emphasizes research in areas of human ecology. One characteristic of man's environment is that it is changing constantly. To conduct quality research requires a skillful blending of research knowledge with a sensitive understanding of the dynamics of the environment. Research methods that require the environment to stand still result in isolated snapshots. Human ecology is not motionless. Neither is it a series of snapshots, each unrelated to the others. Human ecology research must be a dynamic blending of environmental questions from physical, biological, aesthetic, and social points of view. Its methods, standards, and hypotheses emerge directly from the nature and organization of the materials within a specified field. (See Chapter 2 for a conceptual framework.) Pressing and abiding questions of human welfare should be uppermost in the formulation of research purposes and methodology.

Bibliography

Ainsworth, Mary D., and James L. Kuethe. "Texture Responses in the Rorschach and Sorting Test." *Journal of Projective Technique and Personality Assessment* 25:391-402; 1961.

Allen, Ernest M. "Why Are Research Grant Applications Disapproved?" *Science* 132:1532-1534; 1960.

Allport, Gordon W., Philip E. Vernon, and Gardner Lindzey. *Study of Values.* Boston: Houghton Mifflin Company, 1951.

Alper, T., H. Blane, and B. Adams. "Reactions of Middle and Lower Class Children to Finger Paints as a Function of Class Differences in Child Training Practice." *Journal of Abnormal and Social Psychology* 51:439-448; 1955.

American Psychological Association. *Standards for Educational and Psychological Tests and Manuals.* Washington, D.C.: American Psychological Association, 1966.

American Psychological Association. "Technical Recommendations for Psychological Tests and Diagnostic Techniques." *Psychological Bulletin* 51:201-238; 1954, supplement.

American Women. Report of the President's Commission on the Status of Women. Washington, D.C.: 1963.

Angell, Robert C., and Ronald Freedman. "The Use of Documents, Records, Census Materials and Indices." In *Research Methods in the Behavioral Sciences.* New York: Holt, Rinehart and Winston, 1963.

Arny, Clara B. *Evaluation in Home Economics.* New York: Appleton-Century-Crofts, Inc., 1953.

Baldwin, A., J. Kalhorn, and F. Breese. "Patterns of Parent Behavior." *Psychological Monographs* 58:3; 1945.

Baldwin, A., J. Kalhorn, and F. Breese. "The Appraisal of Parent Behavior." *Psychological Monographs* 63:4; 1949.

Bales, R.I. *Interaction Process Analysis: A Method for the Study of Small Groups.* Cambridge: Addison-Wesley Press, 1950.

Barnes, Fred P. *A Guidebook in Research Methods for Practitioners in Education*. Illinois Curriculum Program. Springfield, Ill.: Office of Superintendent of Public Instruction, 1956.

Bennett, J.W., and G. Thaiss. "Survey Research and Sociocultural Anthropology." In *Survey Research in the Social Sciences*, C.Y. Glock, ed. New York: Russell Sage Foundation, 1967.

Birren, Faber. *Light, Color and Environment*. New York: Van Nostrand Reinhold Co., 1969.

Blum, G.S. *The Blacky Pictures: Manual of Instructions*. New York: The Psychological Corporation, 1950.

Bogardus, E.S. "A Social Distance Scale." *Sociology and Social Research* 17:265-271; 1933.

Borek, Ernest. *Man the Chemical Machine*. New York: Columbia University Press, 1952.

Brand, R.H. "Measurement of Fabric Aesthetics." *Textile Research Journal* 791-804; September 1964.

Britt, Stewart H., ed. *Consumer Behavior and the Behavioral Sciences*. New York: John Wiley & Sons, Inc., 1966.

Brodbeck, May. "Logic and Scientific Method in Research on Teaching." In *Handbook of Research on Teaching*. American Educational Research Assoc., N.L. Gage, ed. Chicago: Rand McNally Co., 1963.

Burgess, Ernest W. "Research Methods in Sociology." In *Twentieth Century Sociology*, Georges Curvitch and W. E. Moore, eds. New York: Philosophical Library, 1949.

Burk, Marguerite C. "Food Economic Behavior in System Terms." *Journal of Home Economics* 62:325; May 1970.

Buros, Oscar K. *Personality Tests and Reviews*. Highland Park, N.J.: Gryphon Press, 1970.

Buros, Oscar K., ed. *Sixth Mental Measurements Yearbook*. Highland Park, N. J.: Gryphon Press, 1965.

Buros, Oscar K., ed. *Seventh Mental Measurements Yearbook*. Highland Park, N.J.: Gryphon Press, 1972.

CRM Books. *Developmental Psychology Today*. Del Mar, Calif.: CRM Books, 1971.

Caldwell, Lynton K. "Centers of Excellence for the Study of Human Ecology." *Proceedings of Symposium on Human Ecology*. U.S. Department of Health, Education and Welfare. Warrenton, Va.: Airlie House, 1968.

Campbell, William G. *A Form Book for Thesis Writing*. Boston: Houghton Mifflin Co., 1954.

Cannon, Walter B. *The Wisdom of the Body*. New York: W.W. Norton and Company, Inc., 1932.

Compton, Norma H. *Compton Fabric Preference Test*. Copyright, 1965 (a).

Compton, Norma H. *Compton Fabric Preference Test Manual*. Utah State University Agricultural Engineering Station Special Report 19; August 1965 (b).

Compton, Norma H. "Development of a Fabric Preference Test." *Perceptual and Motor Skills* 22:287-294; 1966.

Compton, Norma H. "Personal Attributes of Color and Design Preferences in Clothing Fabrics." *The Journal of Psychology* 54:191-195; 1962.

Conant, J. *Science and Common Sense.* New Haven: Yale University Press, 1951.

Corey, Stephen M. *Action Research to Improve School Practices.* New York: Teachers College, Columbia University Press, 1953.

Cornell, Francis G. "Sampling Methods." In *Encyclopedia of Educational Research*, Chester W. Harris, ed. New York: Macmillan Company and the American Educational Research Association, 1960.

Cromie, William J. "Home-Made Sounds Can Make Unhappy Home." *Deseret News*, Tuesday, November 14, 1967, p. A13.

Davis, Elwood C. *The Philosophic Process in Physical Education.* Philadelphia: Lea and Febiger, 1961.

Davis, J.A. *Teachers versus Researchers: Locals and Cosmopolitans in Graduate Schools.* Paper for the American Sociological Association meeting, August 1960.

Dicken, Charles F., in *The Sixth Mental Measurements Yearbook.* Highland Park, N.J.: The Gryphon Press, 1965.

Dildine, Glenn C. "Energy — Basis of Living and Learning." *Journal of National Education Association;* April, 1950.

Dollard, John. *Criteria for the Life History.* New York: Peter Smith, 1949.

Dubos, Rene. "The Crisis of Man in His Environment." *Proceedings of Symposium on Human Ecology.* U.S. Department of Health, Education and Welfare. Warrenton, Va.: Airlie House, 1968.

Duvall, Evelyn M. *Family Development.* 2nd ed. Philadelphia: J.B. Lippincott Company, 1962.

Dyer, Doris (adapted by Beatrice Paolucci). "Students' Wives Values as Reflected in Personal and Family Activities." Unpublished master's thesis, Michigan State University, 1963.

Ehrlich, Paul, and Anne Ehrlich. *Population, Resources, Environment — Issues in Human Ecology.* San Francisco: W.H. Freeman & Co., 1970.

Ellwood, Charles A. *Cultural Evolution.* New York: The Century Co., 1927.

Etter, Alfred G. "Man's Noise — the Ultimate Insult." (Excerpted from testimony presented in Chicago at federal noise pollution hearings, 1971.) *Los Angeles Times*, August 8, 1971.

Festinger, L., and D. Katz. *Research Methods in the Behavioral Sciences.* New York: Holt, Rinehart and Winston, 1953.

Festinger, L., S. Schachter, and K. Back. *Social Pressures in Informal Groups.* New York: Harper and Row, 1950.

Fisher, S., and S. Cleveland. "Body-image Boundaries and Style of Life." *Journal of Abnormal Social Psychology* 52:373-379; 1956.

Flanagan, John C. "The Critical Incident Technique." *Psychological Bulletin* 51:327-358; July, 1954.

Flesch, Rudolph. *How To Write Better.* Chicago: Science Research Associates, Inc., 1951.

Flugel, John Carl. *Psychology of Clothes.* London: Hogarth Press, Ltd., 1950.

Frank, Jerome D. "Galloping Technology, A New Social Disease." *Journal of Social Issues* 22:4:1; October, 1966.

Galfo, Armand J., and Earl Miller. *Interpreting Education Research.* Dubuque, Iowa: Wm. C. Brown Co., 1965.

Garrett, Henry E. *Statistics in Psychology and Education.* 6th ed. New York, David McKay Co., 1966.

Glock, Charles Y., ed. *Survey Research in the Social Sciences.* New York: Russell Sage Foundation, 1967.

Good, Carter V. *Essentials of Educational Research.* New York: Appleton-Century-Crofts, Inc., 1966.

Good, Carter V. *Introduction to Educational Research.* 2nd ed. New York: Appleton-Century-Crofts, 1963.

Goodenough, Florence L. "Measurement of Intelligence by Drawings." Yonkers: *World Book,* 1926.

Gorden, Raymond L. *Interviewing Strategy, Techniques, and Tactics.* Homewood, Ill.: The Dorsey Press, 1969.

Gordon, Leonard V. "The Gordon Personal Profile." In *The Sixth Mental Measurements Yearbook.* Highland Park, N.J.: The Gryphon Press, 1965.

Grace, William J., and John C. Grace. *The Art of Communicating Ideas.* New York: The Devin-Adair Company, 1952.

Greenwood, Ernest. *Experimental Sociology: A Study in Method.* Morningside Heights, New York: King's Crown Press, 1945.

Griffiths, Daniel E. *Research in Educational Administration.* New York: Bureau of Publications, Teachers College, Columbia University, 1959.

Grinker, Roy R., ed. *Toward a Unified Theory of Human Behavior.* New York: Basic Books, Inc., 1956.

Gross, Irma H. "Impact of Certain Basic Disciplines on Home Management in Family Living." *Journal of Home Economics* 58:448-452; June, 1966.

Gross, I.H., and E.W. Crandall. *Management for Modern Families.* 2nd ed. New York: Appleton-Century-Crofts, 1963.

Halldane, John F. "Physical Measurement Related to Human Perception and Cognition." *Materials Research and Standards* 8:13; December, 1970.

Hamburger, Walter J., Milton M. Platt, and Henry M. Morgan. "Mechanics of Elastic Performance of Textile Materials Part X. Some Aspects of Elastic Behavior at Low Strains." *Textile Research Journal* 22:695-729; 1952.

Hamley, A.H. *Human Ecology: A Theory of Community Structure.* New York: Ronald Press Co., 1950.

Harlow, H.F. "The Nature of Love." *American Psychologist* 13:673-685; 1958.

Harriman, Philip L. *Handbook of Psychological Terms.* Totowa, N.Y.: Littlefield, Adams & Co., 1965.

Hill, Reuben. "Methodological Issues in Family Development Research." *Family Process* 3:186-206; March, 1964.

Hill, Reuben, and Roy H. Rodgers. "The Developmental Approach." In H.T. Christensen, ed., *Handbook of Marriage and the Family.* Chicago: Rand McNally & Company, 1964.

Hillway, Tyrus. *Handbook of Educational Research.* Boston: Houghton Mifflin, 1969.

Hillway, Tyrus. *Introduction to Research.* 2nd ed. Boston: Houghton Mifflin, 1964.

Hodson, Norma G. "Self-Actualization Through Effective Management of Family Relationships and Resources." Talk presented to American Home Economics Association 58th Annual Meeting, Dallas, Texas, 1967.

Home Economics Research Abstracts. Washington, D.C.: American Home Economics Association, 1969.

Honigmann, John Joseph. *The World of Man.* New York: Harper & Row, 1959.

Horn, Marilyn. *The Second Skin.* Boston: Houghton Mifflin Co., 1968.

Jackson, Robert M., and J.W.M. Rothney. "A Comparative Study of the Mailed Questionnaire and the Interview in Follow-up Studies." *Personnel and Guidance Journal* 39:569-571; March, 1961.

Jennings, H.H. *Sociometry in Group Relations: A Work Guide for Teachers.* Washington, D.C.: American Council on Education, 1948.

Johnson, H. *Johnson Home Economics Interest Inventory.* Ames, Iowa: Iowa State College Press, 1955.

Jung, C.G. "The Need for Roots, An Interview." *Landscape* 14:2; 1965.

Kerlinger, Fred N. *Foundations of Behavioral Research.* New York: Holt, Rinehart and Winston, Inc., 1964.

Klausner, Samuel Z. *On Man in His Environment.* San Francisco: Jossey-Bass, Inc., 1971.

Klopfer, Bruno, et al. *Developments in the Rorschach Technique.* New York: Harcourt, Brace and World, Inc., 1954.

Kluckhohn, Clyde. "Personal Documents in Anthropological Science." In *The Use of Personal Documents in History, Anthropology and Sociology.* Social Science Research Council, 1945.

Kluckhohn, C. "Values and Value-Orientations in the Theory of Action: An Exploration in Definition and Classification." In *Toward a General Theory of Action.* T. Parsons and E.A. Shils, eds. New York: Harper and Row, 1962.

Knapp, David C. The New York State College of Human Ecology at Cornell University. Ithaca, N.Y.: Cornell University, 1970.

Kohlman, E.L. "Development of an Instrument to Determine Values of Home-makers." Unpublished Ph.D. thesis, Iowa State University, 1961.

Lake Placid Conference on Home Economics: Proceedings of Conferences 1 to 10, 1899-1908. Proceedings of the Fourth Annual Conference, 1902. Washington, D.C.: American Home Economics Association.

Leverton, Ruth. "Development of Basic Nutrition Concepts for Use in Nutrition Education." In *Proceedings of Nutrition Education Conference, February 20-22, 1967.* U.S. Dept. of Agriculture Misc. Publication No. 1075, June, 1968.

Lindberg, Joel. "Dimensional Changes in Multi-component Systems of Fabrics: A Theoretical Study." *Textile Research Journal* 31:664-669; 1961.

Lindzey. "On the Classification of Projection Techniques." *Psychological Bulletin* 56:158-168; 1959.

Linton, Ron M. "Strategy for Improvement of the Status of Man in His Environment." *Proceedings of Symposium on Human Ecology.* U.S. Department of Health, Education and Welfare. Warrenton, Va.: Airlie House, 1968.

Lowen, Alexander. *Pleasure.* New York: Coward-McCann, Inc., 1970.

Luckiesh, Matthew, and Frank Moss. *The Science of Seeing*. New York: D. Van Nostrand Co., 1937.

Lurie, W. "Impertinent Questioner — Scientist's Guide to Statistician's Mind." *American Scientist* 46:57; 1958.

Lusk, Graham. *The Elements of the Science of Nutrition*. Philadelphia: W.B. Saunders Company, 1917.

Lynd, R.S., and H.M. Lynd. *Middletown*. New York: Harcourt, Brace & Co., 1929.

Lynd, R.S., and H.M. Lynd. *Middletown in Transition*. New York: Harcourt, Brace & Co., 1937.

McClintock, Michael. "Human Ecology — Implications for Home Economists." Talk presented at 3M Home Economics Seminar, St. Paul, Minn., 1971.

McLuhan, Marshall. *Understanding Media*. New York: The New American Library, Inc., 1964.

McLuhan, Marshall, and Quentin Fiore. *War and Peace in the Global Village*. New York: Bantam Books, 1968.

Maccoby, E.E., and N. Maccoby. "The Interview: A Tool of Social Science." In *Handbook of Social Psychology*, 1st ed., G. Lindzey, ed. Reading, Mass.: Addison-Wesley, 1954.

Machover, Karen. *Personality Projection in the Drawing of the Human Figure*. Springfield, Ill.: Thomas, 1948.

Malinowski, Bronislaw. *Argonauts of the Western Pacific: An Account of Native Enterprise and Adventure in the Archipelagoes of Melanesian New Guinea*. London: Routledge & Kegan Paul, 1922.

Malinowski, Bronislaw. *Coral Gardens and Their Magic*. London: Routledge & Kegan Paul, 1935.

Mander, A.E. *Logic for the Millions*. New York: Philosophical Library, Inc., 1947.

Mann, J. "Experimental Evaluations of Role Playing." *Psychological Bulletin* 53:227-234; 1956.

Mead, Margaret. *Coming of Age in Samoa*. New York: Modern Library, 1953.

Merrill, B. "A Measurement of Mother-Child Interaction." *Journal of Abnormal and Social Psychology* 41:37-49; 1946.

Merton, Robert K. "The Social Psychology of Housing." *Current Trends in Social Psychology*. Pittsburgh: The University of Pittsburgh Press, 1951.

Miller, David W., and Martin K. Starr. *The Structure of Human Decisions*. Englewood Cliffs, N.J.: Prentice-Hall, Inc., 1967.

Modley, Rudolf, and Dyno Lowenstein. *Pictographs and Graphs*. New York: Harper & Row, Inc., 1952.

Murphy, Gardner. *Personality: A Biosocial Approach to Origins and Structure*. New York: Harper, 1947.

Newman, Joseph W. "New Insights, New Progress, for Marketing." *Harvard Business Review* Nov.-Dec., 1957, 95-102.

Nixon, Richard M. President's State of the Union Message, 1970.

Nye, F. Ivan, and Felix M. Berardo. *Emerging Conceptual Frameworks in Family Analysis*. New York: The Macmillan Company, 1966.

Oldfield, R.C. *The Psychology of the Interview.* 4th ed. London: Methuen, 1951.

Ortega, Lourdes. "A Study of Word Recognition and Concomitant Galvanic Skin Responses of a Group of Schizophrenic Patients and of a Group of Graduate Students." Unpublished master's thesis, George Washington University, 1962.

Osgood, C., G. Suci, and P. Tannenbaum. *The Measurement of Meaning.* Urbana, Ill.: University of Illinois Press, 1957.

Pace, C. Robert, and Donald G. Wallace. *A Questionnaire on the Activities, Opinions, and Experiences of College Graduates.* Syracuse: Syracuse University, 1948.

Paolucci, Beatrice. "Decision-Making in Relation to Management in Classes of Home Economics by Beginning Teachers." Unpublished Doctor's dissertation, Michigan State University (as abstracted in *Journal of Home Economics* 49:225; March, 1957).

Park, Robert E., and E.W. Burgess. *Introduction to the Science of Sociology.* Chicago: The University of Chicago Press, 1921.

Parten, M.B. *Surveys, Polls and Samples.* New York: Harper & Row Publishers, Inc., 1950.

Petrie, Asenath. *Individuality in Pain and Suffering.* Chicago: The University of Chicago Press, 1967.

Plihal, Jane, and Marjorie Brown. *Evaluation Materials: Physical Home Environment and Psychological and Social Factors.* Minneapolis: Burgess Publishing Company, 1969.

Pratt, Carroll C. *Annual Review of Psychology.* Palo Alto, Calif.: Annual Reviews, Inc. 12:87; 1961.

Price, Dorothy Z. "Toward Self-Actualization: Managing Resources." *Forum,* Fall/Winter, 1969.

"Proceedings of Symposium on Human Ecology." Department of Health, Education and Welfare, Public Health Service, Consumer Protection and Environmental Health Service. Warrenton, Va.: Airlie House, 1968.

Rice, Ann Smith. "An Economic Framework for Viewing the Family." In *Emerging Conceptual Frameworks in Family Analysis.* F. Nye and F. Berardo, eds. New York: The Macmillan Company, 1966.

Richardson, Lou, and Genevieve Callahan. *The New How to Write for Homemakers.* Ames: The Iowa State College Press, 1962.

Riley, Matilda W. *Sociological Research: A Case Approach.* New York: Harcourt, Brace & World, Inc., 1963.

Rosenberg, Morris. *Society and the Adolescent Self-Image.* Princeton, N.J.: Princeton University Press, 1965.

Rosenzweig, Saul, Edith E. Fleming, and Louise Rosenweig. "The Children's Form of the Rosenzweig Picture-Frustration Study." *The Journal of Psychology* 26:141-191; 1948.

Rummel, J. Francis. *An Introduction to Research Procedures in Education.* 2nd ed. New York: Harper & Row, 1964.

Sarason, Seymour B., et al. *Anxiety in Elementary School Children: A Report of*

Research. New York: John Wiley & Sons, Inc., 1960.

Schachter, S., et al. "An Experimental Study of Cohesiveness in Productivity." *Human Relations* 4:229-238; 1951.

Schlater, Jean D., ed. *National Goals and Guidelines for Research in Home Economics.* A study sponsored by the Association of Administrators of Home Economics, 1970. Michigan State University, East Lansing, Mich.

Schlater, Jean D. "The Management Process and Its Core Concepts." *Journal of Home Economics* 59:2:93-98; February, 1967.

Scoby, Donald R. *Environmental Ethics.* Minneapolis: Burgess Publishing Company, 1971.

Sears, R.R., E.E. Maccoby, and H. Levin. *Patterns of Child Rearing.* Evanston, Ill.: Row, Peterson and Company, 1957.

Selltiz, Claire, et al. *Research Methods in Social Relations.* Rev. ed. New York: Holt, Rinehart and Winston, Inc., 1959.

Shepard, Paul, and Daniel McKinley. *The Subversive Science.* Boston: Houghton Mifflin Company, 1969.

Shindell, Sidney. *Statistics, Science and Sense.* Pittsburgh: University of Pittsburgh Press, 1964.

Shumsky, Abraham. *The Action Research Way of Learning.* New York: Bureau of Publications, Teachers College, Columbia University, 1958.

Slonin, Morris J. *Sampling in a Nutshell.* New York: Simon and Schuster, Inc., 1960.

Social Science Research Council. *The Social Sciences in Historical Study.* A report of the committee on historiography. Social Science Research Council, Bulletin 64. New York, 1954.

Spear, Mary E. *Charting Statistics.* New York: McGraw-Hill Book Co., Inc., 1952.

Stevens, Stanley S. "Mathematics, Measurement and Psychophysics." In *Handbook of Experimental Psychology.* New York: Wiley & Sons, Inc., 1951.

Storer, N.W. *Science and Scientists in an Agricultural Research Organization: A Sociological Study.* Unpublished Ph.D. dissertation, Cornell University, 1961.

Stott, Leland H. "The Longitudinal Approach to the Study of Family Life." *Journal of Home Economics* 46:79-82; February, 1954.

Stott, Leland H. "The Problem of Evaluating Family Success." *Marriage and Family Living* 13:149-153; November, 1951.

Straus, Murray S. "Some Basic Requisites for Research Activity." *Journal of Home Economics* 62:4; April, 1970.

Strong, E. *Manual for Strong Vocational Interest Blanks for Men and Women.* Palo Alto, Calif.: Consulting Psychologists Press, 1959.

Terman, Louis Madison, et al. *Genetic Studies of Genius: I. Mental and Physical Traits of a Thousand Gifted Children.* Stanford, Calif.: Stanford University Press, 1925.

Terman, Louis Madison and Melita H. Oden. *Genetic Studies of Genius: IV. Twenty-Five Years' Follow-Up of a Superior Group.* Stanford, Calif.: Stanford University Press, 1947.

Theodorson, George A., ed. *Studies in Human Ecology*. New York: Harper & Row, 1961.

Thomas, William, and Florion Znaniecki. *The Polish Peasant in Europe and America*. New York: Knopf, 1927.

Thomas, William I. *Source Book of Social Origins*. 6th ed. Boston: Gorham Press, 1909.

Thorndike, Robert L., and Elizabeth Hagen. *Measurement and Evaluation in Psychology and Education*. 2nd ed. New York: John Wiley & Sons, Inc., 1961.

Thurstone, L.L., and E.J. Chave. *The Measurement of Attitude*. Chicago: The University of Chicago Press, 1929.

Titles of Dissertations and Theses Completed in Home Economics. Washington, D.C.: American Home Economics Association, annual compilation.

Torreta, Delfina Marquez. "Somesthetic Perception of Clothing Fabrics in Relation to Body Image and Psychological Security." Unpublished Ph.D. dissertation, Utah State University, 1968.

Travers, Robert M.W. *An Introduction to Educational Research*. 3rd ed. New York: The Macmillan Company, 1969.

Trilling, Lionel. *Freud and the Crisis of Our Culture*. Boston: Beacon Press, 1955.

Underwood, Benton J. *Psychological Research*. New York: Appleton, 1957.

U.S. Department of Health, Education, and Welfare (Public Health Service, Environmental Health Service). *Environmental Health Problems*. Rockville, Maryland: U.S. Dept. HEW, 1970.

Van Bortel, D.G. "Homemaking: Concepts, Practices, and Attitudes in Two Social Class Groups." Unpublished Ph.D. thesis, University of Chicago, 1954.

Walker, Helen M., and Joseph Lev. *Elementary Statistical Methods*. Rev. ed. New York: Holt, Rinehart and Winston, Inc., 1958.

Wapner, Seymour, and Heinz Werner, eds. *The Body Percept*. New York: Random House, 1965.

Webster's New International Dictionary of the English Language. 2nd ed. unabridged. Springfield, Mass.: G. & C. Merriam Co., 1957.

White, Leslie A. *The Science of Culture*. New York: Farrar, Straus and Company, 1949.

Whitney, Frederick L. *The Elements of Research*. 3rd ed. New York: Prentice-Hall, 1950.

Wiener, Norbert. *The Human Use of Human Beings – Cybernetics and Society*. New York: Doubleday Anchor, 1954.

Witkin, H., et al. *Psychological Differentiation*. New York: John Wiley & Sons, Inc., 1962.

Woodworth, Robert S. *Dynamics of Behavior*. New York: Holt, 1958.

Young, Kimball. *Personality and Problems of Adjustment*. New York: Appleton-Century-Crofts, 1940.

Young, Pauline. *Scientific Social Surveys and Research*. Englewood Cliffs, N.J.: Prentice-Hall, Inc., 1966.

Index

639